INTEREST-RATE OPTION MODELS

WILEY SERIES IN FINANCIAL ENGINEERING

INTEREST-RATE OPTION MODELS

Understanding, analysing and using models for exotic interest-rate options

Riccardo Rebonato

John Wiley & Sons
Chichester · New York · Brisbane · Toronto · Singapore

Copyright © 1996 Riccardo Rebonato
Published by   John Wiley & Sons Ltd,
                   Baffins Lane, Chichester,
                   West Sussex PO19 1UD, England

                   National 01243 779777
                   International (+44) 1243 779777

Other Wiley Editorial Offices

John Wiley & Sons, Inc., 605 Third Avenue,
New York, NY 10158-0012, USA

Jacaranda Wiley Ltd, 33 Park Road, Milton,
Queensland 4064, Australia

John Wiley & Sons (Canada) Ltd, 22 Worcester Road,
Rexdale, Ontario M9W 1L1, Canada

John Wiley & Sons (Asia) Pte Ltd, 2 Clementi Loop #02-01,
Jin Xing Distripark, Singapore 0512

Library of Congress Cataloging-in-Publication Data

Rebonato, Riccardo.
    Interest-rate option models : understanding, analysing, and using models for
exotic interest rate options / Riccardo Rebonato.
        p.   cm.
    Includes bibliographical references and index.
    ISBN 0-471-96569-3
    1. Interest rate futures—Mathematical models.   2. Options
(Finance)—Mathematical models.   I. Title.
HG6024.5.R43   1996
332.63'23—dc20   96-22784
                                                                       CIP

British Library Cataloguing in Publication Data

A catalogue record for this book is available from the British Library

ISBN 0-471-96569-3

Typeset in 10/12pt Times by
Mathematical Composition Setters Ltd, Salisbury, Wilts.
Printed and bound in Great Britain by Biddles Ltd, Guildford
This book is printed on acid-free paper responsibly manufactured from sustainable
forestation, for which at least two trees are planted for each one used for paper
production.

To Rosamund

To my parents

Contents

Contents   ix

Acknowledgements

Thanks are due to Mike Sherring and Dr Ian Cooper for their valiant attempts at transforming the mindset of a solid-state physicist into that of an option pricer: how difficult the task has been only they and the author can tell; to my employer, BZW, for providing a conducive and stimulating environment, in which all the topics treated in this book have found a continuous benchmark of relevance and applicability; to Charles Thompson and Dr Vivian Li for performing some calculations; to Dr Thomas Gustavsson, who kindly made available his unpublished thesis: Chapter 5 clearly mirrors his approach in emphasising the importance of the choice of numeraire; to many friends and colleagues, who were kind enough to read (parts of) the manuscript at different stages of its writing, and provided useful comments: among the many I would like to thank Dr Noël Vaillant, Soraya Kazziha, Carl Scott, Paul Ellis and Dr Rowell; it is finally a pleasure to thank Dr Carol Alexander, who made very useful comments on an earlier version of the manuscript.

I am very grateful to my wife for her help and support.

Without all this help the book would have been much the poorer. Needless to say, I remain nonetheless solely responsible for any errors that still occur.

Introduction and outline of the book

In every review of interest-rate derivative instruments it appears to be *de rigueur* to present a table, or the ubiquitous bar chart, displaying the exponential-like growth of this type of product in terms of underlying notional, outstanding deals, or some other measure of volume. The correctness of these statistics and the importance of these measures are undeniable; even more significant, however, has been the *qualitative* change in the type of options which have recently begun to be actively traded in the over-the-counter (OTC) markets.

In the last 10 years or so, 'plain-vanilla' instruments such as caps, floors or European swaptions have been actively traded both by investors, seeking to make profit from their views on the level of future interest rates, and by liability managers and company treasurers in general, attempting to control their interest-rate exposure. The common feature of these European instruments is that their value depends to first order on the *level* of the yield curve, and, therefore, money is to be expected to be made or lost according to whether one's prediction of 'rates' going up or down turns out to be correct. For this type of instruments a simple valuation formula (Black (1976)) gives, under reasonable and intuitively appealing assumptions, a theoretically well-justifiable closed-form solution for the option value. In view of their relative simplicity, and of the fact that, historically, they have been the first success-fully traded interest-rate OTC options, it has become customary to describe as 'first generation' those instruments (caps, floors and European swaptions) for which the Black model provides a closed-form solution.

A common feature of these European options is the fact that they tend to give an exposure at *one point in time* to the underlying forward or swap rate. Also, they are in general poorly suited to express complex views on the steepening or flattening of the yield curve, rather than on its level. Several instruments have therefore been introduced either as stand-alone OTC products, or embedded in swaps or structured notes. So many have been the different types and variations of these 'exotics', that a complete list would be almost impossible to compile; nonetheless one can distinguish at least two important classes: the path-dependent and the barrier options, which can be reasonably regarded as 'second-' and 'third-generation' instruments, respectively.

In the self-standing format, barrier options have for instance been traded as knock-out (knock-in) caps and floors, where the cap or floor disappears (or comes to life) if a given index rate (possibly a swap rate) is above or below a certain level at a pre-specified time. Notice that, since the index rate need not be the same as the forward rate that determines the payoff (for instance, a 3-month LIBOR cap might be knocked out if a 5-year swap rate is above or below a certain barrier level), the relative levels of different portions of the yield curve play an important role in determining the value of the option.

A variation of this knock-out structure in an embedded form can be found in trigger notes, where a certain swap disappears if an index rate is below or above (for yield enhancement or reduction of the paid fixed rate, respectively) a given level. Notice that, also in this case, the 3-month maturity rate can cause the disappearance of, say, a 5-year swap, whose value per unit principal would depend on a longer-maturity swap rate. Once again, the interplay of different portions of the yield curve plays an essential role in determining the value of the embedded option.

If the knock-out opportunities were to occur at several (rather than single) pre-specified times, it is easy to see that the option itself acquires a path-dependent nature, which becomes even more pronounced for those trigger swaps where the principal simply amortises (instead of disappearing) as a function of the path of an index rate: these instruments have been actively traded especially in the US$ market, either as 'yield enhancement' instruments, or in order to hedge the pre-payment risk of mortgage-backed securities. Even by the extremely simple description just given of these type of options, one can easily notice a considerable blurring of the clear-cut distinction proposed before between second- and third-generation instruments.

However they might be described, these instruments have introduced a whole new dimension to the pricing of options dependent on interest rates. On the one hand, in fact, they have required the introduction of models capable of pricing instruments crucially dependent on the correlated movements of different portions of the yield curve. On the other hand, they have highlighted the need to manage the risk of these new exotic options in a manner consistent with the pricing and hedging of the first-generation instruments.

The very concept of the 'underlying' instrument has undergone a subtle but important transformation: the exotic OTC option trader will often hedge his position in the 'third-generation' instrument using not cash instruments (the old 'underlying bond') but an (often rather heady) cocktail of actively traded more elementary *options* (e.g. caps or European swaptions). Whatever model the exotic option pricer has therefore chosen, it must yield the same price for the plain-vanilla hedging options, priced in the market using a different (usually Black's) model. Since the true cost of an option is the cost of the replicating hedge, and since this hedge, in the case of second- or third-generation instruments, is often made up of caps and floors, the perspective of the exotic option hedger is to take the prices of the first-generation options as a given, rather than the product of a possibly questionable model. In this respect the price of a cap for the user of a sophisticated option model is more akin to the price of, say, IBM shares for someone using the Black and Scholes model to price an IBM stock call option: nobody would argue that the value of a call should be lower because the shares are a bit expensive!

In this context, the very success of the Black (1976) model for plain-vanilla options has been both the blessing and the bane of more sophisticated approaches. It is, in fact, essential to emphasise that expert practitioners are all too aware of the limitations of the Black model, and that their 'doctoring' of the one unobservable input (the 'implied' volatility) can well recover a desired option price, but *a priori* this procedure does not tell them anything about the 'intrinsic' correctness of the model. In other terms, its virtually universal acceptance in the market place does not imply a similar acceptance of the underlying assumptions, since distributional features not accommodated by Black's model (for instance, mean reversion, leptokurtosis, etc.) are incorporated in an *ad hoc* way by adjusting the Black's implied volatility. The indubitable simplicity and intuitive appeal of the Black approach have therefore given rise to a situation where any more sophisticated model has 'at least' to recover the Black prices for plain-vanilla instruments, if it is to win any acceptance among practitioners. From this point of view the Black approach has become not an equal-ranking model, which might see its predictions challenged by a more 'realistic' approach, but a benchmark which more advanced methodologies simply cannot ignore.

The need to go beyond Black's closed-form formula (to value, for instance, American options) has always been present, but, as pointed out before, option markets have recently seen the appearance of option payoffs strongly dependent on the imperfect correlation between rates (e.g. yield spread options), on the path followed by the rates (e.g. indexed principal swap), and/or of discontinuous nature (e.g. knock-out caps). The first class of payoffs point to many- (or at least two-) factor models as the way forward. The second shift the emphasis towards Monte Carlo approaches. The latter require, in numeric implementations, a sampling resolution which seriously stretches even one-factor lattice models. The hard lessons learnt by some market practitioners in attempting to risk-manage instruments such as knock-out indexed-principal swaps show that even state-of-the-art model implementations are far from having solved all the problems encountered in the market place.

In the light of these considerations, the book has been structured as follows. After an initial chapter (Chapter 1) which defines and shows how to value the elementary building blocks (swaps, caps, European swaptions, etc.), a statistical argument is presented showing how to reduce in a drastic way the dimensionality of the problem of describing the yield curve dynamics (Chapter 2). Having demonstrated that this reduction of the problem is indeed possible (and reasonable), it is then shown (Chapter 3) why this line of attack of complex interest-rate option problems is actually indispensable. These first three chapters (Part One) are therefore intended to furnish a general motivation for the following material.

Part Two (Chapters 4 and 5) then supplies the theoretical underpinning for all the following treatment, presenting, in the simplest possible way, the probabilistic set-up, the essential elements of stochastic differentiation and integration and the conditions of no-arbitrage. The importance of the choice of the unit of account is stressed throughout this part of the book, with a view to enhancing both the theoretical understanding and the capability to make use of the results so derived in complex practical applications.

Having laid hopefully solid foundations, the discussion becomes more practical in Part Three, which presents the actual implementation tools: lattice methodologies (Chapter 6), the partial differential equation approach (Chapter 7) and Monte Carlo techniques (Chapter 8).

At this point the reader should be in a position fully to appreciate the theoretical, numerical and practical implications of the specific models. Several of these are therefore analysed in detail, both by reviewing and re-obtaining in a coherent way material available in the literature, and by presenting the results of original empirical and theoretical investigations. Rather than attempting an exhaustive review of 'all' the models (a task clearly impossible), different approaches have been taken as representatives of important classes: the chapters of Part Four (from the 9th to the 14th) therefore tackle the Cox Ingersoll and Ross, Vasicek, Black Derman and Toy, Hull and White, Longstaff and Schwartz, Heath Jarrow and Morton and Brennan and Schwartz models, respectively.

The concluding Part Five attempts to bring together the material covered by discussing general features of the models that can be better appreciated after the specific approaches have been presented, and to impart some words of wisdom regarding the pitfalls connected with the choice and the implementation of any given model: Chapter 15 deals with affine models, Chapter 16 with Markovian short-rate processes.

Without pre-empting the concluding remarks to be found in these two chapters, it is appropriate to point out a few salient messages. To begin with, it is the strong (but not uncontroversial) view of the writer that the quality of a model should be assessed on the basis not of the *a priori* appeal of its assumptions (e.g. normal versus log-normal rates), but of the effectiveness of its hedging performance. This has not only practical but also theoretical appeal, since an option price is, after all, nothing but the cost incurred in running the duplicating hedging portfolio.

Furthermore, I shall stress the point that the calibration procedure is an integral part of a model specification, and that it makes little sense to talk about the 'goodness' or 'realism' of a given model, for instance on the basis of its distributional or economic assumptions, without exploring the ease, robustness and reliability of the parameter estimation procedure.

As for the style and the technical level, financial intuition rather than mathematical rigour has been stressed throughout; references have been provided to allow the more mathematically inclined reader to find rigorous proofs for the sometimes sketchy derivations presented in the text. I have found the use of 'his/her' for the possessive pronoun too burdensome; whenever possible I have used the logically incorrect 'their' (as in 'Every student should bring their pens'), comforted by the fact that, what has been deemed to be good enough by Jane Austen, must certainly serve my prose more than adequately. Whenever this slight of hand proved stylistically impossible, I have made use of the pronoun 'his' with the tacit understanding that no specific gender should be implied.

I would consider my task more than satisfactorily accomplished, if, by the end of this work, the reader will not be tempted to paraphrase Oscar Wilde's famous book review: 'Good in parts, and original in parts; unfortunately, the good parts were not original, and the original parts were not good.'

List of symbols and abbreviations

FINANCIAL AND STATISTICAL QUANTITIES

$B(t,T)$—Rolled-up money-market account where £1 is reinvested at the prevailing instantaneous short rate from time t to time T.

$\text{Correl}[a, b]$—Correlation between a and b.

$\text{Covar}[a, b]$—Covariance between a and b.

$E_Q[x(T) \mid \mathfrak{J}(t)]$—Expectation taken at time t on the basis of the information (filtration) $\mathfrak{J}(t)$ and in the probability measure Q of the time-T value of quantity x.

$f(t,s)$—Instantaneous forward rate seen from the time-t yield curve, spanning the infinitesimal period $[s \;\; s + \mathrm{d}t]$, $(s \geq t)$.

$f(t,T_1,T_2)$—Discrete continuously compounded forward rate seen from the time-t yield curve, spanning the finite period $[T_1 \;\; T_2]$, $(t \leq T_1 < T_2)$.

K—Strike price.

$G(i,j,r,s)$—Green's function (Arrow–Debreu price): value at time j and in state i of £1 paid with certainty at time s if state of the world r is attained.

$k(t)$—Reversion speed at time t.

$L(t)$—Consol yield in the Brennan and Schwartz model.

NDTR—Cumulative normal distribution.

P—Probability measure.

$P(t,T)$—Price at time t of a discount bond maturing at time T.

Q—Probability measure.

$r(t)$—Instantaneous short rate at time t.

R—Pratt–Arrow measure of relative risk aversion.

$R(t,T)$—T-maturity spot rate seen from the time-t yield curve.

Std$[a]$—Standard deviation of a.

$v(t,T)$—Price volatility at time t of a discount bond maturing at time T.

$V(t)$—Generic security price at time t.

Var$[a]$—Variance of a.

X—Equilibrium swap rate (in Chapter 1); Strike price elsewhere.

$Z(t)$—Relative price at time t.

$\theta(t)$—Time-dependent drift in the HW models.

θ—Reversion level in the CIR model.

κ—Reversion speed in the CIR model.

$\lambda(x,t)$—Market price of risk as function of state variable x and calendar time t.

μ—Drift of a random variable.

$\sigma(t,T)$—Volatility at time t of an instantaneous forward rate of expiry T.

τ—Tenor of a FRA.

ω—Probabilistic event.

Ω—Probability space.

$\mathfrak{F}_t$—Filtration at time t.

MARKET ABBREVIATIONS

bp—Basis Point (i.e. 1% of a percentage point).
DEM—Deutsche Mark.
ESP—Spanish Peseta.
GBP/GB£—Pound Sterling.
ITL—Italian Lira.
USD/US$—US Dollar.

MODELS AND VARIOUS ACRONYMS

BDT—Black Derman and Toy.
BS—Brennan and Schwartz.
CIR—Cox Ingersoll and Ross.
EFD—Explicit Finite Differences.
FRA—Forward Rate Agreement.
HJM—Heath Jarrow and Morton.
HL—Ho and Lee.
HW—Hull and White.
IFD—Implicit Finite Differences.
LS—Longstaff and Schwartz.
MC—Monte Carlo.
PCA—Principal Component Analysis.
PDE—Partial Differential Equation.
SDE—Stochastic Differential Equation.

PART ONE
THE NEED FOR YIELD CURVE OPTION PRICING MODELS

1
Definition and valuation of the underlying instruments

1.1 INTRODUCTION

The main task of this book is to show how existing option models can be understood, analysed and implemented in order to price and risk-manage 'exotic' interest-rate options. The term 'exotic' is, by itself, far from being unambiguous: while, on the one hand, the financial press tend to extend the adjective to any 'derivative' instrument (thereby including even futures contracts), some traders in the US$ derivatives market, on the other hand, might consider a 10-year American, step-up-coupon swaption with exit penalty a 'commoditised' plain-vanilla instrument. In the context of this book, 'exotic' will be taken to refer to any option whose value cannot be reduced to a closed-form expression, such as, for instance, Black's (1976) celebrated formula. Models, such as the Hull and White (see Chapter 11), which do afford closed-form solutions for certain types of options (typically calls or puts on discount bonds) are, of course, also treated, but the emphasis is laid on the applications that go beyond the important but limited cases for which exact formulae exist.

Before embarking on the treatment of these exotic interest-rate options it is important to have a clear understanding of how the underlying instruments are priced, and of the rather subtle interplay between the prices of the 'underlying' and of the 'derivative' instruments. This is the task undertaken in the present chapter, and in Chapter 3. The attempt has been made to make the treatment as self-contained as possible, and therefore Black's formula is derived in Section 3.2. Readers totally unfamiliar with the fundamentals of option pricing might, however, find it profitable to read at least some chapters from any of the many introductory texts (I cannot think of a better one than Hull's (1992) classic). Finally, the overall treatment would have been more elegant if a completely axiomatic approach had been adopted, by deriving theoretical results first, and applications thereafter. It was feared, however, that in so doing more could be lost in financial intuition than gained in elegance. Chapters 1 to 3 therefore make use of an 'intuitive' understanding of what arbitrage is in order to derive important results, despite the fact that arbitrage is 'properly' defined only in Chapters 4 and 5. Clearly, the earlier derivations (i.e. those in Chapters 1 and 3) are less general than they could have been if presented in the context of the martingale approach. However, the reader would have missed the important issue of the very motivation for yield curve models, presented in Chapters 2 and 3. The simple proofs presented in this chapter should therefore be seen in this light, and profitably revisited before embarking on Part Three.

Broadly speaking, pricing an exotic interest-rate option can be looked at in two distinct ways. Complex interest-rate options can be regarded as tools which allow the investor to express 'sophisticated' views about the future evolution of interest rates. These views, as mentioned in the introduction, can go well beyond simple directional positions ('rates are going to go "up" or "down"'), for which plain-vanilla instruments such as futures and swaps are probably more suited, but can, for instance, express predictions about the steepening or flatting of a yield curve, independently of, or in conjunction with, a change in level; or about the precise timing of a certain yield curve move. In all these cases the investor will reap his rewards if his views were correct *and if these views were different from the market's*. Therefore, in this framework, pricing the market exactly (i.e. recovering the observed market prices within the bid/offer spread) is neither logically necessary, nor, to some extent, desirable. If a model could be trusted to give a fundamentally correct, albeit necessarily simplified, description of economic reality then discrepancies between model and market values would point to possible trading opportunities. Equilibrium models, which attempt to describe the economy as a whole, belong in this class.

At the opposite end of the spectrum there is a pure no-arbitrage approach: in this framework the user who needs to price an exotic interest-rate option will hedge his position using either plain-vanilla options (such as caps or European swaptions) or the underlying 'cash' instruments (bonds, forward rate agreements (FRAs), swaps or futures); the correctness of the prices of the latter will not be questioned, and the value of the exotic options will be regarded as the cost of the replicating hedging portfolio. Clearly, exact recovery of the actually traded market prices of the underlying instrument now becomes all-important. At the risk of oversimplifying the issue, one approach can be seen as an attempt to *explain* prices, the other as using these prices as exogenously given building blocks.

Whatever the approach might be, it will be necessary to recover the implied market values for the underlying instruments using the more sophisticated approaches described in later chapters. (In the context of no-arbitrage models, the procedure is normally referred to as calibration or parametrisation of an interest rate model.) In turn, the market prices of futures, FRAs, swaps, or bond prices are all a function of the discount curve. A discussion is therefore undertaken in this chapter of the issues underlying the construction of a reliable yield curve, and the evaluation from the latter of the market prices of the instruments mentioned above. An excellent (and lengthy) treatment of these topics as far as LIBOR curves are concerned can be found in Miron and Swannell (1991). The next section deals with the conceptual steps involved in the creation of a discount curve, and highlights the methodological similarities and differences in constructing bond and LIBOR yield curves.

1.2 DEFINITION OF SPOT RATES, FORWARD RATES, SWAP RATES AND PAR COUPON RATES

There exist a number of equivalent descriptions of a given market yield curve. Ultimately, spot rates, yields, swap rates, par coupon curves, etc., are all shorthand notations for cash flows that will occur at some future time. These cash flows, in turn, can either be certain, or conditional upon pre-specified states of the world being attained in the future. A title to a single certain cash flow of magnitude X at a known time in the future T is called a **discount bond**, and the amount X is referred to as the **principal**, or **notional**, or **face value**. In certain cases, i.e. especially for short maturities T, these instruments are traded directly in the market. What is more common, however, is to have securities that promise to pay a stream of certain payments at time t_i, often referred to as **coupons**, and a (usually larger) payment on the last payment date (the **maturity date**). These latter instruments are normally called **coupon-bearing bonds**. In the rest of this book, the price at time t of a discount bond maturing at time T will be denoted by $P(t,T)$, and the price at time t of a coupon-bearing bond paying coupons at times t_i, and the principal amount at time T by $Bnd(t,\{t_i\},T)$. Since the problems connected with the possibility of default are not touched upon in this book, and since coupon-bearing bonds are reducible to a suitable bundle of discount bonds with different face values, from the conceptual point of view the collection of prices $P(t,T)$ for any $T \geq t$ fully describes the value to be associated to any collection of certain future cash flows. Since, as mentioned before, pure, risk-free discount bonds are rarely traded in the market, their prices have to be imputed from the prices of the coupon-bearing bonds. Despite these practical difficulties the conceptual advantages arising from assuming that the prices of a continuum of discount bonds are indeed directly available are such that it will always be assumed in the following chapters that this continuum of prices (otherwise known as the **discount function**) have already been obtained. How this can be accomplished is explained in the following sections.

A security that entitles the holder to a given cash flow if a particular, pre-specified, state of the world is attained at one or more future dates is called a **contingent claim** (a more precise definition will be given in Chapter 4). In some situations, despite the fact that the cash flows are uncertain at time t_0, they can be replicated exactly by entering suitable strategies which require only (positive or negative) holdings of discount bonds. If arbitrage (see Chapter 4) is to be avoided, knowledge of the discount function at time t_0 therefore completely determines the prices of this class of contingent claims. Notice that, since the payoffs of these simple contingent claims can be replicated using instruments that pay *certain* cash flows in the future, no statistical assumptions have to be made regarding the probability of occurrence of any future state of the world. In particular, the value of these instruments is independent of any volatility. Contingent claims that can be replicated in this fashion (e.g. FRAs, swaps) are treated in this chapter.

For more general contingent claims, no-arbitrage and knowledge of the discount function are not sufficient to determine their value, and one must also make suitable assumptions about the probability distributions of the random variable(s) that determine the future cash flows. (It will actually turn out that, because of no-arbitrage, assumptions only need to be made regarding the second, or higher, moments of these distributions). Not surprisingly, therefore, the prices of these contingent claims will turn out to be given (Section 4.10) by suitable expectations, taken with respect to the appropriate probability distributions, of future cash flows. Some of these expectations can be easily evaluated with closed-form expressions, using the market discount function and the variance of the random variable(s) which determine the payoffs. These simple, volatility-dependent, contingent claims which admit closed-form solutions (caps, floors and European swaptions) are also treated in this chapter. The rest of the book deals with contingent claims for which such simple solutions are not available (or, as it will be argued in Chapter 3, are of limited use), and whose future cash flows depend on pre-specified future realisations of the discount function. Despite the fact that this definition is perfectly self-consistent, it is more common to express the conditions that trigger future payments in terms of rates. These are therefore defined as follows.

The time-t **continuously compounded discrete spot rate of maturity** T, $R(t,T)$, is defined by

$$P(t,T) \equiv \exp[-R(t,T)(T-t)] \qquad (1.1)$$

$$R(t,T) \equiv -\frac{\ln[P(t,T)]}{T-t} \qquad (1.1')$$

The time-t **continuously compounded discrete forward rate** spanning the period $[T\ T+\Delta t)$, $f(t,T,T+\Delta t)$ is defined by

$$\frac{P(t,T+\Delta t)}{P(t,T)} \equiv \exp[-f(t,T,T+\Delta t)\Delta t] \qquad (1.2)$$

$$f(t,T,T+\Delta t) \equiv -\frac{\ln(P(t,T+\Delta t))-\ln(P(t,T))}{\Delta t} \qquad (1.2')$$

The limits as $T \rightarrow t$, $\Delta t \rightarrow 0$ in Equations (1.1') and (1.2') define the instantaneous short rate, $r(t)$, and the instantaneous forward rate, $f(t,T)$, respectively.

$$r(t) = \lim_{t \rightarrow T} R(t,T) \tag{1.3}$$

$$f(t,T) = \lim_{\Delta t \rightarrow 0} - \frac{\ln(P(t,T+\Delta t)) - \ln(P(t,T))}{\Delta t} = -\frac{\partial \ln(P(t,T))}{\partial T} \tag{1.3'}$$

i.e. the **instantaneous forward rate as seen from the yield curve at time t is equal to (minus) the logarithmic derivative of the time t price of a discount bond of maturity T with respect to its maturity.**

Finally, from (1.3') one can write

$$\int_t^T d \ln P(t,s) = -\int_t^T f(t,s)\, ds = \ln(P(t,T)) - \ln(P(t,t)) \tag{1.4}$$

But, since $P(t,t) = 1$,

$$-\int_t^T f(t,s)\, ds = \ln P(t,T) \tag{1.5}$$

and, finally,

$$P(t,T) = \exp - \int_t^T f(t,s)\, ds \tag{1.6}$$

the **(logarithm of the) price at time t of a discount bond maturing at time T is equal to the integral over maturities of the instantaneous forward rates as seen from the time-t yield curve.**

In complete analogy with the definitions given above, in the case of simple (rather than continuous) compounding, the **simply compounded spot rate** is defined to be

$$R_s(t,T) = \frac{1/P(t,T) - 1}{T - t} \tag{1.7}$$

and the **simply compounded forward rate** spanning the period $[T_1 \; T_2]$, $F(t,T_1,T_2)$ is then defined as

$$F(t,T_1,T_2) = \frac{P(t,T_1)/P(t,T_2) - 1}{T_2 - T_1} \tag{1.8}$$

Having clarified these alternative equivalent ways of describing the value of future cash flows, the next section will tackle the task of associating a value to a contingent claim whose payoffs can be replicated using strategies involving pure discount bonds. It will be assumed throughout that no market frictions are present.

1.3 THE VALUATION OF PLAIN-VANILLA SWAPS AND FRAs

A **plain-vanilla interest-rate swap** is an agreement whereby two parties undertake to exchange, at known dates in the future, a fixed for a floating set of payments (often referred to as the fixed and floating legs of a swap). The **fixed leg** is made up by payments B_i

$$B_i = N_i X \tau_i \tag{1.9}$$

where N_i is the notional principal of the swap outstanding at time t_i, τ_i, usually referred to as the frequency or the tenor of the swap, is the fraction of the year between the ith and the $(i+1)$th payment (therefore approximately equal to $\frac{1}{2}$ or $\frac{1}{4}$ for a semi-annual or quarterly swap)[1], and X is the fixed rate contracted at the outset to be paid by the fixed-rate payer at each payment time. For a plain-vanilla swap each fixed payment B_i occurs at the end of the accrual period, i.e. at time t_{i+1}. See Figure 1.1.

If we denote by $P(0,t)$ the price of a discount bond maturing at time t, the present value of each fixed payment B_i is given by:

$$PV(B_i) = N_i X \tau_i P(0, t_{i+1}) \tag{1.10}$$

As for the **floating leg**, each payment A_i, also occurring at time t_{i+1}, is given by

$$A_i = N_i R_i \tau_i \tag{1.11}$$

where R_i is a shorthand notation for the τ-period spot rate (i.e. the 3-month or 6-month LIBOR rate, for a quarterly or semi-annual swap, respectively) prevailing at time t_i, and covering the period from t_i to t_{i+1}: $R_i = R(t_i, t_i + \tau)$. Times t_i and $t_i + \tau$ are normally referred to as the **reset and payment times** for the ith period, respectively. Clearly, the net present value at a generic time t of each of these floating payments is given by

$$PV(A_i) = N_i R_i \tau_i P(t, t_{i+1}) \tag{1.12}$$

Needless to say, while, at time 0, the magnitudes of the fixed-leg payments are known, and a certain value can therefore be associated to them (Equation

Figure 1.1 The timing of cash flows for a plain-vanilla swap: the realisation at time t_i (reset time) of the spot rate R_i spanning the period $[t_i \ t_{i+1}]$ determines a floating payment per unit principal at time t_{i+1} (payment time) of magnitude $R_i \tau_i$. The tenor τ_i is given by the number of days between t_i and t_{i+1} divided by 360 or 365, as dictated by the appropriate conventions. For a plain-vanilla swap, the fixed payment per unit principal $X\tau_i$ also occurs at time t_{i+1}.

(1.10)), the realisations of the τ-period spot rates R_i at times 1, 2, ..., n are *not* known, and, therefore, for the moment we do not know what value to associate to expression (1.12).

Let us now consider the following strategy: let us purchase at time 0 (today) a discount bond maturing at time t_i, $P(0,t_i)$, and sell (go short of) a discount bond maturing at time t_{i+1}, $P(0,t_{i+1})$. At time t_i the resulting portfolio will have a value $V(t_i)$

$$V(t_i) = P(t_i,t_i) - P(t_i,t_{i+1}) = 1 - P(t_i,t_{i+1}) \qquad (1.13)$$

which, assuming simple compounding over the period $t_i t_{i+1}$, is equal to

$$V(t_i) = 1 - \frac{1}{1 + R_i\tau_i} = \frac{R_i\tau_i}{1 + R_i\tau_i} \qquad (1.13')$$

By Equation (1.12) above, the payer of the floating leg will have to make a payment at time t_{i+1} of present value $V'(t_i)$ at time t_i equal to

$$V'(t_i) = \frac{R_i\tau_i}{1 + R_i\tau_i} \qquad (1.14)$$

Therefore $V(t_i) = V'(t_i)$, i.e. the payoff arising from the floating leg can be perfectly and certainly met by entering the long/short bond strategy suggested before. **At time 0 the commitment to pay R_i in the floating leg and the strategy of holding a bond $P(0,t_i)$ and shorting a bond $P(0,t_{i+1})$ must therefore have the same value:**

$$\mathbf{P(0,t_i) - P(0,t_{i+1}) = R_i\tau_i P(0,t_{i+1})} \qquad (1.15)$$

It follows that, to avoid arbitrage (precisely defined in Chapter 4, but intuitively understandable at this stage as the capability of making certain money without any risk), one can value the floating leg of a swap by setting the unknown quantities R_i equal to the value (notice carefully that no statements about probability distributions or expectations have been used in the argument)

$$R_i = \frac{P(0,t_i)/P(0,t_{i+1}) - 1}{\tau_i} \qquad (1.16)$$

but Equation (1.16) is simply the well-known definition of a simply compounded forward rate spanning the period $[t_i\ t_{i+1}]$, $F(0,t_i,t_{i+1})$ (see Equation (1.8)). Therefore, to avoid arbitrage **the a priori unknown cash flows in the floating leg must be set equal to the projected forward rates.** (The same result can be obtained in a more general way using the approach of Chapter 5, Section 5, where it is shown that, if one uses bonds of maturities t_{i+1} from the current term structure as numeraire, forward rates are driftless.) Notice carefully that the quantities $PV(A_i)$ in Equation (1.12) are stochastic variables, and, as such, possess a certain variance. It is only the present value of each floating reset *plus* the accompanying strategy of long/short bonds that has no variance, and is therefore amenable to a purely deterministic evaluation at time 0.

The **equilibrium swap rate** is then defined as the fixed rate X such that today's present value of the fixed and floating legs are the same:

$$\sum PV(B_i) = \sum N_i X \tau_i P(0, t_{i+1}) = \sum PV(A_i) = \sum N_i F_i \tau_i P(0, t_{i+1}) \quad (1.17)$$

The **equilibrium swap rate** is therefore equal to

$$X = \frac{\sum N_i F_i \tau_i P(0, t_{i+1})}{\sum N_i \tau_i P(0, t_{i+1})} \quad (1.18)$$

i.e. it **is a weighted average of the projected forward rates**. This can be seen more clearly by setting

$$w_i = \frac{N_i \tau_i P(0, t_{i+1})}{\sum N_i \tau_i P(0, t_{i+1})} \quad (1.19)$$

which allows one to rewrite Equation (1.18) as

$$X = \sum F_i w_i \quad (1.20)$$

This expression will be used later in the section.

By the way the equilibrium rate has been obtained it follows that entering the equilibrium swap today has zero cost, since, by definition, the two parties have undertaken to exchange legs of identical value. After an equilibrium swap has been entered, the swap itself will in general no longer have zero value, since interest rates will not, in general, have followed the implied forward curve. It is in fact easy to show that the only values of the joint realisations at time t_1 of the projected forward rates which preserves zero value to an equilibrium swap initiated at time 0 are the values for the same forward rates implied by the yield curve at time 0, i.e.

$$F(t_1, t_i, t_i + \tau_i) = F(0, t_i, t_i + \tau_i) \quad (1.21)$$

where the full notation $F(t, T, T + \tau)$ has been employed to indicate the forward rate from time T to time $T + \tau$, as seen from the yield curve at time t. Notice that, in Equation (1.21), the term $i = 1$ implies that

$$F(t_1, t_1, t_1 + \tau) = R_s(t_1, \tau_1) = F(0, t_1, t_1 + \tau) \quad (1.22)$$

since $F(t, t, T) = R_s(t, T)$; therefore, **in general** (i.e. barring fortuitous cancellations), **for the time-0 equilibrium swap to retain its zero value, the realisation at time t_i of a spot rate must equal the time-0 projected forward rate.**

For the payer of the fixed rate the present value of the swap at time t will be given by

$$NPV_{swap}(t) = -\sum N_i X \tau_i P(t, t_{i+1}) + \sum N_i F_i \tau_i P(t, t_{i+1}) \qquad (1.22')$$

where the $F_i s$ are now the forward rates calculated from the discount curve at time t. As mentioned after Equation (1.16) above, notice carefully that the argument underpinning the derivation is of no-arbitrage nature, and no claim has been made about expectations of future rates.

Further insight into the equilibrium rate can be obtained by expanding the numerator in Equation (1.18) making use of relation (1.16). For a swap with n resets, and final maturity at time t_{n+1}, one can write

$$\sum_{i=1,n} N_i F_i \tau_i P(0, t_{i+1}) = \sum_{i=1,n} N_i \tau_i \left(\frac{P(0, t_i)/P(0, t_{i+1}) - 1}{\tau_i} \right) P(0, t_{i+1})$$

$$= \sum_{i=1,n} N_i [P(0, t_i) - P(0, t_{i+1})] \qquad (1.23)$$

which, for constant principals $N_i = 1$, can be written

$$\sum_{i=1,n} N_i F_i \tau_i P(0, t_{i+1}) = \sum_{i=1,n} P(0, t_i) - P(0, t_{i+1})$$

$$= P(0, t_1) - P(0, t_2) + P(0, t_2) - P(0, t_3) \ldots + P(0, t_n) - P(0, t_{n+1})$$

$$= P(0, t_1) - P(0, t_{n+1}) \qquad (1.23')$$

For a spot-starting plain-vanilla swap the present value of the floating leg of a swap is therefore equal to

$$\sum PV(A_i) = P(0,0) - P(0, t_{n+1}) = 1 - P(0, t_{n+1}) \qquad (1.23'')$$

Notice that the frequency of the plain-vanilla swap does not affect the value of the floating leg, which is therefore the same not only for different day count conventions (ACT/360, ACT/365, 30/360, etc.), but also for a monthly or a yearly swap with same final maturity. **The equilibrium swap rate is therefore given by the ratio of two portfolios of discount bonds:**

$$X = \frac{1 - P(0, t_{n+1})}{\sum N_i \tau_i P(0, t_{i+1})} \qquad (1.24)$$

or, in general, for a swap starting at a future time t, its value at time 0 is

$$X = \frac{P(0, t) - P(0, t_{n+1})}{\sum N_i \tau_i P(0, t_{i+1})} \qquad (1.24')$$

and, therefore, **any yield curve model capable of pricing discount bonds exactly must recover the market swap rates correctly for any choice of the model volatility.**

Notice carefully that this would no longer be the case if a simple modification to the payment provisions were introduced, for instance if the rate determining the payoff in Equation (1.11) were still the τ-period LIBOR reset at time t_i, but the corresponding payments were to occur at any time other than t_{i+1}. In this case the cancellation in Equation (1.23) between $P(0, t_{i+1})$ in the numerator and the denominator would no longer take place, and one would be left with a dependence on the volatility input of a given yield curve model (see Section 5.8 for a discussion of the LIBOR-in-arrears case).

Since a FRA is simply a one-period swap (or, conversely, since a swap is a series of FRAs), the expressions just derived also price this simpler instrument: the net present value of a forward rate agreement, whereby one party undertakes to pay the other at time t_{i+1} (per unit principal) the difference between the τ-period LIBOR resetting at time t_i and an agreed fixed rate X, times the fraction of the year τ covered by the LIBOR spot rate, is simply given by

$$PV(FRA) = [P(0, t_i) - P(0, t_{i+1})] - XP(0, t_{i+1})\tau_i \qquad (1.25)$$

Let us now consider the issuer of a coupon-bearing bond, who, against receipt today of £1, undertakes to pay a fixed coupon X with frequency $1/\tau$, and to repay the principal at maturity t_{n+1}. The coupon liability incurred by the issuer clearly has the same present value as the fixed leg of a swap. As for the principal to be paid back (redeemed) at maturity and received upfront today, their combined present values, $PV(A')$, are given by

$$PV(A') = 1 - P(0, t_{n+1}) \qquad (1.26)$$

Comparing Equation (1.26) with expression (1.23″) one can therefore conclude that **the floating leg of a swap has exactly the same value and plays exactly the same role as the receipt of the proceeds from issuing the bond today, and the accompanying commitment to repay the principal at maturity.**

Whether one is dealing with plain-vanilla swaps or with bullet bonds (i.e. bonds paying regular coupons, without any call or put provisions), their pricing can therefore be completely reduced to a suitable manipulation of pure default-free discount bonds. More precisely, in view of the above it is clear that, apart from credit considerations, the present value of a bond, Bnd, paying n coupons X at regular intervals every τ years until a final maturity at time t_n is given by

$$PV(Bnd) = \sum_{i=1,n} X\tau_i P(0, t_i) + 100 P(0, t_n) \qquad (1.27)$$

Using bond conventions, what has been referred to before as the equilibrium rate is called the **par coupon**, which can therefore be defined as that **particular coupon that prices the bond today exactly at par.** As pointed out before, by moving the last term on the RHS of equation (1.27) to the left one immediately finds the bond equivalent of the present value of the floating leg of a swap. Just as an equilibrium swap struck with a rate X at time t_0 will in general have a non-zero value at a later time t (see Equation (1.22$'$)), a par bond issued at time t_0 will, in bond terminology, trade **at a discount** or **at a premium** at later time t, according to whether the RHS of Equation (1.23) above will add up to more or less than 100, respectively.

1.4 THE VALUATION OF CAPS, FLOORS AND EUROPEAN SWAPTIONS

It will be important for the following to link the variance of the equilibrium swap rates obtained above with the variances of and correlations among the underlying forward rates. To see this more precisely, it is necessary to define first of all a cap, and then a swap option (swaption in the following).

A **cap** is a collection of caplets. A **caplet**, in turn, is a contract which pays at time t_{i+1} the difference between the τ-period spot rate resetting at time t_i, R_i, and a strike price K multiplied by the year fraction τ_i between t_i and t_{i+1}, if this difference is positive, and zero otherwise:

$$\text{Caplet}(t_i + 1) = \text{Max}[R_i - K, 0]\tau \qquad (1.28)$$

No-arbitrage arguments, presented in detail in Chapter 4, show that, for valuation purposes, the unknown future value of the rate resetting at time t_i must be set equal to today's implied forward (the analogy with the case of the FRA is in this respect complete). If, in addition, one accepts the log-normal assumption for the forward rates, one can very easily arrive at the Black model, in which a caplet of expiry t_i struck at K is seen as a call on the forward rate:

$$\text{Caplet} = [F(t_0, t_i, t_{i+1})N(h_1) - KN(h_2)]P(t_0, t_{i+1}) \qquad (1.29)$$

where $N(\cdot)$ denotes the cumulative normal distribution,

$$h_{1,2} = \frac{\ln\left(\dfrac{F}{K}\right) \pm \frac{1}{2}\sigma^2(t_i - t_0)}{\sigma\sqrt{t_i - t_0}} \qquad (1.29')$$

and σ is the percentage volatility of the forward rate. (See Chapter 3 for details of the derivation.) Notice that, despite the fact that the Black formula was originally derived for the particular case of an option on a futures commodity contract, in the context of this book any valuation formula for a call option obtained under the assumption of (i) log-normal distribution for the underlying variable, and (ii) absence of drift in the process for the percentage increment dx/x of the underlying variable will be referred to as a Black formula. The same terminology will therefore apply irrespective of whether the variable x is, for example, a forward rate, or a forward bond price. Needless to say, stating that a certain forward rate is indeed driftless will have to be justified on the basis of no-arbitrage arguments (see Chapter 5).

Let us now consider a call expiring at time T and struck at $1/(1 + X\tau)$ on a discount bond maturing at time $T + \tau$. At option expiry its payoff will be given by

$$\text{Payoff} = \max\left[P(T, T + \tau) - \frac{1}{1 + X\tau}, 0\right]$$

$$= \max\left[\frac{1}{1 + R\tau} - \frac{1}{1 + X\tau}, 0\right] \tag{1.30}$$

where R now indicates the realisation at time T of the τ-period spot rate. Equation (1.30) can be rearranged to give

$$\text{Payoff} = \max\left[\frac{(X - R)\tau}{(1 + R\tau)(1 + X\tau)}, 0\right] \tag{1.31}$$

but, since the quantity $1/(1 + X\tau)$ is known at the outset, the payoff at time T of the call on the discount bond can be written as

$$\text{Payoff} = \frac{1}{1 + X\tau} \frac{\max[(X - R)\tau, 0]}{1 + R\tau} \tag{1.32}$$

i.e. it is identical, to within the proportionality factor $1/(1 + X\tau)$, to the payoff, paid at time $T + \tau$, from a put on the τ-period spot rate resetting at time T, or, in other terms, to a floorlet resetting at time T and paying at time $T + \tau$. Conversely, **a put on the same discount bond (expiring and paying at time T) is equivalent, to within the same proportionality factor, to a T-expiry caplet on the τ-period rate**. The equivalence just established between a caplet (floorlet) and a put (call) on a discount bond will be of great relevance in the context of the calibration of interest-rate models, whenever closed-form solutions are available for calls or puts on discount bonds. (See, in particular, Chapters 9, 11 and 12.)

Going back to Equation (1.29'), one can notice that, given the market practice of pricing caps using the Black formula, there is a one-to-one correspondence between the prices and the volatilities that enter the Black equation. It is therefore common in the market to express the value of a caplet in terms of the 'implied volatility'. One can therefore say that **the market expresses, via a complete set of cap prices, its views about the volatility of the underlying forward rates** and, at the same time, about how the imperfections of the Black model can be accounted for by adjusting the volatility input.

A European swaption is then defined as a contract that gives the holder the right at time t_i to enter a swap (i.e. to pay or receive the fixed rate over the life of the swap) of a given frequency, starting at time t_s and maturing at time t_m at a pre-known rate K:

$$\text{Max}[X - K, 0]B \quad \text{(payer's swaption)} \tag{1.33}$$

$$\text{Max}[K - X, 0]B \quad \text{(receiver's swaption)} \tag{1.33'}$$

with $B = \sum_{k=1,n} P(t_i, t_{i+k}) \tau_k$. Swaptions are priced in the market assuming that forward swap rates, given by expression (1.24) of the previous section, are log-normally distributed, and using the Black model as applied to the forward swap rate X:

$$\text{Receiver's swaption} = [X(t_0, t_i, t_{i+1})N(h_1) - KN(h_2)]B$$

(A justification of the theoretical soundness of this formula i.e. of the reason why one is justified in assuming no drift for the swap rate, will be given in Chapter 5.) The relevant volatility for the Black formula as applied to swaptions is now the volatility of the forward swap rate X. It will be shown in Chapter 4 that, despite the fact that B is in itself a stochastic quantity, as long as one can hedge one's position in the swaption using the forward bond B, the volatility of B does not enter the valuation formula. This is the exact counterpart of the statement that the volatility of the discount bond $P(t_0, t_{i+1})$ in Equation (1.29) does not enter the valuation formula for a caplet. It would be surprising if this were not the case, since a one-period swaption is a caplet. Notice, however, that since the swap rate is given by a linear combination of forward rates (Equation (1.20)), if one assumes the latter to be log-normally distributed — as it is implied by the Black formula as applied to caplets (Equation (1.29)) — then, strictly speaking, a swap rate cannot be log-normally distributed as well. In other terms, while both the cap and the swaption Black valuation formulae can be soundly justified *independently*, the simultaneous pricing of both caps and swaptions using the Black formula (as usually done in the market) is logically inconsistent.

The Black formulae for caps and swaptions reported above constitute the market standard for the valuation of these plain-vanilla instruments. Whatever the 'true' distributions might be, as long as the log-normal distributions are matched, as they are by the pricing procedure, to the first two moments, the impact of this inconsistency is quite small.

Having defined the payoffs of caps and swaptions, one can revisit Equation (1.20), which expresses a swap rate as a linear combination of forward rates. Let us denote the volatilities of forward rate F_i by σ_i. If these forward rates F_i are correlated stochastic quantities characterised by a known covariance matrix (see Chapter 2), then, as long as one can regard the variability with interest rates of the coefficients $\{w\}$ much smaller than the variability of the forward rates $\{F\}$ (in general an excellent approximation), the variance of the swap rate

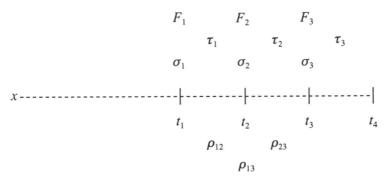

Figure 1.2 The market prices of caplets resetting at times t_1, t_2 and t_3 determine the volatilities σ_1, σ_2 and σ_3 of forward rates F_1, F_2 and F_3, respectively. The European swaption spanning the period $[t_1\ t_3]$ involves forward rates F_1 and F_2, and therefore brings in the correlation ρ_{12}. The European swaption spanning the period $[t_1\ t_4]$ involves forwards F_1, F_2 and F_3, and therefore brings in the additional correlations ρ_{13} and ρ_{23}. The European swaption spanning the period $[t_2\ t_4]$ involving forward rates F_2 and F_3 is only affected by the correlation ρ_{23}. The market prices of the three caplets and the three swaptions together therefore completely specify, at least in principle, σ_1, σ_2, σ_3 and ρ_{12}, ρ_{13}, ρ_{23}.

is simply given by

$$\text{Var}[X] = \sum_i \sum_j w_i w_j \sigma_i \sigma_j \rho_{ij} \tag{1.34}$$

where ρ_{ij} is the correlation coefficient between forward i and forward j. Equation (1.34) shows that, if the covariance matrix of the forward rates is known, then the volatility of the swap rate can be immediately determined. Conversely, within the limits of the approximation stated above, from the variances of a complete series of swap rates one can, at least in principle, directly obtain the underlying covariance matrix. If the volatilities (standard deviations per unit time) of the swap rates are imputed from the traded prices of swaptions, then one can, at least in principle, obtain the market-implied covariance matrix. More precisely, let us consider two caplets, resetting at times t_1 and t_2, and spanning the periods τ_1 and τ_2. Their market prices will indicate (by inversion of Black's formula) the volatilities, σ_1 and σ_2, of the underlying forward rates, F_1 and F_2. See Figure 1.2. Let us then consider the market price of the option to enter the swap covering the period $\tau_1 + \tau_2$. This price will reveal the volatility of the swap rate (again by inverting Black's formula). Via Equation (1.27), and since σ_1 and σ_2 are known from the caplet prices, this will uniquely determine ρ_{12}.

Let us now extend the range of instruments to include a caplet resetting at time t_3. The new underlying forward rate F_3 will introduce correlation terms both with F_1 and with F_2, ρ_{13} and ρ_{23}. *Two* new swaptions are, however, brought into play by the additional forward rate, i.e. the option to enter the swap covering the period $\tau_1 + \tau_2 + \tau_3$, and the option to enter the swap spanning $\tau_2 + \tau_3$. Therefore, Equation (1.34) allows, at least in principle, the determination of the full covariance matrix by including the market volatilities of more and more swap rates. This apparently cumbersome procedure is of crucial importance in the calibration of two-factor models, and will be used, and referred to, extensively in following chapters.

In the present and previous sections (i) swap rates and bond prices have been defined; (ii) their valuation has been expressed in terms of pure discount bonds; (iii) the payoffs and the valuation of the plain-vanilla European options on FRAs and swaps have been defined; (iv) the link between the volatilities of FRAs and swap rates has been highlighted. In order to compute the value of a plain-vanilla swap and of a bullet bond, however, it has been assumed that a market discount function, i.e. a continuum of prices $P(0,t)$, were known. These prices, however, are not directly available in the market, but have to be distilled from the prices of the instruments actually traded. The next section will therefore tackle the complementary problem of determining the prices $P(0,t)$ used in this section, or, as it is commonly said, of determining the market discount function. Strictly speaking, the **discount function** $P(0,t)$ is the function that gives the price today of a discount bond maturing at time t. The **term structure of interest rates** is the function associating to each maturity the value of the (suitably compounded) spot rate from time 0 to the desired maturity. The **yield curve** is the curve which displays the yields of coupon-bearing bonds as a function of maturity. Since, as it is well known (see, e.g., Schaefer (1977), and Section 1.5), these yields depend in general on the coupon of the bond, the yields of par coupon bonds are normally used. Since any of these curves can be obtained from the other (see Section 1.5), the three terms will be used interchangeably.

Although conceptually similar, the creation of the bond and of the LIBOR discount curves are different in important ways. Bonds, in fact, are issued, either by corporate entities or by government issuers, at discrete time intervals with discrete maturities. At any point in time, therefore, one can obtain from the market the prices of bonds which had been priced at par on the day of their issuance, but currently trade at a discount or at a premium. In the swap market, on the other hand, every day one has access to the equilibrium swap rates for swaps of any of a range of benchmark maturities. It is as though par bonds of all these maturities were issued every day. Since, as it will be shown in the next section, knowledge of the par coupon curve (i.e. of the curve describing the par coupon for any possible maturity) is tantamount to knowledge of the (discrete) discount function, it is clear that, for the LIBOR curve, obtaining the latter is little more than an exercise in skilful and careful, but conceptually straightforward, interpolation. Obtaining a reliable LIBOR discount curve is no trivial matter, but the difficulties mainly lie in accounting properly for different conventions in the deposit, futures and swap markets and in interpolating between benchmark maturities in an efficient and consistent way.

When it comes to the bond market, however, the comparative paucity of data changes the very nature of the problem, and forces upon the user the need to employ best-fit estimation techniques. As a result, while major trading houses agree on the LIBOR rates obtained from the discount factor typically to within a basis-point (i.e. a percentage of a percentage point) equivalent in their plain-vanilla rates, much bigger discrepancies arise in the bond curve estimation (to the point, for instance, that the Financial Times Gilt curve published on Mondays is always quoted with its source). The next section therefore tackles the problem of showing how, at least conceptually, the two different term structures of interest rates can be obtained.

1.5   DETERMINATION OF THE DISCOUNT FUNCTION: THE CASE OF BONDS—LINEAR MODELS

Bonds are issued by government and corporate entities. Their market prices reflect not only the implied riskless discount function, but a series of important additional factors, such as the creditworthiness of the issuer, liquidity, tax regimes, institutional preferences or regulatory restrictions. All these are topics of great interest, and a thorough treatment would require a book in its own rights. However, for the pricer of options in a given market (say, options on LIBOR instruments, or options on government bonds of similar coupons, or options on bonds issued by corporate of similar credit quality) the scope can be restricted by using for the estimation procedure homogeneous instruments. This is not a perfect, or even a wholly consistent, solution, but it is adequate for most practical purposes.

Even those investors most superficially acquainted with the bond market have certainly come in contact with the concept of gross redemption yield (GRY), i.e. the internal rate of return of a bond: if $Bnd(T)$ is the price of a bond of maturity T paying a coupon X every τ years, the GRY is defined as

$$Bnd(T) = \sum_{i=1,n} \frac{X\tau_i}{\left(1 + \dfrac{GRY}{\nu}\right)^{vi}} + \frac{100}{\left(1 + \dfrac{GRY}{\nu}\right)^{vn}} \qquad (1.35)$$

where $\nu = 1/\tau$, and, to avoid unnecessary complications, it has been assumed that the valuation is made at the beginning of a coupon period (no accrued interest). The final nail in the coffin of the GRY has probably been driven as early as 15 years ago by Schaefer (1977), who clearly showed the inadequacies of this bond statistic to convey but the most imprecise information about the bond itself. Without repeating the arguments, it will suffice here to say that, by applying the concept of GRY to two bonds of different coupon and maturity, one **discounts payments occurring at the same point in time by different implied discount factors** (the terms $1/(1 + GRY/v)^{vi}$), since in general the GRY will be different for different bonds, **but one discounts payments from the same bond at different points in time by the same rate**. In reality one would wish to do exactly the opposite.

To this effect, one can employ the definition of the τ-period-compounded spot rates $R(0,t)$, given by

$$P(0,t) = \frac{1}{\left(1 + \dfrac{R(0,t)}{v}\right)^{v\tau}} \tag{1.36}$$

and thereby obtain a more satisfactory description of the yield curve, since these rates are no longer bond-specific, but can be used for discounting *any* cash flow occurring at a given point in time. While Equation (1.36) is simply a definition, an argument similar to the one presented in Section 1.3 (i.e. the discrete-time counterpart of Equation (1.16)) shows that the discount bond price $P(0,T)$ can be expressed in terms of forward rates as

$$P(0,T) = \exp\left[-\sum_{i=1,n} F(0,t_i,t_i + \tau)\tau\right] \tag{1.37}$$

where $T = n\tau$, and $F(0,t_i,t_i + \tau)$ is the forward rate obtainable from the term structure at time 0, spanning the period from time t_i, to time $t_i + \tau$, i.e.

$$F(0,t_i,t_{i+\tau}) = \frac{P(0,t_i)/P(0,t_{i+1}) - 1}{\tau} \tag{1.38}$$

A further equivalent description of the yield curve can be given by supplying the par-coupon curve. The par-coupon curve, it will be remembered from the previous section, is the bond equivalent of the equilibrium swap rate (Equation (1.24)), i.e. the ratio of the floating to the fixed leg. Avoiding again, for conceptual simplicity, the case of non-integer periods, and imposing, to lighten notation, $\tau = 1$, let us then consider the par coupon $X(1)$ paid by a bond maturing in one year's time; by rearranging Equation (1.23) one obtains

$$X(1) = \frac{P(0,0) - P(0,1)}{P(0,1)} = \frac{1 - P(0,1)}{P(0,1)} \tag{1.39}$$

whence $P(0,1)$, i.e. the discount factor out to time t_1, can be immediately recovered; moving to a bond issued at par today and paying the par coupon $X(2)$, one can write the ratio of the floating to the fixed leg as

$$X(2) = \frac{1 - P(0,2)}{P(0,1) - P(0,2)} \tag{1.39'}$$

but, since $P(0,1)$ is known from Equation (1.39), $P(0,2)$ can be readily solved for. By this boot-strapping procedure the whole par-coupon curve can be obtained. Therefore, at least conceptually, **supplying the par-coupon curve is equivalent to supplying the discount function** (at least at the discrete points where the coupons are paid).

We have arrived at the conclusion that, while from the *GRY* the discount curve cannot be recovered, **either the set of spot rates $R(0,t)$, or the set of forward rates $F(0,t,t+\tau)$, or the par-coupon curve all give access via simple manipulations to the discount function**. Despite the fact that conceptually there is therefore no distinction between one description or the other, practically the differences are important, since the discount function can be estimated using linear methods, while any of the other equivalent quantities require non-linear procedures. This can be seen as follows.

Let us expand the discount function $P(0,t)$ on the basis of an arbitrarily chosen set of s basis functions $g_k(t)$:

$$P(0,t) = \sum_{k=1,s} a_k g_k(t) \tag{1.40}$$

where a_k is the (as yet unknown) weight corresponding to the k-th basis function. Therefore the price of bond of maturity T_n, Bnd_n, paying (again for simplicity of notation) annual coupons can be written as

$$PV(Bnd_n) = \sum_{i=1,n} XP(0,t_i) + 100P(0,t_n)$$

$$= \sum_{i=1,n} X \sum_{k=1,s} a_k g_k(t_i) + 100 \sum_{k=1,s} a_k g_k(t_n)$$

$$= \sum_{k=1,s} a_k G_{n,k} \tag{1.41}$$

with $G_{n,k} \equiv \sum_{i=1,n} X g_k(t_i) + 100 g_k(t_n)$, or, in vector notation,

$$\mathbf{Bnd = GA} \tag{1.41'}$$

where **Bnd** is the $(nbonds,1)$ vector containing the prices of the $nbonds$ bonds available in the market, **A** is the $(s,1)$ vector containing the coefficients of the s basis functions, and **G** is the $(nbonds,s)$ matrix of coefficients $G_{n,k}$ of Equation (1.41). Equation (1.41') justifies the term 'linear' applied to this type of approach.

If $nbonds = s$, and providing that $Det[\mathbf{G}] \neq 0$, the system provides a unique and 'perfect' solution, where the 'perfect' in this context simply means that all the bonds are exactly priced. More generally, and realistically, $nbonds \gg s$, and therefore

$$\mathbf{A = (G^TG)^{-1}G^TBnd} \tag{1.42}$$

will provide the least-square estimator of A, i.e. of the set of coefficients $\{a\}$

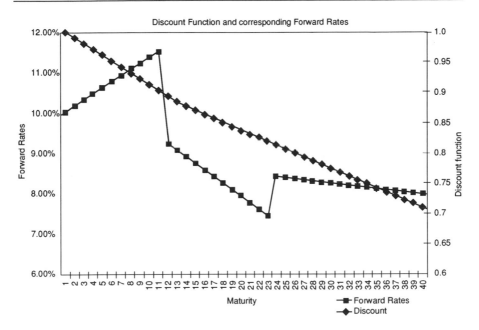

Figure 1.3 A smooth discount function, and the not-so-smooth forward rates that it implies.

such that the sum of the square of the differences between the market and the model prices, i.e. the prices calculated using the lastline of Equation (1.41), is minimised. (The superscripts T and -1, as usual, indicate the transpose and the inverse of a matrix). It is also very easy to incorporate constraints such as the requirement that the discount function should be equal to 1 at the origin, $P(0,0) = 1$, either via the formal use of Lagrange multipliers, or by solving explicitly for one of the coefficients in Equation (1.41).

Since even low-power personal computers can effect the matrix inversion required by Equation (1.42) in a few seconds, the linear approach just described seems to afford a very efficient and rapid way of estimating the discount function. In practice, however, this strategy is fraught with practical difficulties, largely stemming with the very nature of the target function, i.e. the discount function $P(0,t)$. In order to be able to say something more precise, one must examine more carefully the basis functions used for the expansion of the discount function. Many different choices have been proposed (Cubic splines, B-splines, Chebychef polynomials, exponential splines, Bernstein polynomials, etc.). In general, all these basis functions promise, and indeed deliver, a continuous and continuously differentiable discount function at every point. Mathematical continuity can, however, bear surprisingly little resemblance with an intuitive requirement of continuity, especially when it comes to derivatives. These in turn are particularly important since it has been shown in Section 1.2 that

$$f(0,t,t+\varepsilon) = -\frac{\ln P(0,t+\varepsilon)}{\ln P(0,t)}\frac{1}{\varepsilon} = -\frac{\ln P(0,t+\varepsilon) - \ln P(0,t)}{\varepsilon} \simeq -\frac{\partial \ln P(0,t)}{\partial t}$$

(1.43)

i.e. **forward rates are given by (minus) the logarithmic derivative with respect to maturity of the discount bond covering the period from time t to time $t+\varepsilon$.** Unfortunately, functions of very smooth appearance can have still continuous, but not so smooth, derivatives, as shown in Fig. 1.3.

If this is the case, forward rates will also display a rapidly changing, and therefore intuitively implausible, behaviour. For the same reason, forward rates are prone to display a very pronounced dependence on such 'technical details' as the positioning of the knots for B-splines, the number of basis functions, or small variations in the vector of input bond prices. A thorough treatment of these important issues would require more than a chapter. The essential point that should have been conveyed, however, is that direct modelling of the discount function gives rise to a mathematically simple but practically very delicate exercise. The success of the approach will largely depend on the intrinsic suitability of the basis function chosen to describe the behaviour of the discount function. To use a not terribly original, but once again very apt, expression, obtaining reliable forward rates from fitted discount functions can be more of an art than a science.

1.6 DETERMINATION OF THE DISCOUNT FUNCTION: THE CASE OF BONDS – NON-LINEAR MODELS

The difficulties highlighted in the previous section have prompted some researchers to model the spot or forward rates themselves, rather than the discount function. More precisely, one can attempt to expand, say, the continuously compounded spot rates $R(t)$ using a chosen set of basis functions:

$$R(t) = \sum_{k=1,s} a_k g_k(t) \tag{1.44}$$

giving rise for the present value of the bond price (neglecting again for simplicity non-integer periods)

$$PV(Bnd_n) = \sum_{i=1,n} XP(0,t_i) + 100P(0,t_n)$$

$$= \sum_{i=1,n} X \exp(-R(t_i)t_i) + 100 \exp(-R(t_n)t_n)$$

$$= \sum_{i=1,n} X \exp\left[\left(\sum_{k=1,s} a_k g_k(t_i)\right)t_i\right] + 100 \exp\left[\left(\sum_{k=1,s} a_k g_k(t_n)\right)t_n\right] \tag{1.45}$$

Once again the goal will be to change the coefficients $\{\alpha\}$ of expansion (1.44) until, for instance, the sum of the squares of the deviations between model and market bond prices will be minimised. Since, however, the coefficients now appear as arguments of an exponential function, the problem is no longer linear, and there exists no strategy guaranteed to yield the absolute minimum (i.e. the set of parameters that actually minimises the squares of the deviations). Non-linear minimisation algorithms are considerably more laborious to implement. More importantly, those methods that ensure fast convergence are also the most prone to get stuck in local minima. (Conjugate gradients and simulated annealing are two apt and extreme examples of this feature.) To make matters worse, only the most inefficient methods (multi-dimensional simplex) permit to search for a minimum without knowledge of the derivatives of the target function with respect to the optimisation parameters. All the methods which ensure reasonably quick convergence do require (numerical or analytic) evaluation of the derivatives. These, in turn, can be quite time consuming to evaluate, and often algebraically very tedious. 'Smart' methods (such as conjugate gradients) promise stunningly good convergence properties: for a truly parabolic minimum the number of iterations needed should be exactly equal to two! In reality, no minimum is truly parabolic, and fast methods tend to get very close to their target very soon, and use an often infuriatingly large number of iterations to home in to the 'true' solution within the required degree of tolerance.

Slower methods 'ramble around' the coefficient space in a less purposeful manner in the first stages of the optimisation, but, because of this very weakness, are in general better able to explore competing minima.

Both in the case of linear and non-linear methods, the number of basis functions to be used to model either the discount factors or the (spot or forward) rates should be determined on the basis of an enlightened compromise between an oversimplistic description of the target function, and the dangerous tendency to chase every mispriced bond in the market.

For linear models (and, with some qualifications, for non-linear models as well), a useful indication of how many coefficients one 'should' use can be provided by the $\bar{R}^2$ criterion. Let us first define, for a quantity y (the target function, i.e. in this case the bond prices) 'explained' by k variables x_i, $(i = 1, k)$, the quantity R^2 as the ratio between the variance of y explained by the regressors and the total variance of y, i.e.

$$R^2 = \frac{\Sigma \, [y(mod) - y(avg)]^2}{\Sigma \, [y(obs) - y(avg)]^2} \qquad (1.46)$$

(where $y(mod)$ indicates the model prediction for the bond price, $y(obs)$ the corresponding market price, and $y(avg)$ the average of the bond prices). Then

$\bar{R}^2$ is given by

$$\bar{R}^2 = \frac{R^2 - k(n-1)}{(n-1)/(n-k-1)} \qquad (1.47)$$

where k is the number of regressors (parameters), and n the number of observations (the number of bond prices). The imprecise but intuitively suggestive interpretation of the maximum of this statistical indicator is that it displays the 'optimal' number of parameters needed to describe a certain set of data.

Once again, the issue of non-linear minimisation cannot be dealt with in a satisfactory way in a limited space. More simply, the purpose of this section is to highlight the type of issues faced by those users who need to model the bond discount function in order to calibrate the interest-rate models described later on. The different problems encountered when the underlying is a LIBOR-based instrument are mentioned in the following section.

1.7 DETERMINATION OF THE DISCOUNT FUNCTION: THE CASE OF THE LIBOR CURVE

Every day interest-rate market screens display information about three different but interlinked markets: LIBOR borrowing rates, 3-month futures prices and equilibrium swap rates. (Equilibrium swap rates have been defined and treated in Sections 1.2 and 1.3.)

LIBOR (London Inter-Bank Offered Rates) rates are the rates at which high-credit financial institutions can **borrow** in the interbank market for a series of possible maturities, ranging from overnight to, usually, 12 months. (The lending rate is denoted by the acronym LIBID.) In most markets, it is conventional to quote these rates on a **simple compounding** basis.

As for interest-rate (short money) futures, at expiry they assume the value of 100 minus (the 3-month LIBOR rate at expiry multiplied by 100). Day by day, the buyer and seller of a futures contract make or receive a payment in the so-called margin account equal to the difference between the strike price X and the prevailing market value of the futures contract. On expiry date the cash flow occurring between the buyer and the writer of the futures contract is simply the last of the margin-account payments. In other words, all gains and losses are realised, day by day, as they occur. Positive balances in the margin account accrue interest. Even neglecting the effect of this reinvested cash, the equilibrium value of a futures contract (i.e. the value that gives zero value to the contract itself) is different from the equilibrium rate of the underlying FRA. In the latter case, in fact, the payment occurs three months after the expiry of the contract itself. Since, at inception of the contract, the future discount factor from expiry to three months hence is unknown, the relationship between the equilibrium FRA rate and the implied equilibrium futures rate cannot be achieved by discounting by a deterministic quantity (i.e. by a quantity known at contract inception). The correction term which accounts for this difference in payoff timing can easily be obtained using the formalism of Chapters 4 and 5, i.e. by making use of suitable numeraires, and depends on the volatility of the underlying forward rate and on the correlation between this forward rate and the discounting zero-coupon bond. This correction term is normally referred to as the 'futures/FRAs adjustment'. Very good approxima-tions exist for this term (see, e.g. Doust (1995)). For very long-expiry contracts (the US$ market has 3-month futures prices extending to 10 years!) the difference between (100-futures price)/100 and the FRA rate can be as large as 30 basis points, for reasonable choices of the volatility and correlation inputs (see Vaillant (1995)). The initial margin—i.e. the amount of money which both parties have to pay into the margin account at contract inception—is not accounted by this correction term, but is of smaller import.

It is not the purpose of this chapter to go into the intricacies of exact futures pricing. It should be clear, however, that a great amount of care has to be exercised in order to splice together information available from different markets, and that there exists a spectrum of maturities over which more than one type of instrument is traded (LIBOR deposit rates overlap the first futures contracts, and the later-expiry futures contracts overlap the swap market). In theory, once proper account is taken of the exact payoffs, it should be immaterial which type of instruments should be used, since no-arbitrage should ensure the equivalence of the results, however obtained. In practice, not all instruments enjoy the same degree of liquidity; the practice is therefore common to make use of the most liquid assets over the different segments of the yield curve. For many markets this often means using deposit rates to reach the expiry of the first futures contract, and then using a market-dependent number of liquid futures contracts before switching to the market swap rates. Due to this overlap, careful interpolation techniques must be used in order to ensure a 'smooth transition' (and therefore, as discussed above, smooth forward rates). However delicate these techniques might be (see, e.g., Miron and Swannell (1991)), it is clear that the problem is, at least conceptually, much simpler than the estimation of the bond discount function: in the LIBOR market, as mentioned above, day by day there exists the equivalent of a whole series of par-coupon bonds. Not surprisingly, as mentioned above, the agreement amongst practitioners (or, at least, 'good' practitioners) about the LIBOR curves is by far greater than the agreement about the govern-ment par-yield curve.

For the remainder of the book, the 'market' discount function will therefore be taken as uncontroversially available to market participants, despite the fact that, in the light of the last two sections, the assumption is actually more justifiable for the LIBOR curve. The first sections of this chapter have made use of this market discount function to price some elementary underlying instruments. In the chapters of Part Four the price of discount bonds will play a crucial role in the calibration of the various option models.

ENDNOTE

1. Different markets have different conventions (Actual/360, Actual/365, 30/365, etc.) to measure the fraction of the year. Details of the different conventions are clearly presented in Miron and Swannell (1991).

2
Yield curve models: a statistical approach

2.1 STATISTICAL ANALYSIS OF THE EVOLUTION OF RATES

The evolution of the yield curve in its entirety can be described in terms of the dynamics of several equivalent financial quantities, such as, for instance, spot rates, forward rates, or zero-coupon bonds. As long as the transformation laws from one quantity to another are known, the choice of the independent variables is purely a matter of convenience. As shown in the previous chapter, for the three quantities just mentioned, the linking equations are:

$$P(t,T) = \exp\left[-\int_t^T f(t,s)\, \mathrm{d}s\right] \tag{2.1}$$

$$f(t,T) = -\frac{\partial \ln P(t,T)}{\partial T} \tag{2.1'}$$

$$P(t,T) = \exp[-R(t,T)(T-t)] \tag{2.1''}$$

where $P(t,T)$ is the price of a T-maturity discount bond as seen from the yield curve at time t; $f(t,T)$ is the instantaneous forward rate from time T to $T + \varepsilon$ as seen from the yield curve at time t (i.e. the rate which can be contracted at time t for lending/borrowing from time T to time $T + \varepsilon$, with $T > t$); and $R(t,T)$ defines the continuously compounded spot rate from time t to time T. In the following discussion, we shall focus our attention on forward (rather than spot) rates, and consider a finite set of rates of identical tenor spanning the whole maturity spectrum.

All these rates can be regarded as stochastic variables imperfectly correlated with each other, with the degree of correlation normally decreasing with increasing difference in maturity. In the attempt to build a viable model to describe the dynamics of the yield curve, let us therefore consider the case of n

random imperfectly correlated variables $g_i(i = 1, n)$. These random variables could, for instance, represent (absolute or percentage) increments in a forward rate

$$g_i \equiv df_i = \mu_i \, dt + \sigma_i \, dz_i \qquad (2.2)$$

Each term dz_i in Equation (2.2) is a draw from a normal distribution of zero mean and unit variance. Draws at *different times* for the same variable g_i are assumed to be independent of each other:

$$E[dz_i(t) \, dz_i(t + dt)] = 0 \qquad (2.3)$$

Since, however, the variables $\{g\}$ are imperfectly correlated with each other, the increments $dz_i(t)$, $dz_j(t)$ at the same time will display a degree of correlation given by

$$E[dz_i(t) \, dz_j(t)] = \rho_{ij}(t) \, dt \qquad (2.4)$$

where ρ_{ij} represents the correlation between variables i and j. To lighten the notation the dependence on t will often be dropped in the following. (For readers not familiar with stochastic calculus, the precise meaning of expression (2.4) will become clear after Chapter 4.) If, as assumed, a yield curve is described by n (discrete) forward rates, and if the identification is made between the increments in the forward rates and the variables $\{g\}$, then the evolution of these variables $\{g\}$ completely determines the evolution of the yield curve itself. Let us evaluate the covariance between random variables i and j:

$$\mathrm{Covar}[g_i, g_j] = \mathrm{Covar}[df_i, df_j] = E[df_i \, df_j] = E[(\mu_i \, dt + \sigma_i \, dz_i)(\mu_j \, dt + \sigma_j \, dz_j)]$$

$$(2.5)$$

where definition (2.2) has been used to obtain the last equality. When terms in brackets are multiplied through, from ordinary calculus one knows that all terms in dt^2 are infinitesimals of higher order than dt, and therefore 'disappear' in the product. It can be shown from stochastic calculus (Chapter 4) that terms in $dz \, dt$ can also be set equal to zero, and terms $E[dz_i \, dz_j]$ give the contribution in Equation (2.4). Therefore

$$E[df_i \, df_j] = \mathrm{Covar}[df_i, df_j] = \sigma_i \sigma_j \rho_{ij} \, dt \qquad (2.6)$$

$$E[df_i \, df_i] = \mathrm{Var}(df_i) = \sigma_i^2 \, dt \qquad (2.6')$$

In general, if the variables $\{g\}$ do represent changes in forward rates, the drift term, i.e. the expectation, of each random variable will be obtainable from no-arbitrage conditions (see Chapter 5, and Girsanov's theorem in particular), but as far as the covariance matrix is concerned, we can, without loss of generality, assume $\mu_i = 0$.

One can then consider a (random) n-dimensional vector $\mathbf{Vg}$ of components vg_i

$$\mathbf{Vg} = \begin{bmatrix} vg_1 \\ vg_2 \\ vg_3 \\ \cdots \\ vg_n \end{bmatrix} = \begin{bmatrix} \sigma_1\, dz_1 \\ \sigma_2\, dz_2 \\ \sigma_3\, dz_3 \\ \cdots \\ \sigma_n\, dz_n \end{bmatrix} \qquad (2.7)$$

with $vg_i = \sigma_i\, dz_i$. For the case of $n = 2$, several realisations of this vector $\mathbf{V}$ are shown in Figures 2.1–2.3 for the correlation of 0, 0.8 and -0.8, respectively. When the correlation is positive (negative) to a, say, large and positive realisation of the first component there corresponds with great likelihood a large and positive (negative) realisation of the second component. Therefore the vectors will mainly end in the first and third (second and fourth) quadrants (Figures 2.2 and 2.3). If the correlation were zero, there would be no preferential location in any of the quadrants for the extremities of the vectors, as shown in Figure 2.1. If the volatilities were not identical, then the axes of the ellipse would be elongated in the direction of the component with the highest variance.

One of the interesting features of this vector is that **its length L** (or, to be more precise, it Euclidean norm), given by the sum of the squares of all its components

$$L = \Sigma vg_i^2 = dt\, \Sigma \sigma_i^2 \qquad (2.8)$$

is simply equal to the sum of all the individual instantaneous variances (times the term dt, which shall be dropped in the following to lighten notation). We shall make use of this important result later in this section.

Going back to the n-dimensional vector $\mathbf{G}$ of components $g_1 = df_1$, $g_2 = df_2, \ldots, g_n = df_n$, we know from elementary linear algebra that we can then apply a (for the moment generic) transformation, i.e a rotation and, possibly, a stretching of $\mathbf{G}$, by applying the transpose of a matrix $\mathbf{A}[n \times n]$, so as to turn the vector $\mathbf{G}$ into a new vector $\mathbf{Y}$:

$$\mathbf{Y} = \mathbf{A}^T \mathbf{G} \qquad (2.9)$$

or, in algebraic form,

$$y_s = \sum_k a_{ks} g_k \qquad (2.10)$$

The matrix $\mathbf{A}$ is made up of column vectors $\mathbf{a}_s$, $(s = 1, n)$; the jth element of the sth vector, a_{js}, contains the contribution of the jth original variable, g_j, to the sth new variable y_s. These new variables, for reasons which will become apparent in the following, will be called factors. If the original variables $\{g\}$

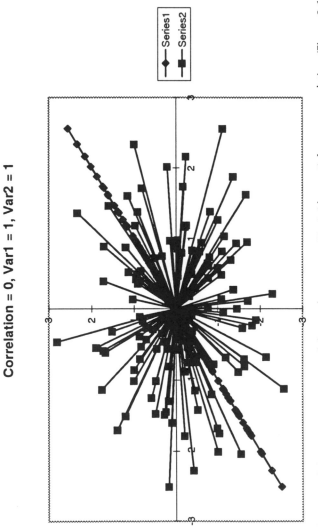

Figure 2.1 Realisations of the two components of the random vectors **Vg** (with $n = 2$) for zero correlation (Figure 2.1), positive (0.8) correlation (Figure 2.2) and negative correlation (-0.8), and equal (unit) variance. Each line corresponds to one particular realisation of the vector. Notice the different unit length along the axes in the graphical representation.

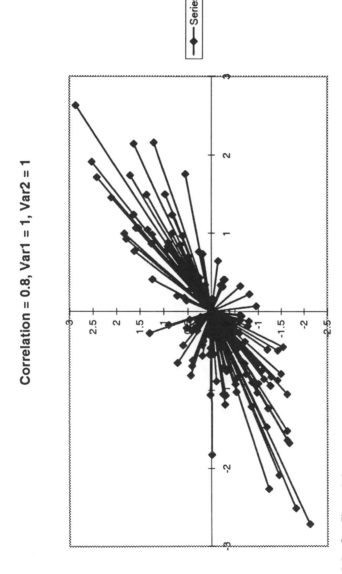

Figure 2.2 See Figure 2.1.

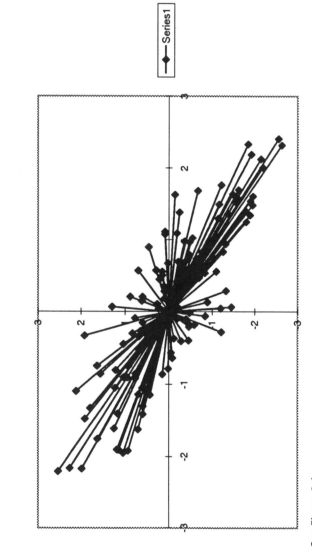

Figure 2.3   See Figure 2.1.

indeed represented increments in forward rates, then the new variables $\{y\}$ would be *increments* in **factors**, expressed as linear combinations of the forward increments. Therefore, with a slightly awkward notation, one can write $y_s = \mathrm{d}(fac)_s$:

$$y_s = \mathrm{d}(fac)_s = \mu_s\,\mathrm{d}t + \sigma_{y_s}\,\mathrm{d}z_s \qquad (2.10')$$

As pointed out above, we shall not be concerned in this chapter with the drift term, but we shall derive below the expression for the variance of the increments in the factors.

From definition (2.10), the covariance matrix element $\mathrm{Cov}(y_r, y_s)$ is given by

$$\mathrm{Cov}(y_r, y_s) = E[y_r\, y_s]$$

$$= E[(\mu_r\,\mathrm{d}t + \sigma_{y_r}\,\mathrm{d}z)(\mu_s\,\mathrm{d}t + \sigma_{y_s}\,\mathrm{d}z)] = E\left[\sum_k a_{ks}g_k \sum_j a_{jr}g_j\right] \qquad (2.11)$$

This result is, so far, completely general, since no requirement as been imposed on the transformation **A**. A particular rotation of special importance is one where all the vectors $\mathbf{a}_s$ are orthogonal to each other, i.e.

$$\sum_k a_{ks}a_{kr} = 0 \quad \text{if } r \neq s \qquad (2.12)$$

If this is the case the matrix **A** is said to be orthogonal, and its inverse is simply equal to its transpose:

$$\mathbf{A}^T = \mathbf{A}^{-1} \qquad (2.13)$$

In this case one can then write

$$Y = A^T G = A^{-1}G \Rightarrow AY = AA^{-1}G = \mathbf{G} = \mathbf{AY} \qquad (2.14)$$

$$g_j = \sum_s a_{js}y_s \qquad (2.14')$$

Using Expressions (2.14), (2.5) and (2.6) the covariance element $\mathrm{Cov}(\mathrm{d}f_i, \mathrm{d}f_j)$ is therefore equal to

$$\mathrm{Covar}[\mathrm{d}f_i, \mathrm{d}f_j] = E[\mathrm{d}f_i, \mathrm{d}f_j] = E\left[\sum_s a_{is}y_s \sum_r a_{jr}y_r\right] = \sigma_i\sigma_j\rho_{ij} \qquad (2.15)$$

(As mentioned before, the term '$\mathrm{d}t$' has been dropped to lighten the notation.) In particular

$$\mathrm{Var}[\mathrm{d}f_j] = \sigma_j^2 = E\left[\sum_s\sum_r a_{js}a_{jr}y_s y_r\right] \qquad (2.16)$$

From Equation (2.8), the length, $L(\mathbf{V}g)$, of the vector $\mathbf{V}g$, i.e. the sum of the variances of the original variables $\{g\}$, is given by

$$L(\mathbf{V}g) = \sum_j \sigma_j^2 = \sum_j E[g_j^2] = E\left[\sum_j \sum_s \sum_r a_{js} a_{jr} y_s y_r\right] = E\left[\sum_s \sum_r y_s y_r \sum_j a_{js} a_{jr}\right]$$

(2.17)

where Equation (2.14′) has been used to substitute out g_j. From the orthogonality condition (2.12), the last summation inside the expectation sign on the RHS is equal to 0 if $s \neq r$. Therefore Equation (2.17) simplifies to

$$\sum_j \sigma_j^2 = E\left[\sum_s y_s^2 \sum_j a_{js}^2\right] = \sum_s E[y_s^2] \sum_j a_{js}^2$$

(2.18)

Let us now impose the further constraint on the transformation matrix $\mathbf{A}$ that the sum over forward rates of the squares of the loadings of each individual factor should add up to 1; or, equivalently, let us impose that the 'length' (Euclidean norm) of each of the vectors $\mathbf{a}_s$ should be exactly 1:

$$\sum_j a_{js}^2 = 1$$

(2.19)

If this is the case, then one obtains for the length, L, of the vector $\mathbf{V}g$

$$L(\mathbf{V}g) = \sum_j \sigma_j^2 = \sum_j E[y_s^2]$$

(2.20)

But, looking back at Equations (2.6), (2.6′) and (2.10′) one can easily see that each expectation on the RHS is simply equal to the variance of the relative factor, i.e. $\mathrm{Var}(y_s) = E[y_s^2]$. We shall denote all these variances by λ_s, i.e. $\mathrm{Var}(y_s) \equiv \lambda_s$. Therefore, the particular transformation $\mathbf{A}$ that we have specified, and which is fully characterized by requiring that the vectors $\mathbf{a}_s$ should be normalised to unity (Equation (2.19)) and orthogonal to each other (Equation (2.12)), rotates the original column vector $\mathbf{V}g$ into a new column vector $\mathbf{V}y$, whose components are the standard deviations of the $\{y\}$ $\sqrt{\lambda_n}$ variables times the independent Brownian increments dw_n:

$$\mathbf{V}y = \begin{bmatrix} \sigma_{y1}\,dz_1 \\ \sigma_{y2}\,dz_2 \\ \sigma_{y3}\,dz_3 \\ \cdots \\ \sigma_{yn}\,dz_n \end{bmatrix} = \begin{bmatrix} \sqrt{\lambda_1}\,dw_1 \\ \sqrt{\lambda_2}\,dw_2 \\ \sqrt{\lambda_3}\,dw_3 \\ \cdots \\ \sqrt{\lambda_n}\,dw_n \end{bmatrix}$$

(2.21)

and **such that the lengths of the two vectors Vg and Vy have been preserved**. And, remembering that the length of the vectors $\mathbf{V}g$ and $\mathbf{V}y$ is given by the sum of the respective variances (Equations (2.20) and (2.8)), one can easily see that **the particular transformation chosen is such that the new variables $\{y\}$ (the increments in the factors) display the same total variance as the original variables (the increments in the forward rates $\{g\}$).**

Since the original covariance matrix of the variables $\{g\}$ (Equation (2.6)), Σ, is real and symmetric it can always be diagonalised by an orthogonal matrix such as $\mathbf{A}$; the procedure is often referred to, in linear algebra parlance, as finding the orthogonal axes of Σ, i.e. finding its eigenvectors and eigenvalues. The requirement that the matrix $\mathbf{A}$ should be orthogonal then allows one to write the covariance matrix $\mathbf{A}$ of the variables $\{y\}$ by inspection:

$$\Lambda = \mathbf{A}^T \Sigma \mathbf{A} \qquad (2.22)$$

where Λ is the *diagonal* matrix of elements λ_s $(s = 1, n)$:

$$\begin{bmatrix} \lambda_1 & & & & & \\ & \lambda_2 & & & & \\ & & \lambda_3 & & & \\ & & & \cdots & & \\ & & & & \cdots & \\ & & & & & \lambda_n \end{bmatrix} \qquad (2.23)$$

So long as all the original variables g_i are linearly independent, i.e. so long as no $\mathrm{corr}(g_i, g_j) = 1$ for $i \neq j$, then all the eigenvalues (variances) λ_s will be distinct. In case of co-linearity, i.e. if any of the original variables can be expressed as a linear combination of the others, then only q eigenvalues will be different from zero, where $\mathbf{q}$ is the number of linearly independent original variables, or, equivalently, the rank of $\mathbf{A}$.

The variables which have so far been referred to as 'factors' are normally called **principal components**. After the transformation, Figure 2.4 shows a large number of realisations (for $n = 2$) of the vector $\mathbf{Vy}$, the transform of the vector $\mathbf{Vg}$, for the case of a correlation ρ between the two original variables of 0.8. Comparing Figure 2.4 with Figure 2.2, one can notice that the axes of the ellipse are now orthogonal to each other, with a different ratio of the variances of the two factors.

Assuming, for the moment, linear independence, so that the matrix $\mathbf{A}$ is of full rank, it is always possible to order the eigenvalues (variances) by magnitude, from the largest downward. (This simply corresponds to permuting the column vectors $\mathbf{a}_s$ (the loadings) in the matrix $\mathbf{A}$.) Since, as we have shown, the total variance, i.e the length of $\mathbf{Vg}$, is preserved by the chosen transformation, one can say that the first principal component accounts for the maximum fraction of the total variance, the second principal component explains the largest part of the *residual* variance, and so on until the n components fully account for all of the original variance.

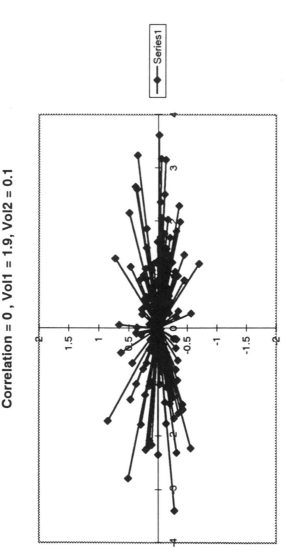

Figure 2.4 A large number of realisations of the two components of the transformed vectors, obtained from the transformation of the original variables whose components are shown in Figure 2.2. Notice that the ratio of the length of the major to the minor axis is very large (indicating that the new variables explain in a very 'effective' way the variability of the original variables), and that the two axes are now orthogonal. The larger the correlation between the two original variables, the larger the ratio of the transformed axes, the greater percentage of the original variability will be explained by the first principal component.

Table 2.1 Degree of Correlation for Changes in US$ Treasury Forward Rates of Different Maturities for the 1987–1994 Period

Maturity (yrs)	0.00	0.50	1.00	1.50	2.00	3.00
0.00	1.00	0.87	0.74	0.69	0.64	0.60
0.50	0.87	1.00	0.96	0.93	0.90	0.85
1.00	0.74	0.96	1.00	0.99	0.95	0.92
1.50	0.69	0.93	0.99	1.00	0.97	0.93
2.50	0.64	0.90	0.95	0.97	1.00	0.95
3.00	0.60	0.85	0.92	0.93	0.95	1.00

In general, the larger the correlation among the original variables, the more efficient the first principal component will be in accounting for the original variance (see Figure 2.4). If the variables $\{g\}$ were (possibly percentage) changes in forward rates, many empirical studies have been carried out of their time series behaviour. A typical example of the statistical properties of forward rates for the US Treasury yield curve in the years 1987/1994 has for instance been analysed by Brown and Schaefer (1994) (using data described in Fisher et al (1994)), who examined changes

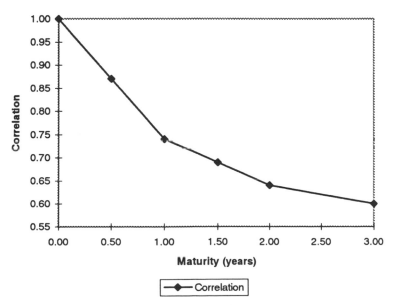

Correlation between instantaneous forward rates

Figure 2.5 Correlation between the spot rate and instantaneous forward rates starting at the times indicated on the x-axis for the US$ Treasury curve 1987/1994.

in instantaneous forward rates of different maturities at monthly intervals. The observed degree of correlation among these forward rates is shown in Table 2.1.

Figure 2.5 shows the degree correlation between the spot rate and the instantaneous forward rates starting at later and later times. As it is apparent, the speed of decorrelation is not constant, and the largest proportion of decoupling occurs between adjacent forward rates.

In the light of the discussion above, the high degree of correlation between the original n variables indicates that a transformation of variables in terms of principal components should be very efficient in order to explain the co-movements of different parts of the yield curve, and that, therefore, a 'brute-force' description of the yield curve dynamics that employed all the underlying variables would be not

Table 2.2 Contributions to the Overall Explained Variance of the Different Principal Components for the UK Rate Data Described in the Text

Principal Component	Explained Variance	Total Variance
1	92.170%	92.170%
2	6.930%	99.100%
3	0.614%	99.714%
4	0.240%	99.954%
5	0.031%	99.985%
6	0.004%	99.989%
7	0.002%	99.991%
8	0.000%	99.995%

Table 2.3 Weights of the Original Variables (i.e. Changes in Rates of Maturities 1 to 8) needed to produce the First Three Principal Components for the Same Data Used to Obtain Table 2.2

Loadings	First Princ Comp	Second Princ Comp	Third Princ Comp
1	0.329	−0.722	0.49
2	0.354	−0.368	−0.204
3	0.365	−0.121	−0.455
4	0.367	0.044	−0.461
5	0.364	0.161	−0.176
6	0.361	0.291	0.176
7	0.358	0.316	0.268
8	0.352	0.343	0.404

only impossibly cumbersome, but also fundamentally wasteful. This has prompted many researchers to apply the principal component analysis described above to model the yield dynamics of most currencies. (See references in Wilson (1994) for a bibliography of several recent empirical studies.) The new variables $\{y_i\}$ produced by these analyses have empirically been observed to be such that

(i)   the first principal component is made up by approximately equal weights $\{a_{i1}\}$ of the original variables, and can therefore be intuitively interpreted as the 'average level' of the yield curve,

(ii) the second is made up by weights $\{a_{i2}\}$ of similar magnitude and opposite signs at the opposite end of the maturity spectrum, and therefore lends itself to the interpretation of being the slope of the yield curve,

(iii) the third is made up by weights $\{a_{i3}\}$ of similar magnitude and identical signs at the extremes of the maturity spectrum, and approximately twice as large and of opposite sign in the middle; this feature warrants the interpretation of the third component as the 'curvature' of the yield curve (remember that the numerical approximation to the second derivative of a function $f(x)$ is given by $f'' \cong (f(x+\mathrm{d}x) + f(x-\mathrm{d}x) - 2f(x))/\mathrm{d}x^2$.

These results are for instance borne out by the principal component analysis of the rates in the UK market in the years 1989/1992 (see Tables 2.2–2.3 and Figure 2.6), where, for clarity of exposition, the original maturity spectrum has been subdivided into eight distinct buckets.

As for the 'explanatory power' of these new variables, in most currencies one then finds (see Table 2.2) that the 'level' often accounts for up to 80–90% of the total variance, and that the first three principal components taken together often describe up to 95–99% of the inter-maturity variability. **The number of independent rates (or linear combinations thereof) needed to describe the dynamics of the yield curve in its entirety can therefore be drastically reduced with little loss of information.**

In the light of these findings, in establishing a framework for option pricing the formulation of a model of the yield curve behaviour has been reduced for tractability to the specification of the dynamics of a few underlying driving factors. Some researchers have adopted a two- or three-variable approach. The Brennan and Schwartz (1982) (Chapter 13) and Heath Jarrow and Morton (1989) (Chapter 14) models are two examples of this pricing philosophy. More commonly, however, a single variable has been chosen to describe the whole yield curve. It must be stressed at this point that this does not mean that the yield curve is forced to move in parallel (see the discussion at the end of the next section), but simply that only one source of uncertainty is allowed to affect the different rates. The individual rates can be affected by changes in the driving variable to a different extent, in as complex a way as the richness of the model can allow.

One-factor models do, however, imply perfect local correlation between movements in rates of different maturities, and, as such, are intrinsically

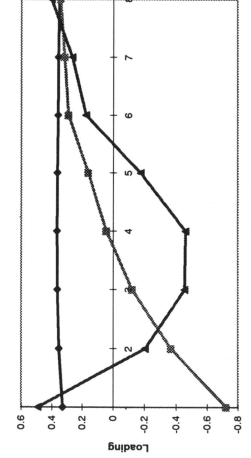
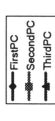

Figure 2.6   Loadings of the original variables to form the first three principal components.

incapable of pricing *simultaneously* and *consistently* instruments which depend on the imperfect correlation between rates. As outlined in the introduction, in the real world, as opposed to the simplified universe of one-factor models, practically all interest-rate options depend in an important way on the decorrelation between rates. (Virtually the only exceptions are caps and some trivial cases of knock-out options.) Academics and practitioners have therefore been looking at sound and easily implementable two- or three-factor models, implicitly or explicitly based on a PC framework, as the natural way of attacking the problem of pricing in a simultaneous and consistent manner at least all the plain-vanilla options (caps and European swaptions) observed in the market. Some of these approaches are discussed in following chapters. Before embarking on the analysis of the individual models, however, it is very important to explore to what extent these higher-dimensionality models based on the assumption that linear combination of forward rates should be taken as driving factors can actually fulfil these hopes. The next section will therefore look at the intrinsic limitations of *any* such low-dimensionality description of the yield curve dynamics (where by 'low-dimensionality model' I mean a model with a small (two or three) number of driving factors). The emphasis of the remainder of this chapter will therefore be on the general, rather than specific, features of this class of models.

2.2 THE EFFECTS OF MODEL DIMENSIONALITY ON OPTION PRICING

As mentioned above, empirical studies have shown that the historically observed correlation between n-month forward rates of different maturities decreases with increasing difference in the maturity of the forward rate (see again Figure 2.5). Furthermore, the decorrelation between forwards maturing n years apart is observed to decrease with the maturity of the first forward (in other terms, the correlation between the 3-month forwards in 1 and 2 years' time is lower than the correlation between 3-month forwards in 9 and 10 years' time).

These empirical observations suggest that an exponentially decaying structure for the correlation function can plausibly describe this qualitative behaviour. Since in the rest of this section the discussion will focus on very general features of low-dimensionality models the following assumptions are made (see Rebonato and Cooper (1995) for a more thorough discussion):

Assumption 1 The yield curve world is fully described by N m-month forwards.

Assumption 2 The correlation ρ between forwards maturing at times T_1 and T_2 is given by an exponentially decaying function of the form

$$\rho(T_1, T_2) = \exp[-\beta(T_2 - T_1)] \tag{2.24}$$

Table 2.4 The Eigenvalues Resulting from the Diagonalisation of the Covariance Matrix (2.25), as Obtained with a Value of ρ of 0.85; the Cumulative Explained Variance is Also Reported

Eigenvalues

0.316	0.118	0.051	0.027	0.017	0.012	0.010	0.008	0.007	0.006

Explained Variance

0.744	0.871	0.920	0.946	0.962	0.973	0.981	0.988	0.995	1.000

Table 2.5 The Eigenvectors Resulting from the Diagonalisation of the Covariance Matrix (2.25), as Obtained with a Value of ρ of 0.85

Eigenvectors

0.300	−0.417	0.447	−0.434	0.384	−0.328	0.255	−0.156	−0.056	−0.006
0.337	−0.401	0.277	−0.046	−0.206	0.407	−0.499	0.400	0.173	0.021
0.361	−0.310	−0.027	0.371	−0.438	0.177	0.263	−0.491	−0.315	−0.052
0.366	−0.162	−0.305	0.408	0.027	−0.436	0.238	0.340	0.454	0.111
0.360	0.007	−0.427	0.068	0.430	−0.106	−0.433	0.027	−0.506	−0.207
0.346	0.169	−0.355	−0.320	0.207	0.427	0.054	−0.360	0.387	0.339
0.317	0.295	−0.124	−0.414	−0.296	0.098	0.384	0.365	−0.106	−0.487
0.285	0.374	0.146	−0.172	−0.393	−0.398	−0.222	0.009	−0.228	0.560
0.247	0.398	0.349	0.197	0.013	−0.162	−0.291	−0.361	0.385	−0.480
0.202	0.359	0.405	0.399	0.384	0.343	0.296	0.254	−0.213	0.213

By virtue of Assumption 2 the correlation structure is therefore fully described by a single decay constant β.

In order to give a concrete focus to the discussion, the special issue has then been addressed of the correlation between a collection of ten 6-month forward rates for the US$ market at the beginning of December 1994, with the first forward maturing in two years' time. These are the forwards that would enter the pricing, for instance, of any 2×5 year swaption, or of any caption to enter a 5-year cap in two years' time, or of any 5-year forward swap amortised or knocked out in two years' time by the realisation of the 6-month spot rate.

Given the structure for the correlation posited by Assumption 2 above, a principal component (PC) analysis can then be undertaken from the covariance matrix obtainable from the cap volatility curve and Equation (2.24) above. More precisely, the element of the covariance matrix corresponding to forwards i and j can be obtained as

$$\text{Cov}[df_i, df_j] = \sigma_i \sigma_j \exp[-\beta(T_j - T_i)] \quad j > i \qquad (2.25)$$

The eigenvalues and eigenvectors of the resulting matrix are shown in Tables 2.4 and 2.5.

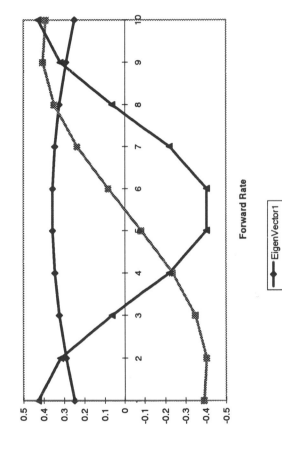

Figure 2.7 The eigenvectors of the covariance matrix. The elements of the nth eigenvector n give the weights that must be assigned to the increments in the forward rates to obtain the nth principal component.

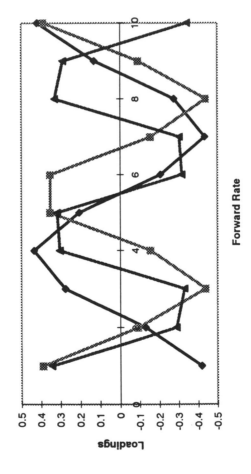

Figure 2.8   See Figure 2.7.

Last Two Eigenvectors

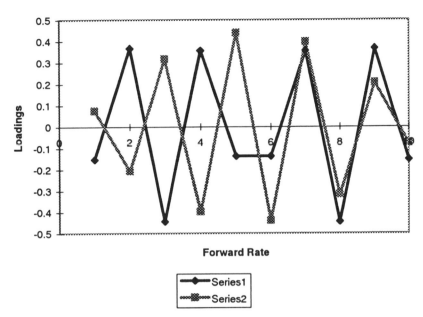

Figure 2.9   See Figure 2.7.

The usual interpretation of the first principal components as level, slope and curvature is borne out by the analysis. But, for this very 'clean' example, in which the covariance matrix was assumed to be known *a priori*, rather than obtained from a noisy time series or imputed from the market prices of swaptions and caps, a more interesting interpretation becomes apparent. Figures 2.7, 2.8 and 2.9 show the weights to be given to the original variables (the forward rates r_i) to obtain the new variables, the PCs y_i.

These figures immediately suggest the interpretation of the eigenvectors as akin to the basis functions in a Fourier series expansion, with each vector contributing higher and higher frequency components. For those readers who might be unfamiliar with Fourier series, it will suffice to say that the loadings needed to obtain higher and higher principal components can be seen as sine or cosine 'waves' of higher and higher frequency. So, the first principal component would correspond to frequency 0, the second to a frequency equal to $\frac{1}{2}$, the third to a frequency of 1, etc. Notice that all the contiguous components of the last eigenvector have opposite signs (corresponding to the maximum (Nyquist) frequency). The relevance of these observations will become apparent later on.

As seen before, the PC transformation can be seen as a rotation of the n-dimensional vector $\mathbf{g}$ by means of (the transpose of) a matrix $\mathbf{A}$ into a new vector $\mathbf{y}$

$$y_s = \sum_{j=1,n} a_{js} g_j \tag{2.26}$$

$$\mathbf{y} = \mathbf{A}^T \mathbf{g} \tag{2.26'}$$

alternatively one can re-obtain the original quantities y by using the matrix $\mathbf{A}$:

$$\mathbf{g} = \mathbf{A}\mathbf{y} \tag{2.27}$$

$$g_i = df_i = \sum_{s=1,n} a_{is} \, d(fac)_s = \sum_{s=1,n} a_{is} y_s$$

As discussed in the previous section, one can mimic the approach of an m-factor PC-based model by restricting the summation in Equation (2.27) to the first $m (m < n)$ terms. Indicating explicitly this dependence on the summation index one can write

$$g(m)_i = df(m)_i = \sum_{s=1,m} a_{is} y_s \tag{2.27'}$$

The total variance explained by the new m variables $g(m)_i$ is clearly smaller than the variance of the original variables r_i, since

$$\Sigma = \mathbf{A}^T \Lambda \mathbf{A} \tag{2.27''}$$

and now the eigenvectors $a_{m+1}, a_{m+2}, \ldots, a_n$ have all been set to zero, so that only the first m eigenvalues $\lambda_s \ (s = 1, m)$ are different from zero. In other terms, the length L (Equation (2.8)) of the original vector has *not* been preserved by the chosen transformation: if we define by $\Sigma(m)$ the 'synthetic' covariance matrix obtained using only the first m components, the sum of the variances of the df_i is now only equal to $\Sigma_{s=1,m} \lambda_s^2$: some variance has been 'lost'. To the extent that the PC approach efficiently accounts for the observed variability it is usually claimed that this loss of information should be small. However, in order to obtain exact cap pricing, the variances, $\mathrm{Var}(df(m)_i)$, are implicitly rescaled, by the calibration procedure of any m-factor model, so as to compensate for the variance 'lost' by carrying out the summation over m rather than n terms.

Having obtained the quantities $g(m)_i$, one can then ask for the correlation structure implied by using only m PCs. To this effect one has to calculate

$$E[df(m)_i \, df(m)_j] \tag{2.28}$$

where each $g(m)_i$ is given by Equation (2.27), and the orthogonality condition between the different y_i can be invoked to reduce Equation (2.28) to

$$\mathrm{Covar}[r_i(m), r_j(m)] = \sum_{s=1,m} a_{is} a_{js} \, \mathrm{Var}(y_s) \tag{2.29}$$

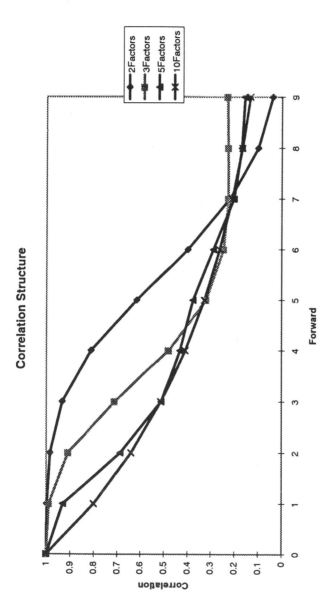

Figure 2.10 The 'synthetic' correlation between the first and subsequent forwards obtainable by retaining a number of factors.

Covariance Surface - 3 Factors

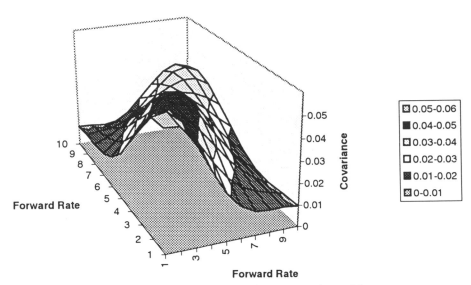

Figure 2.11   The whole covariance matrix for different numbers of factors.

Covariance Surface - 5 Factors

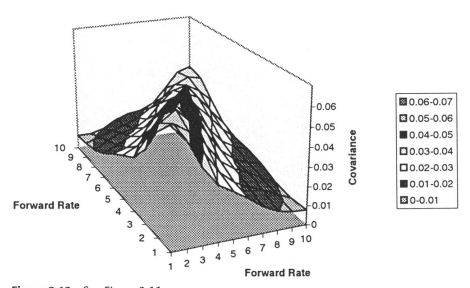

Figure 2.12   See Figure 2.11.

Covariance Surface - 10 factors

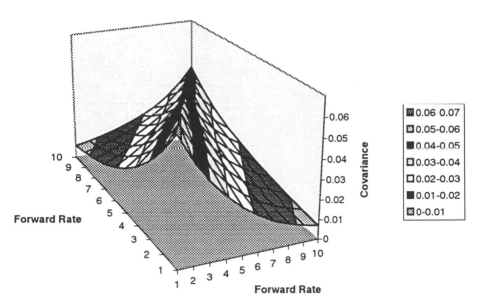

Figure 2.13 See Figure 2.11.

Figure 2.10 provides an illustration of the shape of the correlation between the first and the remaining forwards for different numbers of factors. Figures 2.11 to 2.13 show the shape of the full covariance matrix among all the forwards, obtained using Equation (2.29), again for different numbers of factors. The qualitative shape of the correlation function changes smoothly from having a negative convexity at the short end of the maturity spectrum and a positive convexity at the long end (sigmoid shape) for a small number of factors, to having a positive convexity throughout for a large number of factors. The very interesting qualitative feature then becomes apparent that **any yield-curve model that uses principal components as driving factors is constrained to displaying a sigmoid-like correlation structure. This feature is not a result of the particular assumptions of the specific models, but a general consequence of the low dimensionality of these approaches.** It is actually rather surprising to find that, in order to recover an exponential-like correlation structure, one seems to have to employ a rather high number of principal components (approximately four or five for this example).

Looking at Equation (2.29) one can appreciate the implications of the Fourier series interpretation of the eigenvectors outlined before: keeping in mind that the eigenvalues (i.e. the variances of the principal components) are by construction of decreasing magnitude, one can see that by limiting the set of basis functions to the first m terms one is allowed to construct the model covariance matrix simply by using a linear combination of sine functions of increasing frequency, with positive and monotonically decreasing weights. Not surprisingly, **the model correlation that can be obtained using a constant and a sine wave of frequency equal to half the full maturity span (this is what is implicitly used by a two-factor PC-based model) is constrained to look like a sigmoid.**

It is important to explore both the relevance and the generality of these observations. First of all, since, as mentioned before, PCs are constructed to explain with maximum efficiency the *diagonal* elements of the covariance matrix (see Wilson (1994)), and hence the overall level of the observed variance, it is possible that different approaches such as factor analysis, which explicitly focuses the attention on the *off-diagonal* elements, might give different results.

Furthermore, approaches such as Longstaff and Schwartz's (see Chapter 12), which assume as the second factor a variable which is *not* a linear combination of rates (e.g. the variance of the short rate), could in principle describe the qualitative shape of the correlation function in a more efficient way.

In practice, however, studies conducted on the Brennan and Schwartz (Chapter 13) and on related models (which do not exactly choose the PCs as the driving factors) produce exactly the sigmoid correlation function predicted by this study. More interestingly, the same can be observed in the case of the Longstaff and Schwartz model (see Figure 12.3 in Chapter 12). **It therefore seems plausible to surmise that the observations mentioned above might extend to driving factors other than PCs.** Actually, results obtained by Rebonato and Cooper (1995) show that the derivative of the correlation with respect to the difference in maturities of two forward rates goes to zero as the two forward rates approach each other for any model of the (extremely general) form

$$df(t,T) = \mu\, dt + A(t,T)\, dz_A + B(t,T)\, dz_B \qquad (2.30)$$

The relevance of these findings is quite far-reaching. They imply that it is *a priori* impossible, within the framework of these low-dimensionality approaches, to price correctly *at the same* time all the caps and swaptions observed in the market. (Recall from Chapter 1 that swaption prices embed information about the variances of and the correlations among the underlying forwards.) Actually, a one-factor model could account for all the cap prices, but no arbitrary swaption could be simultaneously and consistently priced. A two-factor model could price at the same time all the caps and one arbitrary swaption, or all the caps and the particular family of swaptions which happen to have the correct expiry time and final maturity implied by the line generated by the intersection of the model and market covariance matrices. This is clearly borne out by Figure 2.14 (the 'Sydney-Opera-House effect'), which shows the market and model swaption prices for a variety of swaptions (US$ market, November 1994) for a modification of the Brennan and Schwartz model exactly calibrated to the cap prices (i.e. to the diagonal elements of the covariance matrix).

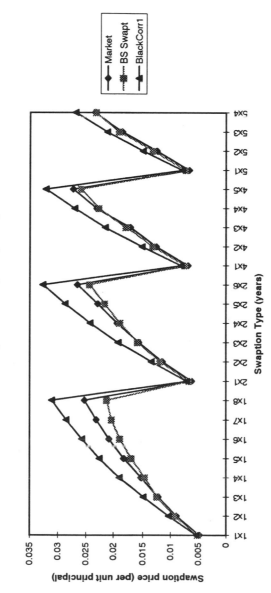

Figure 2.14 The prices of different swaptions (US$ market, December 1994) for a modification of the Brennan and Schwartz model. The series labelled BlackCorr1 shows the swaption prices that would be obtained using the market cap volatilities and perfect correlation between the forward rates.

Notice that, for each swaption series, there is always one intersection point between the market and model curves, corresponding to the line mentioned before. The same figure also shows the option prices that would be obtained with the market cap volatilities if a perfect correlation between forwards were assumed (series BlackCorrl).

This can help to put the whole discussion in perspective: if what one is striving to achieve is consistent simultaneous pricing of caps and swaptions, *any* reasonable decorrelation pattern brings about a significant improvement with respect to any one factor model. The features that are left out are, at the same time, 'finer details' but still important for actual pricing (15–20 bp out of 250).

Notice also the dangers of incorrect parameterisation: if one were to introduce a third factor one *could* obtain the desired correlation shape, but probably at the expense of giving a spuriously large weight to the third component. This would run against the econometric interpretation of the underlying factors, and create a forced fitting to a mis-specified model. As mentioned before, to a small extent this is what is accomplished by all one-factor models: by constructing each forward rate by using a truncated summation as in Equation (2.27′) one is creating new variables $df(m)_i$ which display a smaller variance than the original g_i. By forcing exact pricing of caps one is implicitly rescaling the variance of the first component to match the market data. Due to the lack of structure in the first PC, which is roughly a constant, this has no major effect; the same would, however, no longer be true if one allocated in an arbitrary fashion the variances of the further PCs. Indeed, an exponential-looking correlation structure can be obtained with two factors using implausibly fluctuating (and time-dependent) variances. As usual, blind, brute-force fitting to market quantities has very little in common with a realistic description of the financial world.

Finally, it is interesting to point out that if a single-factor approach is chosen, and *exactly* the same weights are chosen for *the* eigenvector, this implies that the sensitivity of each forward rate to change in the principal component is precisely the same; therefore the yield curve is constrained to move in parallel. If the variables $\{g\}$ are taken to be absolute (rather than percentage) changes in forward rates, this is just what is accomplished by a model, the Ho and Lee, discussed later on (Chapter 10). **As for all one-factor models, they can be seen in a unified manner as different allocations of weights among the various forwards (thereby implying a different sensitivity of each forward to a move in *the* factor), and as different prescriptions on how to make these weights depend on time.**

2.3 A FRAMEWORK FOR OPTION PRICING

Despite the intrinsic limitations of low-dimensionality models outlined in the previous section, analytic and/or numerical tractability has forced upon researchers the need to model the evaluation of the yield curve in terms of the dynamics of a very small number of driving factors. Especially in early approaches *one* specific rate, usually the short rate, $r(t)$, has been chosen as a proxy for the single variable that principal component analysis indicates can best describe the movements of the yield curve. In this approach, after allowing the stochastic component of its process to be of diffusive nature only (no discontinuous jumps), one is led to write explicitly, or implicitly to assume,

$$dr(t) = \mu_r(r(t),t)\, dt + \sigma_r(r(t),t)\, dz \qquad (2.31)$$

where $\mu_r(r(t),t)$ indicates the drift of the short-rate process, $\sigma_r(r(t),t)$ its standard deviation per unit time, and dz is the increment of a standard Brownian motion ($E[dz] = 0$, $E[dz^2] = 1\, dt$).

In this framework, the price of any contingent claim depending on the yield curve as a whole (not only on the short rate) will be a function of calendar time t, of its payoff at expiry or maturity T, and, via Ito's lemma, of the short-rate dynamics only. All the rates of maturity intermediate between the maturity of r and T are accounted for, in this framework, by the process of the short rates, that 'drives' the whole yield curve.

The explicit approach implied by Equation (2.31) above, however, is by no means necessary, or unique. The 'martingale' or 'evolutionary' approach, for instance, pioneered by HJM (Heath, Jarrow and Morton (1987)) takes a continuum of instantaneous forward rates as the building blocks to describe the dynamics of the whole term structure. Equations formally similar to Equation (2.31) above can then be written for each forward rate (the drift terms will be derived in detail in following chapters):

$$df_i(t) = \mu_i(t)\, dt + \sum_{j=1,\ldots,n} \sigma_{ji}(f_i(t),t)\, dz_j \qquad (2.32)$$

where k different sources of uncertainty (factors) are assumed to shock the n forward rates that describe the yield curve ($n \geqslant k$). Notice that despite the fact that in the evolutionary approach n equations appear instead of the single Equation (2.1), the approach still remains simply k factor (with k possibly as low as 1). The principal component analysis mentioned before can then directly provide the volatility inputs for the dynamics of the forward rates.

Given either approach, the task of pricing contingent claims on instruments dependent on the yield curve movements can therefore be reduced to the following conceptual 'ingredients':

(i)   a concrete specification of the process for the driving factor(s) (i.e. a parametric specification of the functional dependence of the drift and the variance of the process on the state variables);

(ii) a way of translating the deterministic and stochastic movements of the driving variable(s) into the deterministic and stochastic movements of the underlying quantities of interest (bonds, forward rates, etc.);

(iii) a way of relating the possible attainable future values of an asset to its present value today, i.e. a discounting procedure.

However, before embarking on the analysis of these different models, a fundamental condition must be imposed concerning points (i) and (ii) above, i.e. on the possible 'allowable' movements for the prices of the instruments (bonds, etc.) which depend on the yield curve. This fundamental condition must be enforced in order to prevent the possibility of arbitrage (as more precisely defined in Chapter 4) between bonds of different maturities, and, more in general, between any two instruments. So many are the possible equivalent formulations of this no-arbitrage condition (Jamshidian (1990) enumerates 14!), that it is very easy to miss the underlying common reasoning. On the other hand, enforcing the no-arbitrage condition in a particular form can be, for a specific model, considerably more straightforward and intuitive than if a different, albeit equivalent, formulation had been chosen. The tasks of presenting the 'classical' (Vasicek (1977)) and 'modern' (martingale) formulation of the no-arbitrage conditions in such a way as to underline their similarity, and to show how they can be directly applied to different types of implementation are therefore undertaken in Chapter 4.

This chapter has so far shown that, with certain caveats, it is indeed reasonable to attempt a description of the joint dynamics of all the interest-rates-dependent instruments observed in the market using a very small number of underlying variables. A very fundamental question, however, still remains to be answered: since, as it has been repeatedly stated, plain-vanilla options (caps and European swaptions) are priced in the market using the Black formula, couldn't it be profitable to extend the same approach to more complicated payoffs? The integration might have to be carried out numerically rather than analytically, but fast computers and efficient integration techniques should make this an easily surmountable problem. In simpler terms: **why does one need whole-yield-curve option models at all?** The issue of the motivation of yield-curve models is therefore raised in the next chapter, in which an attempt will be made to extend a Black-like type of approach to relatively complex payoffs. The purpose of the chapter will be to show that, while conceptually possible, this line of attack is soon doomed to failure due to the dramatic growth in complexity of the resulting partial differential equations, and to virtually insurmountable parameter estimation problems. En route to proving this point, the Black formula will be obtained and some results will be derived, which will be seen to be special cases of the more general no-arbitrage treatment of Chapter 4.

3
A motivation for yield curve models

3.1 INTRODUCTION

Two cases of increasing complexity will be considered in this chapter: the first one will lead directly to the Black (1976) valuation formula; the second will produce an equation which can be formally recast in the same terms as the Black equation, but which will contain 'adjustment' terms on some of the inputs dependent on the correlation between them (see Doust (1995), whose approach has been followed in the remainder of this section). These results are meant to provide a financially intuitive background for the more formal treatment of the no-arbitrage conditions presented in Chapter 4. Furthermore, and possibly more importantly, the two examples provided will help to draw two important conclusions. First of all, it will be shown (Section 2) that the well-known Black (1976) approach can give, for the simple case of a European option on a discount bond, a completely satisfactory treatment of this simple problem, which fully accounts for the stochastic nature of the discounting factor (see also Merton (1973)). Therefore the common claim that the stochastic nature of interest rates forces one to move, for the case of European bond options, to yield-curve models is simply not justifiable. The Black model might indeed have been originally formulated with a deterministic interest-rate framework in mind, but as long as the option is of a European nature, a single discounting rate, completely mapped in the discount bond maturing at the time of the option payoff, is of relevance, and therefore, if suitably interpreted, the Black model can give a perfectly 'correct' answer to this type of European problem.

The second important point (Section 3) is that, to a certain extent, the Black formalism can be retained even for more complicated types of options, at the expense of increasing the dimensionality of the problem, and of introducing a series of correlation terms, which not only soon make the resulting equations rather unwieldy, but introduce correlation terms difficult to estimate or to impute from traded option prices in a consistent manner.

The need and the justification for yield-curve option models should therefore spring rather naturally from the discussion to be found in the following two sections. In addition, the concept of numeraire will be introduced in an 'informal' way, and its link with the hedging and discounting procedure should become more obvious, and assist the intuition during the more formal treatment of Chapters 4 and 5.

Given its function, the present chapter has been positioned before Chapters 4 and 5, despite the fact that extensive use is made of Ito's lemma (introduced in Section 4.8). Readers not familiar with this analytic tool might prefer to postpone the reading of the material here presented until after Chapter 4 (but *before* Chapter 5). Also, it might be beneficial to re-read this chapter after Chapter 5.

3.2 HEDGING A BOND OPTION WITH THE UNDERLYING FORWARD CONTRACT

Let us consider the simple case of an option, O, valued at time 0, struck at X and expiring at time t, on a discount bond maturing at time $T > t$, $P(0,T)$. The example is of greater generality than one might at first surmise, since, as seen in Chapter 1, a variety of instruments, such as caps or floors, can be seen as puts or calls on discount bonds. Our purpose is to determine the partial differential equation (PDE) satisfied by the function, O, which gives the value of the option today. The assumption will be made at the outset that the function O should depend on the forward bond price $FP(t,T) = P(0,T)/P(0,t)$ and on the discount bond $P(0,t)$ in a separable way, i.e.:

$$O(FP(t,T),P(0,t)) = f(FP(t,T))P(0,t) \qquad (3.1)$$

for some function f, as yet unknown (the function f will be shown later in this section to be the solution to a partial differential equation). Let us consider the following hedging strategy:

(i)   a position in the spot bond $P(0,t)$,
(ii) a position in a forward contract on the bond maturing at time T struck at P_0 for delivery at time t. From Chapter 1 we know that the present value of this contract is $(FP(t,T) - P_0)P(0,t)$.

Let us begin by constructing a portfolio, Π, containing 1 unit of the option, 'a' units of the spot bond, and 'b' units of the forward contract:

$$\Pi(t) = O + aP(0,t) + b(FP(t,T) - P_0)P(0,t)$$
$$= fP(0,t) + aP(0,t) + b(FP(t,T) - P_0)P(0,t) \qquad (3.2)$$

The change in the value of this portfolio over a small time dt, i.e. its differential $d\Pi(t)$, will be needed for the ensuing treatment. In order to obtain this quantity one should notice that in ordinary calculus, terms like $dx\, dy$ in the expansion of the differential of the product of two functions, $d(xy)$, disappear. It will be shown in Chapter 4 that, if x and y are stochastic quantities, the double differential term does not disappear, as shown by Equation (3.4') below. Let us then allow $P(0,t)$ and $FP(t,T)$ to be log-normally distributed stochastic variables characterised by an instantaneous variance $P(0,t)^2\sigma P(0,t)^2$ and $FP(t,T)^2\sigma FP(t,T)^2$, respectively (see Equations (3.5) and (3.5′) below).

Over an infinitesimal time dt the increment in the portfolio value will be given by:

$$d\Pi(t) = df\,P(0,t) + f\,dP(0,t) + df\,dP(0,t) + a\,dP(0,t)$$
$$+ b(FP(t,T) - P_0)\,dP(0,t) + b\,dFP(t,T)P(0,t) + b\,dFP(t,T)\,dP(0,t) \tag{3.3}$$

From the following chapters (see, in particular, Section 4.8), two results will be used:

(1) if f is a function of a log-normal stochastic variable x with percentage volatility σ_x, then

$$df = \left[\frac{\partial f}{\partial t} + \frac{1}{2}\sigma_x^2 x^2 \frac{\partial^2 f}{\partial x^2}\right]dt + \frac{\partial f}{\partial x}\,dx \tag{3.4}$$

and

(2) if x and y are two jointly log-normally distributed stochastic variables with correlation ρ, then

$$dx\,dy = \sigma_x \sigma_y xy\rho\,dt \tag{3.4′}$$

Applying these results to Equation (3.3) above, and remembering that the log-normal assumption for $FP(t,T)$ and $P(0,t)$, imply processes of the form

$$\frac{dP(0,t)}{P(0,t)} = \mu_P\,dt + \sigma_P\,dz \tag{3.5}$$

$$\frac{dFP(0,t)}{FP(0,t)} = \mu_{FP}\,dt + \sigma_{FP}\,dz \tag{3.5′}$$

one obtains

$$d\Pi(t) = \left[\frac{\partial f}{\partial t} + \frac{1}{2}\sigma_{FP(t,T)}^2 FP(t,T)^2 \frac{\partial^2 f}{\partial FP(t,T)^2}\right]P(0,t)\,dt$$

$$+ \frac{\partial f}{\partial FP(t,T)}P(0,t)\,dFP(t,T) + f\,dP(0,t)$$

$$+ \frac{\partial f}{\partial FP(t,T)}\sigma_{P(0,t)}\sigma_{FP(t,T)}P(0,t)FP(t,T)\rho_{0,T}\,dt$$

$$+ a\,dP(0,t) + b(FP(t,T) - P_0)\,dP(0,t) + b\,dFP(t,T)P(0,t)$$

$$+ b\sigma_{P(0,t)}\sigma_{FP(t,T)}P(0,t)FP(t,T)\rho_{0,T}\,dt \tag{3.6}$$

where $\rho_{0,T}$ is the correlation between the prices of the discount bond maturing at time t, and the forward bond $FP(t,T)$. All the terms in $dFP(t,T)$ and $dP(0,t)$ are stochastic, i.e. their value is not known with certainty before the move; in general, therefore, the value of the portfolio after a time interval dt will also be a stochastic quantity.

Following the spirit of the original Black and Scholes derivation, however, one can look for those particular holdings of $P(0,t)$ and $FP(t,T)$ that can make the portfolio locally deterministic, i.e. only containing terms in dt. Financially, this corresponds to finding those positions in the forward bond and in the discounting zero that can exactly (instantaneously) neutralise any move in the option price. If one chooses

$$a = -f \tag{3.7}$$

$$b = -\frac{\partial f}{\partial FP(t,T)} \tag{3.7'}$$

and if the forward contract had been struck at $P_0 = FP(t,T)$, then one can immediately verify by direct substitution that (i) only the terms in dt in Equation (3.6) above are retained, and (ii) the initial value of the portfolio thus constructed is exactly 0. Since, in absence of arbitrage (more precisely defined in Chapter 4), a deterministic portfolio of zero value cannot accrue any value over time, d$\Pi(t) = 0$. Therefore, after substituting Equations (3.7) and (3.7'), and after noticing that the term containing the correlation drops out, Equation (3.6) above becomes

$$\frac{\partial f}{\partial t} + \frac{1}{2}\sigma_{FP(t,T)}^2 FP(t,T)^2 \frac{\partial^2 f}{\partial FP(t,T)^2} = 0 \tag{3.8}$$

Equation (3.8) is a purely diffusive parabolic partial differential equation. It will be shown in Chapter 5 (Feynman–Kac theorem) that its solution is given by taking the expectation of the final payoff over a log-normal distribution for the variable $FP(t,T)$. More precisely, if solved with the appropriate boundary conditions for a call option struck at X, Equation (3.8) directly gives the Black formula (see, e.g., Hull (1992)):

$$\text{Call}(FP,X) = P(0,t)[FP(t,T)N(h_1) - XN(h_2)] \tag{3.9}$$

with

$$FP(t,T) = \frac{P(0,T)}{P(0,t)}$$

$$h_1 = \frac{\ln\dfrac{FP(t,T)}{X} + \dfrac{1}{2}\sigma_{FP(t,T)}^2 t}{\sigma_{FP(t,T)}\sqrt{t}}$$

$$h_2 = \frac{\ln\dfrac{FP(t,T)}{X} - \dfrac{1}{2}\sigma_{FP(t,T)}^2 t}{\sigma_{FP(t,T)}\sqrt{t}}$$

and $N(\cdot)$ denotes the cumulative normal distribution.

Several interesting features can be noticed about this result: to begin with, the PDE obtained does not contain $P(0,t)$, and therefore the separation assumption enforced at the beginning was justified. But of greater interest is the fact that if one enters a position in the spot discount bond $P(0,t)$ equal to the *forward* value of the option, $O/P(0,t)$, and if one enters into a position in the forward bond struck at $P_0 = FP(t,T)$, then one has no exposure (**instantaneously**) to changes in the different interest rates of various maturities between 0 and t. In other terms, both the option $(O = fP(0,t))$ and the spot bond maturing at time $T(P(0,T) = P(0,t)FP(t,T))$ can be expressed in terms of units of the same traded asset, in this case the spot bond maturing at time $t(P(0,t)$. It is this common 'numeraire' (defined precisely in Chapter 4, and analysed in detail in Section 5.5) which takes out the exposure to movements in rates between 0 and t.

Notice also that the equation just obtained does not tell one what the fair price for the forward contract should be, and therefore only provides a **relative** pricing. Furthermore, and more importantly, the volatility entering the PDE (3.8) is the price volatility of the **forward** bond (rather than the spot bond). Therefore, if one is 'implying' a volatility from a market option price, one will not gain direct access to the volatility of the cash instrument. The same would have been true if one had considered an option on common stock, rather than on a bond: only the *forward* stock price volatility would have been recoverable from option market prices.

Finally, it is important for future developments to point out that no terms containing the first derivative with respect to, or the drift of, the forward bond price enter Equation (3.8). This indicates that the PDE obtained is of purely diffusive character. It will be shown in Chapter 4 that this is in general equivalent to saying that the forward bond price of log-normal process

$$\mathrm{d}FP(t) = \mu_{FP}(t)\,\mathrm{d}t + FP(t)\sigma_{FP}(t)\,\mathrm{d}z$$

is driftless (i.e. $\mu_{FP} = 0$), or, if suitable technical conditions are met, that its process is a martingale. The implications of this remark will be fully explored in the course of Chapters 4 and 5.

3.3   HEDGING A PATH-DEPENDENT BOND OPTION WITH FORWARD CONTRACTS

A more interesting case will now be considered of a bond option expiring at time t_2 and struck at X on a bond maturing at time T_2, $P(0,T_2)$, but whose principal at expiry will be made to depend on the value at time t_1 of a bond maturing at time T_1, $P(t_1,T_1)$. For instance, the option could disappear (i.e. the principal could go to zero) if, at time t_1, the bond maturing at time T_1 were above or below a given barrier level, but the precise details of the contract are not important, as long as the path dependence is limited to a single realisation of the discount bond in question. A knock-out cap with a single barrier could be modelled this way.

In complete analogy with the treatment of the simple option dealt with above, two similar assumptions will be made at the outset: a separable form will be assumed for the function that gives the present value of the option, and the plausible assumption will be made that the forward option value will depend on the two forward bonds $FP(t_1,T_1) = P(0,T_1)/P(0,t_1), FP(t_2,T_2) = P(0,T_2)/P(0,t_2)$

$$O(FP(t_1,T_1),FP(t_2,T_2),P(0,t_2)) = f(FP(t_1,T_1),FP(t_2,T_2))P(0,t_2) \quad (3.10)$$

The hedging portfolio will now be composed by a position in the discount bond $P(0,t_2)$, a position in a forward contract on the bond maturing at time T_1 struck at F_1 and paying at time t_1, and a position in a forward contract on the bond maturing at time T_2, struck at F_2 and paying at time t_2:

$$\Pi(t) = P(0,t_2)f + aP(0,t_2) + b(FP(t_2,T_2) - F_2))P(0,t_2)$$
$$+ c(FP(t_1,T_1) - F_1))P(0,t_1) \quad (3.11)$$

For the case of a function, f, of two variables, x and y, Ito's lemma gives

$$df = \left[\frac{\partial f}{\partial t} + \frac{1}{2}\left(\frac{\partial^2 f}{\partial x^2}\sigma_x^2 x^2 + \frac{\partial^2 f}{\partial y^2}\sigma_y^2 y^2 + 2\frac{\partial^2 f}{\partial x \partial y}\sigma_x \sigma_y \rho_{xy} xy \right) \right] dt$$
$$+ \frac{\partial f}{\partial x}dx + \frac{\partial f}{\partial y}dy \quad (3.12)$$

where ρ denotes the correlation between the variables x and y. Using this two-dimensional version of Ito's lemma and Equation (3.4′) above, and making the same log-normal assumptions about the distributions of the prices of the forward and discount bonds, one gets for the dynamics of the portfolio $\Pi(t)$:

$$d\Pi(t) =$$

$$\left[\frac{\partial f}{\partial t} + \frac{1}{2}\sigma_{FP(t_1,T_1)}^2 FP(t_1,T_1)^2 \frac{\partial^2 f}{\partial FP(t_1,T_1)^2} + \frac{1}{2}\sigma_{FP(t_2,T_2)}^2 FP(t_2,T_2)^2 \frac{\partial^2 f}{\partial FP(t_2,T_2)^2} \right.$$

$$\left. + \sigma_{FP(t_1,T_1)}\sigma_{FP(t_2,T_2)}FP(t_1,T_1)FP(t_2,T_2) \frac{\partial^2 f}{\partial FP(t_1,T_1)\partial FP(t_2,T_2)} \rho_{F_1,F_2} \right] P(0,t_2)\, dt$$

$$+ \frac{\partial f}{\partial FP(t_1,T_1)} P(0,t_2)\, dFP(t_1,T_1) + \frac{\partial f}{\partial FP(t_2,T_2)} P(0,t_2)\, dFP(t_2,T_2)$$

$$+ f\, dP(0,t_2) + \frac{\partial f}{\partial FP(t_1,T_1)} \sigma_{P(0,t_2)}\sigma_{FP(t_1,T_1)}P(0,t_2)FP(t_1,T_1)\rho_{t_2,F_1}\, dt$$

$$+ \frac{\partial f}{\partial FP(t_2, T_2)} \sigma_{P(0,t_2)} \sigma_{FP(t_2, T_2)} P(0, t_2) FP(t_2, T_2) \rho_{t_2, F_2} \, dt + a \, dP(0, t_2)$$

$$+ b(FP(t_2, T_2) - F_2) \, dP(0, t_2) + b \, dF(t_2, T_2) P(0, t_2)$$

$$+ b\sigma_{P(0,t_2)} \sigma_{FP(t_2, T_2)} P(0, t_2) FP(t_2, T_2) \rho_{t_2, F_2} \, dt$$

$$+ c(FP(t_1, T_1) - F_1) \, dP(0, t_1) + c \, dFP(t_1, T_1) P(0, t_1)$$

$$+ c\sigma_{P(0,t_1)} \sigma_{FP(t_1, T_1)} P(0, t_1) FP(t_1, T_1) \rho_{t_1, F_1} \, dt$$

$$\tag{3.13}$$

where $\rho_{F1,F2}$, $\rho_{t1,F1}$ and $\rho_{t2,F2}$ denote the correlation between the two forward prices, between the forward price $FP(t_1, T_1)$ and the discount bond maturing at t_1 and between the forward price $FP(t_2, T_2)$ and the discount bond maturing at T_2, respectively, and, as before, $\sigma_{FP(ti, Ti)}$ denotes the percentage volatility of the forward bond $FP(t_i, T_i)$, $(i = 1, 2)$.

If the forward contracts had been struck at $F_1 = FP(t_1, T_1)$ and $F_2 = FP(t_2, T_2)$ (so that their present value today is exactly zero), and if the holdings are chosen to be

$$a = -f \tag{3.14}$$

$$b = - \frac{\partial f}{\partial FP(t_2, T_2)} \tag{3.14'}$$

$$c = - \frac{\partial f}{\partial FP(t_1, T_1)} \frac{P(0, t_2)}{P(0, t_1)} \tag{3.14''}$$

then, as before, the portfolio is purely deterministic, and, as can be verified by direct substitution, has zero set-up value. Repeating the argument that a deterministic portfolio of zero initial value must still be worth 0 after a time dt, the condition $d\Pi(t) = 0$ therefore yields:

$$d\Pi(t) =$$

$$\left[\frac{\partial f}{\partial t} + \frac{1}{2} \sigma_{FP(t_1, T_1)}^2 FP(t_1, T_1)^2 \frac{\partial^2 f}{\partial FP(t_1, T_1)^2} + \frac{1}{2} \sigma_{FP(t_2, T_2)}^2 FP(t_2, T_2)^2 \frac{\partial^2 f}{\partial FP(t_2, T_2)^2} \right.$$

$$\left. + \sigma_{FP(t_1, T_1)} \sigma_{FP(t_2, T_2)} FP(t_1, T_1) FP(t_2, T_2) \frac{\partial^2 f}{\partial FP(t_1, T_1) \partial FP(t_2, T_2)} \rho_{F_1, F_2} \right] P(0, t_2) \, dt$$

$$+ \frac{\partial f}{\partial FP(t_1, T_1)} \sigma_{P(0, T_2)} \sigma_{FP(t_1, T_1)} P(0, t_2) FP(t_1, T_1) \rho_{t_2, F_1}$$

$$- \frac{\partial f}{\partial FP(t_1, T_1)} \frac{P(0, t_2)}{P(0, t_1)} P(0, t_1) FP(t_1, T_1) \sigma_{P(0, T_2)} \sigma_{FP(t_1, T_1)} \rho_{t_1, F_1} = 0$$

$$\tag{3.15}$$

or, after cancelling terms in $P(0,t_2)$ and simplifying,

$$
\left[\frac{\partial f}{\partial t} + \frac{1}{2} \sigma_{FP(t_1,T_1)}^2 FP(t_1,T_1)^2 \frac{\partial^2 f}{\partial FP(t_1,T_1)^2} + \frac{1}{2} \sigma_{FP(t_2,T_2)}^2 FP(t_2,T_2)^2 \frac{\partial^2 f}{\partial FP(t_2,T_2)^2} \right.
$$

$$
\left. + \sigma_{FP(t_1,T_1)} \sigma_{FP(t_2,T_2)} FP(t_1,T_1) FP(t_2,T_2) \frac{\partial^2 f}{\partial FP(t_1,T_1) \partial FP(t_2,T_2)} \rho_{F_1,F_2} \right] dt
$$

$$
+ \frac{\partial f}{\partial FP(t_1,T_1)} FP(t_1,T_1) [\sigma_{P(0,T_2)} \sigma_{FP(t_1,T_1)} \rho_{t_2,F_1} - \sigma_{P(0,t_1)} \sigma_{FP(t_1,T_1)} \rho_{t_1,F_1}] = 0
$$

$$(3.15')$$

This equation does not depend on $P(0,t_2)$ or $P(0,t_1)$, as conjectured at the beginning. If the payoff of the forward contract occurred at time t_2 instead of t_1, then the term in square brackets in the last line would be identically zero, and the equation would still be a purely diffusive equation with no drift. In general, however, this will not be the case, and the last term will be retained. Financially this stems from the fact that the option depends, *inter alia*, on $FP(t_1,T_1)$ but not on $P(0,t_1)$ for $t_1 \neq t_2$. Therefore by hedging the 'barrier condition' by entering a forward contract on $FP(t_1,T_1)$ which, by paying at t_1 does depend on $P(0,t_1)$, one is introducing in the hedging portfolio an exposure (to the discount bond maturing at time t_1) to which the original option is not sensitive. This will therefore give rise to the lack of cancellation between the forward/spot bond correlation terms, as shown in the last line of Equation (3.15'). This equation, in particular, shows that this unwanted exposure can be accounted for, and therefore hedged, if we assume to know how moves in the 'undesired' discount bonds are correlated with moves in the bonds on which the contract shows a direct dependence.

However, if one defines a new quantity

$$FP(t_1,T_1)' =$$

$$
FP(t_1,T_1) \exp \left[\int_0^{t_1} \sigma(s)_{P(0,t_2)} \sigma(s)_{FP(t_1,T_1)} \rho(s)_{t_2,F_1} - \sigma(s)_{P(0,t_1)} \sigma(s)_{FP(t_1,T_1)} \rho(s)_{t_1,F_1} \, ds \right]
$$

$$(3.16)$$

or, for constant volatilities and correlations,

$$
FP(t_1,T_1)' = FP(t_1,T_1) \exp[\sigma_{FP(t_1,T_1)} (\sigma_{P(0,t2)} \rho_{t_2,F_1} - \sigma_{P(0,t_1)} \rho_{t_1,F_1}) t_1]
$$

$$(3.16')$$

one can readily verify by direct substitution that Equation (3.15′) becomes

$$\frac{\partial f}{\partial t} + \frac{1}{2} \sigma^2_{FP'(t_1,T_1)} FP'(t_1,T_1)^2 \frac{\partial^2 f}{\partial FP'(t_1,T_1)^2} + \frac{1}{2} \sigma^2_{FP(t_1,T_2)} FP(t_2,T_2) \frac{\partial^2 f}{\partial FP(t_2,T_2)^2}$$

$$+ \sigma_{FP'(t_1,T_1)} \sigma_{FP(t_2,T_2)} FP'(t_1,T_1) FP(t_2,T_2) \frac{\partial^2 f}{\partial FP(t_1,T_1) \partial FP(t_2,T_2)} \rho_{F_1,F_2} \, dt = 0$$

$$(3.16'')$$

i.e. **the adjusted PDE displays again a purely diffusive behaviour (no drift terms)**.

Furthermore, it will be shown in Chapter 5 that, if a variable x is described by a stochastic differential equation of the form

$$\frac{dX}{X} = \mu \, dt + \sigma \, dz \qquad (3.17)$$

then its value at time t, contingent on its value at time 0 being $x(0)$, is given by

$$x(t) = x(0) \exp\left[\int_0^t \left(\mu(s) - \frac{1}{2} \sigma(s)^2\right) ds + \int_0^t \sigma(s) \, dz(s)\right] \qquad (3.18)$$

Looking back at expressions (3.16) and (3.16′) one can see that, in terms of the unadjusted financial variables, both the forward option price and the forward bond price $FP(t_2,T_2)$ display no drift, while the log-normal variable $FP(t_1,T_1)'$ can be interpreted as the original variable $FP(t_1,T_1)$ to which a drift has been superimposed. This additional drift needed to make the PDE a pure diffusion (technically, needed to turn the semi-martingale process for $FP(t_1,T_1)$ into a martingale process, as explained in Chapter 4) is given by the integrand in Equation (3.16) above.

It is also instructive to look at the structure of the 'correction' term given by Equation (3.16): the integrand is equal to the difference between [the covariance between $FP(t_1,T_1)$ and the discounting factor $P(0,t_2)$] and [the covariance between $FP(t_1,T_1)$ and the discounting factor $P(0,t_1)$]; if the payoff were to occur, say, in a currency or via a discount factor totally uncorrelated with the forward price $FP(t_1,T_1)$, then no correction term would have to be included, since, on average, there would be no systematic bias between the behaviour of the hedge and the behaviour of the underlying contract to be hedged. If the correlation were perfect, on the other hand, then the correction term would simply account for the difference in volatility between the different discounting factors. If also the volatility of $P(0,t_1)$ and $P(0,t_2)$ were identical, then no correction term would have to be employed at all (but, in this case, probably $P(0,t_1) = P(0,t_2)$ and the treatment of the previous section would apply).

Chapter 5 will show that these adjustment terms, and, in general, these drift conditions, are nothing but special cases of Girsanov's theorem, which specifies how different quantities grow when the numeraire is switched (more precisely, which specifies the drift transformation which corresponds to the change of measure brought about by switching the numeraire). For the moment, the message of this chapter is much simpler: moving from the case of a simple European option (Section 3.2) to a case where an additional forward price influences the final payoff (Section 3.3), not only has the computational burden increased from a one-dimensional to a bi-variate integration, but the input quantities have become much more cumbersome. For all its elegance, Equation (3.16) tells one nothing about how the correlations and volatilities should be computed. If more forward prices were allowed to affect the payoff of the option it is easy to see how the same approach would lead to more and more complex formal solutions: each hedging forward position would introduce an unwanted exposure to the discount bonds $P(0,t_i)$, not appearing in the option payoff; each of these exposures would in turn give rise to 'adjustment' terms in the relative forwards containing more and more correlations contributions; only the forward contract paying at the same time as the option would result in needing no adjustment, and, once the forward position in the maturity forward were entered, no exposure to the expiry discount bond would remain. However, all the other forward contracts introduced to hedge whatever payoff-sensitive exposure might be triggered by the various $FP(t_i, T_i)$ would need an adjustment.

Can one look more deeply into the 'origin' of these correction terms? Let us consider again for a moment the situation when the correlation among all the different (spot and forward) bonds is exactly unity (this is actually what is implicitly enforced by any one-factor model). In that case, even if introducing additional hedging forward contracts has brought about an unwanted exposure to the discount bonds $P(0,t_i)$ maturing at their payoff times, one would know exactly (**given the perfect correlation**) how the prices of these discount bonds would move relative to the discount bond maturing at option payoff. Therefore these extra exposures would actually bring about no additional risk (at least as long as the volatilities of all the discount bonds were known exactly). In reality, the correlation among different bonds will not be perfect, and the correction term accounts for the relative magnitude (via the volatility) and the relative 'direction' (via the correlation ρ) of the movement of one discount bond with respect to the movement of the discount bond maturing at option payoff time (t_{exp}). As before, this can be looked at as expressing all the assets in units of $P(0,t_{exp})$ ($P(0,t_2)$ for the example just treated), a choice of numeraire which is indeed very 'natural' (to use Doust's (1995) terminology) both for the option and for the forward contract expiring and paying at option maturity, but for no other contract. In a naive approach one could hope to estimate all these unknown correlations either historically or by implying their values from traded instruments. Even for a moderate number of forward exposures in the option payoff, however, the number of unknown terms in the resulting variance–covariance matrix soon defies any reasonably robust historical estimation procedure.

As for the implied approach, it is indeed possible, at least in principle, to impute the 'market' covariance implied by actively traded instruments (see Chapter 1). The task of pricing complex deals, however, exactly boils down to making prices, and hence implying covariances, for instruments which are *not* actively traded. Using the implied approach can therefore supply the user with a number of 'reference points' in the distributional space of the underlying variable; in order to move forward, i.e. to price the non-plain-vanilla structures, one needs to engage in a delicate interpolation (and often extrapolation) exercise.

What is needed is some strong structure to be imposed on the co-movements of the financial quantities of interest; remembering the conclusions of Chapter 2, this structure can be provided by specifying the dynamics of a small number of variables (for instance, the principal components or their proxies). Once the process for these driving factors has been chosen, the variances and correlations among all the financial observables can then be obtained, analytically or numerically as the case might be, as a byproduct of the model itself. The implied co-dynamics of these quantities might result in being simplified to the point of becoming simplistic, but, at least, the pricing of different options and hedging instruments can be undertaken on a consistent basis in the framework of a manageable picture of rate dynamics.

In general, each model will, in turn, display some 'free' or 'fitting' parameters, in numbers varying from two or three to little less than 10. In any case, however, the degrees of freedom will be fewer by an order of magnitude than the statistical quantities needed to estimate nothing more complicated than an option on a 5-year quarterly cap.

This is exactly what interest-rate models offer: by introducing reasonable (or sometimes merely expedient) assumptions on the economy, or some of its variables, a dramatic reduction of the 'fitting' degrees of freedom can be achieved, which not only makes the problem manageable, but which also allows one to focus on the assessment of the correctness of the model specification.

The derivations just presented have ensured an arbitrage-free *relative* pricing. It is, however, both practically important and intellectually rewarding to consider the no-arbitrage conditions in much broader generality. The results arrived at in this chapter will therefore be revisited at the end of Chapter 5, where they will be shown to be special cases of very general and important procedures.

PART TWO
THE THEORETICAL TOOLS

4

The analytic and probabilistic tools

4.1 THE DISCRETE CASE

This and the following chapter will derive the no-arbitrage conditions, and introduce the statistical and financial concepts needed for the task. Many of the theorems that will be used in the practical implementations in later chapters are actually more simply (and elegantly) obtained in continuous time. However, the degree of mathematical sophistication in order to treat 'properly' the continuous-time case is considerably higher than the level needed for the discrete case. The analysis will therefore be carried out for the latter, and the transfer of the results to the continuous case will be accomplished in a rather heuristic manner. The distinction between a heuristic argument and sloppy reasoning is a rather subtle one, especially when the issues, as it is the case for the convergence of the discrete results to the continuous case, are actually rather delicate (see, e.g., Willinger and Taqqu (1991)). It was, however, felt that by explaining in good detail the discrete-time set-up, and in a more cursory way the continuous limit, more could be gained in intuition than would be lost in rigor. As usual, the link with computational methodologies, such as lattices, has been emphasised throughout. If, ultimately, the reader wants to be able to produce, for his original research, fully rigorous and mathematically 'well-justifiable' results, there probably is no alternative but to undertake the study of stochastic calculus applied to finance and option pricing in particular, as treated, to name a few, in Malliaris (1982), Harrison and Pliska (1981), Gardiner (1990), Lamberton and Lapeyre (1991), Oksendal (1995), Duffie (1992) or Dothan (1990). For those readers interested in developing a 'working acquaintance' with the concepts involved, so as to enable them to understand the gist of proofs and arguments found in the literature based on the martingale formalism and to obtain simple results when needed, this chapter should both provide the insight in the underlying financial motivation and further the intuition behind the mathematical theorems. A later section of the next chapter (Section 5.6), in particular, will attempt to make clear the link between the more traditional way of looking at no-arbitrage (as presented in Section 4.5) and the more modern approach. A few worked-out examples will be provided, in order to show how the formalism introduced can easily be brought to yield useful results of direct financial relevance.

Finally, a large proportion of the modern literature on option pricing, even published in journals, such as *Risk* magazine, aimed mainly at a practitioners' audience, is so deeply couched in the martingale formalism that many readers tend to perceive the terminology used as an insurmountable barrier to entry. Therefore the attempt has been made in the present and the following chapters to introduce and define as simply as possible those terms that tend to create the greatest problems. The goal of the writer will have been satisfactorily fulfilled if at least a few readers, scared away in the past by finding in an article that the volatility had to be a non-anticipating function, will continue to plough through their reading, reassured that the expression can be interpreted as asking of the volatility function the rather intuitive requirement that it should not be affected by future, and therefore unknown, events. The wisdom of couching even relatively simple and non-technical results in the formalism borrowed from continuous-time stochastic processes could be debated at length, especially since the need for introducing rather cumbersome concepts often stems from rather 'technical' reasons (Kolmogorov's axiomatic approach to probability is as powerful as elegant, but does not recommend itself for great intuitional appeal). However one might feel about this state of affairs, this tendency seems to be here to stay, and, therefore, at least a passing acquaintance with the terminology, and the underlying ideas, is probably indispensable in order to be able to keep abreast with what is published in virtually all the interesting journals.

4.2 THE PROBABILISTIC SET-UP

Most of the readers are already acquainted with probabilistic concepts (such as, for instance, 'probability density', 'conditional expectation', etc.). The same readers, however, might not be as familiar with (or, perhaps, might never have heard of) concepts such as 'filtration', 'σ-field', etc. This might cause some surprise, since the latter mathematical constructs will be presented in the following as the very building blocks of probabilistic theory. The explanation of this apparent paradox (i.e. ignorance of the foundations, but knowledge of the results derived therefrom) lies in the fact that the more elementary (and intuitively appealing) introductions to probability are based on the so-called 'Frequency' (or 'Classical') approach. The more 'modern'[1] Kolmogorov approach, on the other hand, is completely axiomatic, and is based on set-theoretical concepts (see, e.g., Hatgioannides (1995)). Unlike the Frequency approach, it does not furnish a prescription for explicit calculation of probabilities of events, and 'only' provides the user with *relationships between their probabilities*. Despite this apparent shortcoming, it is ideally suited to deriving the conditions of no-arbitrage, which, as we shall see, depend not on the specific probabilities of occurrence of certain states of the world, but on the possibility or impossibility of these events.

The price to be paid for this is that such a general set-up lends itself but poorly to more quantitative manipulations such as, for instance, differentiation. It will therefore be necessary to introduce a bridging concept (the random variable) capable, at the same time, of allowing with relative ease these operations, and of retaining the original axiomatic structure. The conceptual steps that will be followed can therefore be summarised as follows:

(i) a description of the totality of possible events;
(ii) the definition of those sets of events to which a probability can be associated;
(iii) the introduction of a probability measure which associates to these sets of events a real number between zero and one;
(iv) a mapping of the totality of possible events onto the real numbers.

More precisely, let us consider the case where the particular outcome of an 'experiment' is not known *a priori*, but all the possible outcomes are known before the experiment itself. This situation can be described by means of a finite probability space, which is made up of:

(i) A *state space*, i.e. the totality, Ω, of possible *states of the world* ω_i. In view of the assumed discrete nature of the process, the number of possible states is finite. The economy as a whole will, in general, be described by a number of financial quantities, such as, for instance, securities prices. Each joint realisation of these states variables constitutes a state. To give a financially relevant example, if one assumes that it is possible and reasonable to describe the whole economy in terms of a single variable, r, (see Chapter 2), and if this one state variable is assumed to move, after one time step, from an initial known state $r(0)$ to either of two possible states $r(1,-1)$ or $r(1,1)$ (where the first index specifies the time, and the second the state), then ω_1 is the state of the world corresponding to the state variable being in state $r(1,1)$, ω_2 is the state of the world corresponding to the state variable being in state $r(1,-1)$, and $\Omega = \{\omega_1, \omega_2\}$. A group of states of the world (i.e. a subset of Ω) is called an *event*. For a discrete state space Ω one can then define the collection of subsets A_i of Ω which enjoy the properties (a) of having no elements in common: $A_i \cap A_j = \varnothing$, and (b) such that their union constitutes the whole space Ω: $A_1 \cup A_2 \cup \ldots \cup A_n = \Omega$. Such a collection of subsets is called a *partition*.

(ii) A σ-*field*. This concept is introduced in order to be able to specify those sets of events to which a probability can be associated. While the definition of partition given above could be used for the purpose in the discrete case, problems would arise when Ω is made up of an infinity of states. Let us therefore consider a particular class of subsets of Ω, and more precisely, let us consider the class $\mathfrak{F}$ of subsets of Ω enjoying the following properties:

(a) this class contains Ω itself;

(b) if an event A_i belongs to $\mathfrak{F}$, then its complement also belongs to $\mathfrak{F}$;

(c) if A_1, A_2, ..., A_n belong to $\mathfrak{F}$, then the union $A_1 \cup A_2 \cup ... \cup A_n$ also belongs to $\mathfrak{F}$.

A class of subsets of Ω enjoying the three properties above is called a σ-*field* (or a σ-*algebra*, or a *tribe*). To acquire an intuitive understanding of what the three requirements above entail, let us extend the previous example by one time step, and, for simplicity, let us further assume that an up-move from the state $r(1,-1)$ and a down move from the state $r(1,1)$ lead to the same state $r(2,0)$, i.e. that the 'tree' recombines.

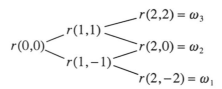

Now, the totality of possible states at time 2 is given by:

$$\Omega = \{\omega_1, \omega_2, \omega_3\}$$

The subsets of Ω are given by

Subset 1	$\{\omega_1, \omega_2, \omega_3\}$
Subset 2	$\{\omega_1, \omega_2\}$
Subset 3	$\{\omega_1, \omega_3\}$
Subset 4	$\{\omega_2, \omega_3\}$
Subset 5	$\{\omega_1\}$
Subset 6	$\{\omega_2\}$
Subset 7	$\{\omega_3\}$
Subset 8	$\{\varnothing\}$

In a financial context, subset, say, 2 would be of relevance, for instance, if one wanted to specify the condition that a certain payoff would occur only if the driving variable r (and therefore, in this one-factor model, the whole universe) were in states $r(2,-2) = \omega_1$ or $r(2,0) = \omega_2$.

For a given space Ω there exist several σ-fields which satisfy the requirements above; the smallest is given by $\{\emptyset,\Omega\}$, where $\emptyset$ denotes the empty set. One can immediately verify, in fact, that this particular σ-field (a) contains Ω; (b) the complement of Ω (i.e. $\emptyset$) belongs to $\mathfrak{I}$, and the complement of $\emptyset$ (i.e. Ω) belongs to $\mathfrak{I}$; (c) the union of $\emptyset$ and Ω also belongs to $\mathfrak{I}$. The largest σ-field is made up by all the subsets of Ω (in general 2^N in number, where N is the number of possible states of the world). It is immediately verified, in fact, that (a) this particular σ-field contains Ω as one of its elements (subset 1); (b) the complement of each of the subsets also belongs to the σ-field made up by all the subsets; (c) the union of as many elements of this σ-field as desired also belongs to this σ-field:

$$\{\omega_1,\omega_2,\omega_3\} \cup \{\omega_i\} = \{\omega_1,\omega_2,\omega_3\} \text{ for any } i$$
$$\{\omega_1,\omega_2,\omega_3\} \cup \{\omega_i,\omega_j\} = \{\omega_1,\omega_2,\omega_3\} \text{ for any } i,j$$
$$\{\omega_1,\omega_2,\omega_3\} \cup \emptyset = \{\omega_1,\omega_2,\omega_3\}$$
$$\{\omega_j,\omega_k\} \cup \emptyset = \{\omega_j,\omega_k\} \text{ for any } j,k$$
$$\{\omega_i\} \cup \emptyset = \{\omega_i\} \text{ for any } i$$
$$\{\omega_i,\omega_j\} \cup \{\omega_j,\omega_k\} = \{\omega_1,\omega_2,\omega_3\} \text{ for any } i \neq j,k$$
$$\{\omega_i\} \cup \{\omega_j,\omega_k\} = \{\omega_1,\omega_2,\omega_3\} \text{ for } i \neq j,k$$
$$= \{\omega_j,\omega_k\} \text{ for } i = j \text{ or } i = k$$
$$\{\omega_i\} \cup \{\omega_j\} = \{\omega_i,\omega_j\} \text{ for } i \neq j$$
$$= \{\omega_i\} \text{ for } i = j \tag{4.1}$$

One can immediately verify that a partition, as defined in (i) above, can be extended to become a σ-field by repeated application to its elements of the fundamental set-theoretical operations of union, intersection and complementation. It is often said that such a σ-field is generated by a *partition* of Ω. The elements of a σ-field $\mathfrak{I}$ are in general called *measurable sets*, and the pair $\Omega,\mathfrak{I}$ is a *measurable space*. As we shall see more precisely later on, loosely speaking, measurable sets are those sets (i.e. collections of elementary events ω) to which a probability of occurrence can be associated.

(iii) Finally we introduce a law $\mathbf{P}(.)$ that associates to each measurable set (i.e. to each element of a σ-field) a real number, and that further enjoys the following properties:

(a) $\mathbf{P}(\emptyset) = 0$, i.e. the real number associated with the empty set is zero;

(b) the real number associated with any event of a σ-field is positive:

$$0 \leqslant P(A) \leqslant +\infty \text{ if } A \text{ belongs to } \mathfrak{I};$$

(c) if $A_1, A_2, \ldots, A_n$ belong to the σ-field $\mathfrak{I}$ and are pair-wise disjoint (i.e. have no events in common) then the real number associated to their union is equal to the sum of the real numbers associated with each individual measurable event, i.e.:

$$\forall A_i A_j \in \mathfrak{F} : A_i \cap A_j = \varnothing \quad \mathbf{P}(\cup A_i) = \sum_i \mathbf{P}(A_i)$$

It is clear that the properties with which this function $\mathbf{P}(.)$ is endowed are very similar to the properties one would intuitively require from a probability function: the 'probability' of the null set is 0; the 'probability' of the union of disjointed events should be equal to the sum of the 'probabilities' of their individual occurrences; each 'probability' should be positive. To complete the identification we simply have to further require that the 'probability' of Ω should add up to 1:

(d) $\qquad\qquad\qquad\qquad \mathbf{P}(\Omega) = 1$

Therefore, a probability is a particular law associating a positive real number to events, and enjoying in addition to conditions (a), (b) and (c) requirement (d). Such a law is often referred to as a *probability measure*. Different probability measures sharing the same null set are called *equivalent* probability measures. Different investors might therefore disagree as to the likelihood of occurrence of different events, but, if their subjective probability measures are equivalent, they would all agree as to which events are possible, and which impossible.

The triplet $\{\Omega, \mathfrak{F}, \mathbf{P})$ is then called a *probability space*, which therefore describes what the possible events are (via Ω), what the measurable events are (via $\mathfrak{F}$), and what probability should be associated to measurable events (via $\mathbf{P}$).

By its very definition, the probability $\mathbf{P}$ operates on (has as domain) elements of a set (events). As such, it does not readily lend itself to manipulations such as differentiation, integration, etc. The next step in our probabilistic set-up is therefore the association of a real number to each set of measurable events (or, more precisely, to each element of a σ-field). Notice that this real number (which can be positive or negative) has nothing to do with the probabilities we have associated with (sets of) events. It is merely a convenient 'label' attached to the various events. Going back to the example considered above, one could assign to each 'up' ('down') move a value of $+1$ (-1), and therefore associate to ω_3 the number 2, to ω_2 0 and to ω_1 -2. The question as to whether the real axis will, in general, provide an adequate mapping (range) for any possible set of (not necessarily) discrete events is an important one, and leads directly to the concept of Borel sets. Without entering into details (see, e.g., Oksendal (1995) or Dothan (1990)) one can simply state the result that it is indeed always possible to define a function RV that establishes a one-to-one correspondence from particular (Borel) sets (σ-fields) of the real line to events in the σ-field $\mathfrak{F}$ generated by Ω. Such a function is normally referred to as a **random variable**. By introducing this concept the translation can then be accomplished from the original probability triplet $(\Omega, \mathfrak{F}, \mathbf{P})$ to $(\Omega', \mathfrak{F}', \mathbf{P}')$, where Ω' is now the real line, $\mathfrak{F}'$ is the σ-field made up of the above-mentioned Borel sets, and $\mathbf{P}'$ is the new probability law now associating a real number between zero and one to the elements of $\mathfrak{F}'$.

4.3 THE FLOW OF INFORMATION

Having established these fundamental concepts, it is then desirable to be able to formalise the idea of information flow; more precisely, one needs, in practical applications, to be able to evaluate conditional expectations, based on the knowledge that certain events have or have not occurred. Later chapters, for instance, will show how these concepts are embodied in the evaluation procedures connected with lattice methodologies.

To develop more formally the intuitive idea of flow of information, one can introduce a family $\mathbf{F}$ of σ-fields, enjoying the property that

$$\mathbf{F} = \{\mathfrak{F}_0 \subseteq \mathfrak{F}_1 \subseteq \mathfrak{F}_2 \subseteq \cdots \subseteq \mathfrak{F}_n\}$$

where the symbol $A \subseteq B$ indicates that the set A is a subset (proper or improper) of A. In other words, each σ-field $\mathfrak{F}_t$ is generated by a partition of Ω at time t: the investor starts at time 0 with $\mathfrak{F}_0 = \{\varnothing, \Omega\}$, i.e. without any knowledge about future realisations of future states of the world; he only knows which events are possible and which impossible. At time 1 his knowledge is increased by the realisation of the state of the world which has actually occurred; by time n all the relevant information has been acquired. The formalism just described accounts for the process of 'learning without forgetting'. The family $\mathbf{F}$ of σ-fields just described is called a *filtration*.

These definitions can be made clearer by considering again a two-step process. Remembering that the elements of a σ-field are the measurable events, a filtration $\mathfrak{F}_k$ indicates the events to which a probability of 0 or 1 can be assigned at time k.

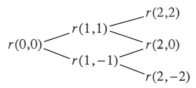

So, as mentioned above, at time 0 the only events whose probabilities are known with certainty are $\varnothing (\mathbf{P}(\varnothing) = 0)$ and $\Omega (\mathbf{P}(\Omega) = 1)$, i.e. we simply know in which state of the world we are, and what the future possible states of the world will be.

At time 1, one will know the prevailing state of the world $(r(1,1)$ or $r(1,-1))$, and, from either state, which states of the world will be reachable over the next time step (i.e. $r(2,2)$ or $(2,0)$ from $r(1,1)$, and $r(2,0)$ and $r(2,-1)$ from $r(1,-1)$).

Therefore, the σ-field $\mathfrak{S}_1$ is made up of the measurable events

$\{\varnothing\}$

$\{\Omega\}$

$\{r(1,1)$ followed by $r(2,2)$, $r(1,1)$ followed by $r(2,0)\}$

$\{r(1,-1)$ followed by $r(2,0)$, $r(1,-1)$ followed by $r(2,-2)\}$

i.e. at time 1 one knows how to associate the probability values 0 or 1 to the events $\varnothing$ and Ω, as before, and to the events $\{[r(1,1)$ followed by $r(2,2)]$, $[r(1,1)$ followed by $r(2,0)]\}$, $\{[r(1,-1)$ followed by $r(2,0)]$, $[r(1,-1)$ followed by $r(2,-2)]\}$:

$$\mathbf{P}(\{[r(1,1) \text{ followed by } r(2,2)], \atop [r(1,1) \text{ followed by } r(2,0)]\}) = \begin{cases} 1 \text{ if } r(1,1) \text{ has occurred} \\ 0 \text{ if } r(1,-1) \text{ has occurred} \end{cases}$$

$$\mathbf{P}(\{[r(1,-1) \text{ followed by } r(2,0)], \atop [r(1,-1) \text{ followed by } r(2,-2)]\}) = \begin{cases} 1 \text{ if } r(1,-1) \text{ has occurred} \\ 0 \text{ if } r(1,1) \text{ has occurred} \end{cases}$$

Finally, at time 2 the σ-field $\mathfrak{S}_2$ is made up of

$\{\varnothing\}$

$\{\Omega\}$

$\{r(1,1)$ followed by $r(2,2)\}$

$\{r(1,1)$ followed by $r(2,0)\}$

$\{r(1,-1)$ followed by $r(2,0)\}$

$\{r(1,1)$ followed by $r(2,-2)\}$

$\{r(2,2)\}$

$\{r(2,0)\}$

$\{r(2,-2)\}$

and by the results of the fundamental set-theoretical operations of union, intersection and complementation on these events, and the investor knows which (series of) events have occurred and which have not. If the evolution of the economy has, for instance, taken place by the state variable moving to state $r(1,1)$ at time 1 and then to state $r(2,0)$ at time 2, the probabilities, for instance, of the fourth element shown above, and, of course, of Ω, have value 1; as for the remaining elements explicitly shown, they all have value 0 (have not occurred). To appreciate how this information could be of importance in practical applications the reader can contrast the two cases of a path-dependent option, or of a simpler option depending only on the final realisation of the state variable.

4.4 THE SECURITIES MARKET

Once the probability space and the flow of information have been defined, one would want a description of the actual securities market. To this effect, one can begin by specifying the *trading horizon T*, i.e. the set of dates on which trading is allowed. In the discrete case the set T will contain a finite number of dates. In a Monte Carlo or in a lattice implementation of an option model the 'trading dates' will be spaced by a time interval Δt.

Then, if there are $K + 1$ securities in the market, one can denote the price of security k at time t if the state of the world ω has occurred by $S(t,k,\omega)$, for any t belonging to the trading horizon. One says that the $(K + 1)$-dimensional stochastic process $S(t)$ is *defined on* $(\Omega,\Im,\mathbf{P})$.

If the economy is indeed described, as it was assumed before, by a single state variable, it must be possible to associate to each realisation of this state variable the prices of all the traded assets. This is exactly what occurs in the case of one-factor models, where a specification of the short-rate dynamics allows to retrieve prices of swaps, caps, etc. (Extension to several driving factors makes the notation more cumbersome, but is conceptually straightforward.) In a one-factor model, to each value $S(t,k,\omega)$ one can therefore associate the probability connected with the path of the underlying state variable. Therefore, if the present state of the world can evolve only to two possible states over one time step, one obtains:

	State 0		State 1	State 2
Security 0	$S(0,0,0)$	|	$S(1,0,1)$	$S(1,0,2)$
Security 1	$S(0,1,0)$	|	$S(1,1,1)$	$S(1,1,2)$
. . .	. . .	|	. . .	. . .
Security K	$S(0,K,0)$	|	$S(1,K,1)$	$S(1,K,2)$

Time 0   *Time 1*

At this point one can introduce the concept of *trading strategy*. A trading strategy is a $(K + 1)$-dimensional vector Θ of holdings of the different securities.

Holding	Security Price
$\theta(0) = 2$	$S(0,0,0) = £2.4$
$\theta(1) = 0$	$S(0,1,0) = £32$
$\theta(2) = -20$	$S(0,2,0) = £0.001$
. . .	. . .
$\theta(K) = 12$	$S(0,K,0) = £16$

A possible trading strategy: at time 0, 2 units (long position) are held of security 0, 0 units of security 1, -20 units (short position) of security 2, ..., 12 units of security K. The vector Θ is therefore made up of $\Theta = \{\theta(0), \theta(1), \theta(2), ..., \theta(K)\}$.

These holdings are known with certainty at time 0, and are going to be adjusted at later times depending on future realisations of the asset prices. The vector of future holdings is therefore itself a random vector. In addition it will be assumed that it is *predictable*; this means that the readjustments of the holdings can only occur *after* the prices have been revealed. In other terms, at time $t-1$ the investor decides what the holdings should be (i.e. based on information contained in $\mathfrak{I}_{t-1}$), waits for a new set of prices to be revealed (whereby the information set is augmented from $\mathfrak{I}_{t-1}$ to $\mathfrak{I}_t$), and *then* readjusts the portfolio holdings. In technical terms one says that the trading strategy is $\mathfrak{I}_{t-1}$-measurable. Intuitively, the condition means that only trading strategies will be considered where no 'peeking ahead' is allowed. Furthermore, remembering that the scalar product of two vectors **A** and **B**, of respective elements $\{a_i\}$ and $\{b_i\}$, is given by

$$\mathbf{AB} = \Sigma a_i b_i$$

one can immediately see that the value V of the trading strategy is given by the scalar product of the vector of holdings Θ and the vector **S** containing the prices of the securities:

$$V = \Theta\mathbf{S} = \Sigma \theta_i S_i$$

Of all the possible predictable trading strategies, we are going to be interested in those which satisfy two further requirements. First of all we want the strategy to be *self-financing*. By this one requires that in readjusting the portfolio weights θ_i no net injections or withdrawals of cash should take place over the trading horizon. Purchases (sales) of one asset must be entirely financed by the proceeds of the net sales (purchases) of the other assets. Therefore:

$$\Sigma \ \theta(t)S(t) = \Sigma \ \theta(t+1)S(t) \tag{4.2}$$

The term $\theta(t+1)$ indicates the portfolio allocation among the various securities (as determined at time t) that will be kept unchanged until the securities prices at time $t+1$ are revealed. At time $t+1$ the value of the portfolio, $V(t+1;\{\theta_i\})$, will be

$$V(t+1) = \Sigma \ \theta(t+1)S(t+1) \tag{4.3}$$

and the net profit or loss over the period will be

$$V(t+1) - V(t) = \Sigma \ \theta(t+1)(S(t+1) - S(t)) \tag{4.4}$$

The second requirement we are going to impose on the trading strategies is that at any point in time the value of the portfolio should be positive or 0:

$$\Sigma \ \theta(t)S(t) \geqslant 0 \quad \forall t \tag{4.5}$$

Notice that negative holdings (i.e. short sales) are allowed, but the investor must be able, at any point in time, to liquidate his position and repay all debts. Predictable self-financing trading strategies such that Equation (4.3) is satisfied are called *admissible*.

The portfolio value as defined above applies to time t, i.e. an expression like Equation (4.4) does not say anything about the *present* value of the portfolio itself. In the context of a deterministic-interest-rate economy (see Chapter 5, Section 3), this creates no problem, since one can indifferently discount by a zero-coupon bond maturing at time t, or by rolling over a money market account, as explained in greater detail later on. In a Black-and-Scholes world, therefore, present valuing by a (deterministic) discount bond is perfectly adequate. Speaking of 'future money' is, however, no longer unambiguous for stochastic interest rates, since each asset, be it a discount bond or a money market account, will in general display a stochastic dynamic. In complete generality, therefore, one can express the present value of any stochastic asset in terms of units of any other, arbitrarily chosen, asset (as long as the latter has strictly positive payoffs at all times). By convention this asset, called the *numeraire asset*, is given the index 0. Relative prices $Z_j(t)$ are therefore given by the ratio of the cash prices $S_j(t)$ to $S_0(t)$, the numeraire asset. With some foresight we numbered the cash prices from 0 to K, so that we can now write

$$Z_j(t) = \frac{S_j(t)}{S_0(t)} \quad \forall j = 1, K \tag{4.6}$$

The price/state matrix now becomes

	State 0	State 1	State 2
Security 0	1	1	1
Security 1	$Z(0,1,0)$	$Z(1,1,1)$	$Z(1,1,2)$
...	...	...	...
Security K	$Z(0,K,0)$	$Z(1,K,1)$	$Z(1,K,2)$

$$\underbrace{\qquad}_{\textit{Time 0}} \qquad \underbrace{\qquad}_{\textit{Time 1}}$$

(4.7)

where $Z(i,j,k)$ indicates the relative price at time I of security j in state k. Notice that the value of the first relative asset is always 1 at all times and in all states of the world, since the value of one unit of the chosen numeraire in terms of itself is always 1. The ratio $1/S_0(t)$ is called the *discount factor*, and, needless to say, is not a constant but a stochastic quantity, and will be different for any different choice of numeraire. Also notice that, since to any different choice of numeraire there corresponds a different present value for any asset, the present-valuing process plays a very important role for stochastic interest-rate economies.

4.5   DEFINITION OF ARBITRAGE IN A DISCRETE COMPLETE MARKET

We are finally in a position to give a first definition of arbitrage within the context of self-financing admissible trading strategies. **Arbitrage is a self-financing trading strategy of zero initial value and of non-zero final value;** i.e. no-arbitrage implies that, if in all the states of the world at time T the portfolio value is greater than or equal to zero

$$V(T,\omega) = \sum_k \theta(T,k)S(T,k,\omega) \geq 0 \qquad (4.8)$$

and in at least one state of the world, say $\tilde{\omega}$, it has a strictly positive value,

$$V(T,\tilde{\omega}) = \sum_k \theta(T,k)S(T,k,\tilde{\omega}) > 0$$

then its set-up cost today must be strictly positive:

$$\Rightarrow \sum \theta(0)S(0) > 0$$

something that gives a positive amount at least in some states of the world, and a negative amount in no states of the world, must cost something today. Or, conversely, **if a portfolio has a zero value today it cannot have positive (or negative) values in all states of the world.**

This definition can be considerably extended. Even the formulation just presented, however, can give a very powerful result. Rather than stating it formally, an example is first presented.

Let us consider the simplest non-trivial case of an economy driven by a single state variable, and in which two assets, $S(t,0,\omega)$ (asset 0) and $S(t,1,\omega)$ (asset 1), are traded. At time 0 a single (known) state of the world prevails (state 0). At time 1 only two possible states can occur (state 1 and state 2). We assume to know what possible values the two assets can have after one time step, but we do *not* assume to know with what probability these possible values can be reached. As before, all investors simply know which states are possible and which are not, i.e. their subjective probability measures are all equivalent. Let us consider a trading horizon comprised of today (time 0) and a single future date (time 1). Let us further require that arbitrage cannot occur in this economy. Therefore condition (4.8) must hold. We construct at time 0 a zero-value portfolio, $V(0,0)$ made up of one unit of asset 1 and of a suitable amount of asset 0. The amount of asset 0 needed in order to give the initial portfolio zero value is $-S(0,1,0)/S(0,0,0) \equiv -k$, with $k > 0$:

$$V(0,0) = -\frac{S(0,1,0)}{S(0,0,0)} S(0,0,0) + 1\,S(0,1,0) = 0 \qquad (4.9)$$

$$= -k \qquad S(0,0,0) + 1\,S(0,1,0) = 0$$

We want to use asset 0 as the numeraire asset. Without restricting the generality we can always choose its value today to be equal to 1:

$$S(0,0,0) = 1$$

At time zero the present value of the portfolio, obviously identical to the portfolio value itself, is clearly given by

$$PV(V(0,0) = -\frac{S(0,1,0)}{S(0,0,0)} + \frac{S(0,1,0)}{S(0,0,0)} = 0 \qquad (4.10)$$

Over a time step the asset values and the portfolio measured in units of asset 1 are shown, respectively, by the following tables:

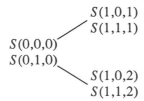

and

$$-S(0,1,0) + S(0,1,0) \begin{cases} -S(0,1,0) + \dfrac{S(1,1,1)}{S(1,0,1)} = -k + \dfrac{S(1,1,1)}{S(1,0,1)} \\[3mm] -S(0,1,0) + \dfrac{S(1,1,2)}{S(1,0,2)} = -k + \dfrac{S(1,1,2)}{S(1,0,2)} \end{cases}$$

where use has been made of the fact that the relative price of the numeraire asset is 1 in all states of the world, and that $S(0,0,0) = 1$.

Let us now consider a very special security for asset 1: a security that pays £1 if state of the world 2 is reached, and 0 otherwise. (As it will be shown in a later chapter such a security is also known as an Arrow–Debreu price, and will play a central role in the construction of computational lattices.) For this particular choice of security 1 the table above becomes

$$-S(0,1,0) + S(0,1,0) \begin{cases} -k \\[3mm] -k + \dfrac{1}{S(1,0,2)} \end{cases}$$

It is at this point that the no-arbitrage conditions come into play. From the definition of arbitrage given above, starting from a zero-value portfolio the portfolio expressed in terms of units of numeraire cannot have positive (or negative) values in both states of the world. But in one of the two states (state 1) we know with certainty, since $k > 0$, that the normalised portfolio value is negative; therefore in state 2 the portfolio value expressed in terms of relative process must be strictly positive:

$$k < 1/S(1,0,2)$$

or

$$\frac{S(0,1,0)}{S(0,0,0)} < \frac{1}{S(1,0,2)} \Rightarrow \frac{S(0,1,0)}{1} < \frac{S(1,1,2)}{S(1,0,2)}$$

where use has been made of $S(0,0,0) = 1$ and $S(1,1,2) = 1$; using the definition of relative prices (Equation (4.6)) one therefore has, at the same time,

$$\mathbf{0 < Z(0,1,0) < Z(1,1,2)} \tag{4.11}$$

Therefore one must be able to write

$$Z(0,1,0) = \lambda_2 Z(1,1,2) \tag{4.12}$$

with $0 < \lambda_2 < 1$. Exactly the same reasoning could have been applied to a security that paid £1 with certainty at time 1 in state 1, and £0 in state 2. If we denote the relative price of this new security $Z^*(i,j,k)$, this would have given rise to an equation of the form

$$Z^*(0,1,0) = \lambda_1 Z^*(1,1,1) \tag{4.13}$$

with $\lambda_1 < 1$. These results are more general than one might surmise, since in our simplified universe **any asset, with any payoff profile in the two possible states of the world, can be obtained as a linear combination of the two primitive securities (Arrow–Debreu prices) that we have just described**. Therefore, for the simple universe we have so far considered, one can write **for any security or combination of securities**

$$Z(0,1,0) = \lambda_1 Z(1,1,1) + \lambda_2 Z(1,1,2) \tag{4.14}$$

with both λ_1 and $\lambda_2 < 1$. The crucial point of this derivation is that the constants λ_1 and λ_2 just obtained are **state specific** and not asset specific. Furthermore, since they are both strictly positive and smaller than 1, after ensuring that $\lambda_1 + \lambda_2$ add up to 1, they can be interpreted as probabilities. Needless to say, by the way they have been obtained, they have little to do with probability in the 'real world', apart from the fact that the probability space subsumed by these 'pseudo-probabilities' has the same null set as the 'real' probability space. It is also clear that, had a different numeraire been chosen, the pseudo-probabilities would, in general, have turned out to be different. Given this probabilistic interpretation, Equation (4.14) above can be viewed as giving the relative price at time 0 as an expectation, taken in this new measure Q' (as opposed to the probability measure Q in the real world) over the possible states ω:

$$Z(0,1,0) = E'[Z(1,1,\omega)] \qquad (4.15)$$

This is an extremely important result: we have shown that, at least for the special case considered here, **if no-arbitrage is to be allowed, there must exist a suitable measure such that the expectation of the future value of relative prices must equal its value today.** Apart from technical conditions this is exactly the requirement for a stochastic process to be a martingale. More precisely, if one considers a finite probability space $(\Omega, \Im, \mathbf{P})$, and a $\Im_n$-measurable process X_n, then the process X is said to be a *martingale* if

$$E'[X_n + 1 \mid \Im_n] = X_n \qquad (4.16)$$

In other terms, if a process is a martingale the best guess as to its expectation over the next time step, contingent on all the information gathered up to time t, is its value at time t. It is easy to prove that this property extends over as many time steps within the trading horizon as desired:

$$E'[X_{n+j} \mid \Im_n] = X_n \quad \forall j \geqslant 0 \qquad (4.17)$$

Therefore the result above can be rephrased as: **if no-arbitrage is to be allowed, then one must be able to construct a probability space such that relative prices are martingales.** (For a mathematically more satisfactory proof see, e.g., Lamberton and Lapeyre (1991) or Duffie (1992). For extensions to the continuous time see, e.g., Dothan (1990).)

A few remarks can enhance the financial intuition behind this theorem: the statement that, in this new measure, the relative price process should be a martingale is tantamount to requiring that the expectation of any relative price at any later time should be the same as its price today. This requirement of zero drift might seem surprising, since it seems to imply no expected return from an asset, but, by recalling the definition of $Z^*(T)$ as *ratios* of traded assets, it can be seen that the martingale requirement is equivalent to imposing the *same* return from both assets. But this is very similar to the old Black and Scholes result, where all assets earn the same (riskless) rate of return. It will become apparent in the next chapter that it is even more similar, nay identical, to the result obtained using the classic (Vasicek) approach: it will be in fact shown that for a particular choice of numeraire (associated with the so-called 'risk-neutral world') every asset earns exactly the spot rate. In other words, the change of measure from Q to Q' tilts the playing field in such a way that the return from each unnormalised asset is the same as the return from the numeraire asset. It can be immediately seen that, since there is no unique choice for the latter, the type and extent of the 'tilting' will have to be different for each numeraire choice.

Needless to say the example presented above is far from being a proof. The latter, however, requires mathematical tools (Separating Hyperplanes Theorem, convex cones, etc.) which are not only relatively sophisticated, but tend to obfuscate the financial intuition to a considerable extent. Despite the fact, however, that, for sake of simplicity, we have worked with a very simple universe (a single driving factor, a single time step, only two possible states after *the* one time step, etc.), a rigorous proof would roughly follow the same conceptual lines. Such a proof can be found, for instance, in Duffie (1992) in a most concise form, in Lamberton and Lapeyre (1991) in much greater detail, or in Dothan (1990) for the continuous time case.

Given the very restrictive conditions enforced for the example presented above no use was made of the concept introduced before of self-financing trading strategy. The conceptual path that leads from the definition of no-arbitrage for self-financing trading strategies to the case of contingent claims is the following (see Gustavsson (1992)).

A *contingent claim* $X(T)$ is first of all defined by specifying its random profile X at time T. For instance, one such contingent claim could be a call option, for which $X(T)$ would be given by $\text{Max}[S(T) - X, 0]$, where the random variable $S(T)$ indicates the realisation at time T of asset $S(t)$.

A contingent claim is then said to be *attainable* if one can always form a self-financing trading strategy $\{\Theta(t)\}$, such that, at expiry T, the option payoff coincides with the payoff provided by the trading strategy, i.e.

$$X(T) = \Theta(T)S(T) \qquad (4.18)$$

If, for any possible contingent claim, it is always possible to create a replicating (i.e. with the same final payoff), admissible, self-financing trading strategy, then the market is said to be *complete*. Notice that this condition is essential for the definition of no-arbitrage that we are presenting. In the simple, two-state, two-asset example that was introduced before the completeness and attainability requirements were disposed of simply by saying that, in our simple universe, any security could be created as a linear combination of the two fundamental building blocks, i.e. the Arrow–Debreu prices.

Given the one-to-one correspondence between contingent claims and admissible self-financing trading strategies, it is possible to express the condition that a contingent claim should be priced by no-arbitrage by requiring that the associated trading strategy should be priced by no-arbitrage; but these are exactly the conditions that were stated and justified in the first part of this section. Therefore, the no-arbitrage conditions obtained so far establish (in discrete time) a series of formal relationships between expectations of particular stochastic variables (the relative prices) and particular trading strategies. The mathematical tools needed to extract quantitative information from these relationships are presented in the following section. For the purpose, the setting will switch from the discrete to the continuous-time case. As mentioned before, this 'transition' is conceptually far from trivial; the rather subtle issues connected with the validity of 'moving to the continuous limit' and the nature of convergence (treated in some detail, for instance, in

Willinger and Taqqu (1991)) will not be addressed, and the validity of this limiting procedure will simply be assumed. References will nonetheless be provided to allow for a mathematically more satisfactory treatment.

4.6 THE CONTINUOUS-TIME LIMIT: A MOTIVATION FOR STOCHASTIC CALCULUS

All the results and the definitions introduced in the previous sections of this chapter referred to the discrete case: time increments were always finite, and the traded securities could attain a finite number of possible states. Despite the fact that a strong case could be made that, in reality, possible securities prices *are* indeed discrete (changing by ticks, basis points, or other similar units), and that trading can only occur with a high but finite frequency, some very powerful results, namely the equivalent of integration and differentiation in ordinary calculus, are most naturally obtained in the case of *continuous* trading. Unfortunately the mathematical formalism required to treat 'properly' continuous-time stochastic processes is considerably more complicated than what is required for the discrete case. Therefore the treatment in the present and the following sections will be more 'heuristic' (an often useful euphemism, in this context, for 'handwaving'). Nonetheless the concepts behind the formalism are of fundamental importance not only in order to acquire the technical tools used extensively in option pricing (first and foremost, Ito's lemma), but also in order to appreciate the underlying equivalence of such methodologies as Monte Carlo simulations, partial differential equations or computational lattices.

   In the previous discussion that led from the definition of no-arbitrage for self-financing trading strategies to the definition of no-arbitrage for contingent claims, it was shown that a very important role (in discrete time) was played by quantities such as

$$\sum_j H_j (Z_j - Z_{j-1}) \tag{4.19}$$

with $\{H_n\}$ a predictable process with respect to a filtration $\mathfrak{I}$, and $\{Z_n\}$ a martingale process of relative prices. If the process of arrival of information can be satisfactorily modelled by a Brownian motion (see Section 4.7), then the discrete time process for Z can be written as

$$\Delta Z(t) = \sigma(t) \, \Delta w(t) \tag{4.20}$$

To give a concrete example, if $\mathbf{H}$ is a vector of holdings of securities, then the sum (4.19) would represent the change in value of a trading strategy, expressed in terms of a particular numeraire. While in the discrete case treated so far the quantity (4.19) is unambiguously defined, serious problems do arise if one attempts to move to the continuous limit. If the flow of information (or,

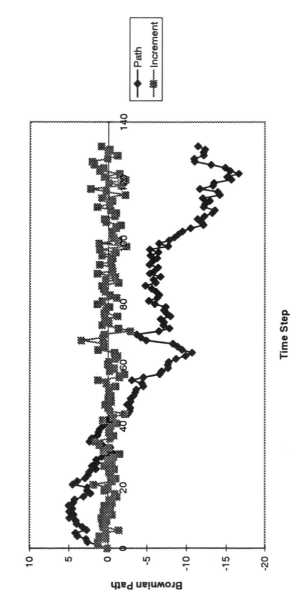

Figure 4.1 A path $w(t)$ starting at 0 and obtained from uncorrelated Brownian increments of identical (unit) variance. As dt tends to zero the path displays continuity, i.e. if the increments are drawn from a distribution that decays to zero 'quickly enough', for a given $\varepsilon > 0$ arbitrarily small, it is always possible to choose a time step dt such that the probability of $|w(t+dt) - w(t)| > \varepsilon$ is negligibly small. The right and left differentials, however, as dt goes to zero are not the same, and the quantity $dw(t)/dt$ does not converge to any unique number.

technically, the filtration) is generated by uncorrelated Brownian increments $dw(t)$, the paths turn out to be continuous everywhere, but nowhere differentiable (see Figure 4.1), i.e. the quantity $dw(t)/dt$ does not tend to any unique value as dt goes to zero. Therefore, despite the fact that the quantity $w(t)$ is a continuous function of time, the limit of Equation (4.19) as dt tends to zero *cannot*, in analogy with ordinary calculus, be written as

$$\int_0^t H(s)\sigma(s)\, dw(s) = \int_0^t H(s)\sigma(s)\, \frac{dw(s)}{ds}\, ds \tag{4.21}$$

On the other hand, moving to the continuous limit does yield, for the case of a Brownian filtration, extremely powerful results (notably, Ito's lemma and Ito's integral). The following section will therefore attempt to give a sense to the LHS of Equation (4.21), i.e. to specify a procedure such that, no matter how small the time interval chosen, a precise value can be associated to the expectation of the integral (4.21) (or of its square). It is worth stressing that our goal in so doing is more limited than with, say, a ordinary (Riemann) integral, where one wants to be able to specify a limiting procedure such that a *number* can be directly associated to the integral itself. In the stochastic case, no procedure can in general be devised such that a unique value, independent of the specific realisation of Brownian increments, can be associated to an equation of the form

$$I(t) = \int_0^t f(s)\, dw(s) \tag{4.22}$$

In a more limited way, the goal of the definition of a stochastic integral is to be able to associate a value independent of the size of the time interval to the *expectation* of (a function of) Equation (4.22). In order to achieve this task, some fundamental properties about random walks and Brownian motions will first be presented in the following section.

4.7 FUNDAMENTAL PROPERTIES OF RANDOM WALKS AND BROWNIAN MOTIONS

Brownian motions can be intuitively regarded as the continuous-time limit of random walks. The analysis will therefore start from the discrete random walk case. The topic of Brownian motions is very rich, and only the specific results needed for the remainder of this chapter (namely the results regarding the quadratic variation of a Brownian motion) will be touched upon.

Let us assume to have a random variable which, at time 0, assumes a value of $X(0)$. For instance, the random variable could be the short rate in a one-factor model. Let us also assume that, after each time step, this random variable can either move up or down by an equal amount. The possibility of the random variable 'not moving' is not allowed.

We can further assume, without restricting the generality of the treatment, that the probabilities of moving 'up' or 'down' should be identical. If this were not the case, the random walk would simply be biased upward or downward to a known extent. Therefore, by subtracting this deterministic drift, one can always reduce oneself to the equal-probability case. The reader will easily recognise a construction extremely similar to the Ho and Lee or, even more so, to the first phase of the tree-fitting procedure proposed by Hull and White (see Chapter 11); if the variable were taken to be the logarithm of the short rate, then the construction would be similar to the BDT model: what is missing in the 'standardised' random walk set up is simply the deterministic drift for the random variable.

Without loss of generality we can further impose that the initial value of the random variable should be 0 (compare again with the Hull and White construction), and that the increment should be of ± 1 (a suitable translation and 'stretching' of the coordinate system can always bring about this condition).

We now have all the ingredients required to define a probability space along the lines of Sections 4.2 and 4.3, where the elementary events, the filtration and the probability measure for this example have been defined.

The essential property characterising the random walk is then that all the *increments* of the random variable should be independent of each other: the fact that the last jump has been 'up' or 'down' has no influence on the probability of the next jump.

From this independence condition two important results follow:

(1) the expectation of the random variable after n moves contingent on its having the value X_0 after m moves ($n > m$) is simply equal to X_0:

$$E[X(n)|\, \Im_m] = X_0(m) \qquad (4.23)$$

In other terms the process $X(i)$ is a martingale.

To obtain the second result, let us now define the quadratic variation at time m of a generic (i.e. deterministic or stochastic) function of discrete time values, $f(j)$, as

$$\mathrm{QVar}[f](k) = \sum_{j=1,k} (f(j) - f(j-1))^2 \qquad (4.24)$$

Then, for the special case when $f(X) = X$, and since for this random variable we have posited $X(j) - X(j-1)$ to be always equal to ± 1 for any j, the second result follows:

(2) the quadratic variation of X after k steps is simply equal to k.

$$\mathrm{QVar}[X](k) = \sum_{j=1,k} (X(j) - X(j-1))^2 = k \qquad (4.25)$$

The importance of this property will become clear as we pass to the continuous limit.

In order to do so, let us begin by increasing the frequency of the jumps, i.e. reducing the time step (which so far had been taken to be 1), and by reducing at the same time the magnitude of each jump. There is an infinity of ways to rescale the problem. **We want to choose** *the* **particular ratio of Δt to ΔX such that the quadratic variation property (4.25) is retained**. To this effect, let us impose that, if the time step decreases by a factor of $K (K = 1/n, n > 1)$, then the magnitude of the jump should be reduced by a factor of $\sqrt{K}$ (compare with the factor $\sigma \sqrt{\Delta t} = \sqrt{\sigma^2 \, \Delta t}$ which appears in Monte Carlo simulations, as discussed in Chapter 8):

$$\Delta t \to K \, \Delta t \tag{4.26}$$

$$\Delta X \to \sqrt{K} \, \Delta X \tag{4.26'}$$

Let us check that, for this particular choice of rescaling, the quadratic variation property (4.25) is indeed recovered for $f(X) = X$: each term $(f_{(j)} - f_{(j-1)})$ is now equal to $\pm \sqrt{K}$ (the original ΔX was 1); its square is therefore simply $K = 1/n$. In order to reach the same point in time k we shall now have to undertake $k/K = kn$ steps. Therefore, as before,

$$\text{QVar}[X](k) = \sum_{j=1,kn} (X(j) - X(j-1))^2 = k \tag{4.27}$$

Since the independence of each increment still holds, also the martingale property is clearly satisfied for this finer random walk.

Moving to the continuous limit, i.e. to the limit as n goes to infinity, or even to the limit as K becomes an arbitrary (i.e. not necessary rational) small number, would now formally require the more complicated treatment for continuous-time stochastic processes; it is, however, intuitively plausible, that, if we define x as some 'suitable' limit of X as the sampling frequency increases, then the properties of independence of increments, of zero conditional expectation, and of quadratic variation equal to the time elapsed still hold. In particular, the chosen scaling ensures that the variance of a Brownian motion is indeed of order $O(\mathrm{d}t)$, and that, therefore, terms in $\mathrm{d}x^2$ should be retained with terms in $\mathrm{d}t$ in any Taylor expansion. It is also by virtue of the precise scaling expressed by Equations (4.26) and (4.26') that, in the course of a Monte Carlo simulation, the contribution arising from the stochastic component of the process neither dominates nor is swamped by the deterministic part, as the size of the time step is changed.

The property just obtained is extremely important, and should be contrasted with the result which will be obtained in Section 9 of this chapter, where it will be shown that for any continuous *deterministic* function (with bounded first derivative) the quadratic variation is always exactly 0, irrespective of the function. This is, in essence, the result of Ito's lemma presented in Section 4.9.

4.8 DEFINITION AND FUNDAMENTAL PROPERTIES OF STOCHASTIC INTEGRALS

Having established some useful properties of Brownian motions and random walks, we are in a position to say something more concrete about expression (4.22), which is, so far, a pure symbol. To this effect let us, first of all, consider a special class of functions $f(t)$, which have the very 'natural' property of being independent of the future behaviour of $w(s)$, for $s > t$. More formally, if $\mathfrak{I}_t$ is the σ-field generated by the Brownian motion $w(s)$ for $s \leqslant t$, then we are going to consider the class of functions which are $\mathfrak{I}_t$-measurable. These functions are also referred to as *non-anticipating* functions. In the context of securities markets, a possible non-anticipating function could be the amount of units of the different securities held at time t_i in a particular trading strategy, based on the information available up to time t_{i-1}. (As we saw in Chapter 4, for admissible strategies reallocations among the various assets can only take place *after* the prices have moved.) Let us then subdivide the interval $[t,T]$ into n subintervals, t_1, t_2, $\ldots,t_{n-1},t_n = T$, and let us choose a point $\tau_j(j = 1,n)$ inside each subinterval (see, e.g., Gardiner (1990)). The procedure is so far identical to the one followed to define 'ordinary' (Riemann) integrals. Let us then define the sum S_n as

$$S_n = \sum_{i=1,n} f(\tau_i)[w(t_i) - w(t_{i-1})] \tag{4.28}$$

If $w(t)$ were a deterministic rather than a stochastic function of time, it is well known that, in the limit as n goes to infinity (in the usual 'nice' manner), the value of S_n converges to a unique value (the Riemann–Stieltjes integral) irrespective of how we choose the points τ_j in the respective subintervals. For the case we are considering, however, it can be easily proven (see, e.g., Gardiner (1990), or Oksendal (1995)) that the choice of sampling point *does* make a difference. Two conventional choices are common:

$$\text{Choice 1: } \tau_i = t_{i-1} \quad \text{(Ito's integral)} \tag{4.29}$$

$$\text{Choice 2: } \tau_i = (t_{i-1} + t_i)/2 \quad \text{(Stratonovich integral)} \tag{4.29'}$$

Whilst the second choice brings about some mathematically 'nice' properties (see, e.g., Gardiner (1990) again), for reasons which will become clear immediately below, the first choice will always be made in the remainder of this book:

$$S_n = \sum_{i=1,n} f(t_{i-1})[w(t_i) - w(t_{i-1})] \tag{4.28'}$$

As with ordinary calculus, having decided how to choose the points inside each interval, one would at this point want to go to the limit as the number of subdivisions becomes larger and larger. As stated before, however, there is no hope of achieving convergence for each individual *finite* sum of the form of Equation (4.28): by the very fact that the increments are random, no two realisations will yield exactly the same path. One could, however, hope that some averaging procedure, applied to a multitude of realisations, could indeed converge to some well-defined quantity. Indeed, with Choice 1 the Ito stochastic integral can be defined as

$$I(T) = \int_t^T f(s)\,dw(s) = \underset{n \to \infty}{\text{lim-ms}}\ S_n$$

$$= \underset{n \to \infty}{\text{lim-ms}} \sum_{i=1,n} f(t_{i-1})[w(t_i) - w(t_{i-1})] \qquad (4.30)$$

where the symbol $\underset{n \to \infty}{\text{lim-ms}}$ indicates the mean-square limit; more precisely, we say that a series $S_n(\omega)$ converges to $S(\omega)$ in the mean square in the probability space Ω where the events ω have a probability density $p(\omega)$ if

$$\lim_{n \to \infty} \int p(\omega)[S_n(\omega) - S(\omega)]^2\,d\omega = 0 \qquad (4.31)$$

Notice that, by Equation (4.30) one has been able to associate to Ito's integral a random variable, not a unique (deterministic) number. As for 'normal' time integrals, however, by varying the upper limit of integration, Ito's stochastic integrals can also be regarded as a function of time, $I(t,\omega)$.

Once a meaning has been associated with the Ito's integral, some mathematically and financially important properties can be easily derived:

(a) **if the process $w(t)$ (the integrator) is a martingale (as it is the case for a Brownian motion) and $f(t)$ (the integrand) a non-anticipating square-integrable function, then Ito's integral is a martingale:**

$$E\left[\int_0^t f(u)\,dw(u)\,|\,\mathfrak{I}_s\right] = \int_0^s f(u)\,dw(u) \quad t > s \qquad (4.32)$$

The intuition is very straightforward: because of its very non-anticipating nature, the integrand function in Equation (4.28′) does not depend on the increment $dw = [w(t_i) - w(t_{i-1})]$. Since, based on the information available at time t_{i-1}, the expectation of dw at time t_i is zero, also the product of the non-anticipating function times the increment will be zero. More formally, dropping the lim-ms sign for ease of notation, one can write (see Lamberton and Lapeyre (1991))

$$E\left[\int_0^t f(u)\, dw(u)\,|\,\Im_s\right] = E\left[\int_0^s f(u)\, dw(u)\,|\,\Im_s\right] + E\left[\int_s^t f(u)\, dw(u)\,|\,\Im_s\right]$$

$$= E\left[\sum_{i=0,s} f(t_{i-1})[w(t_i) - w(t_{i-1})]\,|\,\Im_s\right] + E\left[\sum_{i=s,t} f(t_{i-1})[w(t_i) - w(t_{i-1})]\,|\,\Im_s\right]$$

$$= \sum_{i=0,s} f(t_{i-1})[w(t_i) - w(t_{i-1})] + E\left[\sum_{i=s,t} f(t_{i-1})[w(t_i) - w(t_{i-1})]\,|\,\Im_s\right]$$

$$= \sum_{i=0,s} f(t_{i-1})[w(t_i) - w(t_{i-1})]$$

$$+ E\left[\sum_{i=s,t} f(t_{i-1})[w(t_i)]\,|\,\Im_s\right] - E\left[\sum_{i=s,t} f(t_{i-1})[w(t_{i-1})]\,|\,\Im_s\right] \quad (4.33)$$

where in the third line the expectation sign has been dropped because, at time s, all past realisations up to time s are known. But, if we remember that the function $f(t)$ must be $\Im_{s-1}$ measurable, and that $w(t)$ is a martingale, the two last terms in the second line of Equation (4.33) are identical and therefore

$$E\left[\int_0^t f(u)\, dw(u)\,|\,\Im_s\right] = \sum_{i=0,s} f(t_{i-1})[w(t_i) - w(t_{i-1})] = \int_0^s f(u)\, dw(u) \quad (4.34)$$

which *proves that, under the specified assumptions, Ito's integral is a martingale.*

(b) **under the same assumptions, the expectation of the square of an Ito's integral is equal to the expectation of the Riemann (time) integral of the square of the integrand:**

$$E\left[\int_0^t f(u)\, dw(u))^2\right] = E\left[\int_0^t f(u)^2\, du\right] \quad (4.35)$$

The proof is also straightforward (Lamberton and Lapeyre (1991)): by definition the LHS can be written (dropping again the lim-ms sign) as

$$E\left[\int_0^t f(u)\, dw(u))^2\right] = E\left[\sum_{i=0,t} f(t_{i-1})[w(t_i) - w(t_{i-1})]]^2\right]$$

$$= E\left[\sum_{i=0,t} \sum_{j=0,t} f(t_{i-1})f(t_{j-1})[w(t_i) - w(t_{i-1})][w(t_j) - w(t_{j-1})]\right] \quad (4.36)$$

Let us consider the case of $i < j$ first. In this case care must be taken with the expectation symbol, since quantities revealed at time i will be known at time j; the second line of Equation (4.36) can therefore be rewritten as

$$E\left[\int_0^t f(u)\,dw(u)^2\right]$$

$$= E\left[\sum_{i=0,t}\sum_{j=0,t} f(t_{i-1})f(t_{j-1})[w(t_i) - w(t_{i-1})]E[[w(t_j) - w(t_{j-1})]]\,|\,\Im_{j-1}\right] \quad (4.37)$$

but, since $w(t)$ is a martingale, by a simple manipulation similar to the one carried out in order to prove the property (a) above, the second expectation is equal to 0, making the whole expression (4.37) identically equal to zero. The same result would clearly apply for $i > j$. Therefore, there remains to consider the case of $i = j$:

$$E\left[\int_0^t f(u)\,dw(u))^2\right] = E\left[\sum_i f(t_{i-1})^2[w(t_i) - w(t_{i-1})]^2\right]$$

$$= E\left[\sum_i f(t_{i-1})^2 E[[w(t_i) - w(t_{i-1})]^2\,|\,\Im_{i-1}]\right] \quad (4.38)$$

It is at this point that the results about the quadratic variation of a stochastic function obtained in the previous section are made use of: since the Brownian process $w(t)$ follows a Gaussian distribution of zero mean and variance t, the second expectation is simply equal to $(t_i - t_{i-1})$. Therefore

$$E\left[\sum_i f(t_{i-1})^2 E[[w(t_i) - w(t_{i-1})]^2\,|\,\Im_{i-1}]\right] = E\left[\sum_i f(t_{i-1})^2(t_i - t_{i-1})]\right] \quad (4.39)$$

But the second term is simply the definition of the Riemann integral of the square of the integrand. Therefore, using again the definition of Ito's integral, one obtains the desired result:

$$E\left[\left(\int_0^t f(u)\,dw(u)\right)^2\right] = E\left[\int_0^t f(u)^2\,du\right] \quad (4.39')$$

Apart from the derivation, it is important to stress that, as Equation (4.39') shows, despite the fact that an Ito's integral is a random variable for a fixed t **the expectation of *the square of* an Ito's integral is an ordinary number**.

4.9 STOCHASTIC DIFFERENTIATION: ITO'S LEMMA

Having defined stochastic (Ito's) integrals, we are now in a position to give a meaning, under the usual regularity conditions, to an expression like

$$X(t) = X(0) + \int_0^t \mu(s) \, ds + \int_0^t \sigma(s) \, dw(s) \qquad (4.40)$$

In Equation (4.40) the first integral is an ordinary time integral, while the second (for a 'good', i.e. non-anticipating function $\sigma(t)$) is the Ito integral defined above. We shall call such a process, often symbolically abbreviated as

$$dX(t) = \mu(t) \, dt + \sigma(t) \, dw(t) \qquad (4.40')$$

an **Ito's process** (expression (4.40') is often referred to as the differential form of an Ito's process, or as a stochastic differential equation (SDE)). An expression like Equation (4.40) is ideally suited to Monte Carlo implementations (Chapter 8): as it will be shown, the discrete-time counterpart of the stochastic integral, coupled with the Ito's prescription for the sampling point, gives in fact direct route to the numerical evaluation of Equation (4.40).

If $f(X)$ is a twice-differentiable function of such an Ito's process $X(t)$, then a very important result can be obtained for the differential of $f(X)$:

$$df(X,t) = \frac{\partial f}{\partial X} \, dX(t) + \frac{\partial f}{\partial t} + \frac{1}{2} \frac{\partial^2 f}{\partial X^2} \, dX(t)^2$$

$$= \frac{\partial f}{\partial X} \, \mu(t) \, dt + \frac{\partial f}{\partial t} + \frac{1}{2} \frac{\partial^2 f}{\partial X^2} \, \sigma^2 \, dt + \frac{\partial f}{\partial X} \, \sigma(t) \, dw(t) \qquad (4.41)$$

The last line can be obtained from the first by substituting Equation (4.40) for $dX(t)$ in (4.41), and by using the following stochastic calculus rules, which replace, for functions of stochastic variables, the usual chain rule of ordinary calculus:

$$dt \, dt = 0 \qquad (4.42)$$

$$dt \, dw(t) = 0 \qquad (4.42')$$

$$dw(t) \, dw(t) = dt \qquad (4.42'')$$

The 'new' result, i.e. Equation (4.42''), stems from the result proven in the section devoted to Brownian motions that $w(t)$ has non-zero quadratic variation, and, more directly, from the property (b) of the previous section (see Equation (4.39'). This should be contrasted with the quadratic variation of deterministic functions $f(t)$ (with bounded derivative $\partial f / \partial t$); it is instructive to analyse the difference in some detail: one knows from elementary calculus (Mean Value Theorem) that, after carrying out the usual partition of the interval $[0 \; T]$, one can always find a point τ_i inside each interval i such that the difference of the function at the extremes of the interval itself is equal to the first derivative of the function at τ_i, times the width of the subdivision, i.e.:

$$f(t_i) - f(t_{i-1}) = \frac{\partial f(\tau_i)}{\partial t} (t_i - t_{i-1}) \tag{4.43}$$

Let's now consider the sum

$$\text{QVar}_n = \sum_{i=1,n} [f(t_i) - f(t_{i-1})]^2 = \sum_{i=1,n} \left[\frac{\partial f(\tau_i)}{\partial t} \right]^2 (t_i - t_{i-1})^2 \tag{4.44}$$

which, in the limit as n goes to infinity, will give the quadratic variation of $f(t)$. The last term on the right must be smaller than the square of the maximum value attained by the derivative of $f(t)$ in the interval $[0 \; T]$, times the sum of the intervals squared:

$$\sum_{i=1,n} \left[\frac{\partial f(\tau_i)}{\partial t} \right]^2 (t_i - t_{i-1})^2 \leqslant \text{Max} \left| \left[\frac{\partial f(\tau_i)}{\partial t} \right]^2 \right| \sum_{i=1,n} (t_i - t_{i-1})^2 \tag{4.45}$$

The last summation in Equation (4.45) must, in turn, be smaller than

$$\sum_{i=1,n} (t_i - t_{i-1})^2 \leqslant \sum_{i=1,n} (t_i - t_{i-1}) \, \text{Max}(t_k - t_{k-1}) \tag{4.46}$$

where $\text{Max}(t_k - t_{k-1})$ is the width of the maximum interval in the partition. Since this is just a number (i.e. since it is independent of i) it can be taken out of the summation. As for the sum of all the intervals this must clearly be equal to the full integration range $[0 \; T]$. Therefore

$$\sum_{i=1,n} (t_i - t_{i-1})^2 \leqslant \text{Max}(t_k - t_{k-1})T \tag{4.47}$$

As the partition becomes finer and finer, and QVar_n tends to the quadratic variation of $f(t)$, the right-hand side of Equation (4.47) shrinks to zero, and therefore **for any 'good' deterministic function of time $f(t)$, its quadratic variation is zero**. It is exactly from this difference between ordinary function and functions of random variables that the crucial result (4.42″) originates.

An actual proof of Equations (4.42″), and therefore of (4.41), is not difficult (and can be found, for instance, in Gardiner (1990) or in Lamberton and Lapeyre (1991)), along the same conceptual lines followed to prove Equation (4.35). Rather than reproducing it here, it is worthwhile stressing the crucial importance of Equation (4.41) for financial applications in general, and for option modelling in particular: it is in fact by means of Ito's lemma, as result

(4.41) is often referred to, that it is possible to express the processes for any financial quantity (be it a bond price, a rate or a discount factor) as a function of the (Brownian) driving factor(s) in terms of which one has chosen to describe the economy as a whole. Depending on the model complexity and on the particular type of functional relationship between the state variable and the quantity of interest it may or may not be possible to express the appropriate form of Equation (4.41) as an analytic expression; but, even when closed-form equations are not available and the user has to resort to numerical (e.g. lattice) approaches, it is exactly an implicit form of Ito's lemma that will furnish the dynamics of the derived quantities. Before considering in detail how the no-arbitrage conditions and the stochastic calculus rules just obtained can be put to use to derive powerful results for specific choices of numeraire, which ultimately allow practical implementations of complex models, it is useful to establish a last connection, namely the link between the Ito's processes defined in this section and a particular class of partial differential equations. This connection will prove very useful if one wants to be able to translate, for calculation purposes, from, say, a Monte Carlo approach, ideally tackled with the tools presented in the last two sections, to the finite-differences approach, dealt with in Chapter 7.

4.10   THE LINK BETWEEN ITO'S PROCESSES AND DIFFUSIVE PDEs

Let us consider an asset $S(t)$, a numeraire asset $S_0(t)$, and the associated relative price $ZS(t) = S(t)/S_0(t)$. As we know, if no arbitrage is to be allowed, it must be possible to find a measure Q', equivalent to the real-world measure Q, and dependent on the choice of numeraire, such that all relative prices are martingales. Let us then consider the (spot) price of an option $O(t)$ on $S(t)$. This can also be expressed in units of the same numeraire: $ZO(t) = O(t)/S_0(t)$. This relative option price is a function of the relative stock price, which is, in turn, a random variable. Therefore we can apply Ito's lemma to $ZO = f(ZS)$, giving:

$$dZO(t) = \left[\frac{\partial ZO}{\partial t} + \mu_{ZS} \frac{\partial ZO}{\partial ZS} + \frac{1}{2} \sigma_{ZS}^2 \frac{\partial^2 ZO}{\partial ZS^2} \right] dt + \frac{\partial ZO}{\partial ZS} \sigma_{ZS} \, dw(t) \quad (4.48)$$

where μ_{ZS} and σ_{ZS} denote the drift (under Q') and standard deviation per unit time of the relative price ZS. Since relative prices under Q' must be martingales, μ_{ZS} must be equal to zero. Therefore Equation (4.48) becomes

$$dZO(t) = \left[\frac{\partial ZO}{\partial t} + \frac{1}{2} \sigma_{ZS}^2 \frac{\partial^2 ZO}{\partial ZS^2} \right] dt + \frac{\partial ZO}{\partial ZS} \sigma_{ZS} \, dw(t)$$

$$\equiv \qquad\qquad \mu_{ZO} \qquad\qquad dt + \qquad \sigma_{ZO} \, dw(t) \qquad\qquad (4.49)$$

But, since $ZO(t)$ is itself a relative price, its deterministic growth (μ_{ZO}) must also be zero, and therefore

$$\mu_{ZO} = \frac{\partial ZO}{\partial t} + \frac{1}{2}\sigma_{ZS}^2 \frac{\partial^2 ZO}{\partial ZS^2} = 0 \tag{4.50}$$

Supplemented with the boundary conditions specific to the particular option being considered, Equation (4.50) gives a parabolic, diffusive partial differential equation whose solution satisfies Equation (4.49). More precisely, let us rewrite Equation (4.49) in integral form:

$$ZO(T) = ZO(0) + \int_0^T \mu_{ZO}(t)\,dt + \int_0^T \sigma_{ZO}(t)\,dw(t)$$

$$= ZO(0) + \int_0^T \sigma_{ZO}(t)\,dw(t) \tag{4.51}$$

since ZO must be driftless. Let us now take the expectation, under Q', of both sides of the equation:

$$E'[ZO(T)] = ZO(0) + E'\left[\int_0^T \sigma_{ZO}(t)\,dw(t)\right] \tag{4.52}$$

But the last term on the RHS is the Ito's integral of a good (non-anticipating) function, and as such a martingale; therefore its expectation is simply equal to 0. Therefore, this allows us to say that **the relative price today of the option is simply equal to the expectation, under Q', of its terminal payoff. This result is also known as the Feynman–Kac theorem.**

Notice that the derivation has been presented in terms of *relative* prices. For instance, the numeraire asset could have been chosen to be the discount bond maturing at option expiry. In that case the relative asset price would simply have been the forward price of the asset, and Equation (4.52) would lead directly to the celebrated Black (1976) formula. The only volatility that enters the PDE is therefore the volatility of the *forward* price. (It might be useful, at this point, to revisit Chapter 3.)

Finally, notice that, in order to obtain the Feynman–Kac theorem, one could just as well have worked in spot rather than relative prices; if the discounting had been assumed to be deterministic, however, this would have led to the Black and Scholes formula, of little use for interest-rate options. If the discounting (cash) bond had instead been allowed to be stochastic, this would have made the PDE two dimensional. If Merton's (1973) (Margrabe's (1978)) homogeneity condition had then been invoked to reduce the dimensionality, it would have led exactly to a Black-like formula again, with the resulting volatility given by

$$\sigma_{ZS}^2 = \sigma_S^2 + v^2 - 2\sigma_S v\rho \tag{4.53}$$

with ρ indicating the correlation between the discount bond and the spot asset

S, and v the percentage volatility of the discount bond price. But this is nothing more than what is offered by the relative price (martingale) approach used above, with the only difference that the individual volatilities, and the correlation, need not be specified independently in the latter approach; this makes a lot of sense, since from the price of a traded option it is only the volatility of the forward price (i.e. of the relative price) that can be imputed.

ENDNOTE

1. The common description of Kolmogorov's approach as 'modern' is somewhat puzzling, since it was introduced before the last world war, but the usage has nonetheless remained in the probabilistic literature.

5
The conditions of no-arbitrage

5.1 FIRST NO-ARBITRAGE CONDITION: THE VASICEK'S APPROACH

In the context of interest-rate models, the constraints on the bond price processes necessary to prevent arbitrage were obtained as early as 1977 by Vasicek (Vasicek (1977)). The derivation, sketched in the following, is extremely simple and intuitively appealing. Its main result, i.e. the maturity independence of the market price of risk, directly leads to the PDE approach, which can then be tackled either by explicit analytic solutions, or by the finite-differences methods (see Chapter 7).

The more modern (martingale) approach has a wider scope, in that it does not start from an explicit process for the short rate, and enjoys greater generality by directly allowing a variety of possible numeraires, as described below. It leads naturally to lattice methodologies (Chapter 6) and MC simulations (Chapter 8).

To start with the 'classic' derivation, the original argument used two discount bonds, and was in spirit very similar to the Black and Scholes (Black and Scholes (1973)) approach. It will be slightly modified in the following in order to highlight the width of its scope. Starting from a general Brownian process for the short rate in the real world given by

$$dr(t) = \mu_r(r,t)\,dt + \sigma_r(r,t)\,dz \tag{5.1}$$

Ito's lemma yields for the stochastic differential equation of a bond of maturity T, $P(t,T)$

$$dP(t,T) = \left[\frac{\partial P}{\partial r}\mu_r + \frac{\partial P}{\partial t} + \frac{1}{2}\sigma_r^2 \frac{\partial^2 P}{\partial^2 r} \right] dt + \sigma_r \frac{\partial P}{\partial r}\,dz$$

$$\equiv \qquad\qquad \mu(t,T) \qquad\qquad dt + v(t,T)\,dz \tag{5.2}$$

A portfolio Π can then be created, composed of one unit of bond T_1, and θ_2

units of bond T_2:

$$\Pi(t) = P(t,T) + \theta P(t,T_2) \tag{5.3}$$

The process obeyed by the portfolio is then given by

$$d\Pi = [\mu(t,T_1) + \theta\mu(t,T_2)] \, dt + \left[\frac{\partial P(t,T_1)}{\partial r} \sigma_r + \theta \frac{\partial P(t,T_2)}{\partial r} \sigma_r \right] dz$$

$$\equiv \quad\quad \mu_\Pi \quad\quad\quad\quad\quad\quad dt + \sigma_\Pi \quad\quad\quad\quad dz \tag{5.4}$$

One can easily verify by direct substitution that, if θ is chosen equal to

$$\theta = -\frac{\dfrac{\partial P(t,T_1)}{\partial r}}{\dfrac{\partial P(t,T_2)}{\partial r}} \tag{5.5}$$

the variance of the portfolio identically vanishes: $\sigma_\Pi = 0$; the portfolio thus created, and given by

$$\Pi(t) = P(t,T_1) - \frac{\dfrac{\partial P(t,T_1)}{\partial r}}{\dfrac{\partial P(t,T_2)}{\partial r}} P(t,T_2) \tag{5.6}$$

is therefore purely deterministic.

Multiplying numerator and denominator in the expression giving the holding of the T_2-maturity bond by the volatility of the short rate, σ_r, and remembering from Equation (5.2) above that $\sigma_r \partial P / \partial r = v(t,T)$, one can rewrite Equation (5.6) which gives the instantaneously riskless portfolio as

$$\Pi(t) = P(t,T_1) - \frac{v(t,T_1)}{v(t,T_2)} P(t,T_2) \tag{5.6'}$$

Therefore the holding θ can be more simply rewritten as

$$\theta = -\frac{v(t,T_1)}{v(t,T_2)} \tag{5.7}$$

Notice that our ability to build this deterministic portfolio is not directly predicated on our knowledge of the absolute bond sensitivity to changes in the driving factor, as Equation (5.6) seems to imply, but simply depends on the knowledge of the *ratio* of the bond price volatilities.

Over a small time interval dt the evolution of the portfolio is given by

$$d\Pi(t) = dP(t,T_1) - \frac{v(t,T_1)}{v(t,T_2)} dP(t,T_2) \qquad (5.8)$$

Since, however, the portfolio is by construction now deterministic, it can only earn over dt the instantaneous short rate:

$$d\Pi(t) = r(t)\Pi(t)\, dt \qquad (5.8')$$

Equating Equations (5.8) and (5.8'), and making use of Equation (5.6'), gives

$$dP(t,T_1) - \frac{v(t,T_1)}{v(t,T_2)} dP(t,T_2) = \left[P(t,T_1) - \frac{v(t,T_1)}{v(t,T_2)} P(t,T_2) \right] r(t)\, dt \qquad (5.9)$$

Substituting for $dP(t,T_1)$ and $dP(t,T_2)$ expression (5.2) gives

$$\mu(t,T_1) - \frac{v(t,T_1)}{v(t,T_2)} \mu(t,T_2) = \left[P(t,T_1) - \frac{v(t,T_1)}{v(t,T_2)} P(t,T_2) \right] r(t) \qquad (5.10)$$

Notice that the terms in dz present in Equation (5.2) have cancelled out because of the choice of θ. Rearranging terms gives

$$\mu(t,T_1) - r(t)P(t,T_1) = \mu(t,T_2) \frac{v(t,T_1)}{v(t,T_2)} - r(t)P(t,T_2) \frac{v(t,T_1)}{v(t,T_2)} \qquad (5.11)$$

After dividing throughout by $v(t,T_1)$ one finally obtains

$$\frac{\mu(t,T_1) - r(t)P(t,T_1)}{v(t,T_1)} = \frac{\mu(t,T_2) - r(t)P(t,T_2)}{v(t,T_2)} \qquad (5.12)$$

Notice that Equation (5.12) must hold true for any maturity T_1 and T_2. Therefore the ratio must be equal to a quantity, λ, possibly dependent on r and t, but *independent of maturity*, i.e.

$$\lambda(t,r) \equiv \frac{\mu(t,T) - r(t)P(t,T)}{v(t,T)} \qquad (5.13)$$

By Equation (5.13) the real-world drift of the price of a discount bond, $\mu(t,T)$, differs from the risk-neutral drift $r(t)P(t,T)$ by a quantity which is equal to a pure function of time (and possibly of the short rate), divided by the absolute volatility of the bond price. If one wanted to express the absolute bond drift and volatility in terms of the respective percentage quantities, i.e.

$$\mu = mP \qquad (5.14)$$

$$v = v'P \qquad (5.14')$$

then Equation (5.12) could be rewritten in the more common form

$$\frac{m(t,T_1) - r(t)}{v^1(t,T_1)} = \frac{m(t,T_2) - r(t)}{v^1(t,T_2)} \tag{5.15}$$

i.e. the percentage return on a bond of maturity T differs from the instantaneously riskless rate of return by the function of time (and r) $\lambda(t,r)$. This function is commonly referred to as the **market price of risk**. *If* investors are risk averse, then $\lambda(t)$ will be positive and will represent the excess return over the riskless rate per unit percentage volatility, required by investors in order to compensate them 'correctly' for the extra risk (price volatility) borne by holding a discount bond. This interpretation justifies the name 'market price of risk' for $\lambda(t)$.

If investors were risk neutral, or risk seeking, $\lambda(t)$ would be zero, or negative, respectively. Notice that no-arbitrage arguments, *per se*, cannot determine the sign of the market price of risk: in order to determine when $\lambda(t)$ is positive or negative, one would require access to the utility function of the market investor, which specifies his attitude towards risk. More precisely, one can show (Merton (1990), Elton and Gruber (1991)) that the market price of risk defined above is closely related to the Pratt–Arrow measure of relative risk aversion, $R(U)$, in turn linked to the utility function U by

$$R(U) = -\frac{U''(W)W}{U'(W)} \tag{5.16}$$

where W denotes wealth. As mentioned above, risk aversion (i.e. $U''(W) < 0$) for any strictly increasing utility function ($U'(W) > 0$) gives a positive market price of risk.

One can now go back to Equations (5.2) and (5.12), and equate the drifts on a discount bond, obtaining

$$\frac{\partial P}{\partial r} \mu_r + \frac{\partial P}{\partial t} + \frac{1}{2} \frac{\partial^2 P}{\partial^2 r} \sigma_r^2 = rP + \lambda v(t,T) = rP + \lambda \sigma_r \frac{\partial P}{\partial r} \tag{5.17}$$

Equation (5.17) is a parabolic partial differential equation to which, in the case of a discount bond, the appropriate initial conditions $P(T,T) = 1$ must be added. Recognising, however, that no special use has been made in the derivation up to Equation (5.17) of the fact that $P(t,T)$ represents a *bond* price, one can conclude that the same PDE, supplemented with the appropriate terminal conditions, has to be obeyed by *any* asset traded in the economy, if arbitrage is to be avoided. Different (one-factor) models will produce PDEs of identical structure to Equation (5.8) above, but with different μ_r and σ_r inputs. **This is therefore the fundamental equation that analytic or finite-differences methods set out to solve.** Extension to many factors is conceptually straightforward, and follows exactly the same lines: in general $(n + 1)$ discount bonds, or linearly independent assets, will be required in setting up the portfolio Π in order to neutralize n sources of uncertainty.

5.2 SECOND NO-ARBITRAGE CONDITION: THE MARTINGALE APPROACH

One of the main advantages of the martingale approach is the direct and natural link afforded between the market price of risk, the discounting procedure (choice of numeraire) and the underlying equivalent measures. It is this link, of great conceptual and practical importance, that probably by itself can justify the probabilistic set-up described in Sections 4.1 and 4.2, which could otherwise be regarded as an unnecessarily complicated formalism.

As mentioned before, crucial to the treatment is the choice of a numeraire, defined as the common unit on the basis of which the prices of all the N securities can be expressed. As also mentioned in the previous chapter, any of the N assets can be chosen as numeraire, as long as it has strictly positive payoffs at all times and in all states of the world. In continuous time, asset prices expressed as a function of this numeraire (arbitrarily chosen to be asset 1) can then be written as

$$Z_n^*(t) = \frac{S_n(t)}{S_1(t)} \tag{5.18}$$

Each distinct choice of numeraire will give rise to a different set of relative prices.

Three theorems then constitute the cornerstones of no-arbitrage pricing: the first, for which a simple proof was provided for a particularly simple case, gives the necessary and sufficient conditions for no-arbitrage, as defined in Section 4.5, and holds in complete generality, for any stochastic process describing the shocks which reach the economy; under the specific Brownian assumption for the Wiener processes that generate the filtration $\Im(t)$ (i.e. that describe the flow of information), the second theorem then provides the explicit martingale form for the relative price processes; finally, the third will enable to relate processes obtained using different choices of the numeraire. More precisely:

Theorem 1: A complete market is arbitrage-free if and only if there exists a measure Q^*, equivalent to Q, such that the relative prices $Z^*(t)$ become martingales with respect to $\Im(t)$, i.e.

$$E^*[Z^*(T) \,|\, \Im(t)] = Z^*(t) \tag{5.19}$$

where $E^*[\cdot\,|\,\Im(t)]$ denotes expectation taken at time t with respect to the measure Q^*, contingent on all past and present information up to time t.

Theorem 2 (Representation Theorem) then states that, **under the Brownian assumption for the filtration, any (exponential) martingale $Z^*(t)$ can be indifferently represented as**

$$dZ_n^*(t) = \sigma_n(t)Z_n^*(t)\,dW^*(t) \qquad (5.20)$$

or, in the equivalent integral form, as

$$Z_n^*(t) = Z_n^*(0)\exp\left[\int_0^t \sigma_n(u)\,dW^*(u) - \frac{1}{2}\int_0^t |\sigma_n(u)|^2\,du\right] \qquad (5.20')$$

where $W^*(t)$ is *the* Wiener process in the measure Q^*, and $\sigma_n(t)$ is the volatility of the relative prices. (Extension to several processes is straightforward.) Notice that the second integral is an 'ordinary' (Riemann) integral over time, but the first is a stochastic Ito integral over the Wiener process $W^*(t)$ of the type described in the previous chapter. At the risk of repeating oneself, it is useful to recall that, if one were to perform this latter integral numerically, for instance in the course of a Monte Carlo simulation, one would compute the sum of the products of the volatility at time t_i, $\sigma(t_i)$, times the Wiener increment $\sigma\varepsilon\sqrt{\Delta t}$ connecting time t_i to time t_{i+1}, i.e.:

$$\int_0^t \sigma_n(u)\,dW^*(u) \cong \sum_{i=0,n-1} \sigma(t_i)\varepsilon\sqrt{t_{i+1}-t_1} \qquad (5.20'')$$

with $\varepsilon \in N(0,1)$, and $n = t/\Delta t$, $\Delta t = (t_{i+1}-t_i)$. It is important to remember (see Section 4.8) that, if the function $\sigma(.)$ were evaluated at time t_{i+1} or, for that matter, at any other time, such as $(t_i + t_{i+1})/2$, one would be computing a different integral, converging, as Δt tends to zero, to a different numerical value (the choice of $(t_i + t_{i+1})/2$ for the evaluation time would correspond to the Stratonovich integral: the integral can be mathematically defined, but it does not make much 'physical' or financial sense, in that it requires knowledge at time t of a quantity which will only be revealed at a later time).

For the sake of concreteness, Theorem 3 will be reported at the end of the section, after introducing actual examples of numeraires.

The importance of these rather abstract beginnings can be appreciated by considering two specific choices for the numeraire, namely (i) by discounting each payoff from any asset occurring at time T, $S(T)$, by a discount bond maturing at T, $P(t,T)$ (Section 5.5), or (ii) by dividing the asset price by a rolled-up money market account (for brevity a money market account in the following), where £1 is reinvested at the prevailing short rate from t up to time T (Section 5.4). Before embarking on the analysis of these two cases, however, in order to enhance financial intuition and to appreciate better the implications of the results of the following sections, the next section will deal with the case of a deterministic economy.

5.3 THE CASE OF A DETERMINISTIC-INTEREST-RATES ECONOMY

An economy will, in general, be described as deterministic if the evolution of asset prices is perfectly known at time 0, or, more formally, if the price vector $\{S\}$ is assumed to a deterministic, rather than stochastic, function of time. A *completely* deterministic economy is, of course, of very little interest. As a more interesting case, however, interest-rate-dependent instruments (e.g. bonds, swaps or FRAs) could be assumed to be deterministic, while non-interest-rate-dependent assets (e.g. shares) could be allowed to have a stochastic component. This, for instance, is the classic case treated in Black and Scholes (1973). This approximation can be justified whenever the volatility of one class of assets (the 'stock' prices) affects the present value of a particular contingent claim much more than the volatility of another class of assets (e.g. the discounting bonds). Notice immediately that, if the stochastic asset is assumed to be an interest-rate-dependent instrument (e.g. a bond) but interest rates are treated as deterministic, an obvious inconsistency is introduced.

Assuming deterministic rates is tantamount to imposing zero variance to the processes for the factor(s) driving the yield curve. The no-arbitrage conditions must still hold, but the expectation operator no longer enters the definition. More simply, in fact, one can write, using the same symbols used before (Section 4.5),

$$\Theta(0)S(0) = 0 \Rightarrow \Theta(T)S(T) = 0 \text{ [deterministic economy]} \qquad (5.21)$$

$$\Theta(T)S(T) > 0 \Rightarrow \Theta(0)S(0) > 0 \text{ [deterministic economy]} \qquad (5.21')$$

where $\{S\}$ is a vector of interest-rate-dependent assets, whose future value, in the light of the deterministic character of the yield-curve dynamics, must be computable today. The rest of this section will derive the *a priori* computable future values that interest-rate-dependent instruments must assume in a deterministic-rates economy if (5.21) and (5.21') are to be satisfied. Before embarking on the treatment proper, it is, however, essential to point out that, despite formal similarities, there is an important difference between the results obtained below, and some of the results obtained in Chapter 1: in the treatment of the plain-vanilla instruments, in fact, no claims were made about distributional assumptions (of which a deterministic economy is a special case); it was simply shown that, say, plain-vanilla swaps or FRAs can be valued, in the real world, *as if* forward rates actually did 'come true'. Similar results about forward rates obtained in the remainder of this section, on the other hand, only pertain to the special (deterministic) world described above, and, as such, could not be invoked in order to price plain-vanilla instruments.

With this proviso in mind, let us place ourselves in the context of a interest-rate-deterministic economy, and let us assume that the prices of a continuum of discount bonds of all maturities, $P(0,s)$, are available today. Let us borrow money to purchase a bond of maturity T for $£P(0,T)$, and let us stipulate that no future cash can be injected in or withdrawn from the portfolio made up by the bond and the loan. We have therefore created a zero-cost self-financing trading strategy, to which the no-arbitrage (deterministic) conditions (5.21) and (5.21′) must apply. Let us roll this portfolio over a time step Δt. Our liability (the borrowing) has now increased in value to $£P(0,T) \exp[r(0) \Delta t]$, where $r(0)$ is the short rate prevailing at time 0. If (5.21) is to be satisfied then our asset must have increased its value by the same amount, i.e.

$$P(1 \Delta t, T) = P(0,T) \exp[r(0) \Delta t] \tag{5.22}$$

(Let us suppose that $P(1,T)$ had any other value, say $P'(1 \Delta t, T) > P(1 \Delta t, T)$. One could then reap a riskless profit by liquidating the position, i.e. repaying the loan, which has accrued to a value of $£P(0,T) \exp[r(0) \Delta t]$, and selling the bond for $P'(1 \Delta t, T) > P(1 \Delta t, T) = £P(0,T) \exp[r(0) \Delta t]$.) In plain words, in absence of uncertainty, *any* asset must obviously earn the same (known) return.

Notice that the relationship (5.22) must hold over the first time step also in a stochastic economy in so far as the *expectation* of the bond price is concerned, since, at time 0, the short rate covering the period $[0 \, \Delta t]$ is known with certainty. Matters are, however, different in a deterministic and in a stochastic economy moving from time $1 \Delta t$ to time $2 \Delta t$. In the latter case, in fact, we do not know what short rate will prevail at time $1 \Delta t$, and we can only say that, *if the short rate* at time $1 \Delta t$ *had the value* $r_i (\Delta_t)$, *then* our borrowing would be rolled up from time Δt to time $2 \Delta t$ at the rate $r_i(\Delta t)$, giving for the total liability a value of $£P(0,T) \exp[r(0) \Delta t] \exp[r_i(\Delta t)]$ and hence, our asset, to prevent arbitrage, would also have to be worth $£P(0,T) \exp[r(0)\Delta t] \exp[r_i(\Delta t)]$. But this result only applies *if* the realisation of the short rate at time Δt happened to be $r_i(\Delta t)$ at time Δt. In general, therefore, the value of the T-maturity bond at time $2 \Delta t$ will be obtained by assigning a probability of occurrence to each realisation of the short rate, $g(r_i(\Delta t))$ and by integrating over all possible values

$$P(2 \Delta t, T) = P(0,T) \exp[r(0) \Delta t] \int_0^\infty \exp[r(\Delta t)] g(r(\Delta t)) \, dr(\Delta t) \quad \textbf{[stochastic]}$$

$$\tag{5.23}$$

For the deterministic case, however, we know with certainty that at time Δt the prevailing short rate will have the value $r(\Delta t)$. Therefore Equation (5.23) assumes the much simpler form

$$P(2\,\Delta t) = P(0,T)\exp[r(0)\,\Delta t]\exp[r(\Delta t)\,\Delta t] \quad \textbf{[deterministic]} \qquad (5.23')$$

which can formally be seen as the limit of Equation (5.23) as the distribution $g(r(\Delta t))$ becomes more and more narrowly peaked around $r(\Delta t)$ (i.e. as $g(r(\Delta t))$ approaches the Dirac-δ distribution $\delta(r(\Delta t) - r)$).

Extending the reasoning we are therefore in a position to say that, in the deterministic case, to avoid arbitrage

$$P(n\,\Delta t,T) = P(0,T)\exp\left[\sum_{i=0,\,n-1} r(i\,\Delta t)\,\Delta t\right] \text{[deterministic]} \qquad (5.23'')$$

or, moving to the continuous limit,

$$P(s,T) = P(0,T)\exp\left[\int_0^s r(u)\,\mathrm{d}u\right], \text{[deterministic]} \qquad (5.23''')$$

i.e. **the future value of a bond of maturity T is given by today's value of the bond rolled up at the (known) future values of the short rate**. It will be very instructive to compare this equation with Equation (5.49') of Section 5.5.

Let us now set $s = T$ in Equation (5.23''') above. Then $P(s,T) = P(T,T) = 1$, and therefore

$$P(0,T) = \exp\left[-\int_0^T r(u)\,\mathrm{d}u\right] \qquad (5.24)$$

i.e. **the value of a T-maturity bond today is given by the reciprocal of the value of £1 invested at time 0 and rolled up at the known prevailing instantaneous short rates from time 0 to time T**. But then Equation (5.23''') can be rewritten as

$$P(s,T) = \frac{P(0,T)}{P(0,s)} = \exp\left[-\int_0^T r(u)\,\mathrm{d}u\right] \qquad (5.25)$$

i.e. **the future value of a T-maturity bond is equal with certainty to its forward value today**. One can at this point recall from Chapters 1 and 3 that, in *any* (i.e. not necessarily deterministic) economy, the value $P(0,T)/P(0,s)$ is the *only* strike, if no arbitrage is to be allowed, that gives zero value to a contract to enter into a position in the T-maturity bond at time s (at least in a frictionless economy where agents can take long and short positions in spot discount bonds). Therefore the coincidence of future and forward (no-arbitrage) prices is shown by Equation (5.25) to be valid in the special case of a deterministic economy. It will be shown in Section 5.5 that the same result also holds in the stochastic case for one, and only one, particular choice of numeraire.

Moving from bond prices to forward rates, the τ-period forward rate $f(t,T,T+\tau)$ is in general defined as the rate that, in any economy, gives zero value to the contract made at time t to borrow/lend money from time T to time $T+\tau$. As shown in Chapters 1 and 3, absence of arbitrage dictates that, for any stochastic economy in which an agent can freely take positions in spot discount bonds,

$$f(t,T,T+\tau) = \left[\frac{P(t,T)}{P(t,T+\tau)}-1\right]\bigg/\tau \qquad (5.26)$$

Moving to the limit as τ goes to zero, and switching from simple to continuous compounding, the instantaneous forward rate, now denoted by $f(t,T)$, becomes

$$f(t,T) = \lim_{\tau \to 0} \ln \frac{P(t,T)}{P(t,T+\tau)} \frac{1}{\tau} = \frac{\ln P(t,T) - \ln (P,t+\tau)}{\tau} = -\frac{\partial \ln P(t,T)}{\partial T}$$

$$(5.26')$$

But, in the deterministic case, by Equation (5.25)

$$P(t,T) = \exp\left[\int_t^T r(u)\,du\right]$$

$$(5.25')$$

and therefore Equation (5.26') becomes

$$f(t,T) = r(T) \qquad (5.27)$$

i.e. **future spot rates are equal, in a deterministic economy, to forward rates**. The result given by Equation (5.27) constitutes the essence of the Expectation Hypothesis. It is important to remember the assumptions under which the result has been obtained: it is only in the absence of volatility, in fact, that bond prices reveal, via their logarithmic derivatives, future rates: in the real (uncertain) world, forward rates do not *per se* imply anything about 'real-world' expectations of future rates.

Finally, since the RHS of Equation (5.27) contains no t dependence

$$f(t,T) = f(s,T) = r(T) \quad \forall\, s,t \leqslant T \qquad (5.28)$$

i.e. **in a deterministic economy forward rates do not change over time**.

Having examined the results which apply in the very special case treated in this section, the richer implications brought about by allowing stochastic interest rates should be more fully appreciated. The treatment of the next two sections closely mirrors the general approach to be found in Gustavsson (1992).

5.4 FIRST CHOICE OF NUMERAIRE: THE MONEY MARKET ACCOUNT

The money market account can be defined as

$$B(0,t) = \exp\left[\int_0^t r(s)\, ds\right] \tag{5.29}$$

In words, by Equation (5.29) the rolled-up money market account at time t is the value of £1 invested at time 0 at the prevailing instantaneous short rate (the overnight rate could be a good approximation), and reinvested (with the accrued interest) over each infinitesimal time step dt out to the final time t, always at the prevailing instantaneous short rates. One can immediately notice from the definition that the money market account always has a strictly positive value, and therefore the positivity condition (required for an asset to be a possible numeraire) is satisfied. Relative prices with respect to this numeraire are then given by

$$Z_n'(0,t) = \frac{S_n(t)}{B(0,t)} \tag{5.30}$$

where the prime is a reminder that the expectations and relative prices refer to the numeraire B.

If no-arbitrage is to be allowed, by Theorem 1 a unique equivalent measure Q', implicitly defined by this particular numeraire, must exist such that the martingale condition holds

$$E'[Z_n'(u)\,|\,\mathfrak{F}(t)] = E'\left[\frac{S_n(u)}{B(0,u)}\,\middle|\,\mathfrak{F}(t)\right] = \frac{S_n(t)}{B(0,t)} = Z_n'(t) \qquad \forall u \geq t \tag{5.31}$$

where $E'[\ ]$ indicates expectation taken in the measure Q'. With Equation (5.31) one is standing at time t, up to which time the information ($\mathfrak{F}(t)$) has accumulated. At the very least this information will consist of the value of all the assets at time t, but it could include also all the past prices up to time t. Also, the money market account has been rolled up from some previous arbitrary time 0 to time t. So $B(0,t)$ is a known quantity at time t. By the no-arbitrage theorem the expectation at time t of the ratio of the future cash asset price at u, $S_n(u)$, to the future cash value of the money market account also at time u, $B(0,u)$, is equal to the ratio of the known value of $S_n(t)$ to $B(0,t)$.

Now, $B(0,u)$ can be looked at as the money market account rolled up from time 0 to time t, and then from time t to time u, i.e.

$$B(0,u) = B(0,t)B(t,u) \tag{5.32}$$

Therefore Equation (5.31) can be rewritten

$$E'\left[\frac{S_n(u)}{B(0,u)} \middle| \mathfrak{F}(t)\right] = E'\left[\frac{S_n(u)}{B(0,t)B(t,u)} \middle| \mathfrak{F}(t)\right] = \frac{S_n(t)}{B(0,t)} \qquad (5.31')$$

Given that, at time t, $B(0,t)$ is a known (non-stochastic) quantity and, as such, can be taken out of the expectation operator, one can cancel it from both sides of the equation and write

$$E'\left[\frac{S_n(u)}{B(t,u)} \middle| \mathfrak{F}(t)\right] = S_n(t) \qquad (5.31'')$$

As apparent from Equation (5.31''), the choice of origin 0 is totally arbitrary, and plays no special role. From this point of view, the notation $B(0,t)$ is actually redundant, but it has been chosen to highlight similarities and differences with the numeraire discussed in the following section, where the specification of the time origin becomes essential.

Specialising Equation (5.31'') to the case where the original asset price is today's price of a bond of maturity T, $P(0,T)$, and time u is the maturity of the bond, one readily obtains

$$P(t,T) = E'\left[\frac{P(T,T)}{B(t,T)} \middle| \mathfrak{F}(t)\right] = E'\left[\frac{1}{B(t,T)} \middle| \mathfrak{F}(t)\right] = E'\left[\exp\left(-\int_t^T r(s)\,ds\right) \middle| \mathfrak{F}(t)\right]$$

$$(5.33)$$

where $P(T,T) = 1$ has been used. For $t = 0$

$$P(0,T) = E'\left[\exp\left(-\int_0^T r(s)\,ds\right) \middle| \mathfrak{F}(0)\right] \qquad (5.33')$$

i.e. **today's price of a T-maturity bond is equal to the expectation under Q' of the reciprocal of the money account.** This result can be profitably compared with Equation (5.23) in Section 5.3, which pertained to the case of a deterministic-interest-rates economy:

$$P(0,T) = \exp\left[-\int_0^T r(s)\,ds\right] \qquad (5.24')$$

Equation (5.33') above is one of the most useful and important tools in option pricing, both conceptually and for practical implementations, as will be appreciated, for instance, in the context of all the pricing methodologies which make use (explicitly or implicitly) of the money market account as numeraire. It will suffice for the moment to say that it is by enforcing condition (5.33) that these numerical procedures ensure that expectations of future option payoffs are taken with respect to the correct, but *a priori* unknown, measure Q'.

For future applications it will also be very important to derive the drift on any cash asset price in the measure Q'. To this effect, one can go back to the definition (5.30) and write, after dropping the subscript 'n' to lighten notation,

$$S(t) = Z(0,t)B(0,t) \qquad (5.34)$$

Taking the differential of both sides of the equation gives

$$dS(t) = Z(0,t)\, dB(0,t) + dZ(0,t)B(0,t) + dB(0,t)\, dZ(0,t) \qquad (5.35)$$

In general, as shown in Chapter 4, whenever dealing with stochastic quantities, one cannot set terms such as $dB\, dZ$ to zero, as one would in ordinary calculus. However, for the special case of the money market account, the quantity $dB(0,t)$ can be readily calculated from the definition of B (Equation (5.29)):

$$dB(0,t) = d\left(\exp\left[\int_0^t r(s)\, ds\right]\right)$$

$$= \exp\left[\int_0^t r(s)\, ds\right] \frac{d}{dt}\left[\int_0^t r(s)\, ds\right] dt$$

$$= \exp\left[\int_0^t r(s)\, ds\right] r(t)\, dt = B(0,t)r(t)\, dt \qquad (5.36)$$

(N.B.: in Equation (5.36), the quantity $[\int_0^t r(s)\, ds]$ is simply a function, say, $f(t)$, of its upper integration limit; therefore, evaluating the differential $d(\exp[\int_0^t r(s)\, ds])$ is equivalent to evaluating $d(\exp[f(t)])$, to which the usual rules of differentiation apply.) Notice from Equation (5.36) that, at time t, the quantity $dB(0,t)$ is locally non-stochastic, since the prevailing short rate is known. Therefore in Equation (5.35) the mixed term $dB(0,t)\, dZ(0,t)$ will disappear, leaving

$$dS(t) = Z'(0,t)r(t)B(0,t)\, dt + B(0,t)\, dZ'(0,t)$$

$$= r(t)B(0,t)\, \frac{S(t)}{B(0,t)}\, dt + B(0,t)\, dZ'(0,t)$$

$$= r(t)S(t)\, dt + B(0,t)\, dZ'(0,t) \qquad (5.35')$$

Dividing throughout by $S(t)$ and remembering the definition (5.30) of a relative price one obtains

$$\frac{dS(t)}{S(t)} = r(t)\, dt + \frac{dZ'(0,t)}{Z'(0,t)} \qquad (5.35'')$$

Equation (5.35") shows the very important result that, in the measure Q', **all assets earn the same return, given by the instantaneous short rate**. This was exactly the result obtained in the case of deterministic-interest-rate economy in the previous section, thus justifying the name of 'risk neutral' for this particular measure. That all the returns should turn out to be identical should come as no surprise, after the qualitative discussion which followed Theorem 1; the specific result that this rate of return must be the riskless rate is specific to the particular choice of numeraire.

To be able to say anything more specific about the process (5.35″) one must invoke the Wiener assumption, i.e. one must require that the shocks to the prices can be modelled by a diffusive (no jumps) process. If this is the case then the Representation Theorem 2 applies, and one can write (Gustavsson (1992)) in integral form,

$$Z(0,t) = Z(0,0) \exp\left[\left[\int_0^t \sigma'(s) \, dW'(s)\right] - \frac{1}{2}\int_0^t |\sigma'(s)|^2 \, ds\right]\right] \qquad (5.37)$$

or, using $Z(0,t) = S(t)/B(0,t)$,

$$S(t) = S(0)B(0,t) \exp\left[\left[\int_0^t \sigma'(s) \, dW'(s)\right] - \frac{1}{2}\int_0^t |\sigma'(t)|^2 \, ds\right]\right]$$

$$= S(0) \exp\left[\int_0^t r(s) \, ds\right] \exp\left[\left[\int_0^t \sigma'(s) \, dW'(s)\right] - \frac{1}{2}\int_0^t |\sigma'(t)|^2 \, ds\right]\right] \qquad (5.38)$$

where σ' indicates the volatility of relative prices in the measure Q'.

In differential form Equation (5.37) can be written as (see Equations (5.20) and (5.20′), Section 5.2)

$$\frac{dZ(0,t)}{Z(0,t)} = \sigma'(t) \, dW'(t) \qquad (5.37')$$

which allows one to express Equation (5.35″) as

$$\frac{dS(t)}{S(t)} = r(t) \, dt + \sigma'(t) \, dW'(t) \qquad (5.35''')$$

This result will be of crucial importance in the practical implementation of lattice models, and, specifically, in the context of the construction via forward induction of lattices by means of Green's functions.

Since, by Equation (5.37′), the variable $Z(0,t)$ is log-normally distributed, and since this distributional assumption is compatible with both the cash asset and the numeraire asset being also log-normally distributed, then

$$\sigma'(t) = \sqrt{\sigma(t)^2 + \sigma_B(t)^2 - 2\rho\sigma(t)\sigma_B(t)} \qquad (5.39)$$

where $\sigma_B(t)$ indicates the percentage volatility of the numeraire asset. But since, as shown before, $B(0,t)$ is locally deterministic, the percentage volatility of the numeraire asset, $\sigma_B(t)$, is equal to zero. Therefore $\sigma' = \sigma$, i.e., with choice of numeraire, **the instantaneous percentage volatilities of the relative prices equal the percentage volatilities of the cash prices.**

Another important result that can be obtained in this measure concerns the link between the discount factor and a discount bond. More precisely, imposing that Equation (5.36) should hold for any asset, and therefore for a discount bond of maturity T, one obtains

$$\frac{P(T,T)}{B(0,T)} = \frac{1}{B(0,T)} = \exp\left[-\int_0^T r(s)\,ds\right]$$

$$= P(0,T)\exp\left[\int_0^T v(s,T)\,dW'(s) - \frac{1}{2}\int_0^T |v(s,T)|^2\,ds\right] \qquad (5.40)$$

where, for consistency with the notation employed elsewhere, $v(s,T)$ is the special symbol used to denote volatilities when assets are discount bonds, and indicates the volatility at time s of a discount bond of maturity T. **Expression (5.40) therefore provides the link between the discount factor in the money market account numeraire $(1/B(0,T))$ and the price of a discount bond. As it will be shown later, the discount bond price is equal to the discount factor in the forward neutral measure.** (It is also instructive to compare this result with the deterministic case.) As it will become clearer in the following, the interplay between the discounting procedure and the drift imparted to asset prices is crucial in comparing different choices of numeraire. At a very simple level Equation (5.40) shows that it is not correct, *in Q'*, to discount a payoff occurring at time T from an asset which has grown at the short rate $r(t)$ by the discount bond $P(0,T)$, as it is done, perfectly correctly, within the framework of the Black model.

The important relationship between forward and future prices in the Q' measure can be obtained along the following lines: solving in Equation (5.38) for $B(0,t)$ one can write

$$B(0,t) = \frac{S(t)}{S(0)}\exp\left\{-\int_0^t \sigma'(s)\,dW'(s) + \frac{1}{2}\int_0^t |\sigma'(s)|^2\,ds\right\} \qquad (5.41)$$

Substituting (5.41) in Equation (5.40) and solving for $S(t)$ gives

$$S(t) = \frac{S(0)}{P(0,t)}\exp\left[\int_0^t (\sigma'(s) - v(s,t))\,dW'(s) - \frac{1}{2}\int_0^t |\sigma'(s)|^2 - |v(s,t)|^2\,ds\right] \qquad (5.42)$$

or, for the special case of $S_n(t)$ being a discount bond maturing at $T(T>t)$,

$$P(t,T) = \frac{P(0,T)}{P(0,t)}\exp\left[\int_0^t (v(s,t) - v(s,t))\,dW'(s) - \frac{1}{2}\int_0^t |v(s,T)|^2 - |v(s,t)|^2\,ds\right]$$

$$\qquad (5.42')$$

showing that **future prices** ($S_n(t)$ or $P(t,T)$) **differ, in Q', from the forward prices** ($S_n(0)/P(0,t)$ or $P(0,T)/P(0,t)$), **by the exponential terms in (5.42) and (5.42'), respectively.** Once again, this result can be profitably compared with the equivalent equation obtained in the context of a deterministic economy, and with the results presented in the next section. Finally, more insight can be gained by expanding the square in the right-most exponential in Equation (5.42) and obtaining

$$S(t) = \frac{S(0)}{P(0,t)} \exp\left[\int_0^t (\sigma(s) - v(s,t))\, dW'(s) - \frac{1}{2}\int_0^t |\sigma(s) - v(s,t)|^2\, ds\right]$$

$$\times \exp\left[\int_0^t (\sigma(s) - v(s,t))v(s,t)\, ds\right]$$

$$(5.42'')$$

Notice now that the middle line is the representation of a martingale (Theorem 2) with volatility $\sigma_n(t) - v(s,t)$. If, following Gustavsson (1992), we call this martingale $M(t)$, then

$$S(t) = \frac{S(0)}{P(0,t)} M(t) \exp\left[\int_0^t (\sigma(s) - v(s,t))v(s,t)\, ds\right] \qquad (5.43)$$

Now, $E'[M(t)\,|\,\mathfrak{F}_0] = M(0) = 1$, and therefore

$$E'[S(t)\,|\,\mathfrak{F}_0] = \frac{S(0)}{P(0,t)} E'\left[M(t)\exp\left\{-\int_0^t (\sigma(s) - v(s,t))v(s,t)\, ds\right\} | \mathfrak{F}_0\right] \quad (5.44)$$

Remembering that the expectation of the product of two variables is equal to the product of the expectations plus the covariance between the two variables ($E[a\,b] = E[a]\,E[b] + \text{Covar}[a,b]$), Equation (5.44) becomes

$$E'[S(t)\,|\,\mathfrak{F}_0] = \frac{S(0)}{P(0,t)} E'\left[\exp\left\{-\int_0^t (\sigma(s) - v(s,t))v(s,t)\, ds\right\} | \mathfrak{F}_0\right]$$

$$+ \text{Covar}'\left[M(t), \exp\left\{-\int_0^t (\sigma(s) - v(s,t))v(s,t)\, ds\right\}\right]$$

$$(5.45)$$

If one can be justified in neglecting the covariance term (as it might to some extent be the case, for instance, for options on stocks), one can therefore see that whether future prices are higher or lower than forward prices depends on the difference in volatilities. In the case of interest-rate products, however, payoffs and discounting are, in general, always correlated, and the covariance term will therefore make an (often very important) contribution. Once again, the comparison with the deterministic case is quite illuminating.

5.5 SECOND CHOICE OF NUMERAIRE: DISCOUNT BONDS

A second important choice of numeraire is a discount bond, and, with this choice of numeraire, one can write

$$Z_n''(t,T) = \frac{S_n(t)}{P(t,T)} \quad \forall T \geq t \tag{5.46}$$

(Notice that in this section a slightly different perspective is taken to the one found in Gustavsson (1992). This explains the difference in notation.) In complete analogy with the case of the money market account, one places oneself at time t, where one observes the cash price $S_n(t)$ and, with the present choice of numeraire, one now chooses from the time-t term structure any of the available discount bonds. Every choice of bond maturity corresponds to a different numeraire, and hence a different equivalent measure, $Q''(T)$. The full notation with both arguments for the relative prices is, unlike the money market account case, now absolutely necessary, since, at time s $(s > t)$, a new set of discount bonds will become available: if at time t a bond of residual maturity $(T - t)$ had been chosen, $P(t,T)$, at time s the numeraire becomes a different asset, i.e. the bond $P(s,T)$ of residual maturity $(T - s)$.

Specialising Equation (5.46) to today (time 0) one can write

$$Z_n''(0,t) = \frac{S_n(0)}{P(0,T)} \tag{5.46'}$$

By Theorem 1, discounting by a zero-coupon bond implies, for no-arbitrage, the choice of a measure Q'', equivalent to the real-world measure Q, such that relative prices become martingales, i.e.

$$E''[Z_n''(t,u)|\mathfrak{F}_s] = Z_n''(s,u) = E''\left[\frac{S(t)}{P(t,u)}\Big|\mathfrak{F}_s\right] = \frac{S(s)}{P(s,u)} \quad \forall u \geq t \geq s \tag{5.47}$$

or, for today's term structure,

$$E''[Z_n''(t,u)|\mathfrak{F}_0] = Z_n''(0,u) = E''\left[\frac{S(t)}{P(t,u)}\Big|\mathfrak{F}_0\right] = \frac{S(0)}{P(0,u)} \quad \forall u \geq t \tag{5.47'}$$

As mentioned above, any bond could have been chosen as numeraire asset in Equation (5.47) among the ones available at time s. If the one bond maturing at time $u = t$ had been chosen, then

$$E''\left[\frac{S(t)}{P(t,t)}\Big|\mathfrak{F}_s\right] = E''[S(t)|\mathfrak{F}_s] = \frac{S(s)}{P(s,u)} \tag{5.48}$$

and, for $s = 0$,

$$E''\left[\frac{S(t)}{P(t,t)}\,\middle|\,\tilde{\mathfrak{F}}_0\right] = E''\,[S(t)|\tilde{\mathfrak{F}}_0] = \frac{S(0)}{P(0,u)} \tag{5.48'}$$

showing that **the expectation of future asset prices is, in Q″, identical to the forward asset prices themselves,** or, in other words, that **in Q″ forward asset prices are martingales.** This result should be compared with Equation (5.45) and with the deterministic case. Notice that the choice of the bond maturing at time $t = u$ is far from being fortuitous. Financially it corresponds to the situation of hedging a cash flow known to occur at a single known point in time in the future with a discount bond maturing exactly at this time. If the money market account were used, one would be rolling one's hedge day by day, and would therefore be exposed to changes in interest rates from 0 to u (it might be useful to reconsider the examples in Chapter 3 after this discussion). The link between the different ways of discounting, and of constructing one's hedge, can be further seen as follows (Gustavsson (1992)). Let us solve for the cash price in the two measures: from the no-arbitrage conditions (5.31″) and from Equation (5.47) above one can write

$$S(t) = B(0,t)E'\left[\frac{S(u)}{B(0,u)}\,\middle|\,\mathfrak{F}(t)\right] \tag{5.49}$$

$$S(t) = P(t,u)E''\left[\frac{S(u)}{P(u,u)}\,\middle|\,\mathfrak{F}(t)\right] \tag{5.49'}$$

By equating (5.49) and (5.49′) one obtains

$$E'\left[S(u)\frac{B(0,t)}{B(0,u)}\frac{1}{P(t,u)}\,\middle|\,\mathfrak{F}(t)\right] = E''\left[\frac{S(u)}{P(u,u)}\,\middle|\,\mathfrak{F}(t)\right] \tag{5.50}$$

where on the left-hand term both $B(0,t)$ and $P(t,u)$ have been taken under the expectation sign since they are both known quantities at time t. Therefore,

$$E''[S(u)E|\,\mathfrak{F}(t)] = E'\left[S(u)\frac{B(t,u)}{P(t,u)}\,\middle|\,\mathfrak{F}(t)\right] \tag{5.51}$$

or, using the well-known covariance result $(E[ab] = E[a]\,E[b] + \text{Covar}[a,b])$,

$$E''[S(u)|\,\mathfrak{F}(t)] = E'[S(u)|\,\mathfrak{F}(t)]E'\left[\frac{B(t,u)}{P(t,u)}\,\middle|\,\mathfrak{F}(t)\right] + \text{Covar}'\left[S(u),\frac{B(t,u)}{P(t,u)}\right] \tag{5.51'}$$

The second term on the first line gives the expectation of the ratio of the two different numeraire assets. As for the last term, remembering that $P(t,u)$ is a known quantity at time t, it is clear that **the contribution from this term comes from the correlation between the asset payoffs and the numeraire asset (and, hence, the discounting factor)**. This important observation could be profitably revisited in conjunction with the discussion regarding a caplet payoff and the drift of the relative forward rate, presented at the end of the next section.

In analogy with the reasoning that led to Equations (5.35″) and (5.38′), the rate of return on an asset $S(t)$ in the measure Q'' can also be easily obtained: starting from definition (5.46) one can in fact write

$$S(t) = Z''(t,T)P(t,T) \qquad (5.52)$$

and, after differentiating,

$$dS(t) = dZ''(t,T)P(t,T) + Z''(t,T)\,dP(t,T) + dZ''(t,T)\,dP(t,T) \quad (5.53)$$

The last term is always equal to zero, since dP is of bounded variation. Therefore, dividing both sides by $S(t)$,

$$\frac{dS(t)}{S(t)} = \frac{dP(t,T)}{P(t,T)} + \frac{dZ''(t,T)}{Z''(t,T)} \qquad (5.54)$$

Now,

$$f(t,T) = -\frac{\partial(\ln P(t,T))}{\partial T} \qquad (5.55)$$

and, therefore, as long as the price of a discount bond depends on t and T only via the difference $(T-t)$

$$\frac{dP(t,T)}{P(t,T)} = \frac{\partial(\ln P(t,T))}{\partial t}\,dt = -\frac{\partial(\ln P(t,T))}{\partial T}\,dt \qquad (5.56)$$

and therefore

$$\frac{dS(t)}{S(t)} = f(t,T)\,dt + \frac{dZ''(t)}{Z''(t)} \qquad (5.57)$$

i.e. **the drift on any asset (notice that there is no n-dependence on any specific asset) is equal to the instantaneous forward rate expiring at time T**.

Using the Representation Theorem for exponential martingales one can then write

$$Z''(t,T) = Z''(s,T) \exp\left[\int_s^t \sigma''(u)\, dW''(u) - \frac{1}{2}\int_s^t |\sigma''(u)|^2\, du\right]$$

$$= \frac{S(t)}{P(t,T)} = \frac{S(s)}{P(s,T)} \exp\left[\int_s^t \sigma''(u)\, dW''(u) - \frac{1}{2}\int_s^t |\sigma''(u)|^2\, du\right] \quad (5.58)$$

If one were to choose for numeraire the bond maturing at time t

$$\frac{S(t)}{P(t,t)} = S(t) = \frac{S(s)}{P(s,T)} \exp\left[\int_s^t (\sigma''(u)\, dW''(u) - \frac{1}{2}\int_s^t |\sigma''(u)|^2\, du\right] \quad (5.59)$$

The first term in square brackets on the right-hand side is the forward price as seen from the term structure at time s, and the exponential term is a martingale. Now consider the case when $S(t)$ is a bond maturing at a later time T $(s < t < T)$. Then

$$P(t,T) = \frac{P(s,T)}{P(s,t)} \exp\left[\int_s^t v''(u,T)\, dW''(u) - \frac{1}{2}\int_s^t |v''(u,T)|^2\, du\right] \quad (5.60)$$

where $v''(u, T)$ indicates the time-u volatility of the relative price of a bond maturing at time T in measure Q'', i.e **the volatility of a forward bond price**. Notice carefully that σ'' is different from the volatility of the cash (i.e. non-relative) discount bond, or, for that matter, from the volatility of the relative process of the same discount bond in the measure Q', σ'.

Starting from the definition (5.46), and making the same log-normal assumptions, the volatility of the relative price of asset n is given by

$$\sigma_n''(t) = \sqrt{[\sigma_n(t)^2 + v(t,T)^2 - 2\rho\sigma_n v(t,T)}} \quad (5.61)$$

which relates relative price volatilities to cash price volatilities. But since, as we saw, in Q' relative and cash prices display the same volatility, Equation (5.61) provides a link also between the relative price volatilities in the two measures. When applied to the case of discount bonds, Equations (5.60) and (5.61) together give

$$P(t,T) = \frac{P(s,T)}{P(s,t)} \exp\left[\int_s^t \sqrt{v(u,T)^2 + v(u,t)^2 - 2\rho v(u,T)v(u,t)}\; dW''(u)\right.$$

$$\left. - \frac{1}{2}\int_s^t |v(u,T)^2 + v(u,t)^2 - 2\rho v(u,T)v(u,t)|^2\, du\right] \quad (5.62)$$

Now, if $\rho = 1$ (a reasonable approximation for bonds, corresponding to a description of the economy in terms of a one-factor model), one gets

$$P(t,T) = \frac{P(s,T)}{P(s,t)} \exp\left[\int_s^t (v(u,T) - v(u,t))\, dW''(u)\right.$$

$$\left. -\frac{1}{2} \int_s^t (|\,v(u,T) - v(u,t)\,|^2)\, du\right] \tag{5.63}$$

Notice the difference in the rightmost term with the equivalent term in Equation (5.42′)

$$P(t,T) = \frac{P(s,T)}{P(s,t)} \exp\left[\int_s^t (v(u,T) - v(u,t))\, dW''(u)\right.$$

$$\left. -\frac{1}{2} \int_s^t (|\,v(u,T)\,|^2 - |\,v(u,t)\,|^2)\, du\right] \tag{5.42′}$$

If the Brownian motion $dW'(u)$ were transformed into $dW'(u) + v(u,t)\, du$, then, after expanding the square in the time integral in Equation (5.63), and multiplying $[v(u,T) - v(u,t)]$ by $dW'(t) + v(u,t)\, du$ in Equation ((5.42′), one can observe that the expressions for $P(t,T)$ in the two measures coincide. In other words, **the two measures are simply related by a drift transformation**:

$$dw'(t) = dw''(t) + v(t,T)\, dt \tag{5.64}$$

The following section will show that this result, i.e. the fact that the equivalent measures associated with the different numeraires are linked by a simple drift transformation, is of general validity. For the moment, in so far as the two particular measures examined in this and the previous sections are concerned, since Ito's lemma shows that the volatility of the forward rate, σ_f, is equal to the derivative of the bond volatility with respect to bond maturity

$$\sigma_f = \frac{\partial v(t,T)}{\partial T} \tag{5.65}$$

one immediately notices that, under the log-normal assumption for bond prices and in the money market account measure Q' forward rates are not martingales, but display a drift given by $v(t,T)\, \partial v(t,T)/\partial T$. This result will be re-derived and much expanded upon in the chapter devoted to the HJM model (Chapter 14).

5.6 THE GENERAL LINK BETWEEN DIFFERENT MEASURES

The previous section has shown that the link between the two measures Q' and Q'' is via a drift transformation like Equation (5.64). For Wiener processes, this result is actually of general validity, and constitutes the third 'cornerstone' (Girsanov's theorem) mentioned in Section 5.2. More precisely, one can show (Gustavsson (1992)) that:

(i)   taken two equivalent measures, Q' and Q, they are linked by a strictly positive, continuous, linear functional ρ (the Radon–Nikodym derivative), such that

$$E'[Z'(u)|\,\Im(t)] = E[\rho(u)Z'(u)|\,\Im(t)] \qquad (5.66)$$

This functional is sometimes symbolically denoted by $\rho = dQ'/dQ$, emphasising its intuitive interpretation as the 'change in one measure for a change in the second measure'.

(ii) The functional $\rho(0)$ is the identity transformation, i.e. $\rho(0) = 1$, simply implying that *all* expectations today (see Equation (5.66)) must have the same value.

(iii) The functional $\rho(t)$ is a martingale, and, as such, by (ii) above,

$$\rho(t) = \exp\left[\int_0^t q(s)\,dW'(s)\,ds - \frac{1}{2}\int_0^t |q(s)|^2\,ds\right] \qquad (5.67)$$

(iv) **Wiener process $W'(t)$ in the original measure Q' is transformed, under the measure Q, into**

$$W(t) = W'(t) - \int_0^t q(s)\,ds \qquad (5.68)$$

where $q(t)$ is the volatility that appears in the process for $\rho(t)$.

Let us try to explore more precisely the implications of these results. For the sake of concreteness, let us continue to indicate by Q' the measure relative to the money market account, and by Q any other measure (possibly even the real-world measure). We know from Section 5.4, Equation (5.38′), that, in Q',

$$\frac{S(t)}{B(0,t)} = \frac{S(0)}{B(0,0)}\exp\left[\int_0^t \sigma(s)\,dW'(s) - \frac{1}{2}\int_0^t |\sigma'(s)|^2\,ds\right]$$

$$= S(0)\exp\left[\int_0^t \sigma(s)\,dW'(s) - \frac{1}{2}\int_0^t |\sigma'(s)|^2\,ds\right] \qquad (5.69)$$

since $B(0,0) = 1$. By Equation (5.68) above

$$dW'(s) = dW(s) + q(s)\,ds \qquad (5.68')$$

which, substituted into Equation (5.69) gives

$$S(t) = \frac{S(0)}{B(0,t)} \exp\left[\int_0^t \sigma(s)\, dW'(s) + \int_0^t \sigma(s)q(s)\, ds - \frac{1}{2}\int_0^t |\sigma'(s)|^2\, ds\right]$$

$$= S(0) \exp\left[\int_0^t r(s)\, ds + \int_0^t \sigma(s)\, dW'(s) + \int_0^t \sigma(s)q(s)\, ds - \frac{1}{2}\int_0^t |\sigma'(s)|^2\, ds\right]$$

$$= S(0) \exp\left[\int_0^t (r(s) + \sigma(s)q(s))\, ds + \int_0^t \sigma(s)\, dW'(s) - \frac{1}{2}\int_0^t |\sigma'(s)|^2\, ds\right]$$

$$(5.69')$$

where the definition of $B(0,t)$ has been substituted in the second line. Notice that Equation (5.69) above does not refer to a relative price, but gives the value at time t of the spot (real-world) price of asset S. In the real world the process for S will have the form

$$\frac{ds(t)}{S(t)} = \mu(t)\, dt + \sigma(t)\, dz \qquad (5.70)$$

and therefore

$$S(t) = S(0) \exp\left[\int_0^t \mu(s)\, ds + \int_0^t \sigma(s)\, dW'(s) - \frac{1}{2}\int_0^t |\sigma'(s)|^2\, ds\right] \qquad (5.71)$$

Comparing Equations (5.69) and (5.71) one can see that

$$\exp\left[\int_0^t (r(s) + \sigma(s)q(s))\, d(s)\right] = \exp\left[\int_0^t \mu(s)\, d(s)\right] \qquad (5.72)$$

or, in other words,

$$\mu(s) = r(s) + q(s)\sigma(s) \qquad (5.72')$$

But this is exactly the result obtained in the Vasicek treatment (Section 5.1, Equation (5.13)), **with $q(s) = \lambda(s)$, where the quantity $\lambda(s)$ has been shown to be the market price of risk.** This latter quantity therefore assumes the double interpretation of the return compensation above the riskless rate per unit risk on the one hand, and of the transformation that links together the real-world and the risk-neutral measures, on the other.

5.7 AN INTUITIVE DISCUSSION

A few examples can perhaps make the above discussion more concrete. Let us first consider the case of the evaluation of a simple caplet of expiry t and maturity

T. With Black's model each final payoff is probability weighted by the log-normal distribution of the corresponding forward rate and then discounted by a bond of maturity T. Notice that, given this choice of numeraire, no drift is assumed for the caplet forward rate. Notice also that large payoffs (corresponding to high realisations of the forward rate, and weighted by their log-normal probability distribution) are discounted using the same discount bond as lower-rate payoffs. Let us consider, on the other hand, a lattice approach, such as the BDT model presented later (Chapter 10), which enforces the same (log-normal) distributional assumptions as the Black model, but discounts each final payoff along the actual path followed by the short rate to reach the appropriate state of the world at maturity, i.e. using a rolled-up money market account. Unlike in the Black case, by so doing large payoffs (corresponding to high realisations of the forward rate) are discounted using larger realisations of the money market account, and vice versa. **Yet, despite *identical* variance at expiry and *different* discounting, lattice approaches give the same value as Black's model for the caplet.** Now, the price today of the caplet is given by an expectation, and the same distributional assumptions (in so far as the variance is concerned) are made by the two models. Furthermore, for the log-normal case, the value of an expectation can only depend on the drift and the variance of the underlying variable. Therefore, the fact that, despite different discounting, the same price is recovered can only occur because a different implicit drift is imparted to the underlying variable in the two measures. How this implicit drift of the forward rate can actually be obtained is given by Girsanov's theorem, but it is important to notice that it is this change in drift that exactly compensates for the different discounting (i.e. numeraires) in the two approaches, or, more precisely, which accounts for the covariance between the payoff and the discounting.

More insight can be gained by revisiting Chapter 3, and in particular the example presented in Section 3.2. We considered in that case an option with payoff dependent on two forward bond prices and occurring at the expiry of the second. The hedge had been created using two forward contracts, the second with reset and payment times identical to the option, and the first giving rise to a payment at a time when no cash flows deriving from the option occurred. We found that, in the valuation formula we obtained, the second forward needed no adjustments, but we also found that, if we wanted the resulting PDE to display purely diffusive behaviour, the first forward had to be transformed according to expressions (3.16) and (3.16'). We identified the reason for this adjustment term in the fact that a position in the first forward contract introduced an exposure to a discounting zero, $P(0, t_1)$, absent in the option payoff. We can reinterpret this analysis in terms of the results of this section: the numeraire chosen is the forward bond from t_2 to T_2; with this numeraire, the forward price resetting at time t_2 and maturing at T_2 is 'naturally' driftless (i.e. a martingale); the same does not apply to any other forward price. In particular, the forward from t_1 to T_1 displays the drift correction given by (3.16).

If we had introduced in the option payoff the dependence on more and more forward prices, but retained the same option payoff time, we would have introduced as many additional hedging forward contracts, each bringing in an 'unwanted' dependence in the overall portfolio on their discounting; each forward but the last would therefore be endowed with a drift; correlation terms between the discounting bonds, $P(0,t_i)$ and the forwards $P(t_i,T_i)$ would have to be introduced to render the resulting PDE driftless. It is intuitively easy to see that, by increasing the number of 'intervening' forwards, one is continuously moving towards the measure where the money market account becomes the numeraire and infinitely many forwards can affect the option payoff.

5.8 A WORKED-OUT EXAMPLE: VALUING A LIBOR-IN-ARREARS SWAP

In order to show how the no-arbitrage conditions obtained in the previous sections can directly lead to concrete restrictions and explicit valuation formulae in the pricing of specific contingent claims, a simple example is worked out in full in the following. Two results will be obtained in this section using the martingale formalism: first it will be shown, following a different route, what was already proven in Chapter 1, namely that forward rates can be treated as martingales if one is pricing plain-vanilla swaps; and then the actual correction to be applied to a LIBOR-in-arrears swap (i.e. a swap for which reset time and pay time coincide) will be worked out in detail.

To begin with the plain-vanilla case, let us consider the following strategy:

(i) at time 0 a bond of maturity t_1 is purchased;
(ii) at time t_1 the certain pound paid by this bond is invested (at the spot rate prevailing at time t_1) into a bond maturing at time t_2 (this part of the strategy has zero value today);
(iii) at time 0 $(1 + X\tau)$ units of a bond maturing at time t_2 are sold, with $\tau = (t_2 - t_1)$.

The value of the strategy S at time 0 is:

$$S(0) = P(0,t_1) - (1 + X\tau)P(0,t_2) \tag{5.73}$$

The value of the strategy at time t_2 is:

$$S(t_2) = (1 + R(t_1,t_2)\tau) - (1 + X\tau) = (R(t_1,t_2) - X)\tau \tag{5.74}$$

where the first term in brackets in the middle expression arises from the reinvestment of the bond proceeds from time t_1 to time t_2, and $R(t_1,t_2)$ indicates the spot rates prevailing at time t_1 for maturity t_2.

Let us now consider a FRA expiring at time t_1 and paying at time t_2, struck at X. Its payoff at time t_2 is

$$(R(t_1, t_2) - X)\tau \qquad (5.75)$$

and therefore, since the t_2-time payoffs of the FRA and of the strategy coincide, the value today of the FRA itself must be the same as the value of the strategy:

$$NPV(FRA(0)) = S(0) = P(0, t_1) - (1 + X\tau)P(0, t_2) \qquad (5.76)$$

Let us choose for numeraire a bond maturing at time t_2. In the probability measure under which the relative prices implied by this numeraire are martingales, the expectations and the drifts implied by this choice of numeraire will be denoted by Q', E' and μ', respectively. Then one can write

$$E'\left[\left. \frac{S(t)}{P(t, t_2)} \right| \Im_0 \right] = \frac{S(0)}{P(0, t_2)} \qquad (5.77)$$

where, as usual, $\Im_0$ (usually omitted in the following to lighten notation) indicates that the expectation is taken contingent upon information available at time 0. For $t = t_2$ in Equation (5.77) one obtains

$$E'\left[\frac{(1 + R(t_1, t_2)) - (1 + X\tau)}{1} \right] = E'[R(t_1, t_2)]\tau - X\tau \qquad (5.78)$$

since $P(t_2, t_2) = 1$. Enforcing Equation (5.77) one obtains

$$E'[R(t_1, t_2)]\tau - X\tau = \frac{P(0, t_1)}{P(0, t_2)} - (1 + X\tau) \qquad (5.79)$$

and, therefore, after defining the forward rate at time 0 spanning the period $[t_1 \ t_2]$ as

$$f(0, t_1, t_2) = \frac{\dfrac{P(0, t_1)}{P(0, t_2)} - 1}{\tau} \qquad (5.80)$$

one obtains

$$E'[R(t_1, t_2)] = f(0, t_1, t_2) \qquad (5.81)$$

One also knows that $R(t_1, t_2) \equiv f(t_1, t_1, t_2)$ and therefore

$$E'[f(t_1, t_1, t_2)] = f(0, t_1, t_2) \qquad (5.82)$$

i.e., as we already know, **the forward rate $f(0, t_1, t_2)$ displays no drift μ' under Q' from time 0 to time t_1.**

Let us now consider the case of a LIBOR-in-arrears FRA. As mentioned above, for this instrument the LIBOR setting occurs at the *payoff time* of the FRA, i.e. reset and pay times coincide at time t_1. To analyse the situation, let us now switch numeraire to a bond maturing at time t_1. Quantities under the martingale measure with this choice of numeraire will be denoted by ". Enforcing the no-arbitrage condition now gives

$$E'' \left[\frac{S(t)}{P(t,t_1)} \Big| \mathfrak{I}_0 \right] = \frac{S(0)}{P(0,t_1)} \tag{5.83}$$

or, for $t = t_1$ (using Equation (5.73) for $S(t_1)$ and $S(0)$),

$$E'' \left[\frac{1 - (1 + X\tau)P(t_1,t_2)}{1} \right] = \frac{P(0,t_1) - (1 + X\tau)P(0,t_2)}{P(0,t_1)} \tag{5.84}$$

After rearranging and cancelling this gives

$$E''[P(t_1,t_2)] = E'' \left[\frac{1}{1 + R(t_1,t_2)\tau} \right] = \frac{P(0,t_2)}{P(0,t_1)} = \frac{1}{1 + f(0,t_1,t_2)\tau} \tag{5.85}$$

and, therefore, using the result (5.82) obtained in the measure which used $P(0,t_2)$ as numeraire,

$$E'' \left[\frac{1}{1 + R(t_1,t_2)\tau} \right] = \frac{1}{1 + f(0,t_1,t_2)\tau} = \frac{1}{1 + E'[R(t_1,t_2)]\tau} \tag{5.86}$$

Equation (5.86) explicitly shows the link between the expectations in the measures Q' and Q''. As before $R(t_1,t_2) = f(t_1,t_1,t_2)$, and therefore

$$E'' \left[\frac{1}{1 + f(t_1,t_1,t_2)\tau} \right] = \frac{1}{1 + f(0,t_1,t_2)\tau} = \frac{1}{1 + E'[f(t_1,t_1,t_2)]\tau} \tag{5.87}$$

If one defines

$$z(t,t_1,t_2) = \frac{1}{1 + f(t,t_1,t_2)\tau}$$

Equation (5.87) shows that

$$E''[z(t_1,t_1,t_2)] = z(0,t_1,t_2) \tag{5.88}$$

and therefore

$$\mu_z'' = 0 \quad \text{(under } Q'') \tag{5.89}$$

Considering $f(t,t_1,t_2)$ as a function of $z(t,t_1,t_2)$, Ito's lemma gives, in general (i.e. without specifying to which measure the drift corresponds),

$$\mu_f = \frac{\partial f}{\partial z} \mu_z + \frac{1}{2} \sigma_z^2 \frac{\partial^2 f}{\partial z^2} = \frac{\partial f}{\partial z} \mu_z + \frac{\sigma_z^2}{\tau z^3} \tag{5.90}$$

But, for the measure Q'', given Equation (5.89) above, this drift simplifies to

$$\mu_f'' = \frac{1}{2}\sigma_z^2\frac{\partial^2 f}{\partial z^2} = \frac{\sigma_z^2}{\tau z^3} \qquad (5.91)$$

Let us now make a log-normal assumption for the distribution of the forward rates. Using Ito's lemma again, applied to $z = z(f)$ as expressed by its definition, one obtains for the standard deviation per unit time of z,

$$\sigma_z = -\frac{\sigma_f f \tau}{(1+f\tau)^2} \qquad (5.92)$$

Substituting in (5.91) one finally obtains

$$\mu_{f(0,t_1,t_2)}'' = \sigma_f^2 f^2 \tau z = \frac{\sigma_f^2 f^2 \tau}{1 + f(0,t_1,t_2)\tau} \qquad (5.93)$$

which therefore shows that, in valuing a swap with LIBOR set in arrears each projected log-normal forward must be 'corrected' by the term

$$f(0,t_1,t_2)_{\text{adj}} = f(0,t_1,t_2)\exp\left[\frac{\sigma_f^2 f \tau}{1 + f(0,t_1,t_2)\tau}\,t_1\right] \qquad (5.94)$$

PART THREE
THE IMPLEMENTATION TOOLS

6
Lattice methodologies

6.1 JUSTIFICATION OF LATTICE MODELS

Ho and Lee (1986) (HL in the following) and Black Derman and Toy (1990) (BDT in the following) pioneered the use of arbitrage-free computational lattices for the evaluation of interest-rate options. Their methodology has enjoyed vast popularity due to the in-built capability of their models to price exactly any received market set of discount bonds, and for the intuitional appeal of their approaches which bear formal, if not very deep, similarities with the Cox–Ross–Rubinstein (1979) binomial model. In this chapter it will be shown how their intuitively appealing methodology can be rigorously justified (Section 6.1), and that it can afford, combined with the techniques of forward and backward induction, a very efficient computational tool (Sections 6.2 and 6.3). The results of Chapters 4 and 5 will be drawn upon, both to justify the procedures, and to construct the necessary Green's functions. The reader, who is certainly acquainted with and probably already using interest-rate trees, might feel at the end of Section 6.1 a bit like Molière's *bourgeois gentilhomme*, who, without knowing it, had been speaking in prose throughout his life. The purpose of the first section, however, which will present in a sometimes notationally awkward fashion what is, after all, an algorithmically very simple procedure, is not to pursue a 'tedious argument of insidious intent' for its own sake, but to furnish the user with a solid understanding of the theoretical underpinning of the methodology. Despite, or perhaps because of, the intuitive appeal of tree constructions it is in fact easy to fail fully to understand *why* the procedure works, and, consequently, what its strengths and weaknesses are. Lest the wood might be missed for the trees, two main tasks will be tackled in this section: i.e. to show that the averaging/discounting procedure (i) is indeed equivalent to evaluating a security's price as the *expectation* of its *discounted* payoff (despite the fact that, in the algorithm, averaging is carried out *before* discounting); and (ii) actually carries out (in a very efficient way) the discounting along *each* possible path occurring in the tree, without duplication of effort. The appropriate numeraire associated with the methodology is therefore the discrete counterpart of the rolled-up money market account.

Since computational lattices are, by construction, discrete, an arbitrarily large, but finite, number of discount bonds are assumed to describe the term structure. The starting point for yield-curve lattice models is therefore an exogenous set of discount bond prices $\{P_i(\cdot)\}\,(i=1,N)$ observed in the market. The assumption is then often made that the securities prices are driven by a single factor[1], and that this driving factor is the short rate; further, as elsewhere in this book, it is assumed that the short-rate process can be described by a Brownian diffusion. The value of the short rate today, i.e. at time 0 and in state 0, $r(0,0)$, is known from the price of $P(0,0,1\,\Delta t)$:

$$r(0,0) = -\frac{\ln P(0,0,\Delta t)}{\Delta t} \tag{6.1}$$

(where $P(i,j,T)$ indicates the price in state j and at time i of a bond of maturity T). In addition, the user will in general know, either from a historical or 'implied' estimation, the time-dependent (absolute or percentage) volatility of the short rate. No explicit knowledge is, however, required about its drift. The short rate itself (HL) or its logarithm (BDT) are then allowed, from today's value, to move up or down with equal probabilities to two, as of yet undetermined, states $r(1,1)$ and $r(1,-1)$ (where, again, the first index denotes the time and the second the state). See the construction of Figure 6.1.

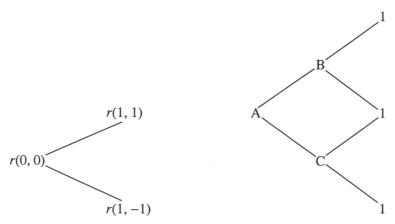

Figure 6.1 $r=(0,0)$ is known at time 0 from Equation (6.1); the value of the short rate in the up state at time 1 Δt, $r(1,1)$, is linked to $r(1,-1)$ by Equation (6.2) or Equation (6.2'); B is given by $\frac{1}{2}(1+1)\exp[-r(1,1)\,\Delta t]$; C is given by $\frac{1}{2}(1+1)\exp[-r(1,-1)\,\Delta t]$; A is given by $\frac{1}{2}(B+C)\exp[-r(0,0)\,\Delta t]$.

The general strategy, both with lattices and with finite-differences grids (or, for that matter, with Monte Carlo simulations), is to ensure that, after a 'move' of the state variable, the correct expectations and variances should be recovered. As mentioned above, one assumes to have direct *a priori* knowledge of the variance of the short-rate process at any point in time (we shall see later on how this can be imputed from market prices), but one does not impose a pre-known drift to the short rate. As usual, the latter will be implicitly determined by ensuring that no-arbitrage opportunities should be allowed, and will be a function of the particular numeraire chosen. This, in turn, will be shown to be, for short-rate lattices, a discrete-time approximation of the rolled-up money market account.

One should notice that it is both the unconditional *and* the conditional (local) second moments that have to be matched. In other words, it is not enough to ensure that, given today's value for the short rate, its unconditional variance at time $i (E[((r(i) - (E[r(i)|\Im_0])^2|\Im_0])$ should have the correct value. (In the following, whenever the short rate is written as a function of a single argument, as in $r(i)$, it is meant as a function of time; if written as $r(i,j)$ it is explicitly meant to be a function of time and state.) One also has to make sure that, given the fact that the short rate at time i and in state j has assumed the particular value $r(i,j)$, the conditional second moment of the distribution originating from this new origin $(E[((r(k) - (E[r(k)|\Im_i])^2|\Im_i])$ should also have the correct (forward) value. In particular, the moment-matching will have to be enforced for any move from state (i,j) to the two adjacent states $(i+1, j-1)$, $(i+1, j+1)$. Since, clearly, ensuring that this latter condition is satisfied automatically guarantees that all the conditional and unconditional variances are correctly recovered, while the converse is in general not true, **the construction of computational lattices entails the matching of all the instantaneous conditional variances (and, implicitly, expectations)**.

Concentrating on the variance first, one can start from the 'root' of the tree, i.e. at $r(0,0)$. The two possible values attainable, with equal probability, over one time step will be denoted by $r(1,-1)$ and $r(1,1)$. In general, for any two (equal-weight) sample values A and B from an arbitrary distribution, their sample standard deviation is simply given by $|A - B|/2$. Given the Gaussian assumption for the process of the short rate (HL), or of its logarithm (BDT), their separation, i.e. $r(1,1) - r(1,-1)$, (HL), or $\ln(r(1,1)) - \ln(r(1,-1))$ (BDT) can be immediately determined from the knowledge of the absolute or percentage volatility of the short rate at time $t(0)$, $\sigma(0)$. Using the simple expression given above for the sample standard deviation, for the BDT and the HL case one in fact immediately obtains

$$\sigma\sqrt{\Delta t} = \frac{r(1,1) - r(1,-1)}{2} \Rightarrow r(1,1) = r(1,-1) + 2\sigma\sqrt{\Delta t} \quad \text{[normal (HL) case]}$$

(6.2)

$$\sigma\sqrt{\Delta t} = \frac{\ln r(1,1) - \ln r(1,-1)}{2} \Rightarrow r(1,1) = r(1,-1) \exp[2\sigma\sqrt{\Delta t}]$$

$$\text{[log-normal (BDT) case]} \quad (6.2')$$

respectively. Equations (6.2) and (6.2') determine the relative separation of the (logarithms of) the two rates. What remains to be determined is the absolute level of the two rates, a unique function, via Equations (6.2) and (6.2'), of either $r(1,1)$ or $r(1,-1)$. Clearly, determining the absolute level of the two rates is tantamount to imposing their conditional (and, for the first time step, also unconditional) expectation. The construction can be pictorially seen as the moving up and down of a rigid rod of length $r(1,1) - r(1,-1)$: the length of the rod gives the variance, and its location in r-space the expectation.

In order to determine the absolute level of, say, $r(1,-1)$ the following procedure can be employed: one can construct another tree representing bond prices in the same states of the world described by the short-rate tree, and, in addition, extending one extra time step (i.e. in the example treated so far, up to time $2\,\Delta t$). Figure 6.1 shows where states A, B and C in the bond tree correspond to states $r(0,0)$, $r(1,1)$ and $r(1,-1)$ in the short-rate tree, respectively. If one then considers a bond of maturity $2\,\Delta t$, which therefore pays with certainty £1 in all states of the world at time $2\,\Delta t$, one can ask for the price of this bond at time $1\,\Delta t$ in state, say, 1, i.e. for $P(1,1,2\,\Delta t)$. (In the notation for the bond prices, the first argument denotes the time, the second the state of the short-rate tree, and the last the maturity of the discount bond.) From the results of Chapter 4, we know that, in continuous time, this price is given by the conditional expectation, in the appropriate measure, of a certain payment of £1 at time $2\,\Delta t$. If one discounts using a rolled-up money market account, this conditional expectation is given by

$$P(1,1,2\,\Delta t) = E'_{t=\Delta t}[1 \exp - \int_{\Delta t}^{2\,\Delta t} r(s)\, ds \,|\, r(\Delta t) = r(1,1)] \qquad (6.3)$$

(A slight liberty has been taken with the notation, since 'r' denotes the short rate both in the continuous, $r(t)$, and in the discrete, $r(i,j)$, case. It is hoped that no ambiguities should arise). In discrete time the integral from time Δt to time $2\,\Delta t$ is equivalent to a single step, over which the short rate is known to be in state $(1,1)$. Therefore the short rate itself can be taken out of the expectation sign, giving

$$E'_{t=\Delta t}[1 \exp(-r(1,1)\,\Delta t) \,|\, r(\Delta t) = r(1,1)]$$

$$= \exp[-r(1,1)\,\Delta t]E_{t=\Delta t}[1 \,|\, r(\Delta t) = r(1,1)] \qquad (6.3')$$

By virtue of the Brownian assumption, and since we have assumed equal probabilities of $\frac{1}{2}$ for the 'up' and 'down' jump, the last expectation is therefore approximated, in discrete time and using a binomial lattice, by

$$E'_{t=\Delta t}[1\exp(-r(1,1)\,\Delta t)|\,r(\Delta t)=r(1,1)]$$
$$=\exp[-r(1,1)\,\Delta t](1\tfrac{1}{2}+1\tfrac{1}{2})=\exp[-r(1,1)\,\Delta t] \quad (6.3'')$$

With a binomial lattice one is therefore approximating the whole integration over a distribution by a sampling carried out over as few as two points. Therefore the value at time $1\,\Delta t$ and in the state corresponding to $r(1,i)(i=1,-1)$ of a bond maturing at time $2\,\Delta t$ is simply given by the one-period discount factor obtained using rate $r(1,i)$.

Let us now call $P(1,1,2\,\Delta t;r(1,1))$ and $P(1,-1,2\,\Delta t;r(1,-1))$ the value at time 1 of a discount bond maturing at time $2\,\Delta t$ in the 1 (up) and -1 (down) states of the world, respectively (the parametric argument $r(i,j)$ which appears in the notation for the discount bond price now specifies on which rate(s) the latter depends).

Continuing the same reasoning, the expectation as of time 0 of the price of a $2\,\Delta t$-maturity discount bond, which will depend on $r(1,1)$, $r(1,-1)$ and $r(0,0)$, $P(0,0,2\,\Delta t;r(1,1),r(1,-1),r(0,0))$, must then be given by

$$P(0,0,2\Delta t;r(1,1),r(1,-1),r(0,0))$$
$$=E'_{t=0}[\exp-\int_0^{2\Delta t}r(s)\,\mathrm{d}s]=E'_{t=0}[\exp-\int_0^{\Delta t}r(s)\,\mathrm{d}s\exp-\int_{\Delta t}^{2\Delta t}r(s)\,\mathrm{d}s]$$
$$=\exp[-r(0,0)\,\Delta t]E'_{t=0}[\exp-\int_{\Delta t}^{2\Delta t}r(s)\,\mathrm{d}s] \quad (6.4)$$

where, in the last line, the first step has been discretised. But, from Equations (6.3') and (6.3'') above,

$$\exp[-r(0,0)\,\Delta t]E'_{t=0}[\exp-\int_{\Delta t}^{2\Delta t}r(s)\,\mathrm{d}s]$$
$$=\exp[-r(0,0)\,\Delta t][\mathrm{prob}(0\to1)P(1,1,2\,\Delta t)+\mathrm{prob}(0\to-1)P(1,-1,2\,\Delta t)]$$
$$(6.5)$$

(where $p(0,\to\pm1)$ is the probability of going from state 0 to state $+1$ or -1), and therefore

$$\textbf{P(0,0,2}\,\Delta t;r(1,1),r(1,-1),r(0,0))=$$
$$\exp[-r(0,0)\,\Delta t]\tfrac{1}{2}\{P(1,1,2\,\Delta t)+P(1,-1,2\,\Delta t)\} \quad (6.6)$$

As mentioned before, the (admittedly rather cumbersome, but, hopefully, useful) notation employed for the first term in Equation (6.6) emphasises that the discount bond price $P(0,0,2\,\Delta t)$ depends and $r(0,0)$, $r(1,-1)$ and $r(1,1)$. However, since $r(0,0)$ is known from Equation (6.1), since the prices $P(1,\pm1,2\,\Delta t)$ are related to $r(1,1)$ and $r(1,-1)$ by Equations (6.3), (6.3') and

(6.3''), and since the two rates at time 1, $r(1,1)$, $r(1,-1)$, are linked by the relationships (6.2) and 6.2') above, the price $P(0,0,2\,\Delta t)$ **can be seen to be a function of a** *single* **unknown**, i.e. $r(1,-1)$ (or $r(1,1)$) only. Therefore one can write

$$P(0,0,2\,\Delta t; r(1,1), r(1,-1), r(0,0)) = P(0,0,2\,\Delta t; r(1,-1)) \qquad (6.6')$$

This function of a *single* variable can now be equated to the observed market price of a two-year discount bond, thereby uniquely determining the value for $r(1,1)$ (or $r(1,-1)$). The resulting equation admits close solution for the HL model, or requires a simple numerical algorithm (e.g. Newton–Raphson) for the BDT approach.

It is easy to see that the extension of the rate tree by one time step will introduce a single new unknown and one more equation. All the rates in the $(i+1)$ states of the world j at time i are in fact linked by

$$r(i,j+1) = r(i,j-1) + 2\sigma\sqrt{\Delta t} \quad \text{[HL, normal case]} \qquad (6.7)$$

$$r(i,j+1) = r(i,j-1)\exp[2\sigma\sqrt{\Delta t}] \quad \text{[BDT, log-normal case]} \qquad (6.7')$$

and therefore, given the value of the volatility at time $(i-1)\,\Delta t$, they can all be expressed as a function of, say, $r(i,-i)$. The unit payoffs from a bond maturing at time $i+1$ can then be discounted to time i using all and only the rates $r(i,j)$ (all a function of, say, $r(i,-i)$ via Equations (6.7) and (6.7')), and from time i to time 0 using *already determined rates*. This model value for a $(i+1)\,\Delta t$-maturity bond can then be compared with the corresponding market value, and the single unknown, $r(i,-i)$, adjusted accordingly.

By analysing the procedure just presented, several features should be apparent: first of all, each process of averaging and discounting carries out numerically the integration needed to produce a discounted expectation. It so happens that the numerical integral just described is carried over as few as two points, but there is nothing special about *bi*nomial branching, or about the specific values chosen for the probabilities. Any scheme (possibly multinomial and/or with state-dependent unequal probabilities) could be used, as long as the two first moments of the short rate distribution were correctly recovered. The effectiveness of these more complex schemes is a numerical but not a conceptual issue.

Furthermore, going back to Equation (6.5) above, it is clear that the following conceptual strategy would be followed, in continuous time, to compute the expectation at time 0 of the reciprocal of the exponential of the short rate from time 0 to time $2\,\Delta t$: one would have to integrate over the probabilities of occurrence (i.e. to calculate the expectation) of the values of the expectations of [the reciprocal of the exponential of the short rate], contingent on the fact that these expectations originate from each individual realisation at time Δt of the short rate itself. (Some apologies are certainly due to the reader at this point, who might be forgiven for thinking that the above sentence is possibly the most awkward ever written in the English language; on the other hand, one might say it is not English at all.) For once, expressing the same concept in symbols might result in a more readable expression:

$$E'_{t=0}[\exp - \int_0^{2\Delta t} r(s)\,ds] = \exp[-r(0,0)\,\Delta t] \int p(r(0,0) \to r(\Delta t, x))E'_{t=\Delta x}$$

$$\times \left[\exp - \int_{\Delta t}^{2\Delta t} r(s)\,ds \,|\, r(\Delta t) = r(\Delta t, x) \right] dx \quad (6.8)$$

where $p(r(0,0) \to r(\Delta t, x))$ represents the probability that the short rate should move from state 0 at time 0 to state x at time Δt. In turn, expression (6.8) can be rewritten as

$$\exp[-r(0,0)\,\Delta t] \int p(r(0,0) \to r(\Delta t, x))E'_{t=\Delta x}\left[\exp - \int_{\Delta t}^{2\Delta t} r(s)\,ds \,|\, r(\Delta t) = r(\Delta t, x) \right] dx$$

$$= \exp[-r(0,0)\,\Delta t] \int p(r(0,0) \to r(\Delta t, x))$$

$$\times \left[\int p(r(\Delta t, x) \to r(2\Delta t, w))(\exp - \int_{\Delta t}^{2\Delta t} r(s)\,ds)\,dw \right] dx \quad (6.9)$$

Clearly, in Equation (6.9) the value of $r(s)$ at time Δt in the innermost integral is equal to $r(\Delta t, x)$. If one wanted to carry out numerically the first integration (over dx) in the context of a binomial lattice methodology, the integration over the probabilities of occurrence of states 1 and -1 would simply be achieved by assigning equal ($\frac{1}{2}$) probabilities to both events, reducing Equation (6.9) to

$$E'_{t=0}\left[\exp - \int_0^{2\Delta t} r(s)\,ds \right] = \exp[-r(0,0)\,\Delta t]$$

$$\frac{1}{2} \int p(r(\Delta t, 1) \to r(2\,\Delta t, w))\left(\exp - \int_{\Delta t}^{2\Delta t} r(s)\,ds \right) dw$$

$$+ \frac{1}{2} \int p(r(\Delta t, -1) \to r(2\,\Delta t, w))\left(\exp - \int_{\Delta t}^{2\Delta t} r(s)\,ds \right) dw \quad (6.10)$$

In the middle line the value of $r(s)$ at time Δt, i.e. the lower integration limit, is now equal to $r(\Delta t, 1)$ and, similarly, the value of $r(s)$ at time Δt in the last line is equal to $r(\Delta T, -1)$. Finally, if the integration over dw were carried out numerically using a binomial lattice methodology one would obtain

$$E'_{t=0}\left[\exp - \int_0^{2\,\Delta t} r(s)\,\mathrm{d}s\right] = \exp[-r(0,0)\,\Delta t]$$

$$\{\tfrac{1}{2}[\tfrac{1}{2}\exp[-r(\Delta t,1)\,\Delta t] + \tfrac{1}{2}\exp[-r(\Delta t,1)\,\Delta t]]$$

$$+ \tfrac{1}{2}[\tfrac{1}{2}\exp[-r(\Delta t,1)\,\Delta t] + \tfrac{1}{2}\exp[-r(\Delta t,-1)\,\Delta t]]\}$$

$$= \exp[-r(0,0)\,\Delta t]$$

$$\{\tfrac{1}{2}\exp[-r(\Delta t,1)\,\Delta t] + \tfrac{1}{2}\exp[-r(\Delta t,-1)\,\Delta t]\} \qquad (6.11)$$

Therefore the repeated expectation needed to compute the value at time 0 of a $2\,\Delta t$-maturity bond can be simply approximated in a binomial lattice as

$$P(0,0,2\,\Delta t) = \exp[-r(0,0)\,\Delta t]$$

$$\{\tfrac{1}{2}\exp[-r(\Delta t,1)\,\Delta t] + \tfrac{1}{2}\exp[-r(\Delta t,-1)\,\Delta t]\} \qquad (6.11)$$

Notice that, despite the fact that only *two* terms appear in curly brackets in Equation (6.12), the discounting (see Equation (6.11)) along each of the *three* possible paths has been accounted for. Generalising the observation, one can say that

(i)   **the averaging/discounting procedure from time n back to the tree root actually accounts for discounting along *each* possible path that can occur in the lattice, and the along-the-path discounting is therefore correctly associated with the (discrete counterpart of) the rolled-over money market account; and**

(ii)   **the binomial procedure which leads to Equation (6.6) in effect carries out an n-dimensional integration by using two points for each one-dimensional integration, and by arranging, via recombination, the integration points in such a skilful way that the number of these one-dimensional integrals only grows linearly (rather than exponentially) with the number of time steps.**

Finally, before concluding this preliminary section on binomial lattices, it is worthwhile noticing that, by the way lattice methodologies have been described, the commonly made statement that models like BDT or HL 'do not depend on the market price of risk' should actually be rephrased as 'do not require an *a priori* explicit knowledge of the market price of risk', or, equivalently, 'do not require an *a priori* explicit knowledge of the drift of the short rate'. The tree-fitting procedure described above, in fact, actually endows the unknown (time-dependent) function describing the market price of risk with as many degrees of freedom as there are market discount bonds, and implicitly determines the values of the this function which allow exact pricing of the market bonds.

6.2 IMPLEMENTATION OF LATTICE MODELS: BACKWARD INDUCTION

The 'naive' procedure just described allows the determination of a tree for the short rate such that market discount bonds are exactly priced by construction. As discussed above, the procedure can be shown to be equivalent to determining the change in drift required by Girsanov's theorem if arbitrage is to be avoided: by matching all the market bond prices, one has effectively ensured that all the expectations have been taken with respect to the (*a priori* unknown) correct probability measure implied by the chosen numeraire. As we know, this equivalent measure can only differ from the real-world measure by a drift transformation; and indeed the drift, i.e. the *absolute* position of, for instance, $r(1,1)$ and $r(1,-1)$ (as shown above, their position *relative* to each other is determined by the variance condition), has been determined by the construction outlined above. Notice, incidentally, that no use has been made so far of the result that, when the rolled-up money market account is the numeraire, all assets earn the riskless return over time dt; this result will be the key to the evaluation of the Green's functions necessary to carry out the forward induction (Section 6.3).

Notice also that the drift transformation is a function of the pre-chosen volatility of the short rate (we shall see later on how this degree of freedom can be pinned down). In other words, an identically perfect match to bond prices would have been obtained (by construction) for any exogenous choice of the volatility of the short rate. However, the shape of the yield curve (as determined by the prices of its discount bonds) is a function *both* of expectation of future rates *and* of future volatility (see Section 7.1). Therefore, even if the universe were indeed a one-factor world, driven by a Markovian short rate, the exact matching of the market bond prices cannot tell the user anything about the appropriateness of the chosen volatility, and therefore of the imputed risk-adjusted drift. In other words, the user cannot know, *simply* by virtue of the correct pricing of the market discount bonds, that the 'correct' expectations are implicitly carried out. This point will be revisited in detail in the chapter devoted to the BDT model, where it will be shown that information about, for instance, market cap prices must be brought into play.

For the moment, let us assume that the 'correct' volatility has somehow been guessed, and that, therefore, the expectations of the bond prices have indeed been taken in the appropriate measure. If this is the case, after the tree has been built, the user can evaluate the conditional or unconditional expectation of any payoff occurring at any point in time. It was in fact shown in Chapter 5, Section 4, that the price at time t of any security of known time-T payoff is given by the (risk-neutral) expectation of the discounted payoff, contingent upon the information available at time t. Therefore, for a generic security V of known payoff $V(T)$ at time $T = n \, \Delta t$, one can write

$$V(n - 1, j) = E\left[V(n \, \Delta t)\exp\left[-\int_{(n-1)\Delta t}^{n \, \Delta t} r(s) \, ds\right]\middle| r((n - 1) \, \Delta t) = r(n - 1, j)\right]$$

$$= \exp\left[-\int_{(n-1)\Delta t}^{n \, \Delta t} r(s) \, ds\right] E[V(n \, \Delta t)]$$

$$= \exp[r(n - 1, j) \, \Delta t]\tfrac{1}{2}(V(n, j + 1) + V(n, j - 1)) \qquad (6.13)$$

(Once again, a single argument denotes a quantity in continuous time, and the exponential has been taken out of the expectation sign because at time $(n - 1) \, \Delta t$ it is a known quantity.) Notice that the *expectation* of a *discounted* payoff is actually evaluated, in a binomial tree, by *first* discounting and *then* averaging. The correctness of the procedure stems from the fact that, when taking each conditional expectation, the short rate that determines the one-period discounting is always known in that particular state of the world, and the term $\exp[-r \, \Delta t]$ can therefore always be taken outside the expectation operator.

By repeating the evaluation of these conditional expectations all the way to the root of the tree (i.e. to the state $(0,0)$) as shown in the previous section one finally obtains the value of the security characterised by the known payoff at time T. The procedure just described is often referred to as *backward induction*. The name stems from the fact that it can be seen as the discrete-time equivalent of the backwards Kolmogorov equations, which, for diffusion problems, permit to obtain the original distribution of a particle (i.e. its position at time 0), given its probability distribution at a later time. The counterpart of the procedure would be to derive, starting from an initial Dirac-delta (i.e. perfectly localised) distribution of a rate, or, in other terms, from the knowledge of the short rate today, its distribution at a later time. This is exactly what was accomplished, albeit in a rather cumbersome way, by the procedure described in the previous section when the short-rate construction was extended from time step 1 to time step 2. The equations which allow to accomplish this task are often referred to as *forward* (Fokker–Plank) equations, and their implementation in the context of computational lattices is described in the following section.

For the moment it is important to notice a strength and a weakness of backward induction: to begin with, in each state and at each point in time the user has knowledge of a (conditional) *expectation*. Therefore at each node it is easy to determine whether an early exercise opportunity, which should take place whenever intrinsic value is greater than the residual option value, should be taken advantage of or not. Backward induction is therefore ideally suited to tackle the case of American options. By the same token compound options (i.e.

options on options, as found, for instance in the case of captions) can be very easily accommodated. As pointed out before, the backward-induction procedure is after all equivalent to the evaluation, for an n-step tree, **of an n-dimensional integral**, where each conditional integration is carried out by using only two (very carefully chosen) points.

On the other hand backward induction can but poorly handle the case of path-dependent options (Section 8.1 mentions how this shortcoming can, to a certain extent, be circumvented, at least for suitably benign cases.) The problem clearly stems from the fact that, when evaluating a conditional expectation at time i and state j, the user has full information about what happened at later times (i.e. for times greater than i), but cannot say how that particular state of the world 'has been reached': a variety of paths, along which payoff-dependent conditions might have occurred, will in general converge at any given node (i,j) from the tree root at $(0,0)$. For these situations, Monte Carlo techniques, notoriously cumbersome to tackle American options, come to the fore.

6.3 IMPLEMENTATION OF LATTICE MODELS: FORWARD INDUCTION

It is apparent, from the 'naive' presentation given in Section 6.1, that fitting further time slices of the interest-rate tree as suggested above entails traversing the same portions of the lattice over and over again. But, thanks to the no-arbitrage conditions obtained in Chapter 5, there is a way to avoid this duplication of labour. As shown before, in fact, in the measure associated with the rolled-up money market account all assets, and hence discount bonds, earn the short rate over a time step Δt. To see how this can be of assistance in the construction of the tree, let us define $G(i, j, s, t)$ as the value at time j and state i of a security paying £1 in state s and time t $(t > j)$. These quantities are known in financial literature as Arrow–Debreu prices (see, e.g., Jamshidian (1991)), and bear an obvious discrete-time similarity to the Green's functions of physics, which describe the response to the unit (Dirac-delta) stimulus for linear systems. A special case of these Arrow–Debreu prices is today's value of a security paying £1 at (s,t), i.e. if state s at time t is reached, and zero otherwise. This security will be denoted in the following by $G(0,0,s,t)$. Notice that the assumption of market completeness in Section 4.5 ensures the possibility of actually constructing these single-payoff securities by linear combinations of traded assets. Given this assumed market completeness and absence of arbitrage, the price today, $V(0,t)$, of a generic security whose payoff £$v(s,t)$ only depends on the state attained at a given time t must be given by

$$V(0,t) = \sum_s G(0,0,s,t)v(s,t) \tag{6.14}$$

In particular, for a discount bond maturing at time T, Equation (6.14) must reduce to

$$P(0,T) = \Sigma_s \, G(0,0,s,T) \qquad (6.14')$$

Therefore, **knowledge of the Arrow–Debreu prices completely determines the value of a discount bond**.

The first task of this section is to show that, in the computational trees so far considered, knowledge of the Green's function for all states at time t, $G(0,0,(.),t)$, immediately determines the value of the Green's function for all states at the next time step, $G(0,0,(.),t+\Delta t)$. To this effect, one makes use of the fact that, for the chosen numeraire, *all* assets earn the short rate over time Δt. The argument then proceeds as follows. If one knew, at time t and in state $j-1$, the Green's function $G(0,0,j-1,t)$ and, in the same time-state node, the value of one pound paid at time $t+\Delta t$ in state j, i.e. $G(j-1,t,j,t+\Delta t)$, one would immediately know how to calculate the value today of this certain pound, i.e. $G(0,0,j,t+\Delta t)$: by the very definition of Green's functions it would be given by $G(0,0,j-1,t)G(j-1,t,j,t+\Delta t)$. But $G(j-1,t,j,t+\Delta t)$ is simply equal to $\frac{1}{2}[\exp[-r(j-1,t)\,\Delta t]]$ (see Figure 6.2), and $G(0,0,j-1,t)$ is already known from the already fitted tree (i.e. from the previous step of the forward-induction procedure). On the other hand, in a binomial tree, the only non-zero elements of $G(k,t,j,t+\Delta t)$ are those corresponding to $k=j-1$ (the case just analysed) and $k=j+1$ (for which similar reasoning applies). Therefore from Figure 6.2 it is easy to see that the price of a security paying £1 in state j at time $t+\Delta t$ and £0 everywhere else is given by

$$
\begin{aligned}
G(0,0,j,t+\Delta t) = &\tfrac{1}{2}(0+1)\exp[-r(j+1,t)\,\Delta t]G(0,0,j+1,t) \\
&+ \tfrac{1}{2}(1+0)\exp[-r(j-1,t)\,\Delta t]G(0,0,j-1,t) \qquad (6.15)
\end{aligned}
$$

Therefore, **knowledge of the Arrow–Debreu prices and of the short rates at time t completely determines all the Arrow–Debreu prices at time $t+\Delta t$**.

Furthermore, as shown in Section 6.1, all rates at time t are a unique function, via the volatility, of a *single* value of the short rate (see Equations (6.2) and (6.2')). Therefore, by virtue of Equation (6.8) not only can one express a model price of a bond maturing at time $n\,\Delta t$ as a function of a single unknown rate (say, $r(n,-n)$, as shown before), but the traversing of already fitted portions of the lattice can be avoided by simple multiplication by the appropriate (already calculated) Green's functions. (To get the whole procedure started one puts $G(0,0,0,0)=1$, since the value £1 today is, of course, just £1.) **The computational savings afforded by this technique reduce the number of operations from $O(N^3)$ to $O(N^2)$.**

This apparently 'merely' technical advantage can actually make the

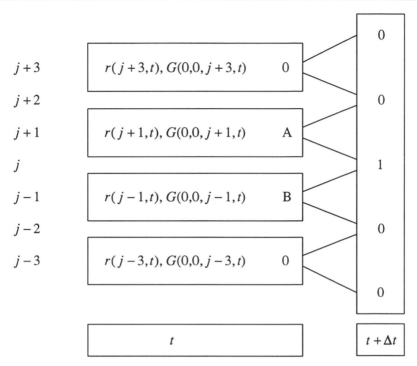

Figure 6.2 The Green's function $G(0,0,j,t+\Delta t)$ is given by the sum of A $G(0,0,j+1,t)$ and B $G(0,0,j-1,t)$; A and B are given by $\frac{1}{2}(0+1)$ $\exp[-r(j+1,t)\,\Delta t]$ and $\frac{1}{2}(1+0)$ $\exp[-r(j-1,t)\,\Delta t]$, respectively; $G(0,0,j+1,t)$ and $G(0,0,j-1,t)$ are known.

difference between being able to use a computational lattice in real trading situations and having to use it as an interesting but hopelessly cumbersome research tool.

The present chapter has therefore shown that the intuitively appealing lattice methodologies can be fully justified as numerical procedures which carry out the repeated expectations needed to evaluate the price of any security in the correct measure. Furthermore, it has been shown that the backward induction procedure is a particularly efficient integration method since an n-dimensional multiple integral is evaluated using $O(n)$ one-dimensional integrations. Finally, the simplicity of the forward tree construction has been illustrated by introducing the Arrow–Debreu prices, i.e. the financial equivalent of physics' Green's functions.

These features should be kept in mind while comparing lattice methodologies with the PDE and Monte Carlo approaches described in the next two chapters.

ENDNOTE

1. Extension to several factors is conceptually straightforward; it must kept in mind, however, that the computational cost grows with the power of the number of factors, thereby making more than two- or three-factor models of virtually impossible implementation. This well-known drawback of lattice methodologies (and of finite-differences schemes) is often referred to as 'the curse of dimensionality'.

7

The partial differential equation (PDE) approach

7.1 THE UNDERLYING PARABOLIC EQUATION AND THE CALIBRATION ISSUES

It was shown in Chapter 4 (Section 10) that, associated with any Brownian process, there exists a parabolic (diffusion) partial differential equation (PDE). If this result is coupled with the no-arbitrage constraints outlined in Section 6.5, one obtains, for the simple case of the driving factor being the short rate[1], an equation of the form

$$\frac{\partial V(r,t,T)}{\partial r}\mu_r + \frac{\partial V(r,t,T)}{\partial t} + \frac{1}{2}\frac{\partial^2 V(r,t,T)}{\partial r^2}\sigma_r^2$$

$$= rV(r,t,T) - \lambda(r,t)\sigma_r\frac{\partial V(r,t,T)}{\partial r} \tag{7.1}$$

where $V(r,t,T)$ is the price of any traded asset (allowed, in general, to depend on the state variable(s), calendar time and a maturity or expiry time), $\lambda(r,t)$ is the market price of risk (which, as seen before, can be a function of calendar time and of the state variable(s) but not of the specific instrument V), and μ_r and σ_r indicate the drift and the standard deviation per unit time of the short rate, respectively.

Historically the PDE approach has been the first line of attack to solve the problem of the valuation of interest-rate options: as early as 1977 Vasicek (1977) introduced a normal mean-reverting model, followed by CIR's square-root-volatility process for the mean-reverting rate (Cox, Ingersoll and Ross (1985), see Chapter 9), and Brennan and Schwartz's two-factor model (Brennan and Schwartz (1982), see Chapter 13). Lately the approach has enjoyed a renewed interest due to the LS model (Longstaff and Schwartz

(1992)), and to the HW Extended Vasicek approach (Hull and White (1990a)), reviewed in Chapters 12 and 11, respectively.

Equation (7.1) is the same for any instrument and for any one-factor model. Different solutions arise from (i) different initial and boundary conditions which uniquely characterise different securities (e.g. for discount bonds the condition $P(T,T) = 1$ must hold); and (ii) from concrete model specifications, as embodied in the functional form for the dependence on time and on the state variable of the drift, the market price of risk and the variance. Normally this dependence is given in parametric form, i.e. by specifying a particular functional form, and by allowing for n parameters $\{\alpha_n\}$ (with n ranging from a few to about a dozen). For suitably simple (and expedient) specifications of the functional forms for the market price of risk, for the drift and for the variance, and for straightforward boundary conditions (e.g. discount bond or simple calls) analytic solutions can sometimes be found. Even in these few cases nothing more complicated than an American option will force upon the user the need for numerical solutions.

It is important to stress that Equation (7.1) holds true in the 'real-world' measure; therefore the drift that appears in it is not risk-neutrally or forward-neutrally adjusted, but is the drift in theory observable in the real world. This observation has rather far-reaching consequences: it is in general true, in fact, that the common feature of these models is that the set of parameters $\{\alpha_i\}$ (e.g. reversion speed, reversion level, volatility, etc.), which describes the 'real-world' process for the short rate, enter the PDE for an interest-rate-dependent instrument *together* with the market price of risk. The solutions of the accompanying PDEs will therefore contain coefficients which are combinations of the real-world quantities *and* the market price of risk. Therefore, estimating the $\{\alpha_i\}$ from time-series analysis of rates observed in the 'real-world' measure is not sufficient in order to determine the coefficients of the PDE, and access is needed to market instruments (e.g. bonds) which price the risk connected with the variability of the underlying factor(s).

Two routes therefore remain open: one can first undertake a time-series estimate, using market data, of the 'real world' parameters $\{\alpha_i\}$ that best account for the available historical data. Thereafter, one can obtain an estimate of the market price of risk by cross-sectional best fit to the observed prices of, say, bonds on a given day.

Alternatively, one can dispense with the time-series analysis altogether, and attempt to determine the non-linear *combinations* of the $\{\alpha_i\}$ and of the market price of risk that cross-sectionally best account for the observed bond prices. (The latter approach bears clear conceptual similarities with the procedure of obtaining the 'implied' volatility when using the Black and Scholes formula.)

The price to be paid if the first route is followed is that, in general, the market prices of traded instruments will not be exactly recovered. The second approach, however, is not without its own dangers. These can be seen as follows. Since a discount bond price is given by the expectation of the discounted maturity payoff,

$$P(t,T) = E_t'\left[\exp\left[-\int_t^T r(u)\,du\right]\right]$$

and since the discounting function is non-linear in the short rate, in general **the yield of a T-maturity bond will depend not only on expectations of the future rates but also on future volatility.** The implications of this can be intuitively appreciated with a simple numerical example: let us consider two universes, one with a volatility for the short rate of 5%, and one with a volatility of 30%. Let us also assume that, in both these worlds, the trading intervals are 1 year ($\Delta t = 1$), and that the only traded instruments are one- and two-year discount bonds. The yield curve is therefore fully described by the prices of these two discount bonds, which are assumed to be the same in universe 1 and 2 ($P(0,1) = 0.90909$ and $P(0,2) = 0.82644$). In order to obtain some numerical values, let us further make some assumptions regarding the distribution of the short rate (e.g. log-normal). Employing the procedure described in Chapter 6, and after imposing equal probabilities for an 'up' and a 'down' jump we can therefore obtain the elementary tree depicted in Figure 7.1. By construction, both universes have the same term structure, but one can easily calculate that the expectation of the short rate after 1 year is different for the 5% and the 30% volatility cases, and equal to 10.002% and 10.078%, respectively.

This clearly shows that, as stated above, both volatility and expectations of

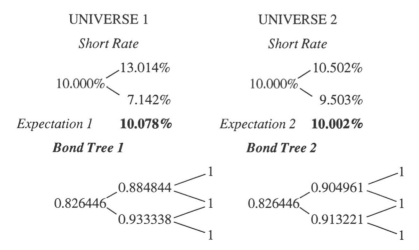

Figure 7.1 Expectations of the short rate after one year for two worlds with the same term structure but different volatilities (see text for details).

future rates contribute to the shape of the yield curve, and that an infinity of possible combinations of these two 'ingredients' can account for an observed term structure of rates. This very important observation will be revisited in later chapters (see, in particular, Chapter 9 and Chapter 12). For the moment it will be sufficient to notice that, if the model were correctly specified and the 'market noise' not too severe it would, of course, be immaterial whether the 'historical' or the 'implied' route were followed. In practice, however, attempting an exclusively cross-sectional estimate of the PDE coefficients has inherent dangers: if the deterministic part of the short-rate process is too simple to allow for complex patterns of expectations of rates, an inordinate burden would be put on the shoulders of the volatility component in order to attempt to recover the observed term structure. Humped yield curves have been known to create problems with simple approaches such as CIR or Vasicek. But it should always be remembered that even 'rich' models which allow for more complex yield-curve shapes can give no guarantee that the correct apportioning will be accomplished by a cross-sectional procedure between yield-curve curvature arising from rate expectations and from future yield volatility.

In order to gain confidence about the reliability of the coefficients, a time-series inspection of their daily cross-sectional estimates is often very useful. Due to the fact the $\{a_i\}$ are often estimated in conjunction with the *a priori* unknown market price of risk, it can be difficult to say anything very precise from the numerical values themselves, but such tell-tale indications as wildly fluctuating estimates over consecutive days can often point to a mis-specified or mis-estimated model.

Needless to say, the features just highlighted are *not* logically connected with PDE approaches, but apply to any model. In practice, however, the cross-sectional estimation of the parameters (and sometimes of the unobservable state variables) tends to be associated for practical reasons with the PDE approach rather than with tree-based methodologies. These caveats, which will be explored at greater length in the context of the discussion of specific models, are therefore well worth bearing in mind before attempting any analytic or numerical solution to equations such as (7.1) above, which mix 'real-world' (i.e. econometrically accessible) parameters with the non-directly observable market price of risk.

Once reasonable confidence has been obtained in the robustness of the parameterisation, if the functional form of the factor's process gives rise to a PDE which admits a closed-form solution for the required boundary conditions, the computational advantages are obvious. Less obvious, but just as important, is that considerable computational savings can be accomplished with closed-form models even if numerical methods, such as finite differences, have to be employed, as it might be the case, for instance, if one wanted to check for early exercise opportunities: since at each node both the coefficients and the state variables are known, all quantities, in fact, such as swap rates, which can be expressed as a function of linear combinations of discount bonds (see Chapter 1), can be evaluated analytically on a node-by-node basis. This can be contrasted with non-analytic models, where, in order to obtain, say, a swap rate at time i and state j, the values in that state of the world have to be *numerically* obtained for all the discount bonds needed for the evaluation of the swap rate itself.

The preferred procedures for the numerical integration of PDEs have tended to be linked to finite-differences schemes, either in the implicit (IFD)) or the explicit (EFD) formulation. These are therefore reviewed in the following sections.

7.2 FINITE-DIFFERENCES (FD) APPROXIMATIONS TO PARABOLIC PDEs

The starting point for the following discussion will be a parabolic partial differential equation of the form:

$$\frac{\partial V}{\partial t} + \frac{1}{2}\sum_i\sum_j \frac{\partial^2 V}{\partial x_i \partial x_j}\sigma_i\sigma_j\rho_{ij} + \sum_i \frac{\partial V}{\partial x_i}\mu_i = a\,V \qquad (7.2)$$

where $V = V(t, x_1, x_2, \ldots, x_n)$ represents the value of a contingent claim, function of time and of n stochastic state variables (Wiener processes) $\{x_i\}$, $\mu_i(x_i, t)$ are the drifts of the n variables, $\sigma_i(x_i, t)$ their standard deviations per unit time, and ρ_{ij} the correlation between process i and process j. Qualitatively, the second term represents a *diffusive* component, which gives rise to the spreading of an initial distribution, and the third term describes an *advective* component, which is responsible for a 'translation' of the solution function over time. For the sake of simplicity the first part of the discussion will deal with a single driving variable, x, often referred to as the 'space variable'. The forward (Fokker-Plank) and backward (Kolmogorov) equations are two special cases of Equation (7.2) above. The former describes how an initial distribution for V evolves forward in time (often starting from a Dirac-delta distribution at the origin): it is the equation implicitly used, in its finite-time counterpart, when forward fitting a tree (see Chapter 6, Section 3). The latter brings back a terminal distribution at time T to an earlier time t (possibly 0): it is the equation implicitly used in a tree when backward discounting cash flows to earlier time steps (Chapter 6, Section 2). The rest of the discussion will be mainly focused on the backward (Kolmogorov) equation.

A backward parabolic PDE must be supplemented by *initial conditions*, which, despite the somewhat deceptive name, describe the value of the variable V at the *final* time T; and by *boundary conditions*, which prescribe how the function V, or its derivatives, behave at the necessarily finite integration boundaries of the grid of the space variable, more precisely described later on.

Nothing specific has been said about the drift and volatility functions μ and σ, such as their absolute or percentage character. It is useful to effect, whenever possible, such transformations (for instance the well-known logarithmic transformation discussed in the following) that reduce the equation above to having coefficients independent of the state variables (see, e.g., Hull and White (1990b)).

In general, FD approaches, whether implicit or explicit, can be most profitably seen as an attempt to discretise the continuous-time partial differential equations that govern a particular phenomenon by substituting finite differences for partial derivatives. These finite-time approximations are by no means unique, since, as explained further on, the partial derivatives of interest can be substituted for in the computational scheme by time-centred or time-forward differences, by space-centred and space-forward differences, and by various combinations thereof. Superficially minor differences in how these approximations are implemented (moving, for instance, from a space-centred to a space-forward differencing scheme) can determine the success (stability) or failure (instability) of the whole procedure. Stability, in turn, is determined by the convergence properties of a given scheme. Explicit criteria whose fulfilment give necessary and/or sufficient conditions for stability abound in the PDE literature. Given the vastness of the topic, that could well warrant a book in its own right, only the most common and relevant stability conditions for the specific parabolic PDEs encountered for interest-rate options will be treated in the following.

To make the discussion more concrete, let us first of all restrict the analysis to the one-dimensional case and define an integration mesh, with calendar time on the horizontal axis, sampled from today (time 0) to the final expiry of the option (time T) at N points, spaced by an interval $T/N = \Delta t$. The state variable driving the yield curve (typically the short rate) will then be sampled at $(2m + 1)$ points (from $-m$ to m), spaced by Δx, and arranged on the vertical axis, for each time observation point. (Since much of the work on FD schemes is borrowed from physics-related literature, where the corresponding parabolic PDEs describe the heat diffusion equation, the variable x is often referred to as the 'space' coordinate.) Notice that, while the choice of the range of the time variable is totally unambiguous, [0 T], an *a priori* choice must be made about which values of the state variables are too high or too low to be of interest: more precisely, whenever the space (short-rate) variable assumes values such that the option of interest is too deeply in- or out-of-the-money, the PDE collapses to an easy-to-guess solution, which can be substituted for, as shown more precisely later on, on the upper and lower boundaries of the mesh.

Before considering the different schemes in any detail, it is necessary to distinguish between *initial* and *boundary* conditions. As mentioned before, despite the name the former are applied at the *final* time slice, i.e. for each node of the mesh at time T. For the case of a simple discount bond, for instance, the initial conditions would have the form $V(x_0 + i \, \Delta x, N \, \Delta t) = 1$, $i = -m,m$, where V denotes the value function, sampled discretely at $2m + 1$ points, and x_0 is the 'centre' value of the space (rate) variable in the finite mesh. Since, for a given mesh, each point is uniquely determined by two integers i and j along each axis, the value function V will often be denoted by $V(i,j)$, with the first index representing the space, and the second the time coordinate, respectively.

As explained below, values of the function at time $k \, \Delta t$ are obtained by backward induction from the 'neighbouring' values of the function at time $(k + 1) \, \Delta t$. (See Figure 7.2.)

This creates problems for the upper and lower values of the function for any time smaller than T, i.e. for $V(\pm m, k) \; \forall k < N$, since they would depend on values at $\pm(m + 1)$ not sampled by the mesh. The practice is therefore common to substitute directly for $V(\pm m, k)$ values coming from one's specific knowledge of the security being priced. For the case of a call option, for instance, for the very deeply in-the-money region the ratio of time value to intrinsic value is

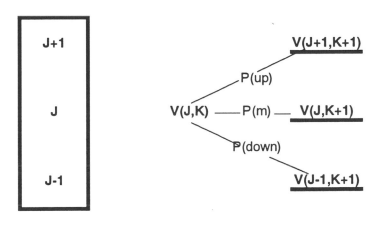

Figure 7.2 Explicit finite differences: the values $V(j,k+1)$, $V(j+1,k+1)$ and $V(j-1,k+1)$ at time $(k+1)$ linked by Equation (7.11) to the value $V(j,k)$ at time k, and the probabilistic interpretation of the procedure. The values underlined have already been calculated when updating the value $V(j,k)$ at time k.

very small; therefore substituting for $V(m,k)$ intrinsic value would entail a very small error. In this region, therefore, the first derivative (delta) is virtually linear, and the curvature (gamma) almost zero; these values can also be directly substituted in the FD scheme. Conversely, for the same case of a call, little error would be incurred by neglecting altogether the very small time value that deeply out-of-the-money options possess, i.e. by setting $V(-m,k)$, as well as the first and the second derivatives, to zero. The validity of these approximations clearly depends on the size of the mesh, and on the spacings Δt and Δx. Unfortunately, for many FD schemes these two quantities are not independent if stability is to be achieved, and, as explored later on, this can have important computational consequences.

Finally, while, for simplicity, the space variable has so far been associated with the short rate, it is actually more common to work on a suitable transformation of the short rate itself, so chosen as to make its variance stationary, or at least independent of the state variable. The simplest such transformation is $x = \ln(r)$, which turns the absolute volatility for the short rate σr into the absolute volatility for the logarithm σ. Hull and White (1990b) suggest general strategies in order to accomplish this transformation. In the following, unless explicitly stated, it will always be assumed that this transformation has been carried out, following the general methodology outlined at the beginning of the next section.

7.3 THE EXPLICIT FINITE-DIFFERENCES SCHEME

The parabolic PD equation obeyed, in the real world, by the price of a generic security V for the case of a single lognormal driving factor (the short rate) is given by

$$\frac{\partial V}{\partial t} + \frac{1}{2} \frac{\partial^2 V}{\partial r^2} \sigma^2 r^2 + \frac{\partial V}{\partial r} (\mu_r - \lambda \sigma) = r V \qquad (7.3)$$

for a SDE for the short rate of the form

$$dr = \mu(r,t) r \, dt + \sigma(r,t) r \, dz \qquad (7.4)$$

In general, given the heteroskedastic nature of process (7.4), a new variable $\phi = \phi(r,t)$ is sought, displaying stationary volatility. By applying Ito's lemma

$$d\phi = \mu_\phi \, dt + \sigma r \frac{\partial \phi}{\partial r} \, dz \qquad (7.5)$$

with

$$
\mu_\phi = \frac{\partial \phi}{\partial t} + \mu_r r \frac{\partial \phi}{\partial r} + \frac{1}{2} \frac{\partial^2 \phi}{\partial r^2} r^2 \sigma^2
$$

For the sought transformation $\sigma r \, \partial\phi/\partial r$ should be a constant (or, at least, should not depend on the state variable). For the simple case when $\sigma(r,t) = \sigma(t)$ (independent of r), it is easy to see that the transformation $\phi = \ln(r)$ ($\partial\phi/\partial r = 1/r$) indeed gives the desired constant coefficient to the stochastic component of the process, and the PDE above simply becomes

$$
\frac{\partial V}{\partial t} + \frac{1}{2} \frac{\partial^2 \phi}{\partial \phi^2} \sigma^2 + \frac{\partial V}{\partial \phi} (\mu_\phi - \lambda\sigma) = r\, V
$$

$$
\equiv \frac{\partial V}{\partial t} + \frac{\partial^2 V}{\partial \phi^2} a^2 + \frac{\partial V}{\partial \phi} b = r\, V \tag{7.6}
$$

The grid construction referred to above can then be repeated for the variable ϕ instead of r. With reference to the mesh depicted in Figure 7.2 one can then approximate the time derivative by the *time-forward* approximation

$$
\left.\frac{\partial V}{\partial t}\right|_{t=i\Delta t,\, \phi=\phi_0+j\Delta\phi} = \left.\frac{\partial V}{\partial t}\right|_{i,j} \cong \frac{V(i+1,j) - V(i,j)}{\Delta t} \tag{7.7}
$$

As for the space derivatives, in the explicit FD scheme (EFD) they can be approximated by

$$
\left.\frac{\partial V}{\partial \phi}\right|_{i,j} \cong \frac{V(i+1,j+1) - V(i+1,j-1)}{2\Delta\phi} \quad \textbf{EFD} \tag{7.8}
$$

$$
\left.\frac{\partial^2 V}{\partial \phi^2}\right|_{i,j} \cong \frac{V(i+1,j+1) - V(i+1,j-1) - 2V(i+1,j)}{\Delta\phi^2} \tag{7.9}
$$

while for the implicit FD (IFD) scheme they are approximated by

$$
\left.\frac{\partial V}{\partial \phi}\right|_{i,j} \cong \frac{V(i,j+1) - V(i,j-1)}{2\Delta\phi} \quad \textbf{IFD} \tag{7.8'}
$$

$$
\left.\frac{\partial^2 V}{\partial \phi^2}\right|_{i,j} \cong \frac{V(i,j+1) + V(i,j-1) - 2V(i,j)}{\Delta\phi^2} \tag{7.9'}
$$

Notice that all the values at time $i+1$ are known at time i, either from the initial conditions if $i+1 = N$, or from the previously updated time slice if

$i + 1 < N$. Therefore for the EFD case the only unknown quantity at time i is exactly the quantity $V(i,j)$ being updated, which appears in the time derivative. One can therefore rewrite Equation (7.6) as

$$\frac{V(i+1,j) - V(i,j)}{\Delta t} + \frac{a}{\Delta\phi^2}[V(i+1,j+1) + V(i+1,j-1) - 2V(i+1,j)]$$

$$+ \frac{b}{2\Delta\phi}[V(i+1,j+1) - V(i+1,j-1)] = r\,V(i,j) \qquad (7.10)$$

with a and b implicitly defined by Equation (7.6). After collecting terms in $V(i,j)$, $V(i+1,j)$, $V(i+1,j+1)$ and $V(i+1,j-1)$, Equation (7.10) can be rewritten as

$$V(i,j) = \frac{1}{1+r\Delta t}\left[V(i+1,j+1)\left(\frac{a\Delta t}{\Delta\phi^2} + \frac{b\Delta t}{\Delta\phi}\right)\right.$$

$$\left. + V(i+1,j-1)\left(\frac{a\Delta t}{\Delta\phi^2} - \frac{b\Delta t}{\Delta\phi}\right) + V(i+1,j)\left(1 - \frac{2a\Delta t}{\Delta\phi^2}\right)\right]$$

$$\equiv \frac{1}{1+r\Delta t}[V(i+1,j+1)p_{\text{up}} + V(i+1,j-1)p_{\text{down}} + V(i+1,j)p_{\text{m}}]$$

$$(7.11)$$

where the coefficients p_{up}, p_{m} and p_{down} have been defined to be

$$p_{\text{up}} = \frac{1}{1+r\Delta t}\left(\frac{a\Delta t}{\Delta\phi^2} + \frac{b\Delta t}{\Delta\phi}\right) \qquad (7.11')$$

$$p_{\text{m}} = \frac{1}{1+r\Delta t}\left(1 - \frac{2a\Delta t}{\Delta\phi^2}\right) \qquad (7.11'')$$

$$p_{\text{down}} = \frac{1}{1+r\Delta t}\left(\frac{a\Delta t}{\Delta\phi^2} - \frac{b\Delta t}{\Delta\phi}\right) \qquad (7.11''')$$

respectively. From a technical point of view one can notice that, for the chosen transformation, the coefficients p_{up}, p_{m} and p_{down} are independent of the state variable ϕ and can therefore be calculated once and for all, rather than 'on the fly' during the backward induction process. But it is conceptually more important to notice that the choice of the symbols p_{up}, p_{m} and p_{down} for these three coefficients, clearly suggestive of a probabilistic interpretation, was not without a certain degree of foresight, since one can immediately verify that it is always true that

$$p_{up} + p_m + p_{down} = 1 \qquad (7.12)$$

If, furthermore, p_{up}, p_m and p_{down} are all positive, then the interpretation of these coefficients as (risk-adjusted) 'probabilities' of moving to an up, middling or down state is warranted. In addition, if one compares two binomial moves on a binomial lattice with a single trinomial move on a FD mesh, one can immediately notice the fundamental similarity between the two approaches (see Figure 7.3.)

An approach like the one described in the chapter devoted to lattice methodologies, and routinely implemented for models like BDT, is in fact tantamount to prescribing *a priori* the probabilities, and achieving the matching of the moments by moving the grid coordinates; a finite-differences scheme, on the other hand, pre-assigns these coordinates and strives to find the probabilities that ensure the matching of the moments.

Furthermore, one can prove (Ames (1977)) that **sufficient condition for convergence of the EFD scheme is that all the coefficients (i.e. 'probabilities')** p_{up}, p_m and p_{down} **should simultaneously be positive.** The intuition behind this requirement is quite easy to grasp: Equation (7.11) implicitly enforces the matching of the first two moments (conditional expectation and variance) of the quantity V. Whenever the expectation lies outside the range $[V(i+1,j-1)V(i+1,j+1)]$, no positive choice for all the 'probabilities' can produce $E[V] = p_{up}V_{up} + p_m V_m + p_{down}V_{down}$ (the notation $V_{up,m,down}$ should be self-evident). In other terms, **the EFD scheme will break**

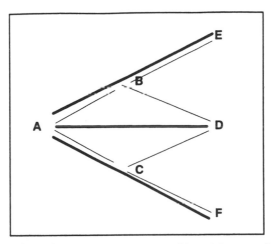

Figure 7.3 The similarity between two steps in a binomial tree, which reach from A the three points E, D and F, and a single backward move in the EFD method, which links E, D and F with A.

down exactly when its mapping onto a trinomial recombining lattice fails to be possible. It is also clear from this discussion what the 'dangerous' situations are: since the mesh is fixed *a priori*, with each time slice carrying space coordinates exactly at the same levels, the expectation condition will fail to be satisfied whenever the growth of V over one time step is too large, thus bringing the expectation above or below the highest or lowest grid point (respectively) in the time slice 'in front'. Binomial or trinomial trees are free from this problem, since the locations of the space coordinates for each time slice is determined in the forward induction procedure on a time-slice-by-time-slice basis by the location of the 'tree-bottom' so as to ensure appropriate centring. Within the context of EFD schemes, in high-drift environments (e.g. steep yield curves) one must therefore either resort to shorter time steps (so as to limit the growth over Δt) or to wider space steps (so as to capture the expectation). Needless to say the first remedy increases the computational burden, while the second makes the resolution coarser. Similar restrictions apply for the variance: the largest possible standard deviation for the three value V_{up}, V_m and V_{down} achievable by varying p_{up}, p_m and p_{down} is $\frac{1}{2}[V_{up} - V_{down}]$ (this corresponds to the degenerate choice of $p_{up} = p_m = 1/2$ and $p_{down} = 0$). If $(\frac{1}{2}[V_{up} - V_{down}])^2 \Delta t$ is smaller than the variance over the time step Δt, the matching of the second moment is also impossible.

A more precise analysis along this line of reasoning shows that the requirements for stability are

$$\mu_\phi < \frac{\sigma^2}{\Delta \phi} \tag{7.13}$$

$$\sigma_\phi < \frac{\Delta \phi^2}{\Delta t} \tag{7.13'}$$

An alternative solution to this problem has been put forward by Hull and White (1990a) who recommend to branch from node (i,j) to the three nodes $(i+1, k+1)$, $(i+1,k)$, $(i+1,k-1)$, where k is an integer, possibly different from j, so chosen as to ensure that the expectation falls within the sampled values. The procedure is discussed in greater detail in the chapter devoted to the HW model.

Little has been said so far about the treatment of the values $V(i \pm m)$, apart from the recommendation to substitute on the edges of the mesh values derived from one's *a priori* knowledge of the option payoffs in limiting cases. After the discussion above, however, it should be intuitively clear that the procedure will be successful as long as the approximated values do not 'contaminate' values in earlier time slices for space coordinates closer and closer to the centre of the mesh. This, in turn, will depend crucially on the speed of propagation of 'information' implied by the PDE and on the $\Delta t / \Delta \phi$ ratio of the mesh. Again, high variances and large drifts will make the treatment of boundary conditions more delicate.

7.4 THE IMPLICIT FINITE-DIFFERENCES SCHEME

As mentioned above the 'only' difference between explicit and implicit FD approaches is the replacement of space-forward with space-centred derivatives. See Equations (7.8) and (7.9) and Figure 7.4

This apparent minor variation makes a big difference, since three unknown values ($V(i,j+1)$, $V(i,j)$ and $V(i,j-1)$) now appear in the equation for $V(i,j)$. Since $V(i,j)$ will in turn appear in the equations for $V(i,j+1)$ and $V(i,j-1)$, the above choice for the space derivatives gives rise to a tri-diagonal system of equations. Its solution, working one's way from one end upwards, is *per se* trivial, but unfortunately the intuitively appealing correspondence with a tri-nomial branching process characterised by 'transition probabilities' is lost. On the other hand, it can be shown that the IFD scheme is unconditionally stable for any choice of Δt and $\Delta \phi$, and can therefore compete in flexibility with the modified-branching EFD procedure. Its main appeal, however, is linked to the fact that, for *two* space variables (see, e.g., the Brennan and Schwartz model) one of the most powerful numerical schemes is the Hopscotch method, which

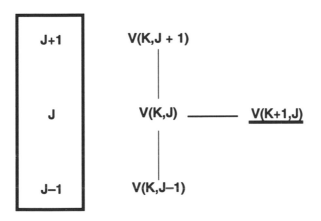

Figure 7.4 Implicit finite differences: updating the value $V(k,j)$ requires knowledge of $V(k,j+1)$, $V(k,j-1)$ and $V(k+1,j)$. Only the value underlined has already been calculated when updating the value $V(k,j)$ at time k.

consists of using an alternation of implicit and explicit procedures for successive time slices (Gourlay and McKee (1977)). Already for as few as two-dimensions, FD schemes require a somewhat careful numerical implementation, especially in so far as handling of the boundary conditions is concerned. Probably for three, and certainly for more driving factors, Monte Carlo approaches, reviewed in the next chapter, provide a more efficient way of obtaining option prices.

ENDNOTE

1. Extensions to the case where there are several driving factors are conceptually straightforward, and follow exactly the same conceptual lines outlined in Section 5.1.

8

Monte Carlo approaches

8.1 INTRODUCTION

It was pointed out in the introductory section that a large number of actively traded OTC interest-rate options display path-dependent features in their payoffs. Recently Hull and White (1993b) have shown that there exists a whole class of derivative products whose value can be efficiently calculated within the framework of any recombining tree methodology. There are some important restrictions to the validity of their approach, some of technical, and some of fundamental nature; to begin with the latter, in order for the approach to be computationally viable it is essential that the value at time $t + \Delta t$ of the path function, $F(t + \Delta t)$, which determines the payoff should be computable from the value of the path function itself at time t, $F(t)$, and of the state variable(s). An example of such a function could, for instance, be the average of (a function of) the state variable(s), since knowledge of the value of this average up to time t and of the possible realisations of the state variable(s) over the next time steps clearly specify in a unique way the possible values of the average.

In addition, for practical computational reasons, at most one path function can be considered: an average-rate index-amortising cap, for instance, would probably be outside the practical, if not theoretical, reach of the approach.

It is not only these rather esoteric (and, after all, rather rare) options that call for a more general technique than computational lattices can afford: one of the most interesting approaches to option pricing, in fact, is the Heath Jarrow and Morton methodology (Chapter 14), which draws part of its richness from the very fact that the short-rate process is, in general, non-Markovian (see Chapter 16). Special cases of the HJM approach do exist, in which this extra complexity can be eliminated, but it can be shown (see Chapters 14 and 16, and Carverhill (1993)) that, by so doing, one is actually implementing a model virtually indistinguishable from the Extended Vasicek (Chapter 10) or the Black Derman and Toy (Chapter 9). For the general, i.e. non-Markovian, Heath

Jarrow and Morton approach the very nature of the path dependency is actually such that it cannot be handled by the Hull and White technique within the framework of *any* recombining tree methodology.

Since the early 1990s, practitioners have therefore turned their attention to non-recombining (bushy) trees, and to the Monte Carlo method. The latter technique, well known and widely used in statistical physics since the 1960s, was introduced into the option area by Boyle (1977); due to its rather unsatisfactory convergence properties, and to its being ill-suited to handle American, and in general compound, options, until recently it has tended to be regarded as a rather inelegant, 'brute force' or last-resort method. The great popularity enjoyed by the HJM approach, coupled with increased computational power, has, however, brought the Monte Carlo technique into the limelight, and given new impetus to research into the so-called variance reduction strategies. The remaining sections of this chapter therefore introduce the method within the context of the pricing and hedging of interest-rate options; indicate how, by using suitable techniques, its estimates can be made substantially more accurate; and show how the method's greatest limitation, i.e. the inability to handle American options, can, to some extent, be overcome.

8.2 THE METHOD

The idea behind the technique is extremely simple, and intuitively appealing. The starting point is a model for the evolution of interest rates as a function of n state variables. The processes for a series of stochastic quantities, $\{X_i(t)\}$, assumed to be driven by n factors, can then be written as

$$dX_i(t) = \mu_i(t,X_i(t)) \, dt + \sum_{k=1,n} \sigma_{ik}(t,X_i(t)) \, dz_k(t) \qquad (8.1)$$

where, as usual, dz_i is a Brownian motion, $(E[dz_i] = 0, \ E[dz_i \, dz_j] = \rho_{ij} \, dt])$ and μ_i and σ_{ik} indicate the drift and volatilities of X_i, respectively. Given the initial values of the quantities X_i (which could be, e.g. forward rates, spot rates or asset prices) at time 0, i.e. given the vector $\{X_i(0)\}$, it was shown in Chapter 4 that, as long as the functions σ_{jk} are 'well behaved', the value at a later time t of the quantities X is given by

$$X(t) = X(0) + \int_{s=0}^{t} \mu_i(s,X_i(s)) \, ds + \int_{s=0}^{t} \sum_{k=1,n} \sigma_{ik}(s,X_i(s)) \, dz_k(s) \qquad (8.2)$$

Notice that the first integral is an 'ordinary' (Riemann) integral over time, but the second is a stochastic (Ito) integral. The whole idea behind the Monte Carlo technique is nothing more than replacing these two integrals by their discrete-time counterparts:

$$\int_{s=0}^{t} \mu_i(s, X_i(s)) \, ds \cong \sum_s \mu_i(t_s, X_i(t_s)) \Delta t_s \tag{8.3}$$

$$\int_{s=0}^{t} \sum_{k=1,n} \sigma_{ik}(s, X_i(s)) \, dz_k(s) \cong \sum_s \sum_{k=1,n} \sigma_{ik}(t_s, X_i(t_s)) \Delta z_k(t_s) \tag{8.4}$$

and therefore to evolve the vector $\{X(0)\}$ through time using the equation

$$X(t_s + \Delta t) = X(t_s) + \mu_i(t_s, X_i(t_s)) \Delta t_s + \sum_{k=1,n} \sigma_{ik}(t_s, X_i(t_s)) \Delta z_k(t_s) \tag{8.5}$$

In Equation (8.5) t_s indicates one of the discrete points in time into which the interval $\{0 - t\}$ has been subdivided, $\sigma_{ik}(t_s, X_i(t_s))$ are the volatility functions evaluated at time t_s, and the Wiener increment $\Delta z_k(t_s)$ is approximated by

$$\Delta z_k(t_s) \cong \varepsilon_k \sqrt{\Delta t} \tag{8.6}$$

where ε indicates a random draw from a standardised (i.e. $N(0,1)$) normal distribution[1]. Notice carefully that specifying that the volatility functions should be evaluated at time t_s is not pedantic: while for ordinary (e.g. Riemann) integrals it is in the limit immaterial which point is chosen within the integration interval Δt_s, stochastic integrals will converge to different values according to how the sampling point is chosen. In particular, two possible, and plausible, choices, i.e. to effect the sampling at t_s or at $(t_s + t_{s+1})/2$, give rise to the Ito and the Stratonovich integrals, respectively. While the latter might have some desirable mathematical properties, that make it more 'similar' to 'ordinary' integrals, it requires foreknowledge of financial quantities at a future point in time. If we require, on the grounds of financial intuition, that $\sigma(t)$ should be a non-anticipating function, then Ito's integral, and its discrete-time counterparts, Equations (8.5) and (8.6), are the correct tools to use.

Evolving the quantities of interest from time 0 to the final payoff time T constitutes one realisation, which, for given functional forms of the drifts and variances, is therefore completely specified by the $T/\Delta t$ Gaussian draws. The terminal value of the state variables and of whatever statistic has been accumulated along the path then allows the evaluation of the time-T payoff. This has to be discounted back to time 0 and, as customary, the discounting procedure must be consistent with the chosen numeraire. As usual, the conceptually crucial part of the calculation is to ensure that the correct terminal distribution is achieved (i.e. that expectations are taken in the correct measure). Since each different way of discounting implies a different measure, the term 'correct' only makes sense once the discounting procedure is specified. In principle, discounting by a discount bond maturing at option payoff could be employed, as long as quantities such as forward rates or prices were assigned the correct (zero) drift. However, the martingale condition only holds for payoffs occurring at the maturity of the discounting bond. Therefore, with this type of discounting no payoff-sensitive manipulations can be accomplished along the path. For instance, the simple case of a knock-out bond option treated in Section 3.2 cannot be implemented using zero drift for the forward rate and discounting by a zero-coupon bond. In other words, those situations where a MC simulation can be implemented with this choice of numeraire and zero drift for the forward rates, offers nothing more than a cumbersome (and expensive) way of performing numerically the integral given analytically for European options by Black's result. If, however, one discounted using the money market account, and used the appropriate (non-zero) drifts for forward rates, any intermediate condition can be imposed along the path. The drawback is that the terminal payoffs must be present valued (*before* averaging) using the specific path followed by the short rate, and that the drifts of the forward rates are not zero.

Needless to say, Monte Carlo being a technique rather than a model, its 'ingredients' (i.e. drifts and variances) must be obtained from the separate choice of a no-arbitrage model. A later section, for instance, will show how to obtain the drift consistent with the BDT model; or, to give a different example, with the HJM approach, also reviewed in the following, the forward rate drifts turn out to be simply related to discount bond variances. In any case, once the desired model has been chosen, specific quantities will have to be evolved over time. If one uses the money market account as numeraire, one knows, in fact, from the results of Section 5.4, that in this measure all *assets* grow with a drift equal to the short rate, $r(t)$, and that forward rates display a non-zero drift. In addition, the money market account will have to be reinvested along each path in order to provide the necessary discount factor. To this effect the process for the short rate must also be known. Equation (10.3') of Section 10.2 or Equations (14.37) and following of Section 14.5 provide the relevant expressions for the BDT and HJM models, respectively. Once the present valuing has been carried out, the option value from each realisation can be accumulated, and the average after N realisations can be taken. This average gives an unbiased estimator of the 'true' option value.

The MC technique therefore is yet another route to perform the numerical integration of the final payoff function times the appropriate probability distribution. In this respect, its similarities with lattice or PDE methodologies (in turn even more closely related) are quite apparent. The methodological differences, however, are the sources of both its strengths and its weaknesses. To begin with, in a binomial lattice methodology the probability of reaching the topmost node after n steps is 0.5^n; for a weekly tree extending out to five years this implies that the topmost path has a probability of occurrence of 5×10^{-79}; in turn, this implies that the highest and lowest values of the short rate sampled by a realistic weekly BDT tree of this maturity can be as high and as low as 10,100% and 0.0060%, respectively, for the example above (GB£

curve, May 1994, 20% vol.). For this same tree the short-rate spacing around the forward rate can be as coarse as 40 basis points. Clearly, a naive log-normal binomial lattice methodology affords a very inefficient procedure to take the expectation of any function likely to vary rapidly around the centre of the distribution, as it is the case, for instance, with barrier options. To compound the problem, if one wants to achieve a finer sampling in rate space, one is forced, within a tree framework, to increase the number of time steps as well, thereby paying a n^2 price, despite the fact that the accuracy of the integration is known to depend mainly on the fineness of the r-space sampling, and not on a high number of time steps.

The MC approach is free from all these problems: time steps can be tailor-made; the sampling of the distribution is finest around the forward rate (or price, as appropriate); each path has the same probability of occurrence of $1/$(no. of realisations). Furthermore, it is known that, if one wanted to tackle a multi-factor model, MC is probably *the* method to perform high-dimensional numerical integrations, since its (not negligible) computational cost grows roughly linearly with the number of driving factors.

These advantages are not without price, at least for 'naive' implementations: to begin with, in order to increase by a factor n the accuracy of the MC estimate, n^2 as many simulations have to be carried out. Furthermore, deltas and gammas are arduous to obtain, since they are numerically obtained as differences of noisy quantities. As for deltas or other statistics, a useful procedure consists of using the same series of random numbers to evaluate the option values for two slightly different initial values of the quantity with respect to which differentiation is sought. By this procedure, biases in each individual realisation should to a large extent cancel when taking the difference between the 'up' and 'down' simulation. It is actually not rare to obtain, for relatively simple problems, deltas more accurate than the prices.

Apart from these 'technical problems' a more fundamental limitation of MC approaches stems from the fact that they are intrinsically ill-suited to tackle American (free-boundary) problems. The reason for these shortcomings are not difficult to understand: as explained in greater detail in Section 8.4, in order to decide at any time t before option expiry whether the intrinsic value of the option at time t is worth more or less than the expectation of its future payoffs, the (probability-weighted) values of not yet realised paths should be available. Unlike the cases of lattices, where the final payoff is evolved towards the root using backward induction (Kolmogorov equations), MC makes use of forward induction (Fokker–Plank equations); the respective strengths and weaknesses of the two approaches in so far as path-dependent and free-boundary problems are concerned exactly stem from what is known about the past and the future at each point in time. Very recently, some attempts have been made to adapt MC techniques to American option problems. A sketchy review of some current lines of thought on the topic is presented in Section 8.4.

Another important restriction on the possible uses of MC procedures for interest-rate options stems from the fact that, in order to compute payoffs along the path, one must be able to recover the relevant swap rates, bond prices, etc., from the values of the evolved quantities. This constitutes no problems for models, like the HJM (Chapter 14) which evolve the full yield curve. If, however, only the drifts and variances of the state variables are explicitly known *a priori*, then one must be able to recover at each time/space point the required quantities from the evolved variables. To give a concrete example, if one is dealing with a one-factor short-rate model, one must be able to recover the yield curve at time t from $r(t)$ and the Brownian draws from 0 to t. This, however, is in general only possible for the so-called affine models (see Chapter 15). The important class of log-normal models, on the other hand, for which analytic results are virtually non-existent, do not lend themselves to an explicit mapping from the short rate to the yield curve. Their implementation in a MC framework is therefore either impossible, or requires rather drastic approximations.

Of these three sources of difficulties—difficulty in handling American options, restriction to the evolution of affine models, and slowness of convergence—the latter has been given the greatest attention and many powerful techniques, generally referred to as variance reducing, have been proposed.

In order to treat in a consistent manner these techniques, let us first denote (Boyle (1977)) by $V(y(T))$ the present value of an option dependent on the realisation at time T of an arbitrary function y of the state variable X (extensions to several variables are conceptually straightforward), and by $h(y,T)$ its (arbitrary) distribution function at time T, only satisfying

$$\int h(y)\,dy = 1 \tag{8.7}$$

Notice that the function y could, in general, depend on all the realisations of the state variable from 0 to T. In order to emphasise this feature, it will often be denoted in the following as $y(X(t))$, $0 \leqslant t \leqslant T$. As for the evolution of X, it is given by an expression like Equation (8.8)

$$X(t_s + \Delta t) = X(t_s) + \mu_i(t_s, X(t_s))\,\Delta t_s + \sum_{k=1,n} \sigma_{ik}(t_s, X(t_s))\,\Delta z_k(t_s) \tag{8.8}$$

Notice that, even if the distribution of the underlying variable X is assumed to be known *a priori*, the user will in general not know the final distribution of the complex (usually, for MC applications, path-dependent) function $y(X(t))$, $0 \leqslant t \leqslant T$, that gives rise to the option payoff, and, after division by the terminal value of the numeraire, to the present value of the option. As an example, one might be interested in the terminal (time-T) distribution generated by the paths of those forward rates X that, from time 0 to time T, have not fallen below a given barrier level at pre-specified reset times. Or, to give another example, the function $y(X(t))$, $0 \leq t \leq T$, could be the average of the values $X(t)$ encountered along a particular path from 0 to T. Clearly, for the simple case of a European option, $y(X(T)) = X(T)$. Therefore, as stated in the previous section, the purpose of the MC approach (or, for that matter, of *any* option pricing methodology) is to obtain an approximation for the final distribution of the function h, given the distribution of X over time. Once this is obtained, the option value can be calculated as

$$\int V(y)h(y)\,dy \equiv V^*$$ (8.9)

It is worthwhile pointing out how the same value could be arrived at by repeated integrations over the *known* distribution of the underlying variable. Let us consider the simple case of a call option, V, struck at K, on the average of the realisations at time $T/2$ and at time T of the underlying variable X. To each realisation of X at time $T/2$ one could associate the probability $h(X(T/2))$ dX, known from the assumed distributional properties of X. The probability of occurrence of a value $X''(T)$, contingent on $X(T/2) = X'(T/2)$, would also be known from the distributional assumptions about X. Therefore

$$V = \iint \frac{1}{B} p\left(X\left(\frac{T}{2}\right) = X' \mid X(0) = X_0\right) p\left(X(T) = X'' \mid X\left(\frac{T}{2}\right) = X'\right)$$

$$\times \text{Max}\left[\frac{X' + X''}{2} - K, 0\right] dX'\, dX''$$ (8.10)

where $p(X(t) = X^* \mid X(\tau) = X^{**})\, dX^*$ indicates the probability that, given its known distributional properties, the variable X should attain the value X^* at time t, contingent on its having attained the value X^{**} at time $\tau(\tau < t)$, and $1/B$ is the appropriate discount factor. Clearly, if the average had to be taken over n realisations, the integral would have become n dimensional, and, very soon, even skilfully implemented non-MC numerical techniques would fail to provide a viable way to calculate the necessary repeated expectations. Therefore the MC technique, simply by using the user's distributional knowledge about X in order to produce its evolution over time, obtains the equivalent of an n-dimensional integration (see Equation (8.10) above) by carrying out a single (Equation (8.9)) explicit one-dimensional integration (at least for one-factor models). Notice, however, that, despite the computational simplicity of expression (8.9), the underlying problem is truly n dimensional, since, in order to arrive at $h(y)$, n multiple integrations still have to be implicitly carried out.

As for the practical evaluation of V^*, an estimate can be obtained by drawing a large number (n) of sample values $y_i(T)$ from the terminal distribution $h(y)$, and by calculating

$$V_{\text{est}} = \frac{1}{n} \sum V(y_i) \qquad (8.11)$$

(Notice that the function V indicates the *present value* of the terminal payoff, and that, therefore, the division by the numeraire has already taken place.) Since, by the central limit theorem, the sum of a 'large' number of independent variables, however distributed, approaches a normal distribution, it follows that the standard deviation of the estimate (for large n) is approximately equal to

$$\text{std}(V_{\text{est}})^2 = \frac{1}{n} \sum (V(y_i) - V_{\text{est}})^2 \qquad (8.12)$$

and the distribution of V_{est} tends to a normal distribution with mean equal to V^* and variance equal to $\text{std}(V_{\text{est}})^2/n$:

$$V_{\text{est}} \in N\left(V^*, \frac{\text{std}(V_{\text{est}})^2}{n}\right) \qquad (8.13)$$

(Strictly speaking, the quantity $\sum (V(y_i) - V_{\text{est}})^2$ should be divided by $(n-1)$. Given the magnitude of n, dividing by n instead is of no consequence.) This expression clearly shows that, in order to reduce the standard deviation of the estimate by a factor of, say, 10, 10^2 more draws have to be carried out. Alternatively, Equation (8.13) also shows that, instead of increasing n (the 'naive' approach), one can attempt to reduce the standard error by attempting to reduce $\text{std}(V_{\text{est}})$. This is the route taken by the variance-reduction techniques, a few of which are reviewed in the following section.

8.3 VARIANCE-REDUCTION TECHNIQUES

One of the simplest variance-reduction techniques is the *contravariate* method. One starts, with this approach, from the knowledge of the analytic expression for the value, G, of a 'similar' option. For concreteness, one can, for instance, think of the option to be evaluated using the MC technique as an average rate caplet, and the 'known' option as a plain-vanilla caplet. The value of the simple option is given by the integral of the *same* function V (i.e. in this example, the cap function, which associates to a final rate, be it spot or average, the present value of the maximum of zero and the difference between the rate itself and the strike) over the distribution $f(X)$ (in the case of the 'similar' option $y(X) = X$) of the terminal realisations of the spot rate:

$$G = \int f(X)V(X)\,\mathrm{d}X = \int f(y)V(y)\,\mathrm{d}y \qquad (8.14)$$

Notice that, while the distribution $h(y)$ appearing in Equations (8.8) and (8.9) is, in the context of this specific example, the distribution of the *average* of the spot rates, and, as such, *a priori* unknown, $f(y)$ is known from the outset from the known distributional properties of X. The quantity G (in the case of the present example a plain-vanilla caplet) can therefore be calculated exactly. Therefore one can write, by adding and subtracting G,

$$V^* = \int V(y)h(y)\,dy + G - \int f(y)V(y)\,dy = G + \int [h(y) - f(y)]V(y)\,dy \quad (8.15)$$

If one values the last integral using the naive MC technique, one can obtain

$$V_{cv} = G + (V_{est} - G_{est}) = V_{est} + (G - G_{est}) \quad (8.16)$$

where G_{est} is obtained using the equivalent of Equation (8.11). The contravariate estimate of V_{cv} is seen to be equal to the naive estimate (V_{est}), corrected by the error that the naive estimate produces in evaluating G. From Equation (8.16) the variance of V_{cv} is therefore given by

$$\mathrm{Var}(V_{cv}) = \mathrm{Var}(V_{est}) + \mathrm{Var}(G_{est}) - 2\,\mathrm{Covar}(V_{est}, G_{est}) \quad (8.17)$$

where the result has been used that the variance of G is zero since, by assumption, it can be analytically evaluated. The variance of V_{cv} will be smaller than the variance of the 'naive' estimate V_{est} as long as $\mathrm{Covar}(G_{est}, V_{est}) > \mathrm{Var}(G_{est})/2$, or, equivalently,

$$\mathrm{Correl}(G_{est}, V_{est}) > \frac{1}{2}\sqrt{\frac{\mathrm{Var}(G_{est})}{\mathrm{Var}(V_{est})}} \quad (8.18)$$

As intuitively obvious, the contravariate technique will prove valuable when the 'simple' option closely matches the payoff of the 'exotic' option, since the underlying idea (see Equation (8.15)) is based on the cancellation of shared estimation errors. The textbook example is the case of the estimation of an option on the *arithmetic* average of log-normally distributed variables, using as control variate the same option on the *geometric* average of the underlying variables (whose distribution can be evaluated analytically). If the control option were uncorrelated with the exotic no benefit would be reaped from the procedure. If negatively correlated, the procedure could even produce an *increased* variance of the estimate. Notice, however, that, since it is possible to evaluate during the simulations all the terms which appear in Equation (8.18), one can always tell whether the variable G chosen for the contravariate technique is actually bringing about an improvement.

Another variance-reduction technique (Clewlow and Carverhill (1994)) which rests on the similar idea of finding quantities highly correlated with the option value to estimate is the Martingale Variance Reduction (MVR) approach. The idea is very simple: notice, to begin with, that, if M is a stochastic quantity of zero expectation, then the estimator

$$M_{\text{est}} = \frac{1}{n} \sum M(X_i)$$ (8.19)

will, of course, also be centred around 0. Therefore, if one were to evaluate

$$M_{\text{estMVR}} = \frac{1}{n} \sum [V(X_i) + M(X_i)]$$ (8.20)

this would still give an unbiased estimator of V^*. The same is true for any linear combination of martingales:

$$E[V_{\text{estMVR}}] = E\left[\frac{1}{n} \sum [V(X_i) + \beta_1 M_1(X_i) + \beta_2 M_2(X_i) + \ldots + \beta_k M_k(X_i)]\right] = V^*$$

(8.21)

If judiciously chosen, however, the standard error of the estimator can be significantly reduced. For the purpose, let us in fact choose, in complete analogy to what was done before, an option of present value G, as 'similar' as possible to the one that we want to value with the MC/MVR technique, and such that an analytic formula for its valuation is available. Having chosen G, let us now create the following martingales:

$$MX_1(t + \Delta t) = MX_1(t) + \frac{\partial G}{\partial X}(\Delta X(t) - E[\Delta X(t)|\Im_t])$$ (8.22)

$$MX_2(t + \Delta t) = MX_2(t) + \frac{\partial^2 G}{\partial X^2}(\Delta X(t)^2 - E[\Delta X(t)^2|\Im_t])$$ (8.22′)

In expressions (8.22) and (8.22′) let us first of all notice that the terms $\partial G/\partial X$ and $\partial^2 G/\partial X^2$ are known *a priori*, given the fact that G was chosen to be an option of known analytic value. Furthermore, from Equation (8.26) at each point in time one can easily evaluate both $E[\Delta X(t)|\Im_t]$ and $E[\Delta X(t)^2|\Im_t]$, the former from the drift of the process, and the latter from its variance (the symbol $\Im_t$ emphasises that both these quantities have to be evaluated at time t). Since from the semi-martingale $\Delta X(t)$ its drift (i.e. its expectation $E[\Delta X(t)|\Im_t]$) is subtracted step by step, the resulting quantity $(\Delta X(t) - E[\Delta X(t)|\Im_t])$ is clearly a martingale. In the limit as Δt goes to zero, the expression

$$\sum \frac{\partial G}{\partial X}(\Delta X(t_i) - E[\Delta X(t_i)|\Im_t])$$

which gives $MX_1(T)$, therefore tends to a stochastic (Ito's) integral. This, in turn, was shown in Chapter 4 to be a martingale itself. Similar considerations apply to MX_2. (Both MX_1 and MX_2 can be 'started' from $MX_1 = MX_2 = 0$.) Finally, the quantities $\Delta X(t)$ and $\Delta X(t)^2$ are easy to evaluate during the course of the simulation. Therefore, we have so far shown that, by adding these new martingale variates to the original estimate, we will cause no 'harm' (i.e. our estimator will still be unbiased). At worst, we could be wasting computer time in sampling irrelevant quantities[2]. But it is intuitively clear that, by choosing the delta and the gamma of the 'approximating' function as the integrand of the Ito's integral computed during the course of the simulation, we are, in fact, 'taking away' quite a substantial portion of the randomness of the option to be evaluated. The estimate of the option price then is

$$V_{\text{estMVR}} = E\left[\frac{1}{n}\sum [V(X_i) + \beta_1 M_1(X_i) + \beta_2 M_2(X_i) + \dots + \beta_k M_k(X_i)]\right] \quad (8.23)$$

What still remains to be specified is how to choose the variables β_i. To this effect let us consider the vector $\mathbf{P}$:

$$\mathbf{P} = \begin{bmatrix} P^1(T) \\ P^2(T) \\ \vdots \\ P^n(T) \end{bmatrix} \quad (8.24)$$

made up by the n final payoffs of the option, the matrix $\mathbf{X}$, where $X_i^j(T)$ denotes the realisation of the ith martingale variate at expiration time T for the jth simulation,

$$\mathbf{X} = \begin{bmatrix} 1 & X_1^1(T) & X_1^2(T) \\ 1 & X_2^1(T) & X_2^2(T) \\ \dots & \dots & \dots \\ 1 & X_m^1(T) & X_n^2(T) \end{bmatrix} \quad (8.25)$$

and the vector β

$$\beta = [V_{\text{estMVR}} \quad \beta_1 \quad \beta_2] \quad (8.26)$$

Since one can clearly write

$$\begin{matrix} \mathbf{P} & = & \mathbf{X} & \beta \\ (n,1) & & (n,3) & (3,1) \end{matrix} \quad (8.27)$$

a least-square estimate of β is given by

$$\beta_{\text{est}} = (\mathbf{X}^T\mathbf{X})^{-1}\mathbf{X}^T\mathbf{P} \quad (8.28)$$

where, as usual, the superscript T indicates transpose, and the superscript $[^{-1}]$ inverse. Equation (8.28) therefore gives the 'best' combination of the parameters $\{\beta\}$ which can afford the maximum achievable variance reduction for the estimate of the option price.

Little more can be said about variance-reduction techniques based on the idea of taking advantage in a skilful way of the high degree of correlation between the target and a known option without examining the specific details of each individual problem. A second class of techniques, however, exists which rely, in order to achieve the desired reduction in variance, on the strong *negative* correlation between two estimates. The simplest of these antithetic methods consists of running two simulations in parallel, the first when a series of Gaussian random draws $\{z_i\}$, and the second with the series of draws $\{-z_i\}$. Given that, if z is a zero-mean, unit-variance random variable, then also $-z$ is a zero-mean, unit-variance random variable also the second series of draws constitutes a feasible realisation for the Brownian process to be simulated. Therefore the antithetic estimate

$$V_{\text{est at}} = \tfrac{1}{2}[V_{\text{est}}(\{z\} + V_{\text{est}}\{-z\})] \qquad (8.29)$$

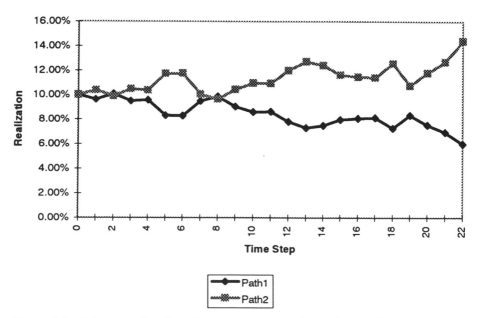

Antithetic Paths

Figure 8.1 A log-normal path with its mirror image, obtained using the same random draws with opposite signs.

(where $V_{\text{est}}(\{z\})$ is the naive estimate obtained using Equation (8.11) and the random draws $\{z\}$) is also an unbiased estimator of the true option value, of variance

$$\text{Var}(V_{\text{est at}}) = \tfrac{1}{4}[\text{Var}(V_{\text{est}}(\{z\})) + \text{Var}(V_{\text{est}}(\{-z\}))]$$
$$+ \tfrac{1}{2}\text{Covar}[V_{\text{est}}(\{z\}), V_{\text{est}}(\{-z\})] \tag{8.30}$$

As long as the covariance between $V_{\text{est}}(\{z\})$ and $V_{\text{est}}(\{-z\})$ is negative, as it will be for the choice of antithetic variable here suggested, the overall variance will have been substantially reduced. Intuitively, as shown in Figure 8.1, the reduction in variance stems from associating to each 'outlier' the opposite and mirror-image 'outlier', thereby cancelling to some extent the biasing effects of both. This technique is particularly effective when the integration is carried over a symmetric range, and the value function is approximately linear, as in the case of the evaluation of the present value of a swap; in this case, in fact, to each 'abnormally' high and positive realisation there corresponds an 'abnormally' high and negative value. In the case of options this anti-correlation is less pronounced, more and more so as the option is out-of-the-money, and an increasing fraction of zero outcomes occur.

8.4 HANDLING AMERICAN OPTIONS

American options are notoriously difficult to evaluate using forward-induction procedures such as Monte Carlo. As it is well known, the problem stems from the fact that, along a given path at time t, the expectation of future payoffs is not available. Backward-induction methods such as tree methodologies, for which expectations of future payoffs are readily available, suffer from the 'symmetric' problem of poor handling of path-dependent options: one method knows only about the past, the other about the future.

In theory, expectations *could* be evaluated using MC: from each time/state point reached during the course of a simulation where the expectation is needed a 'new' MC simulation could in principle be started, until the next exercise time is reached (see Figure 8.2). At this point, and from each of the sub-paths, yet another MC simulation would have to be started, and so on. Needless to say, the dimensionality of the underlying integration, which requires a number of paths growing exponentially with the number of exercise possibilities, is such that the procedure in this naive form is totally impractical.

The problem, however, can be made considerably simpler by combining forward and backward induction. Let us consider first the case of a Markovian one-dimensional model, and, for the sake of concreteness, let us assume that the underlying variables evolved through the simulation are forward rates; let us also consider the case when the option to be valued is an American swaption. Despite the fact that the following treatment would apply to the

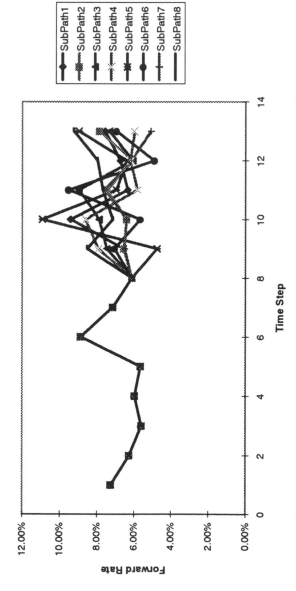

Figure 8.2 A simple illustration of how an American option could, *in principle*, be evaluated using only forward induction: at time step 14 path 1 reaches the first early exercise opportunity. A number of secondary paths then originate from this point until the second exercise opportunity is reached. At this point further sub-paths (not shown) would have to originate from each of the 'primary' sub-paths. The number of paths increases exponentially.

case of any interest-rate model implemented using Monte Carlo, the discussion will be cast with the HJM approach in mind, since it constitutes the most popular and important model to require MC for a general implementation. This section could therefore be profitably re-read after completing Chapter 16.

Under these assumptions, the 'normal' MC procedure can first be followed in order to obtain the sampled future values of a European option expiring at the last exercise opportunity (time T). For the specific case here examined these values will be determined by the realisations of the τ-tenor caplet expiring at time T, and paying at time $T + \tau$. These sampled values will be denoted by $V(i,T)$, where the index i indicates that the value is associated to path i. Following each path one can then move backwards to the previous exercise opportunity (time $T - 1$). Let us assume, for the moment, that it is possible to associate to the value of the realisation at time $T - 1$ of the forward rate $f(T - 1,T,T + \tau)_i$ the discounted expectation of all the payoffs $V(k,T)$ occurring at time T ($k = 1, 2, \ldots, \text{NMC}$). The symbol $f(T - 1,T,T + \tau)_i$ indicates the forward rate at time $T - 1$ expiring at time T and maturing at time $T + \tau$ associated with path i, and NMC is the number of MC simulations. Notice that, given the chosen numeraire, the discounting will have to be carried out along the specific path i from T to $T - 1$. At point $(i, T - 1)$, the yield curve is fully described by $f(T - 1,T - 1,T - 1 + \tau)_i$, i.e. the spot rate of tenor τ at time $T - 1$, and $f(T - 1,T,T + \tau)_i$. Therefore the intrinsic value of the two-period swaption is also available, and one can calculate the maximum of this intrinsic value and of the expectation (assumed, for the moment, to have already been computed). This maximum value $V(T - 1,i)$ can then be associated with the state i at time $T - 1$. Notice that, for a general, i.e. not necessarily Markovian, one-factor model the individual values of the particular series of random draws up to time $T - 1$ uniquely specify the values at time $T - 1$ of all the forward rates. For a general (non-Markovian) model, however, the converse is not true: knowledge that the forward rate $f(T - 1,T,T + \tau)_i$ has assumed a particular value is not enough to identify the value of the remaining forward rates. There are several states of the world (i.e. several series of random draws $\{Z_k\}$) associated with the same forward rate $f(T - 1,T,T + \tau)_i$. It is at this point that the one-factor *and* Markov assumptions come into play: if the underlying process is Markovian, knowledge of $f(T - 1,T,T + \tau)_i$ completely determines $f(T - 1,T - 1,T - 1 + \tau)_i$ and, therefore, the intrinsic value. If this is the case it is therefore unambiguous to associate the value function $V(T - 1,i)$ to, say, forward $f(T - 1,T,T + \tau)_i$.

Once this is done, one can completely forget about the function $V(T,i)$ since all the relevant information (the maximum of intrinsic value and expectation of future values) is contained in $V(T - 1,i)$; one can therefore move backwards using exactly the same procedure through earlier and earlier exercise opportunities. Despite the fact that nothing has been said about how the expectation can indeed be computed, it is intuitively clear that iteration of the procedure outlined above should entail the evaluation of N one-dimensional integrals (for N exercise opportunities) rather than one N-dimensional integral (as the naive procedure mentioned above would have implied).

The question remains open of how to evaluate the (discounted) expectation of the time-T value function at point $(i, T-1)$. Several procedures have been proposed (see Boyle, Broadie and Glasserman (1995) for a recent review), none of which has so far won total acceptance. Qualitatively, one of the most popular ideas behind these approaches is to make use of the paths encountered during the forward-induction procedure in order to approximate the expectation by using a skilful 'bundling' of the paths: all the paths that 'went through' a small window of values at times $T-1$ are considered to have originated from a single 'point'; the values V associated with their realisations at time T can therefore be approximately associated with a single value of the state variable(s) at time $T-1$, and expectation can therefore be approximately evaluated. Details are given in Tilley (1993). Needless to say, the computational *and* memory requirements of this approach are rather formidable. For more than one state variable, the procedure proposed by Barraquand and Martineau (1995) can be more practicable: the idea is to replace partitioning of the state variables space with a partitioning of the payoff space. Boyle, Broadie and Glasserman (1995) show that, although appealing, the procedure may fail to converge. Despite these caveats, practical tests have so far indicated that the procedure might give more accurate results than theoretical considerations would seem to indicate.

The area is the subject of intense research at the moment, especially in order to tackle the case of non-Markovian interest-rate processes.

ENDNOTES

1. One of the advantages of the MC technique is that it allows sampling from arbitrary, i.e. not necessarily normal, distributions. This feature has been made use of for stochastic volatility models (Hull and White (1987)) or for mixed Brownian–Poisson processes. Since conceptually no substantial difference is introduced by allowing for a different–distribution, the discussion in this chapter is restricted to the case of Wiener processes.
2. Notice, however, that the worst possible case would be of a totally uncorrelated control option (which would give a vector β of zeros), not the case of a perfectly anti-correlated control option that (via a β of -1) would *perfectly* correct any estimation error.

PART FOUR
ANALYSIS OF SPECIFIC MODELS

9
The CIR and Vasicek models

9.1 GENERAL FEATURES OF DESIRABLE INTEREST-RATE PROCESSES

In the previous chapters some fundamental properties of interest-rate models have been analysed. In particular, the conditions obtained in Chapters 4 and 5 specify how the price of various securities can (stochastically) vary over time as a function of the underlying factor so as to preclude the possibility of arbitrage. Nothing specific, however, has been said about the dynamics of the underlying driving variables. In order to analyse the properties of individual models, one must, therefore, inject some informational content into the specification of the short-rate process. This is the task of Part IV of this book. For the sake of simplicity, one-factor models will be examined first.

The first stepping-stone in the construction of a one-factor model is the specification of a reasonable form for the stochastic process of the driving factor. If this single variable is the short rate, the distributional properties implied by its stochastic process are of direct interest, since they can give some indication as to how 'reasonable' the chosen process is. The main features that one would like to observe in the short-rate behaviour predicted by any model, and in the implied term structure, are:

(i) the dispersion of the short rate should be consistent with one's expectations of 'likely' values over a given time horizon: in particular rates should not be allowed to become negative, or to assume 'implausibly' large values;

(ii) very high values of rates, on historical terms, tend to be followed by a decrease in rates more frequently than by an increase; the converse is observed to be true for 'unusually' low rates; a mean-reverting process has therefore been suggested to account for this behaviour;

(iii) rates of different maturity are imperfectly correlated, the degree of correlation decreasing more sharply at the short end of the maturity spectrum than towards the end: ideally, the decrease in correlation with maturity implied by a model should be more pronounced in going from, say, 6 to 12 months, than in going from 20 years to 20 years and 6 months;

(iv) the volatility of rates of different maturity should be different, with shorter rates usually displaying a higher volatility;

(v) the short-rate volatility has been observed to lack homoskedasticity: in other words, the level of volatility has been observed to vary with the absolute level of the rates themselves. Chan *et al.* (1991) find that the best exponent β in the expression for the volatility of the short rate σr^{β} (see below) should be around 1.5.

These, of course, are only some rather crude specifications of what a 'reasonable' process should look like. In setting out these *desiderata*, a liberal use has been made of terms such as 'reasonable', 'unlikely', 'usually', etc., reflecting the fact that it is very difficult, or hardly possible, to assign precise quantitative prescriptions; even the requirement that interest rates should always be positive was, albeit for a brief period of time, disobeyed in Switzerland in the 1960s.

Since no known one- or multi-factor model manages to capture all these features at the same time, what is really important, when it comes to the choice and the practical implementation of a particular model, is not so much going through a 'checklist' of met requirements, but appreciating what features are essential for a given application, and which can be dispensed with: if, for instance, one wanted to price a yield spread option, the degree of correlation between rates might very well be more important than preventing interest rates from becoming negative. In valuing deeply out-of-the-money options the differences between a normal or log-normal distribution might be more relevant than a correct specification of the term structure of volatilities. Most challenging of all, if one attempts to create a comprehensive option pricing system (including, for instance, caps, floors, swaps, European swaptions, and exotic options) in order to permit global aggregation and management of interest-rate exposure, one will be confronted with the task of choosing a coherent and internally consistent option pricing framework capable of tackling in a 'satisfactory' way all the different types of options present in the portfolio. Looking back at the conditions set out before, the degree of compromise from the 'ideal' model might be very considerable indeed.

In addition to the need of compromising between the desirable features of different models when it comes to complex implementations of option pricing systems, a further word of caution should be introduced, against ranking models on the basis of how many of the above criteria are met. The ultimate test of an option pricing model is its capability to determine the statistics (such as the delta and gamma risk measures) that enable one to construct a riskless portfolio, and thereby capture the option price it implies (see Chapter 5); in other terms, the hedging test is the ultimate and totally unambiguous criterion on the basis of which one can asses the superiority of one model with respect to another. The history not only of finance, but also of 'harder' sciences like physics, is full of apparently 'poor' models (i.e. models with assumptions that looked *a priori* unpalatable) which have performed remarkably well. Conversely, innumerable approaches apparently incorporating more 'advanced' or 'realistic' features have failed to live up to their promises. Every user of a model, of whatever nature, must be well aware that it *never* accounts for all known aspects of a given phenomenon. What is less obvious to recognise is that very often it is only possible to tell *ex post facto* (i.e. after comparing predictions and observations) which elements of discrepancy from reality have unacceptable consequences, and which can be readily accommodated.

The general features of interest rates described above should therefore be taken as a guideline in devising new models, in improving upon existing ones, and in gauging where results should be taken with a particularly large grain of salt. With this qualification in mind, one can attempt to understand more clearly the structure of models such as CIR or Vasicek (analysed in this chapter) by considering, for instance, the problem of how to ensure that interest rates should not disperse 'too much'. If one focuses attention, in fact, on a relatively short time horizon (e.g. a few weeks or months) one can obtain, for instance by looking at recent past history, sensible estimates of the expected variance of the process over this time. If, however, one assumes the variance so estimated to derive from a normal or a log-normal short-rate process with constant volatility (standard deviation per unit time) of the form

$$dr = \mu_r\, dt + \sigma_r\, dz \quad \text{or} \tag{9.1}$$

$$\frac{dr}{r} = \mu'_r\, dt + \sigma'_r\, dz \tag{9.1'}$$

(with μ, μ' functions possibly of time but not of the level of the short rate) one can easily observe that these distributions associate, after periods of a few years, very sizeable probabilities to the occurrence of values for the short rate far above and below what past experience suggests to be reasonable (see Figures 9.1 and 9.2). In particular, as shown in Figure 9.2, if one uses a constant short rate volatility of 20% and an initial flat term structure at 10% one obtains the appreciable cumulative probability of 5.5% that the short rate should be above 50% in 10 years' time. As noticed before, one can easily verify that, for normal rates, there is a non-zero probability that rates might become negative.

In order to obviate this problem, two main avenues are open: one can either make the volatility of the short-rate time decaying, or one can impose an explicit mean-reverting drift to the short-rate process. The first line of approach

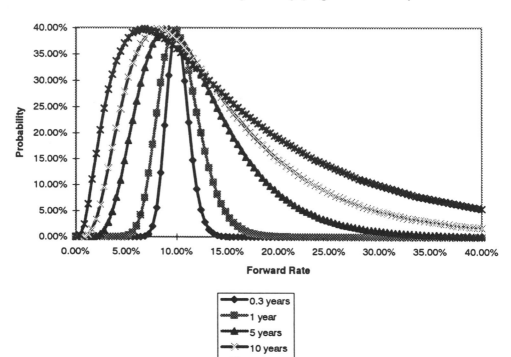

Figure 9.1 The distribution probability for a log-normally distributed forward rate of time-0 value of 10% after several time intervals.

is followed by models like BDT or Ho and Lee (Chapter 10), the second by models belonging to the Vasicek/CIR family (Chapters 9, 11 and 12). If the choice is made to impart a time-decaying behaviour to the volatility of the short rate, one is essentially specifying, as of time 0, the unconditional variance of the short rate process for future times in such a way that one's uncertainty about future rates does not continue to grow unboundedly over time. To see this more clearly, one can write for the total (unconditional) variance of the short-rate process originating at time 0

$$\text{Var}[r(t)] = \int_0^t \sigma(s)^2 \, ds \qquad (9.2)$$

For $\sigma(s) = \sigma_0$ the variance of the short rate grows linearly with time:

$$\text{Var}[r(t)] = \sigma_0^2 t \qquad (9.2')$$

Probability Density (Normal Case)

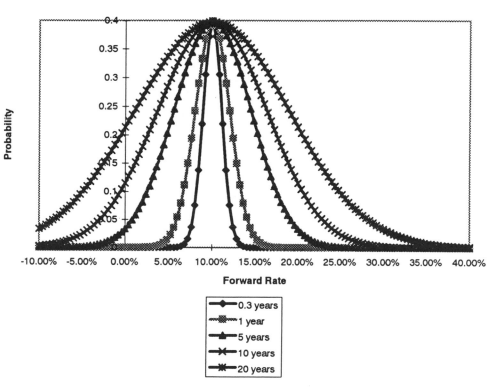

Figure 9.2 The distribution probability for a normally distributed forward rate of time-0 value of 10% after several time intervals.

For a time-decaying volatility, for instance of the form $\sigma(t) = \sigma_0 \exp[-\nu t/2]$, one can write

$$\mathrm{Var}[r(t)] = \sigma_0^2 \int_0^t \exp[-\nu s]\, ds = \frac{\sigma_0^2}{\nu}\,(1 - \exp[-\nu t]) \qquad (9.3)$$

One can then define the *average forward variance* $\sigma(t, T_1, T_2)$ from time T_1 to time T_2 as seen from time t by

$$\sigma^2(t, T_1, T_2) = \frac{\int_0^{T_2} \sigma^2(s)\, ds - \int_0^{T_1} \sigma^2(s)\, ds}{T_2 - T_1} = \frac{\int_{T_1}^{T_2} \sigma^2(s)\, ds}{T_2 - T_1} \qquad (9.4)$$

For $\sigma(t) = \sigma_0$ or $\sigma(t) = \sigma_0 \exp[-\nu t/2]$ this gives

$$\sigma^2(t,T_1,T_2) = \sigma_0 \qquad (9.5)$$

$$\sigma^2(t,T_1,T_2) = \frac{\sigma_0^2}{\nu} \frac{\exp[-\nu T_1] - \exp[-\nu T_2]}{T_2 - T_1} \qquad (9.5')$$

respectively.

Two things are worth noticing: first of all, that if the unconditional variance for a later time T_2 is smaller than the unconditional variance for an earlier time T_1, this would imply (Equation 9.4) a negative forward volatility, i.e. it would be equivalent to saying that we 'know more' about a later time T_2 than an earlier time T_1, which is clearly unacceptable. Even if this 'entropy' condition is not violated, however, by looking at Equation (9.5') one can immediately observe that, for $T_1, T_2 \gg t$, the forward volatility, albeit always positive, tends to zero. While the unconditional variance, as seen from time zero, has an acceptable (strictly non-decreasing) shape, the user might therefore not be happy with the implications of a time-decaying volatility in so far as the *future* increase of uncertainty is concerned. In order to appreciate the importance of this feature, one can examine the market implied Black volatilities (see Figure 9.3) (as obtained, for instance, from cap prices); one can then observe that the undesired dispersion of rates is achieved by assigning, possibly after an initial hump, a decaying behaviour to the volatility of forward rates of increasing maturities. If that were not the case, the buyer of a long-dated cap who believed rates to remain, in some imprecise way, 'clustered' about some mean level, would be paying for interest-rate protection against scenarios (say, rates at 50%) subjectively deemed of virtually impossible occurrence.

Notice, however, that, when pricing a cap as a collection of Black caplets, each individual (driftless) forward rate is evaluated in its own measure, implied by the discount bond used as numeraire. In other terms, the individual components of a cap have no 'interaction' with each other, and it makes no sense to distinguish between an unconditional variance and a forward volatility: for each individual caplet, the only quantity of relevance, as far as the stochastic component of the process is concerned, is the total dispersion of the forward rate at option expiry, however this might have been arrived at. On the other hand, we have seen in Part I, Chapter 3, that the very reason for introducing yield-curve models is to be able to tackle situations where payoff-dependent events occur throughout the life of a certain instrument. If this is the case, the path of forward volatilities that make up a given terminal distribution *does* make a difference, since intermediate events will be assigned, in general, different variances. Depending on the specific application, a reasonable behaviour for forward volatilities can therefore be very important.

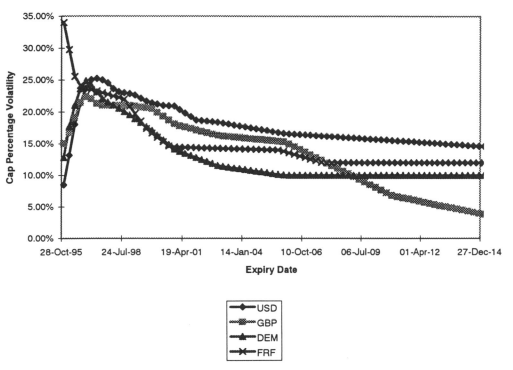

Figure 9.3   Market cap volatilities for several currencies.

The alternative route in order to avoid 'excessive' dispersion of rates is to make the *deterministic* term of the short-rate process take on the burden of preventing rates from 'spreading' too much. In order to achieve this, the suggestion has been put forth by several authors that the short rate should follow a mean-reverting process, i.e. that when the short rate is above (below) a long-term level it should experience a downward (upward) pull towards this level. This long-term level can, but need not, be a function of time.

A whole class of models can thus be obtained, of the general form

$$dr_S = a(r_S, t)[b(t) - r_s]\, dt + r_S^\beta \sigma\, dz \tag{9.6}$$

where σ is a constant, and the exponent β contributes to the determination of the distributional properties of the short rate. In particular, $\beta = 0$ implies 'normal' rates (Vasicek), $\beta = \frac{1}{2}$ gives the CIR model and $\beta = 1$ implies 'log-normal' rates.

The choice of β can be dictated by a compromise between analytic tractability $(\beta = 0)$ and reasonableness of the resulting distribution. The empirical issue of which exponent gives the best description of the interest-rate process has not been settled yet, although Chan et al's (1991) results mentioned above seem to indicate that a higher β might describe observed rates better. A lot will be said in following chapters (see, in particular Chapter 15) about strengths and weaknesses of the two approaches to limiting excessive dispersion of rates, especially in conjunction with the parameterisation procedures. For the moment, it will suffice to keep the considerations outlined above in mind while analysing the CIR model.

9.2 DERIVATION OF THE CIR AND VASICEK MODELS

A unified derivation is given in the following of the Cox Ingersoll and Ross (CIR) (1985a) and Vasicek (1977) models. It should be pointed out, however, that CIR original derivation is quite different, and ensures that their model enjoys features which are not shown to follow from the present derivation. Namely, following Brown and Dybvig (1986) we shall simply enforce the condition of no-arbitrage between bonds, without addressing the issue of whether there exists an equilibrium economy consistent with the model. CIR prove this to be the case for their model, and show in a concrete case how failure to meet the conditions satisfied by their model can lead to situations of non-equilibrium. Their derivation and the implications of the equilibrium character of their description of the economy will be presented in the chapter devoted to the Longstaff and Schwartz model (Chapter 12).

To conform with CIR notation, some of the symbols used in the previous section will be changed, and a mean-reverting process will be described as

$$
\begin{aligned}
dr &= k(\theta - r)\,dt + \sigma r^{\beta}\,dz \\
&= \mu_r\,dt + \sigma_r\,dz
\end{aligned} \tag{9.7}
$$

In the context of one-factor models (the first part of the derivation therefore applies to the Vasicek as well as the CIR model), the price of a default-free discount bond is a function of present time t, maturity T, and the chosen factor, i.e. the short rate:

$$
P = P(r,t,T) \tag{9.8}
$$

For this discount bond, one can write

$$
\frac{dP}{P} = \mu_P(r,t,T)\,dt + v(r,t,T)\,dz \tag{9.9}
$$

where $v(r,t,T)$ is the time-t percentage price volatility of a discount bond maturing at time T. Using Ito's lemma one obtains

$$\frac{dP}{P} = \frac{1}{P}\left[\frac{\partial P}{\partial r}\mu_r + \frac{\partial P}{\partial t} + \frac{1}{2}\frac{\partial^2 P}{\partial r^2}\sigma_r^2\right]dt + \frac{1}{P}\left[\frac{\partial P}{\partial r}\sigma_r\right]dz$$

$$= \left[\frac{1}{P}\frac{\partial P}{\partial r}k(\theta - r) + \frac{1}{P}\frac{\partial P}{\partial t} + \frac{1}{2}\frac{1}{P}\frac{\partial^2 P}{\partial r^2}(\sigma\sqrt{r})^2\right]dt + \left[\frac{1}{P}\frac{\partial P}{\partial r}\sigma\sqrt{r}\right]dz$$

$$(9.10)$$

From Equations (9.9) and (9.10) it follows that

$$v(r,t,T) = \frac{1}{P}\frac{\partial P}{\partial r}\sigma r^\beta \qquad (9.11)$$

At this point one can make use of the no-arbitrage condition obtained in Chapter 5, Section 1,

$$\mu_P(r,t,T) = r + \lambda^*(r,t)v(r,t,T) \qquad (9.12)$$

which, combined with Equation (9.11), and dropping the subscript 'r' for σ, gives

$$\mu_P(r,t,T) = r + \lambda^*(r,t)\frac{1}{P}\frac{\partial P}{\partial r}\sigma r^\beta \qquad (9.13)$$

Equating terms in dt in Equations (9.9) and (9.10) and using Equation (9.13) one gets

$$\frac{\partial P}{\partial r}k(\theta - r) + \frac{\partial P}{\partial t} + \frac{1}{2}\frac{\partial^2 P}{\partial r^2}(\sigma r^\beta)^2 = rP + \lambda^*(r,t)\frac{\partial P}{\partial r}\sigma r^\beta \qquad (9.14)$$

At this point the two models impose different functional forms for the market price of risk (λ^*), and for the exponent β. Namely,

$$\text{in the CIR model} \qquad \beta = \tfrac{1}{2}, \quad \lambda^*(r,t) = \frac{\lambda_0 r^{\frac{1}{2}}}{\sigma}$$

$$\text{in the Vasicek model} \quad \beta = 0, \quad \lambda^*(r,t) = \lambda_0$$

with λ_0 a (different) constant in both models.

Thus Equation (9.14) can be rearranged to give for the CIR model

$$rP + \frac{\partial P}{\partial r}(\lambda_0 + k)r = \frac{\partial P}{\partial r}k\theta + \frac{\partial P}{\partial t} + \frac{1}{2}\frac{\partial^2 P}{\partial r^2}\sigma^2 r \qquad (9.15)$$

while for the Vasicek model one obtains

$$rP = \frac{\partial P}{\partial r} [k(\theta - r) - \lambda_0 \sigma] + \frac{\partial P}{\partial t} + \frac{1}{2} \frac{\partial^2 P}{\partial r^2} \sigma^2 \qquad (9.16)$$

The following treatment will focus on the theoretical and empirical implications of the CIR rather than of the Vasicek model. This choice is partly motivated by the fact that the latter model has met with less interest from academics and practitioners since, as explained in previous sections, it allows for negative interest rates. In this context it should, however, be remembered that what really matters for the purpose of option evaluation is not so much the possibility for interest rates to assume negative values, but the total (integrated) probability for rates to be below zero. As it will be discussed later, if the negative-interest-rate problem is viewed in this light, models such as the Vasicek or the Ho and Lee have probably been too heavily penalised, and their greater analytic tractability should warrant them closer attention. A stronger criticism of the Vasicek (but not of the Ho and Lee or the Hull and White) model is that the possible shapes of the yield curve that can be obtained are rather limited (see also the discussion in Chapter 15, Section 2), therefore making practical implementation potentially very difficult, especially for market yield curves, such as found, for instance, for UK gilts, which often display very complex shapes. With this proviso in mind, the analysis of the Vasicek model is deferred until the discussion of the Hull and White normal model, which can fit exactly any yield curve, and which includes the Vasicek model as a special case.

Concentrating therefore on the CIR model, the partial differential Equation (9.15) has to be solved subject to the boundary condition

$$P(r,T,T) = 1 \quad \forall T \qquad (9.17)$$

A solution satisfying this initial condition is given by (CIR (1985))

$$P(r,t,T) = A(t,T) e^{-B(t,T)r} \qquad (9.18)$$

where

$$A(t,T) = \left\{ \frac{\phi_1 e^{\phi_2 \tau}}{\phi_2 [e^{\phi_1 \tau} - 1] + \phi_1} \right\}^{\phi_3} \qquad (9.19)$$

$$B(t,T) = \frac{e^{\phi_1 \tau} - 1}{\phi_2 [e^{\phi_1 \tau} - 1] + \phi_1} \qquad (9.20)$$

$$\phi_1 = \sqrt{(\kappa + \lambda)^2 + 2\sigma^2} \qquad (9.21)$$

$$\phi_2 = \frac{\kappa + \lambda + \phi_1}{2} \tag{9.22}$$

$$\phi_3 = \frac{2\kappa\theta}{\sigma^2} \tag{9.23}$$

$$\tau = T - t \tag{9.24}$$

The solution of the partial differential equation as expressed by Equation (9.18) emphasises that the value at time t of a discount bond of maturity T, $P(r,t,T)$, depends, apart from t and T, only on the state variable r, today's value of the short rate (and, of course, on the parameters chosen to represent its stochastic process). The future evolution of this rate, as described by the stochastic process (9.7), is completely captured by the pre-exponential term $A(t,T)$ and by the argument $B(t,T)$.

It is also interesting to notice that κ, θ and λ do not occur in these equations separately, but only in the combinations $\kappa\theta$ and $\kappa + \lambda$. Therefore one cannot determine these quantities individually simply using, in however skilful a way, prices of traded securities; in particular the market price of risk remains unrecoverable. This is analogous, as Brown and Dybvig (1986) point out, to the fact that, by observing stock option prices, one can obtain the variance but not the 'true' (i.e. non-risk-adjusted) drift of the generating process for the underlying.

9.3 ANALYTIC PROPERTIES OF THE CIR DISCOUNT FUNCTION

To enhance intuition about the implications of the model, one can first of all explore the behaviour for large and small times to maturity of the discount function. To this effect, one can expand the exponentials in Equations (9.19) and (9.20): remembering that

$$e^x - \sum_0^\infty \frac{x^n}{n!} \tag{9.25}$$

one can write

$$A(t,T) \cong \left\{ \frac{\phi_1(1 + \phi_2\tau)}{\phi_2(1 + \phi_1\tau - 1) + \phi_1} \right\}^{\phi_3} = \left\{ \frac{\phi_1 + \phi_1\phi_2\tau}{\phi_2\phi_1\tau + \phi_1} \right\}^{\phi_3} = 1 \quad [\tau \ll 1] \tag{9.26}$$

$$B(t,T) \cong \frac{1 + \phi_1\tau - 1}{\phi_2(1 + \phi_1\tau - 1) + \phi_1} = \frac{\tau}{1 + \phi_2\tau} \quad [\tau \ll 1] \tag{9.27}$$

This latter quantity, for small values of τ, behaves like τ itself. Equation (9.18) is therefore almost identical, for these values of τ, to

$$P(r,t,T) = 1e^{-r(t-T)} \tag{9.28}$$

which shows, as one should intuitively expect, that, for the very short times, the discount bond can be obtained by a unit of currency discounted at the short rate for the appropriate (short) time. For longer times to maturities, the stochastic process specified in (9.7) modifies both the 'unit of currency' $[1 \Rightarrow A(t,T)]$ and the discounting rate $[r \Rightarrow rB(t,T)]$.

By similar manipulations one can obtain the discount rate on a consol bond. Since the discount rate (in this case, identical to the yield to maturity), in fact, is given by $R_T = \log(P(t,T)/\tau$, one can write

$$\lim_{T \Rightarrow \infty} R_T = \lim_{T \Rightarrow \infty} -\frac{\ln Ae^{-Br}}{\tau} = -\frac{\ln (A) - Br}{\tau} \tag{9.29}$$

Since furthermore

$$\ln (A) = \ln\left(\left\{\frac{\phi_1 e^{\phi_2 \tau}}{\phi_2 [e^{\phi_1 \tau} - 1] + \phi_1}\right\}^{\phi_3}\right) = \phi_3 \{\ln (\phi_1) + \phi_2 \tau - \ln(\phi_2 [e^{\phi_1 \tau} - 1] + \phi_1)\} \tag{9.30}$$

and

$$\lim_{T \Rightarrow \infty} e^{\phi_1 \tau} - 1 = e^{\phi_1 \tau}$$

$$\lim_{T \Rightarrow \infty} \phi_2 [e^{\phi_1 \tau} - 1] + \phi_1 = \phi_2 e^{\phi_1 \tau} \tag{9.31}$$

$$\lim_{T \Rightarrow \infty} \log(\phi_1) + \phi_2 \tau = \phi_2 \tau$$

it follows that

$$\lim_{T \Rightarrow \infty} \ln(A(t,T)) = \tau(\phi_2 - \phi_1)\phi_3 \tag{9.32}$$

Using the results above one can see immediately that

$$\lim_{T \Rightarrow \infty} B(t,T) = \phi_2 \tag{9.33}$$

and that, therefore, the consol discount rate is asymptotically given by

$$R_\infty = -\frac{\ln(A) - Br}{\tau} = (\phi_1 - \phi_2)\phi_3 \tag{9.34}$$

This consol yield is therefore a constant which, incidentally, is not identical to the long-term reversion level θ, although it is proportional to it via the factor κ/ϕ_2. Equally important, as can be verified by straightforward algebraic manipulations, is to notice that the volatility parameter σ^2 can be obtained as

$$\sigma^2 = 2(\phi_1 - \phi_2)\phi_2 \qquad (9.35)$$

For the purpose of comparison with empirical results (reported in Section 6), it is worthwhile stressing that the consol yields (R_∞) to which yield curves of different spot rates but same reversion levels converge is a function of the volatility of the short-rate process, and, as noticed above, is not equal to the reversion level itself: if that were the case, from an estimation of $\kappa\theta$ one could impute the reversion speed κ, and from the latter the market price of risk using the combination $\kappa + \lambda$. Equations (9.33) and (9.34) together provide important links with (almost) observable financial quantities. These links will be exploited in the following in order to assess the realism of the description of the yield-curve dynamics afforded by the CIR model.

As for the shapes that the term structure described by Equation (9.18) can assume, CIR (1985a) show in their original paper that when the short rate today (the spot rate) is below the consol yield the term structure is uniformly rising, while it is falling for the spot rate above $\kappa\theta/(\kappa + \lambda)$. For intermediate values of the short rate, the yield curve is humped. See Figures 9.4, 9.5 and 9.6. It should be noted that the most complex shape is therefore that of a term structure that rises first and then decreases.

A decreasing—increasing—decreasing yield curve (such as the one displayed, for instance, by the UK gilt market in the years 1990/1992) is therefore not obtainable. In concluding this section devoted to the analytic properties of the CIR discount function, it is also important for future discussions to point out that, for reasonable values of the volatility and of the long-term reversion level, the obtainable 'hump' is of quite limited extent (see again Figures 9.4 to 9.6).

9.4 BOND OPTIONS IN THE CIR MODEL

The evaluation of bond option prices in a CIR framework is particularly interesting, in that it is possible to obtain a closed-form solution for the case of a T-maturity European call on an s-maturity discount bond $P(r,0,s)$, struck at K. The terminal condition for the price of such an option is

$$C[r,T,s,K] = \text{Max}[P(r,T,s) - K,0] \qquad (9.36)$$

where $P(r,T,s)$ is the price at time T of the s-maturity discount bond on which the option is written. Without entering into algebraic details, the rest of this section will show how a closed-form expression for options on discount bonds in the context of the CIR model can be obtained using the same kind of

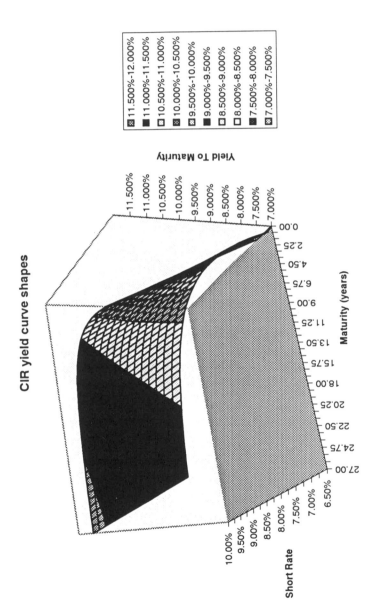

Figure 9.4 Different shapes of yield curve obtainable with the CIR model with $\kappa = 0.3$, $\lambda = 0$ and $\nu = 0.5$ for different values of the initial short rate. Figures 9.4, 9.5 and 9.6 were obtained, *ceteris paribus*, with volatilities of $\sigma = 0.15$, 0.3 and 0.4, respectively. Notice how the curve becomes significantly more humped with increasing volatility. See the text about the relevance of this observation, and Section 6 in particular.

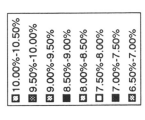

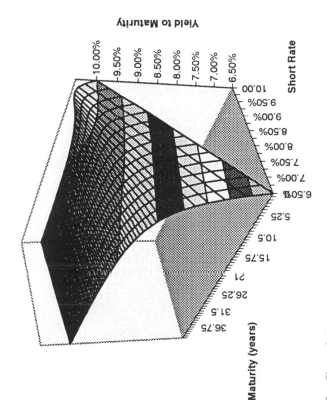

CIR yield curve shapes

Figure 9.5 See Figure 9.4.

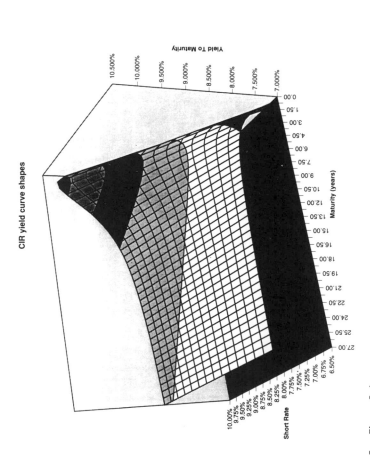

Figure 9.6 See Figure 9.4.

reasoning which leads, under different distributional assumptions, to the Black formula for log-normal bond prices.

From Chapters 3, 4 and 5 we know that, if one uses as numeraire (i.e. for discounting payoffs) the discount bond maturing at time T, forward prices are martingales. We also know (Feynam–Kac theorem, Chapter 4) that in this case the value today of a European option is given by the discounted expectation (in the appropriate measure) of the terminal distribution,

$$C(0) = P(0,T)E[\text{Max}(P(T,s) - K,0)] \qquad (9.37)$$

For a call option on a generic asset S struck at K, the expectation to be evaluated is in general of the form

$$\int_K^\infty S(T)f(S,T)\,\mathrm{d}S - \int_K^\infty Kf(S,T)\,\mathrm{d}S \qquad (9.38)$$

where $f(S)$ denotes the probability density of the variable S at time T. If bond prices were log-normally distributed (which is *not* the case for the CIR model), then it is well known that the two integrals above are given by the cumulative normal distribution evaluated for two standardised values, $h1$ and $h2$, given by

$$h(1,2) = \frac{\ln\left(So \exp\left[\int_0^t \mu_{1,2}(s)\,\mathrm{d}s\right]\right) - \ln(X)}{\sigma\sqrt{t}} \qquad (9.39)$$

If one is working with spot prices, and one uses the rolled-over money market account as numeraire, then assets grow at the riskless rate, giving

$$h(1,2) = \frac{\ln\left(So \exp\left[\int_0^t r(s)\,\mathrm{d}s \pm \frac{1}{2}\int_0^t \sigma^2(s)\,\mathrm{d}s\right]\right) - \ln(X)}{\sigma\sqrt{t}} = \frac{\ln\left(\frac{So}{X}\right) + rt \pm \frac{1}{2}\sigma^2 t}{\sigma\sqrt{t}} \qquad (9.40)$$

i.e. the well-known Black and Scholes formula. Notice that, for a model like the CIR, what can be evaluated, once the parameters are given, are the *spot* prices for the discount bonds $P(0,T)$ and $P(0,s)$ (see Equation 9.18), while the expectation in Equation (9.37) is taken over *future* values of $P(T,s)$. What conceptually remains to be made is the link between future and forward prices. To this effect, one can notice that, as long as one is simply interested in European options, and therefore one chooses to discount payoffs by $P(0,T)$, then from Chapter 5 we know that forward prices (which *can* be evaluated as $P(0,s)/P(0,T)$ from today's yield curve) are martingales. If one still retains the log-normal assumption, and one discounts by $P(0,T)$, then $\mu = \pm 1/2\sigma^2 t$

and

$$h(1,2) = \frac{\ln \dfrac{FP}{X} \pm \dfrac{1}{2}\sigma^2 t}{\sigma\sqrt{t}} \tag{9.40'}$$

with $FP = FP(0,T,S) = P(0,s)/P(0,T)$.

If, finally, instead of being log-normal, forward bond prices have the distribution (straightforwardly if tediously obtainable using Ito's lemma) implied by the square-root process for the short rate, the same reasoning still applies. In this case one can show that, by taking the expectation of terminal condition (9.36) over the rate distribution at time T one obtains the valuation formula

$$C[r,0,T,s,K] = P(r,0,T)[FP(r,T,s)\chi^2(h_1) - K\chi^2(h_2)] \tag{9.41}$$

where χ^2 is the non-central chi-squared distribution,

$$h_1 = \left(2r^* [\varphi + \psi + B(T,s)]; \frac{4\kappa\theta}{\sigma^2}, \frac{2\phi^2 r e^{\gamma(T-t)}}{\phi + \psi + B(T,s)}\right) \tag{9.42}$$

$$h_2 = \left(2r^* [\varphi + \psi]; \frac{4\kappa\theta}{\sigma^2}, \frac{2\phi^2 r e^{\gamma(T-t)}}{\phi + \psi}\right) \tag{9.42'}$$

and

$$r^* = \frac{\ln \dfrac{A(T,s)}{k}}{B(T,s)}$$

$$\gamma = \sqrt{(\kappa + \lambda)^2 + 2\sigma^2}$$

$$\psi = \frac{\kappa + \lambda + \gamma}{\sigma^2}$$

$$\varphi = \frac{2\gamma}{\sigma^2(e^{\gamma(T-t)} - 1)}$$

Expression (9.41) has been written in a slightly different form than in the original CIR derivation to emphasise the similarity with reasoning underpinning the derivation of the Black formulation and with the similar expression obtained for the Hull and White models: $P(r,0,T)$ is in both cases a discount bond present-valuing the terminal option value to today, $P(r,T,s)$ is the forward bond price, and the χ^2 distribution has taken the place of the normal cumulative distribution.

The option valuation expression presented above displays the usual feature of an option value monotonically increasing with option maturity. It is interesting to note, however, that, unlike the case of Black–Scholes stock options, the value of a call is a *decreasing* function of interest rates: while the usual effect of a lower present value of the strike is in fact still present, this is more than offset by the depression in the bond price from an increase in rates. The CIR model can be usefully compared in this respect with the Longstaff and Schwartz approach (see Chapter 12).

Analytic expressions for the discount function and especially for calls on discount bonds are of great value not only in the course of option pricing, but even more so in the calibration phase since, as already shown, caps and floors can be expressed as suitable puts and calls, respectively, on discount bonds. The next section will therefore build on these results in order to tackle the issue of model calibration.

9.5 PARAMETERISATION OF THE CIR MODEL

Having examined the theoretical properties of the CIR model, it remains to consider its practical implementation and its performance. In this light, there are at least two distinct ways to look at the CIR model. According to one view, that will be referred to as the 'fundamental' approach, the model provides a picture of a stylised equilibrium economy, in which interest rates are endogenously determined, and are a function, among other factors, of a specified market price of risk. As mentioned before, this aspect of the CIR model is not borne out of the derivation presented in Section 2 of this chapter. The reader is referred to the original paper (CIR (1985a)) in order fully to appreciate the scope and implication of the original derivation. (See also Chapter 12 for an outline of the argument, there presented in the context of the LS model.) If the specification of the economy were correct, if the process chosen for the short rate were the 'true' one and, finally, if one had access to the utility function of the investors in the market, the model would be totally specified, and would endogenously produce the observed term structure of interest rates. There would be no need to supply, for instance, the rates of different maturities, since these would be a byproduct of the model.

In reality none of the above is known *a priori*. In particular, the utility function, necessary to derive the market price of risk, has historically proven particularly difficult to estimate empirically. Given its simplicity and its parsimonious nature the CIR model approached in this 'fundamental' way could provide some interesting insight about how interest rates are determined in the context of an equilibrium economy. The option prices and the risk management statistics it implies, however, due to the sources of uncertainty mentioned above, can be, at best, of qualitative character.

In order to price interest-rate-sensitive instruments one needs a much more quantitative description of reality. A second approach to the model has therefore been developed, which I will call the 'applied' or, using a term borrowed from the physical sciences, the 'phenomenological' approach. In this approach, one assumes to have correctly identified the general structure of the laws governing a given phenomenon (in this case, the dynamics of the yield curve), but one recognises that the detailed knowledge of how the parameters of this descriptions could be arrived at *ab initio* (i.e. from more fundamental quantities, such as the utility function) is still not available. One therefore resorts to fitting the free parameters of the model to known observable quantities (for instance the yield curve), in the hope, if the original choice of the model functional form and structure were correct, to obtain 'empirically' those quantities that cannot be computed directly.

Specifically, in the case of the CIR model, it is recognised that the term structure of interest rates, as described for instance by Equation (9.18), is a function of one state variable, the short rate, and three parameters, ϕ_1, ϕ_2 and ϕ_3.

Notice carefully that, as observed before, even if the CIR model were an exact description of the state of the world, from bond option prices one could not recover quantities such as the market price of risk. Therefore, even in this 'ideal' case, the true dynamics of the short-rate process, i.e. its reversion speed and the reversion level, would not be recoverable from the prices of traded assets, since κ, θ and λ always appear in the combinations $\kappa\theta$ and $\kappa + \lambda$. Conversely, simply by observing the 'true' ('real-world') history of interest rates, even in a perfect CIR universe, and obtaining, with however sophisticated a statistical model, either the speed of reversion, or the long-term reversion level, or both, would be *per se* of no use for the parameterisation of the model: since the market price of risk would still be unknown, neither ϕ_1, nor ϕ_2 nor ϕ_3 could be recovered.

It is therefore clear that, in order to obtain the parameters that allow a complete specification of the model, one needs quantities that price the source of uncertainty in the economy. These quantities are, for instance, the prices of bonds or the yields they imply.

Exogenously, a set of discount bond yields of different maturities can therefore be chosen (possibly a whole yield curve), and the attempt can then be made to determine those values of the parameters and of the state variable which 'best' describe the observed term structure. If, once again, the CIR model were a perfect and true specification of the real world it would be irrelevant which and how many rates one chose in order to determine the parameters of the model (as long as one chose at least as many rates as parameters to be fitted; choosing more rates than parameters would simply give rise to redundant identities). Since, however, everybody recognises that the model is, at best, a reasonable description of reality, the exogenous rates will not be exactly obtainable: if we have more rates than degrees of freedom, one can at best hope to achieve a good fit of the calculated and observed term structure, and discrepancies between model and observed prices are certainly to be expected. Two important questions therefore arise, regarding

(i) how important these mis-specifications are; and
(ii) what the implications of these 'pricing errors' are: is there any way to decide whether these discrepancies are pointing to the fact that the model is 'poor', or that some of our fundamental assumptions are violated, e.g. the hypothesis that the markets are behaving 'inefficiently'? In other words, can we discover whether the discrepancies are pointing to a poorly specified model or to trading opportunities?

(Notice that the latter question is by no means specific of the CIR model, and can, and has been, addressed in the context of several other approaches. See, for instance, Brennan and Schwartz (1982).)

One way to answer these questions is to estimate cross-sectionally (i.e. using the synchronous values of many different bonds) the observable parameters of the model (ϕ_1, ϕ_2 and ϕ_3) for a series of days, and then examine the time series of estimated parameters. More specifically, if one defines

$$\chi^2 = \sum_i [TMP_{\text{obs},i} - TMP_{\text{mod},i}(r; \phi_1 \phi_2 \phi_3)]^2 \qquad (9.43)$$

where $TMP_{\text{obs},i}$ is the observed total market price of bond i, and $TMP_{\text{mod},i}$ is the model price for bond i, obtained by discounting each cash flow (coupons and principal) using the CIR discount function, then one can attempt to determine the set of parameters $\{\phi\}$ that makes the expression above as small as possible.

The estimation parameter estimation is not straightforward, since the function to minimise (i.e. the sum of squared deviations between observed and model bond prices) is a strongly non-linear function of the quantities to estimate and the optimisation is constrained by the requirement that σ^2 should be strictly positive (see Equation (9.43)). Delicate and complicated as these estimation techniques might be, we can side-step the technical issues (see, for instance, Chapter 1), and assume, for the rest of the discussion, that the correct estimates have been produced, day by day, by the chosen algorithm.

In the CIR formulation, the parameters are not a function of time, and the estimation procedure should produce, were the model correct, exactly the same estimates day after day (to within statistical noise, perhaps due to the bid/offer spread of bond prices). In reality, we expect these parameters not to be exactly constant over time. How can we assess whether their fluctuations are 'reasonable', especially when we do not have any intuitive feeling for the sensitivity of the observable quantities to these parameters? Fortunately, a suitable combination of the ϕs gives rise to an 'almost' observable quantity, i.e. the volatility of the short rate:

$$\sigma^2 = 2(\phi_1 - \phi_2)\phi_2 \qquad (9.44)$$

With the procedure mentioned before of examining time serially the cross-sectionally obtained parameters, we can recover a series of volatilities over a given time period. If our estimation procedure was unconstrained, we can first of all examine whether the obtained volatilities at least turn out to be positive. We can then see whether their values lie in a 'plausible' range, and finally if their variation is 'smooth' over time.

This approach to the assessment of the quality and trading usefulness of the CIR model has been followed by several authors. Their findings are reported in the following section.

9.6 THE CIR MODEL: EMPIRICAL RESULTS

The task of assessing the empirical validity of interest-rate models in general, and of the CIR model in particular, is of obvious importance. Before embarking on the specific examinations of the tests carried out to assess the performance of the various models it is important to have a clear idea of how their parameters influence observable market variables, such as discount bond prices or volatilities. This is particularly important in the case of equilibrium models, such as the CIR or the Longstaff and Schwartz (see Chapter 12), which actually *price*, albeit imperfectly, market bond prices, rather than taking them as input exogenous variables. As it is shown in the following, these equilibrium models contain specific assumptions about the dynamics of the driving factor(s), which in turn determine the attainable shapes of the yield curve, and, at the same time, apportion in different ways the contributions to the curvature of the yield curve to future expectations of rates, and to future expectations of volatility. This can be seen more clearly as follows: a given yield curve is completely specified by a series (in the limit by a continuum) of discount bond prices. These directly imply a series of spot rates, which obviously depend on future expectations of future rates. However, the shape of the yield curve depends also on future expectations of the volatility of the driving factor (the short rate, in the CIR case). To see this, let us draw on the results obtained regarding lattice methodologies (Chapter 6), and let us consider, for simplicity, a one-factor lattice model, such as the BDT or HL (the specific model is immaterial) reviewed in the following: revisiting the construction presented in Chapter 7, Section 1, let us assume that two discount bonds, of maturity 1 and 2 years, are traded in the market, denoted as 'disc1' and 'disc2' in Figure 7.1, of respective prices of 0.9090 and 0.8264. The same figure shows two possible binomial rate trees, constructed on the basis of two different assumptions for the short-rate volatility, i.e. of 5% (vol1) and of 30% (vol2). The actual construction of the trees will be illustrated in detail in later chapters, but we already know from Chapters 6 and 7 that the rate trees are built in such a way that (i) discounting the known final payoff of 1 at time 2 to the present time along the tree gives the observed market price of a two-period discount bond, and (ii) the desired short-rate volatility at time 1 is obtained. If one makes use of the fact that the (pseudo)-probabilities of transition from a given value of the rate to the up and down state are both $\frac{1}{2}$, one is in the position to evaluate the (risk-neutral) expectation of the future short rate at time 1. As shown in Figure 7.1, this expectation has the values of 10.078% and 10.002% for vol2 and vol1, respectively. Therefore, **the same discount bond prices** (0.9090 and 0.8264) **imply different expectations of future rates for different future volatilities.** Conversely, **given the same expectations of future rates, different future volatilities would produce different discount bond prices.** More formally, a two-year zero-coupon bond price is the expectation at time 1 of the one-year discount factor:

$$\text{disc2} = \frac{1}{1 + r_0} E'_{r_1} \left[\frac{1}{1 + r_1} \right] \tag{9.45}$$

and, given the non-linear dependence of the forward discount factor on the short rate,

$$E'_{r_1} \left[\frac{1}{1 + r_1} \right]$$

depends on the rate volatility at time 1. Looking again at the example of Figure 7.1, a market price of disc2 = 0.8264 could equivalently be seen as implying an expectation of the future short rate of 10.002% and of a volatility of 5%, or an expectation of future rates of 10.678% and of a volatility of 30%. Therefore, fitting to market yield curves the parameters of models like the CIR or the Longstaff and Schwartz (see Chapter 12), which incorporate parameters describing both the dynamics of the short rate and the volatility, means attempting to disentangle from the observed market prices the rate expectations from the volatility expectations.

The example just shown indicates that, if volatility and short-rate expectations are independent exogenous variables, an infinity of combinations can be found giving rise to the same observed market values. Specifying a joint dynamics for the two variables (as is done in the Longstaff and Schwartz model), or, at least, linking the values of the volatility to some of the parameters of the rate dynamics (CIR), reduces to some extent the degrees of freedom. Room for ambiguity, however, still remains: for models like the Vasicek, the CIR (or their Hull and White extensions), the higher the reversion speed, the smaller the effect of the volatility on the shape of the yield curve (see Chapter 15, and Figure 15.2 in particular). For the specific case of the CIR model, one can write:

$$dr = \left[(\kappa + \lambda)\left(\frac{\kappa\theta}{\kappa + \lambda} - r \right) \right] dt + \sigma\sqrt{r}\, dz = [\kappa(\theta - r) - \lambda r]\, dt + \sigma\sqrt{r}\, dz \quad (9.46)$$

which shows that changing the reversion speed κ, does not affect the volatility parameter $\sigma = 2(\varphi_1\varphi_2 - \varphi_2^2)$. Therefore, **high values of the reversion speed coupled with low values of the volatility have virtually the same effect on yields as low values of the reversion speed associated with high volatility.**

These simple remarks point out that any fitting procedure of model parameters to market prices of bonds must be taken with a considerable degree of caution. To begin with, if a model like the CIR does not allow for a complex pattern of rate expectations, the attempt to obtain, say, a markedly humped yield curve will put on the volatility all the burden of reproducing the desired curvature (see again Figures 9.4, 9.5 and 9.6). If one looks at the problem in this light, the incapability of producing certain shapes of the yield curve displayed by the CIR model should be regarded as a blessing in disguise, since, at least, it clearly signals the inadequacies of the model, rather than 'camouflaging' its shortcomings by an inappropriate apportioning of the curvature contributions to volatility and rate expectations. 'Richer' models, such as the Longstaff and Schwartz, are, from this point of view, more flexible but also more 'dangerous'.

In addition, for those shapes of the yield curve that can 'naturally' be accounted for by models like the CIR there remains the above-mentioned ambiguity in the choice of reversion speed and volatility parameters. Fits of similar numerical quality can therefore be obtained with radically different sets of parameters: these differences, immaterial in the pricing of the discount bonds, might very well be important in the evaluation of hedge statistics in the context of option pricing. Nothing more specific can be said without undertaking the actual analysis of empirical data reported in the following for the CIR model, and in later sections for the Longstaff and Schwartz. These caveats, however, should always be kept in mind in the assessment of these results.

In order to examine in detail to what extent empirical studies have validated or rejected the CIR model, it is important to remember what constraints are implied by the model on the yield-curve dynamics. Strictly speaking, the CIR model is described by one state variable, the short rate, and three parameters. As mentioned before, a suitable combination of these three parameters yields the volatility of the short rate. Furthermore, the long rate is not allowed by this model to vary with time, but is strictly a constant. With these features of the model in mind, how can the CIR model be tested? One can first of all assume that liquidity effects, maturity preferences or coupon/capital gain taxation either play no role in determining the price of a bond, or have been appropriately accounted for in distilling (Chapter 1) a 'market' yield curve. With this proviso in mind if the CIR model perfectly described reality, all bond prices for all maturities and coupons observed in the market on any day could be exactly reproduced (at least to within a bid/offer spread) with a single set of parameters (for concreteness, out of the numerous combinations of these three parameters we can choose $\kappa + \lambda$, $\kappa\theta$ and σ). Furthermore, having estimated these three parameters (which have no explicit time dependence) on a given business day, if one knew the change over one day of the only stochastic variable, i.e. the short rate, the same set of parameters would exactly give all bond prices on the following day, without any need for further estimation. The CIR model, after all, purports to describe the evolution of *the* factor that drives the whole yield curve.

This is the strongest test to which the CIR model could be put. If one chooses such a purist's approach, the model will certainly not withstand the test: the parameters estimated for a given day will certainly not give exactly the market prices of all bonds on the following day, even if one were given the fore-knowledge of the experienced change in the short rate; furthermore, on any one day, not all the prices can, in general, be perfectly described by a single set of parameters; the fact that a minimum-least-squares procedure has to be employed to determine the parameters automatically means that, in a fundamental sense, either the model is 'wrong' or the market is 'imperfect'. Since, in reality, however, nobody expects the CIR, or for that matter any one-factor, model to be exactly 'true', a more constructive approach is to try to assess from market data whether the approach suggested by CIR gives a 'reasonable' description of reality. Indications that their specification of the dynamics of the yield curve might be substantially correct would be inferred if, for instance, the long rate remained 'almost' constant; if the least-square cross-sectional fit to market bond prices were of 'good' quality, and substantial discrepancies were evenly distributed across maturities; if the parameters providing this best fit on a given day were 'sufficiently similar' to the parameters estimated for a following day, and their variation, if at all present, 'smooth enough'; if the volatility were 'roughly' constant over time, and 'not too different' from the historical observed volatility.

All these criteria have been used in empirical studies, and will be referred to in the following. Before presenting the most interesting results, however, it must be mentioned that the CIR model has been tested both against data from instruments dependent on nominal rates and against data from real rates instruments (notably, index-linked bonds in the UK market). The conclusions drawn from assuming the CIR assumptions to apply to real or nominal rates have been somewhat different. For a useful, albeit by now incomplete, survey of empirical findings, Section 4 of Brown and Schaefer (1991) is recommended.

One of the first and more extensive studies of the CIR model was carried out by Brown and Dybvig (Brown and Dybvig (1986)) for nominal US bonds, who set out a testing methodology then followed by several other authors (see, e.g., Barone, Cuoco and Zautnik (1990) for nominal Italian data, Brown and Schaefer (1991) for index-linked British bonds or de Munnick and Schotman (1992) for nominal Dutch bonds).

A common feature of most of these studies is that the instantaneous short rate is significantly different from a reasonably chosen market short rate (e.g. the mean yield of US Treasury Bills with maturity less than 14 days). In Brown and Dybvig's study the long rate compares favourably with the yield of long bonds. Since this yield, however, changes over time, while the long rate is assumed by the model to be a constant, this fact, from a rigorous point of view, actually testifies against the model.

What is probably more damning is the fact that the time series of the cross-sectional estimates of the three parameters ($\kappa\theta$, $\lambda + \lambda$ and σ) tend to be very far from smooth. Despite the fact that, strictly speaking, nothing can be said *a priori* about the magnitude of these quantities, such erratic behaviour of the fitting parameters is a tell-tale indication of the fact that the optimisation procedure is trying to 'twist' a wrong model into an observed data set.

In this rather bleak scenario, however, an intriguing feature stands out from several studies: if one estimates cross-sectionally the variance parameter σ and the short-rate, and then regresses the time series of estimates of $\sigma\sqrt(r)$ against the observed time-series standard deviation, one finds (Brown and Dybvig (1986)) a slope insignificantly different from unit, and an intercept insignificantly different from zero. In other words, **the interest-rate volatility estimated from cross-sections corresponds well to the standard deviation obtained from time series**. One could be led to conclude, simply on the basis of this finding, that despite all its shortcomings, the CIR model seems to be able to capture a rather fundamental (and subtle) feature of reality. It will be shown in Chapter 15 that this enthusiasm should be considerably dampened, and that the intriguing parallel between the cross-sectional and time-series variances could actually be less striking than it might *prima facie* appear.

What is to be made of the most problematic of the empirical findings, namely the lack of stability of the estimation parameters? As stated before, the immediate conclusion is that one is trying to force 'reality' into a seriously wrong box. Anybody who has tried a 'brute force' fitting of n experimental data points with a set of 'undoctored' polynomials of degree up to n, knows the instabilities of the coefficients upon small variation of the data values, and the unpleasant behaviour away from the constrained points. It should, however, be remembered that even the most celebrated of models, i.e. the Black and Scholes approach, would certainly display low stability of the volatility parameter for long enough option maturities. Still, practitioners compensate for the true stochastic nature of volatility by using the Black and Scholes method, and adjusting its volatility parameter over time to reflect changing market conditions. Nor is parameter instability a specific problem of the CIR model: as will be discussed later on, one formulation of the Hull and White 'extended' models (very similar to the CIR/Vasicek models, but allowing for time-dependent, rather than constant, speed of reversion and long-term reversion level) suffers from similar problems. One might therefore be tempted to argue that if the goal of a model is not so much to describe term structure movements correctly, as to provide a tool for effective pricing and hedging, then models like CIR, or, for that matter, also Vasicek, might prove very valuable. While the argument has a certain appeal in so far as *pricing* is concerned, the ability of a model to produce useful hedging information hinges on its ability to predict in a substantially correct way the dynamics of the yield curve. From this point of view the findings reported above at least indicate that great care should be taken in risk-managing an option position using a CIR framework. This point will be further addressed in the chapter on the Longstaff and Schwartz model (Chapter 12).

From a practical point of view, a further worrying feature of the CIR and, *a fortiori*, of the Vasicek model is the fact that observed yield curves are often poorly reproduced, given the limited flexibility of the function which describes the discount factor. A bond option could therefore be struck on a mispriced underlying bond, and some form of correction must be employed, if reasonable option values are to be obtained. The problem is made more acute by the fact that most options are written with relatively close-to-the-money strikes, where the effect on the option value of a small variation in the price of the underlying bond is particularly pronounced. Which yield curves have satisfactorily been described by the CIR or Vasicek models are, basically, a matter of luck: the US, the Dutch and the Italian yield curves have been fitted to acceptable precision, while, before the change in shape brought about in September 1992 by Black Wednesday, the UK gilt yield curve had been for years recalcitrant to the CIR fitting.

Finally, it is interesting to note that the study by de Munnick and Schotman (1992) has found virtually identical quality of fit for the Vasicek and the CIR model using data from the Dutch bond market. Also structural parameters of the model, such as the implied volatility, turned out to be virtually identical in their study. These findings should pose a further word of caution against dismissing or endorsing a model on the basis of isolated distributional features (such as the possibility of negative rates).

10
The Black Derman and Toy model

10.1 INTRODUCTION

Chapter 6 has shown that it is possible to construct computational trees in such a way that (i) all the implied zero-coupon bond prices match the prices observed in the market (Section 6.1); (ii) the repeated averaging/discounting algorithm can be justified as a discrete-time implementation of the condition that ensures the absence of arbitrage (Section 6.2); (iii) by using the financial equivalent of Green's functions the forward-induction procedure can be accomplished in a very efficient way (Section 6.3). These sections have therefore tackled the conceptual and technical aspects of the lattice models. In order to assess their actual performance, the Black Derman and Toy model (Black, Derman and Toy (1990), BDT in the following) has been singled out for attention, partly for its popularity among practitioners, partly for the simplicity of its calibration and partly because straightforward analytic results, available, for instance, in the case of the Ho and Lee model, are not available. Much of what will be said in the following sections specifically about the BDT model, however, could, and should, be extended to other similar models.

The BDT model is a one-factor model algorithmically constructed in such a way as to price exactly any set of market discount bonds without requiring the explicit specification of investors' risk preferences. As a consequence, (plain-vanilla) swap rates, which can be expressed as linear combinations of discount bonds, can be priced exactly for any volatility input. While these features are shared by the HL model, the BDT approach further assumes a log-normal process for the short rate. Besides preventing negative rates, this assumption allows the volatility input to be specified as a percentage volatility, thereby following market conventions and making model calibration to cap prices much easier. This latter point is less trivial than it might seem, at least for 'real' (e.g. non-flat) term structure, as discussed in connection with the HW model

(Chapter 11, Section 4). Therefore, as will be shown in detail later on, *simultaneous* fitting to the yield curve *and* to cap (*or* swaption) volatilities is conceptually straightforward and computationally very easy to achieve.

The price to be paid for all these positive features is, on the one hand, numerical (log-normal distributions hinder analytic tractability), and, on the other hand, conceptual: by the very fact that the model is specified algorithmically, it is rather 'opaque' as to its implications and hidden assumptions, regarding, for instance, the nature of its mean reversion. The next section will therefore attempt to unravel the implicit features of the BDT model, with a view to understand better its strengths and weaknesses.

10.2 ANALYTIC CHARACTERISATION

In Chapter 6 the construction of a discrete lattice for a general one-factor (Markovian) interest-rate model was presented in detail. Since the BDT model falls in this category, the steps will not be repeated here. The continuous-time equivalent of the BDT short-rate process will instead be analysed, by writing the process for the short rate in the form

$$r(t) = u(t) \exp(\sigma(t)z(t)) \tag{10.1}$$

where $u(t)$ is the median of the short-rate distribution at time t, $\sigma(t)$ the short-rate volatility, and $z(t)$ a standard Brownian motion. Needless to say, it is the function $u(t)$, implicitly obtained by the tree construction outlined in Chapter 6, that allows the correct pricing of an arbitrary set of market discount bonds. For normal models, such as the HL or the Hull and White models reviewed in Chapter 11, the median $u(t)$ can be obtained analytically; for log-normal processes, however, no closed-form expressions are available which allow to construct the tree from the market forward rates and the process volatility without having to make use of the forward-induction procedure. Considerable insight into the model can, however, be obtained by converting Equation (10.1) to its stochastic incremental form: after applying Ito's lemma to $r = r(t, z(t))$, with $z(t) = [\ln(r(t)) - \ln u(t)]/\sigma(t)$, one easily obtains

$$dy(t) = \{c(t) + a(t)[w(t) - y(t)]\} \, dt + \sigma(t) \, dz \tag{10.2}$$

with

$$y(t) = \ln[r(t)]$$
$$w(t) = \ln[u(t)]$$
$$c(t) = \partial w(t)/\partial t$$
$$a(t) = -\frac{\partial \ln[\sigma(t)]}{\partial t}$$

(Similar expressions are known in the literature; Equation (10.2) above, however, makes explicit the link with the median of the distribution; the median, in turn, can be readily obtained from the tree once it has been built.)

As the expression above shows, if the volatility is assumed to be constant, $a(t) = 0$ and the model does not display any mean reversion: in this case the logarithm of the short rate evolves by simple diffusion with a drift which follows the logarithm of the median, as implicitly determined by the forward-induction tree-fitting procedure. If, on the other hand, the volatility is decaying with time, the reversion speed will be positive, and will cause a reversion of $y(t)$ to $w(t)$. For instance, if the volatility of the short rate were to evolve according to the simple law

$$\sigma(t) = \sigma(0) \exp(-vt), \quad v > 0 \tag{10.3}$$

then Equation (10.2) can be rewritten as

$$dy(t) = \{ c(t) + v[w(t) - y(t)] \} \, dt + \sigma(t) \, dz \tag{10.3'}$$

clearly displaying the reversion of the logarithm of the short rate to a time-dependent reversion level, roughly given by the level of the (logarithm of the) forward rates. As shown in greater detail later on, it is by allowing for a general time-dependent short-rate volatility that the BDT model can simultaneously recover a whole series of market (Black) cap prices, often displaying a declining implied (Black) volatility. Furthermore, since swap rates, by the BDT construction exactly recoverable, are also approximately log-normally distributed, the model allows for pricing of swaptions very similar to what was obtained by the Black model (see, however, Chapter 16 about the precise distributional assumptions implied by the BDT model for forward and swap rates).

From Equations (10.3) and (10.3') one can see that the assumption of decaying short-rate volatility is required to prevent the unconditional variance of the short rate, $\sigma(t)^2 t$, from increasing with t without bounds, which would be inconsistent with the mean-reverting character of the short-rate process. Since, however, for a given drift, it is the unconditional variance of the short-rate process that largely determines today's values of caplets, by allowing greater flexibility for the $\sigma(t)$ function, the prices of as many caps as desired can be simultaneously and easily obtained. It is important to notice, as will be shown in detail in Section 10.5, that it is also possible, although slightly more cumbersome, to obtain simultaneous fitting to the prices of a series of options to enter, at different times, the same-maturity swap. It is in general, however, not possible to match *at the same time* cap and swaption prices; this is no specific shortcoming of the BDT model, but rather reflects the intrinsic limitation of any one-factor model, which, as such, implies perfect instantaneous correlation between different rates: while, in fact, a cap is a portfolio of independent options (caplets), a swaption is an option on a linear combination of forward rates (see Chapter 1), and therefore dependent on their imperfect correlation.

A feature which is instead specific to the BDT model, as opposed to one-factor models in general, is the fact that the term structure of volatility is completely determined by the specification of the future volatility of the short rate. This simply stems from the fact that the reversion speed, which by and large determines the volatility of rates of different maturities, is not an independent parameter (as, for instance, in the HW model) but is a unique function of the short-rate volatility, as shown by Equation (10.2) above (see, for a more general discussion, Chapter 15). The implications of this feature will be examined in a later section of this chapter.

10.3 ASSESSING THE REALISM OF THE BDT MODEL

Further sections will explore how easily the BDT model can be made to reproduce market data for cap and swaption prices. Given, however, the inherent dangers of forcing a model to yield results that it is ill-suited to obtain, it is important to ascertain what observable market features are 'naturally' recoverable using the BDT approach. In other words, since any parameterisation procedure should ideally provide little more than the 'fine tuning' of a fundamentally correct phenomenological model, the task of assessing the overall realism of the BDT approach is undertaken in this section.

One of the most obvious shortcomings of the BDT model is the rather artificial link between the future volatility of the short rate and the term structure of volatilities. Figure 10.1 shows the volatility of yields of maturities from 3 months to 10 years for a recent market US$ curve, for different values of the decay constant ν, and for a value of $\sigma(0)$ similar to that observed at the short end of the cap market. For positive values of the decay constant, as implied by declining Black volatilities, yields of long maturities display less variability than short-maturity yields, in overall agreement with market observations.

Exact match of the volatilities of yields of different maturities should not be expected and, if ever actually observed, should be regarded as little more than fortuitous; the observations reported above, however, indicate that, with the positive reversion speed needed to reproduce market cap prices, the qualitative shape of the term structure of volatilities as seen from today's yield curve is by and large correctly captured by the BDT model.

Another very important test of the overall 'realism' of the model, and, in a way, its ultimate acid test, is its hedging performance. Within the framework of any approach hedging can be accomplished either 'within the model', i.e. by attempting to neutralise the exposure to the model driving factor(s), or

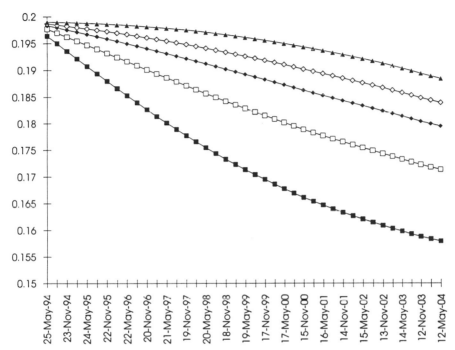

Term structure of volatility for different decay constants (USD 22 Feb 94)

Figure 10.1 Volatility of yields of different maturities (US$, 22 Feb 1994) with decay constant ν (top to bottom) = 0, 0.02, 0.04, 0.08, 0.16, and $\sigma_0 = 20\%$.

'outside the model', i.e. by obtaining price changes with respect to exogenous shocks, which, *per se*, could have a virtually zero probability of occurrence within the model itself. Examples of such exogenous shocks could be rigid shifts in the yield curve, or shocks to individual forwards. The 'outside model' procedure is clearly conceptually inconsistent, but a lot of confidence is needed to embrace the 'in-model' approach, since, within the framework of any one-factor model, one could hedge an exposure to a 10-year yield with an overnight deposit! Despite the fact, however, that exogenous shocks will in general be used for practical hedging purposes, in-model hedging tests can give very useful indications about the realism of the model itself.

Technically, obtaining in-model hedge parameters is straightforward. By evolving backwards in the tree any two assets, A and B, to time $1\,\Delta t$ (i.e. to time step 1), one can obtain their relative hedge ratios through their sensitivities to the short rate (see Table 10.1 below):

$$\frac{A(\text{up}) - A(\text{down})}{B(\text{up}) - B(\text{down})} = \frac{\dfrac{A(\text{up}) - A(\text{down})}{r(\text{up}) - r(\text{down})}}{\dfrac{B(\text{up}) - B(\text{down})}{r(\text{up}) - r(\text{down})}} \tag{10.4}$$

Gammas can be similarly obtained by considering the asset prices at time 2 Δt, and the corrections for the small theta effect introduced are, in practical applications, both small and straightforward. The issues connected with the evaluation of derivatives in the framework of BDT model will be analysed later on. For the present purposes, from Equation (10.4), one can easily derive the sensitivity of bond prices (and hence yields) of different maturities to changes in the short rate. In contrast with the term structure of volatilities, these sensitivities in general show little dependence on the decay constant v. They are instead strongly dependent on the shape of the yield curve, as displayed by Figure 10.2 for several market yield curves.

Upward sloping term structures (e.g. US$ and GB£ in 1994) tend to produce an 'elasticity' above 1; the reverse is true for declining yield curves (e.g. IT Lira and Pesetas in the last quarter of 1993). This should come as no surprise, given the percentage nature of the BDT volatility.

With these sensitivities, one can then carry out what is probably one of the most stringent tests of a model's 'realism'. Armed with the yield sensitivities obtained using Equation (10.4) above and with the foreknowledge of the day-by-day actual experienced changes in the short rate, one can predict the changes in yields of any maturity, and compare the model answers with the market outcome. This analysis, carried out for several currencies for the period 1990–1993 with decay constant chosen to give an overall acceptable fit to market cap prices, provided the results summarised in Figure 10.3. The

Table 10.1

| $t = 0$ | $t = 1$ |

Sensitivities of yields of different maturities

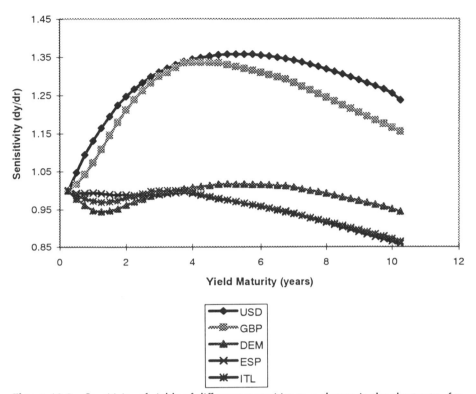

Figure 10.2 Sensitivity of yields of different maturities to a change in the short rate, for the yield curves of US$, GB£, DEM, ITL and ESP (24 Feb 1994, top to bottom at the right-end extreme). On this date, the GB£ and US$ yield curves were upward sloping, the DEM curve humped, and the ITL and ESP curves inverted.

correlation between experienced and predicted yield changes is, by construction, perfect at the short end, and decreases with yield maturity.

Whenever a yield curve displays steepening or flattening the agreement between observed and experienced yield changes is obviously poor, given the one-factor nature of the model: **by and large, in the BDT model yields tend too move in far too parallel a fashion**. See Figures 10.4, 10.5, 10.6 and 10.7.

In the Ho and Lee model with constant (absolute) volatility, yields move exactly in parallel. The BDT model allows for the possibility of more complex changes in the yield-curve shape. The greater structure and flexibility afforded by the BDT approach, however, is so intimately linked with the shape of the yield curve as to make the quantitative implications rather suspect. This important test therefore strongly cautions against blind in-model hedging.

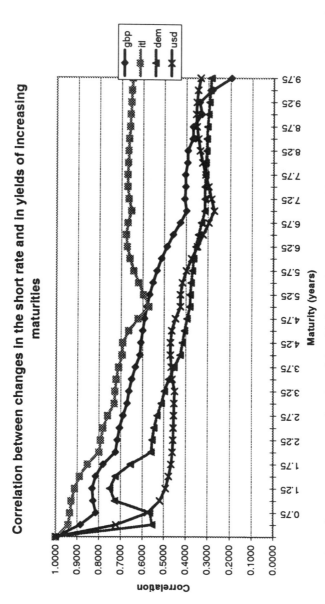

Figure 10.3   Correlation between experienced and model yield changes for increasing yield maturity using a choice of σ_0 and ν to give a good fit to cap prices: top to bottom ITL, US$, DEM and GB£.

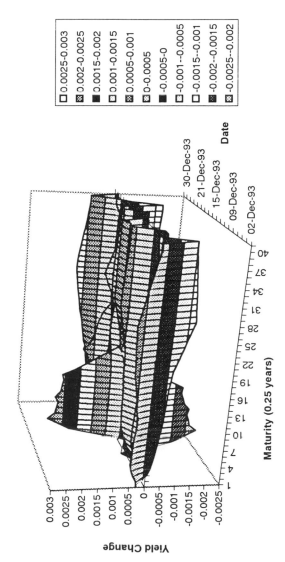

Figure 10.4 Experienced and predicted (next figure) yield-curve changes for the US$ swap market for the month of March 1994. Notice not only the greater complexity of the experienced changes (as one would expect) but also the absence of changes in slope (or curvature) in the predicted series.

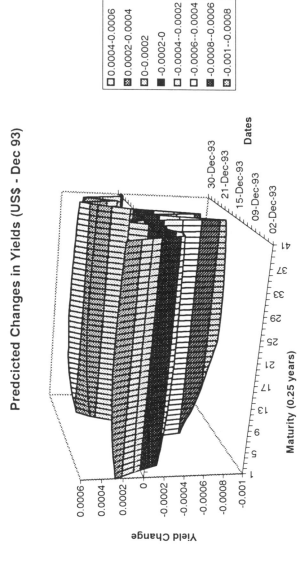

Figure 10.5   See Figure 10.4.

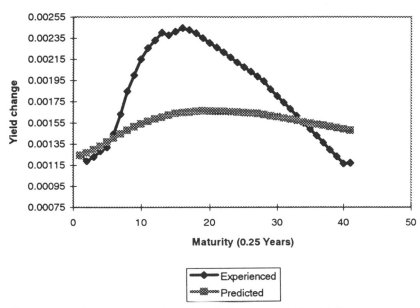

Figure 10.6 Experienced and predicted changes in yields of different maturities for the GB£ curve of 28 Mar 1994. Notice how the predicted changes roughly capture the overall level of the changes.

The BDT model has therefore been shown to enjoy several positive features, but to suffer from two important shortcomings: substantial inability to handle conditions where the impact of a second (tilt) factor could be of relevance; and inability to specify the volatility of yields of different maturities independently of the future volatility of the short rate. The former is unavoidable for any one-factor model; whether and to what extent the latter could be of relevance for a specific option (e.g. a long-maturity swap with principal determined by a short-maturity index) will be discussed in later chapters. Furthermore, nothing has so far been said about the *evolution over time* of the term structure of volatilities. This important topic will be addressed in the context of time inhomogeneous models (Chapter 15).

10.4 DERIVATIVES IN ONE-FACTOR MODELS: THE BDT CASE

It was mentioned in the previous section that the evaluation of derivatives in the BDT model deserves careful consideration. Following BDT's (1990)

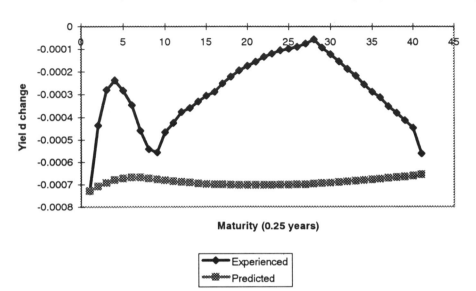

Figure 10.7 Experienced and predicted changes in yields of different maturities for the DEM curve of 17 Mar 1994. It comes as no surprise that the BDT predictions should fail satisfactorily to account for such a complex change in yield curve (with curvature and slope both playing an important part).

original working paper, let us therefore consider the following instruments:

(i)   a T-maturity coupon-bearing bond B;
(ii) a call on this bond struck at X;
(iii) a put on the same bond struck at X,

and let us consider the strategy consisting of

(i)   buying the bond;
(ii) buying the put;
(iii) selling the call.

The bond B will pay n coupons C between now and the expiration time t(opt) of the option ($n = 1$ in the graph below).

$$0\text{-}\,\text{-}\,\text{-}C_1\text{-}\,\text{-}\,\text{-}\,\text{-}\,\text{-}\,|\text{-}\,\text{-}\,\text{-}C_2\text{-}\,\text{-}\,\text{-}\,\text{-}\,\text{-}\,\text{-}\,C_3\text{-}\,\text{-}\,\text{-}\,\text{-}\,\text{-}\,C_4 + \text{Principal}$$
$$t_0 \qquad t(C1) \qquad t(\text{opt})$$

The vertical bar in the graph above indicates the option maturity, and t_0 the present time. Given the strategy chosen, no matter what the prevailing state of the world will be, at option expiry the cashflow from the chosen portfolio will be an amount of currency equal to the strike X with certainty. The total certain payoffs from this strategy will therefore be (i) a coupon C_1 at time $t(C_1)$, and (ii) the strike X at time $t(\text{opt})$. Therefore the payoffs from the original portfolio are identical to the payoffs from a portfolio made up of a discount bond with face value C_1 maturing at $t(C_1)$, and a discount bond maturing at time $t(\text{opt})$ with face value X. If more coupons had intervened between t_0 and $t(\text{opt})$ each would contribute a discount bond. All these zero-coupon bonds can be collectively described as $\{Z_i\}$. One can therefore write

$$P - C + B = \Sigma Z_i \qquad (10.5)$$

where P, C and B indicate the put, the call and the coupon-bearing bond, respectively. The BDT model prices correctly by construction any discount bond; therefore the RHS of Equation (10.5) is correctly priced; **therefore put/call parity is satisfied**.

Let us now consider the hedge ratios, i.e. the 'amount of' coupon-bearing bond needed to hedge (within the model) a call or a put on the bond itself. Differentiating each term in (10.5) with respect to the underlying, B, one obtains:

$$\frac{\partial P}{\partial B} - \frac{\partial C}{\partial B} + \frac{\partial B}{\partial B} = \frac{\partial \Sigma Z_i}{\partial B} = \Delta_{\text{call}} - \Delta_{\text{put}} = 1 - \frac{\partial \Sigma Z_i}{\partial B} \qquad (10.6)$$

The last term on the RHS represents the sensitivity of the portfolio of discount bonds to changes in B. Due to the different choice of numeraire, this term is absent in any Black-like price model, for which the relationship

$$\Delta_{\text{call}} - \Delta_{\text{put}} = 1 \quad \text{(Black model)} \qquad (10.6')$$

always applies. The same type of reasoning can be applied to the gamma sensitivity: differentiating again expression (10.6) with respect to B, one obtains

$$\frac{\partial^2 P}{\partial B^2} - \frac{\partial^2 C}{\partial B^2} = \frac{\partial^2 [\Sigma Z_i]}{\partial B^2} = \Gamma_{\text{put}} - \Gamma_{\text{call}} = \frac{\partial^2 [\Sigma Z_i]}{\partial B^2} \qquad (10.7)$$

Therefore, unlike again the case of the Black model, the gamma exposure of a call is, in general, *not* equal to the gamma of the put, and, depending on the magnitude of the term on the RHS of Equation (10.7) **can be positive or negative**.

Clearly, for a short option on a long bond both

$$\frac{\partial [\Sigma Z_i]}{\partial B} \quad \text{and} \quad \frac{\partial^2 [\Sigma Z_i]}{\partial^2 B}$$

tend to be very small, and therefore the two sensitivities look more and more like the corresponding Black derivatives. Conversely, the more distant the

Table 10.2   The At-the-Money Call and Put Deltas on a 10-year Discount Bond (US$ LIBOR Curve) for Different Expiries. The Quantity in the Last Column is Identically Equal to 1 in the Black Model

Expiry	Delta Call	Delta Put	Delta Call– Delta Put
0.25	0.49003	−0.48996	0.97999
0.50	0.47623	−0.48112	0.95736
1.00	0.45190	−0.45733	0.90923
2.00	0.40348	−0.40441	0.80789
3.00	0.35588	−0.34912	0.70501
4.00	0.30800	−0.29313	0.60113
5.00	0.26194	−0.24095	0.50290
6.00	0.21294	−0.18748	0.40041
7.00	0.16276	−0.13626	0.29902
8.00	0.11086	−0.08766	0.19853
9.00	0.05646	−0.04213	0.09859

maturity of the option, the more time there is for the effect of the discounting (i.e. for the reciprocal of the BDT numeraire, the money market account) to become important. For a *very* long option it is clear that the uncertainty stemming from the optionality itself can be dwarfed by the impact of the discounting. Notice that these conclusions should not be taken to imply that the Black model is wrong, but stem from the different choice of numeraires in the two approaches. Table 10.2 shows this effect by analysing the deltas of at-the-money call and put options of different expiries on a 10-year maturity discount bond (US$ LIBOR curve 24/Feb/95—Vol. 20.00%).

10.5 CALIBRATING THE BDT MODEL: PRICING FRAs, CAPS AND SWAPTIONS USING LATTICE MODELS

The previous sections considered in some detail the issue of how to assess, in the framework of a 'fundamental' approach, the degree of realism of the BDT model. This section tackles the problem of fitting in an efficient way the BDT curve to option market prices. In particular, given the liquidity and importance of caps (floors) and European swaptions, special attention will be devoted to these instruments. In order to accomplish this task, however, it is essential to explore how the price of such instruments as forward rate agreements, caps or European swaptions can be obtained in a systematic way using computational trees. Once again, the specific case of the BDT model will be considered in some detail, but the general principles can easily be applied to different models.

The most elementary building block of caps and swaptions is a forward rate agreement (FRA), described in Chapter 1. For a 'plain-vanilla' FRA of tenor τ, the payment occurs τ years after the reset, i.e. the delay between reset of the index rate and the corresponding payment is equal to the maturity of the index rate. (Typically τ is 0.25 (quarterly) or 0.5 (semi-annual).) This payoff at maturity time T ($T = t_{\text{reset}} + \tau$) per unit principal is therefore given by

$$FRA = (R - X)\tau \qquad (10.8)$$

where τ, as before, is the tenor of the cap, X is the strike, and R is the index rate at expiry.

Remembering (Chapter 1) that the time-0 forward rate f spanning the period i to $i + 1$ is given by

$$F = \frac{\dfrac{P_i}{P_{i+1}} - 1}{\tau} \qquad (10.9)$$

the net present value of an individual FRA was there obtained to be given by

$$NPV(FRA) = \tau(F - X)P_{i+1}$$

$$= \tau\left(\frac{P_i}{P_{i+1}} - 1\right)\frac{1}{\tau}P_{i+1} - X\tau P_{i+1} = P_i - (1 + X\tau)P_{i+1} \qquad (10.10)$$

where P_k is a discounting zero maturing at time k, i and $i + 1$ indicate reset and payment time, respectively, and the other symbols have the usual meaning. Equation (10.10) shows that the net present value of a FRA can be expressed as a linear combination of zero-coupon bonds; these, in turn, are exactly priced by construction in a BDT (or HL) framework. Hence **a FRA is exactly priced by the BDT model**. The same can be said for a swap, which is simply a collection of FRAs. Since the construction of the BDT rate tree is (within numerical error) exact for any volatility, the pricing of a swap is independent of the choice of volatility. (Incidentally, one should notice carefully, as pointed out in Chapter 1 and in the last section of Chapter 5, that, strictly speaking, FRAs set in arrears are not priced by a BDT tree independently of volatility.)

When it comes to options on FRAs, one must distinguish between portfolios of options on FRAs (i.e. caps seen as a collection of caplets), and options on portfolios (linear combinations) of FRAs (forward rates), i.e. swaptions.

Let us consider first of all the simpler case of a portfolio of options, for instance a collection of caplets, making up a cap. The payoff of each individual caplet is determined by the outcome of a τ-maturity rate R reset at time t, and occurs at time $T = t + \tau$

$$\text{Caplet } (T) = \tau \operatorname{Max}[(R - X), 0] \qquad (10.11)$$

At reset time t (corresponding, in BDT discrete time increments, to time step $i = t/\Delta t$), where the reference rate R is observed, one needs to know the distribution of the values of R (e.g. the 6-month LIBOR rate for a semi-annual cap) in the different states of the world. Needless to say, this will in general be different from the short rate which is evolved through the tree, apart from the coarsest of lattices (for practical pricing implementation at least monthly, and often weekly, time steps are in general required). The problem therefore arises of how to associate to each node (i,j) a value for R. But, in each state of the world j at time i the value of this reference rate can easily be obtained by noticing that, at each node (i,j), R_{ij} is given by the ratio of the floating to the fixed leg originating from that node, i.e. by

$$R_{ij} = \frac{P(i,j,i) - P(i,j,i + \tau/\Delta t)}{P(i,j,i + \tau/\Delta t)\tau} = \frac{\dfrac{1}{P(i,j,i + \tau/\Delta t)} - 1}{\tau} \tag{10.12}$$

where $P(i,j,k)$ denotes the value of a k-maturity discount bond at time i in state of the world j. In Equation (10.12) the quantity $P(i,j,i)$ is therefore simply equal to 1. As for $P(i,j,i + \tau/\Delta t)$, i.e. the discount bond at time i maturing after $\tau/\Delta t$ time steps, it is, in general, equal to the risk-neutral expectation of the reciprocal of the money market account (or, rather, of its discrete-time counterpart) taken from the yield curve corresponding to state j:

$$P(i,j,i + \tau/\Delta t) = E'\left[\exp - \int_0^\tau r(s)\,\mathrm{d}s \,\middle|\, r = r(i,j)\right] \tag{10.12'}$$

In turn, this expectation is simply obtained by discounting a unit payoff occurring N time steps after time i back to rate r_{ij}, where N is equal to $\tau/\Delta t$. More precisely, the expectation is evaluated by placing £1 in the $(N + 1)$ of the $(N + i + 1)$ lattice states at time step $i + N$ 'connected with' node (i,j), and then by carrying back this payoff, using the usual averaging/discounting procedure, all the way to node (i,j). As explained in Chapter 6, Section 1, it can be shown that the averaging/discounting procedure is indeed equivalent to discounting along each path, and therefore one can rest assured that the correct (money market account) discounting is indeed carried out. Once Equation (10.12') has been evaluated and the reference rate calculated one must still remember that the actual payoff will actually take place at option *maturity*, i.e. after N time steps, and, therefore, the value of the each payoff (10.11) must be multiplied by the (state-dependent!) discounting factor $P(i,j,i + \tau/\Delta t)$. This quantity, however, has already been computed, state by state, in the evaluation of the reference rate (Equation (10.12')). Therefore, for each state j at option expiry time i, one can create an array $V(i,j)$ given by

$$V_{ij} = \tau \, \mathrm{Max} \left[\frac{\dfrac{1}{P(i,j,i+\tau/\Delta t)} - 1}{\tau} - X, 0 \right] P(i,j,i+\tau/\Delta t) \qquad (10.12'')$$

which contains the value at node (i,j) of the caplet resetting at time $t(i \, \Delta t)$. Finally, in order to obtain the present value of the caplet, the array $V(i,j)$ has to be discounted in the usual manner back to the origin.

For options on a combination of rates, i.e. for instance, for swaptions (see again Chapter 1), what determines the payoff is the difference between the swap rate SR, and the strike rate at expiry. More precisely, the expiry t payoff of a (payer's) swaption is given by

$$\mathrm{Swaption} = \mathrm{Max}[SR - X, 0]B \qquad (10.13)$$

where B is the value of an annuity originating at option expiry, and made up by as many and as frequent payments of X as there are fixed payments in the underlying swap. In Chapter 1 it was shown that, for a plain-vanilla swap, the swap rate SR is given by the ratio of the floating leg to the fixed leg. These were in turn shown to be given by

$$\mathrm{Floating\ leg} = P(t) - P(T) \qquad (10.14)$$

and

$$B = \mathrm{Fixed\ leg} = X \sum_{i=0,n} P(t + i\tau)\tau \qquad (10.14')$$

respectively, where τ is equal to the tenor of the swap, and $T = t + n\tau$ is its maturity. Since the annuity $(10.14')$ is a collection of zero-coupon bonds, the value of B at state (i,j) is obviously priced exactly by the tree as the sum of expectations as the one seen in Equation (10.13). What remains to be determined is therefore the swap rate, SR. However, if one rewrites Equation (10.13) as

$$\mathrm{Swaption} = \mathrm{Max}[SR - X, 0]B = \mathrm{Max}\left[\frac{\mathrm{Float}}{B} - X, 0 \right] B = \mathrm{Max}[\mathrm{Float} - XB, 0]$$

$$(10.13')$$

one can interpret a European swaption as an option to exchange a floating-rate bond (Float) for a fixed-coupon bond (XB). Since the value of the floating leg is given by $P(t) - P(T)$, and, at each node, $P(t) = 1$, all that is required for the evaluation of the expectation at time i and state j of the value of the floating leg is the expectation $E_t[P(T)|r_{ij}]$ contingent on the short rate at time i being in state j. This can be accomplished exactly as shown above for the caplet. Similar considerations apply to the fixed leg. Evaluation of these two quantities then allows computation of the payoff function given by Equation (10.13′); this, in turn, then simply has to be discounted to the origin to give the present value of the swaption.

Both caps and swaptions can therefore be easily computed using BDT lattice trees. Their values, however, will obviously depend on the input volatility of the short rate. As it will be shown, cap prices can be recovered exactly, as can, under specific circumstances, some swaption prices. It will, however, become apparent that, due to the intrinsic one-factor nature of models such as the BDT, it is in general not possible to match *at the same time* both cap *and* swaption prices.

The price of a cap is the sum of the prices of the individual caplets. Let us assume that market prices for caps (of a given tenor) of all maturities are available; i.e. let us assume that the market prices of 6-month, 1-year, 18-month … caps with 6-month tenors are available (for simplicity, the $n + 1$th cap is assumed to have exactly the same reset dates as the nth cap, plus an additional one). For any one-factor model which exactly fits the interest-rates term structure and which allows for a deterministically time-varying volatility, these market prices suggest the following procedure: from the first caplet one can obtain by a trial-and-error procedure the implied volatility of the suitable underlying variable, which, in the case of a BDT model, would be the future volatility of the short rate from time 0 to expiry (6 months in this example) of the first cap(let). By construction, given the tree and this constant volatility over the first 6-month period, the first cap(let) is therefore perfectly priced. Moving on to the second cap price, one can construct the first 6 months of the tree using the previously determined flat volatility, and then search numerically for the constant volatility of the short rate to be used from 6 months to 1 year in order to reproduce the observed market price of the 1-year cap. By so doing, both the 6-month and the 1-year cap are therefore exactly priced by construction. Clearly the procedure can be extended to any cap maturity, since each new maturity always introduces a single new number to be determined, and does not 'spoil' the quantities previously determined. While these considerations are of general validity for any lattice model, for the case of BDT the procedure is even simpler, and the calibration can be accomplished almost instantaneously. Since market caps are priced using the Black formula, and since this, in turn, assumes log-normal forward rates, the market assumptions are very similar with the BDT framework, which displays 'almost' log-normal forward rates (see, however, Chapter 16 for a more precise discussion). Furthermore, by specifying a volatility $\sigma(t)$ in the BDT approach, one is imposing the unconditional variance of the short-rate distribution to be $\sigma(t)^2 t$; but, since at option expiry the forward rate which enters the Black formula becomes a spot rate, the BDT volatility $\sigma(t)$ is (almost) exactly the variance implied by the Black model price. **Tree calibration to market prices of caps can therefore be carried out almost by inspection.**

If one is not interested in pricing consistently *a series* of caplets, and is only interested in a single cap, a unique flat volatility value per all the caplets (rather than a time-varying function) can, of course, price that specific individual cap. However, one must be very careful in using these 'average volatilities': let us assume, to illustrate the dangers, that a four-period cap can be priced with an average (flat) volatility over the four periods of, say, 20%. Let us also assume that a five-period cap can be priced with, say, an 18% volatility. These two combined pieces of information have a strong implication for the implied forward volatility of the short rate from period 4 to period 5. If one priced the first four periods of the 5-year cap with the constant volatility of the four-period cap (i.e. 20%) one can easily compute the remaining variance added by the 5th period, and one can derive the implied forward volatility. But, for low enough values of the market price of the five-period cap, no solution might be found, i.e. only a zero or negative volatility could satisfy the constraints. (The situation is closely reminiscent of the possibility of negative forward rates often found when describing a yield curve in terms of gross redemption yields.) This implies that, for a given model, average volatilities cannot decline too sharply.

While the first procedure described above is therefore constructed to produce in most cases admissible short-rate volatilities when pricing consistently different caps, the 'average volatility' method is not guaranteed to yield meaningful results. The situation, once again, is very similar to discounting cash flows using a gross redemption yield or spot rates.

The issue of the time dependence of the volatility of the short rate in the BDT model warrants more careful analysis. As explained previously (see Section 9.1), the BDT model achieves mean reversion by allowing for the short-rate volatility to decline with time. One essential feature of mean-reverting models is that rates do not assume 'implausibly' large values over very long time horizons. In practical terms, they embody our expectation that the possible values explored by the short rate over, say, the next 30 years should not be significantly different from the range of values encountered over, say, a 40-year period. In general, when using a declining function for the future volatility of the short rate, care must be taken to ensure that the resulting model is viable. In particular, one's information about future financial quantities at a later time t'' must always be less than the equivalent information regarding an earlier time t'. Our loss of information is translated in a diffusion model by an increase in the variance of the process. Therefore, the increase in variance from time t' to time in t'' due to the passage of time must not be reduced to zero or allowed to become negative. Since the volatility used at each time i in a BDT tree produces a process for the short-rate of *total* (uncondi-

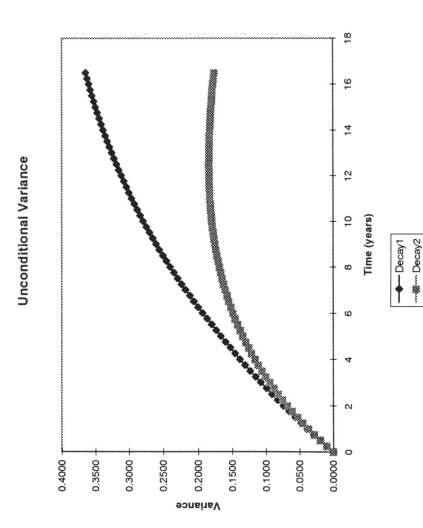

Figure 10.8 The unconditional variance implied by a declining short-rate volatility of functional form $\sigma(\tau) = \sigma 0 \exp[-\nu\tau]$, with $\sigma = 20\%$, $\nu = 0.0180$ and $\nu = 0.040$. Notice that for the higher value of the decay constant ν ('Decay2' in the graph) the unconditional variance is not a monotonically increasing function of time, implying that, as of time 0, more is known about a future time t'' than about an earlier time t'.

tional) variance given by

$$\text{Var}(r; t = i \, \Delta t) = \sigma(t)^2 i \, \Delta t \tag{10.15}$$

the following relationship (a similar relationship links spot rates of different maturity if negative forward rates (and hence possibilities of arbitrage) are to be avoided: $r(t'') > r(t')t'/t''$) must hold:

$$\sigma(t'')^2 > \sigma(t')^2 \frac{t'}{t''} \tag{10.16}$$

Figure 10.8 illustrates what happens when the decrease in volatility is too sharp: the resulting BDT tree might imply that we know more about a future time t'' than about an earlier time t'.

In practice one observes that by following the first procedure, the implied short-rate volatility curve obtained from the market is generally declining over time, possibly after an initial hump (see Figure 9.3). As pointed out above, a declining volatility of the short rate implies a mean-reverting BDT distribution of rates. This is paralleled by the market practice, in the context of the commonly adopted Black model, of using declining *forward* rates volatilities. Both 'stratagems' attempt to avoid in a simple way an excessive dispersion of the rates which would make long-dated caps 'too' expensive: a constant-volatility BDT tree might assign significant probabilities to implausibly high rates (see Figures 9.1 and 9.2), and a cap priced off this tree would therefore offer 'unnecessary' protection. The remarks made in Section 9.1 regarding Black volatilities and yield-curve-model volatilities in general apply very clearly to the BDT case. In particular, correct obtainment of today's prices of an arbitrary number of market caps should not disguise the fact that, for a declining implied (Black) volatility, the forward volatility (Equation (9.4)) will tend to smaller and smaller values, thus implying an asymptotically deterministic model.

As for European swaptions, as pointed out above, they can be indifferently regarded as options to pay or receive the fixed leg of a swap in exchange for the floating leg, or as options on the underlying forward swap rate. A forward swap rate, in turn, for a swap with tenor τ, has been shown in Chapter 1 to be a linear combination of τ-period forward rates. Hence, as stated before, a swaption can be priced as an option on a combination of forward rates.

Looking at a swaption in this light shows one of the biggest problems of swaption valuation in the framework of any one-factor model. In any such model, in fact, all rates are perfectly correlated, and, if the short-rate process were assigned the volatilities needed to price the market caps, the forward equilibrium rate volatility would therefore be overstated by such a model (see Chapter 1 again): roughly speaking, one-factor models do not allow for the possibility that one forward rate might be moving up while another might be declining. Market prices of swaptions clearly reflect this imperfect correlation between rates, as one can readily observe, at least in liquid markets, by comparing the observed cap and swaption volatility curves. In the context of the BDT model, it is not difficult, for an individual swaption, to adjust the overall volatility in such a way as to ensure that the BDT tree produces the same swaption price as observed in the market. Problems creep in, however, as one considers in conjunction caps and swaptions, or a series of swaptions, since the model is intrinsically inadequate to reproduce the overall variance–covariance matrix of the forward rates (see Chapter 2, Section 2).

As long as one is interested in pricing a single European swaption (and one is ready to misprice the 'underlying' caplets), then the distributional assumptions of the BDT model are, once again, of great help. The swap rate implied by the BDT tree is in fact *approximately* log-normal, and bounded by zero from below. Therefore the BDT distributional assumptions are very similar to the assumptions underlying the Black model, as used in the market for swaptions. Furthermore, since the volatilities of yields of different maturities display rather small variations, **a very good guess to the swap rate volatility can be obtained by using for the desired unconditional variance of the short-rate, i.e. by using for $\sigma(t)$ the implied swap rate volatility obtainable from the Black swaption prices**.

As pointed out above a *generic* series of swaps cannot be consistently priced by any one BDT tree. There are situations, however, when the BDT model can still be reasonably calibrated to yield market results, even in the case of several swaptions. Let us consider, in fact, a series of swaptions to enter at different time swaps, all terminating on the same calendar date, e.g. a 6-month swaption into a 3.5-year swap, and 1-year swaption into a 3-year swap, etc. This is of greater relevance than one might initially surmise, since these are the European swaptions underlying a callable bond, or a fixed-maturity American swaption. In this situation, it is possible to describe the short-rate volatility as a time-varying function (for practical purposes a step-wise continuous function will do) such that, in the example above, the first constant value for the volatility spans the time steps between time 0 and 6 months, and the constant level of the volatility is chosen in such a way as to give the correct market price for the first swaption; the second step then goes from 6 months plus 1 time step to 1 year, and its level is determined so as to achieve a match of the second swaption market price; the procedure is continued until all the swaptions are priced. This approach allows the introduction of as many degrees of freedom as market values to be matched in such a way that each new segment does not 'spoil' the values obtained for swaptions of shorter maturity.

The positioning of the boundaries of the step function is crucial: if the first constant segment covered a period between time 0 and, say, 9 months, in general an exact match of the market values will not be obtained. This result is not as intuitively obvious as one might at first surmise: Figure 10.9 compares the volatility fitting for a cap and for a series of swaptions, and clearly shows

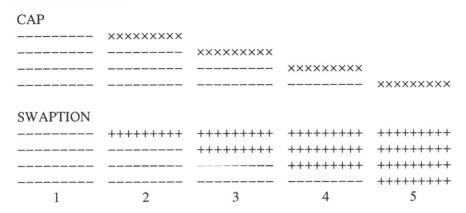

Figure 10.9 The successive periods involved by a series of caplets (×××) and by a series of swaptions with option life indicated by (−−−) and swap residual life shown by (+++). All the swaps into which the options give a right to exercise mature on the same calendar date. Notice how new ××× segments do not affect previous periods, while different +++ segments overlap. Each section (1 to 5) corresponds to one tenor (6 months for the example above).

that, while in the fitting of cap volatilities non-overlapping periods are used in turn, the same is not true for a series of swaptions.

If one had to price a generic set of swaptions, i.e. not necessarily swaptions maturing at the same calendar date, no procedure will produce, within a BDT approach, all the market prices. How important this might be depends on specific cases, but, in general, the effect cannot be safely neglected.

The possibility to adjust the volatility curve in such a way as to 'force' the BDT model to price specific swaptions as the market does not obscure the fact that the model has intrinsic shortcomings for all those options where imperfect correlation between rates plays an important role. Under these circumstances users should therefore be particularly careful in interpreting the results. Needless to say, there is nothing special about the BDT model in so far as this aspect is concerned, since all one-factor models (e.g. the more complex Extended CIR or Vasicek) display the same deficiency.

Depending on what the most important shortcoming of the BDT approach might be perceived to be, several avenues are open for 'better' pricing: if the imperfect correlation among rates implied by the model were deemed to be the essential missing ingredient (e.g. for a spread option) then a two-factor model, such as the Longstaff and Schwartz (Chapter 12), the Heath Jarrow and Morton (Chapter 14) or the Brennan and Schwartz (Chapter 13), would be the obvious way forward; if the impossibility to prescribe independently the future volatility of the short rate and the term structure of volatilities were perceived to be of importance for a particular option, then the time-dependent Hull and

White model (Chapter 11) could provide the answer; if the lack of control upon the future evolution of the term structure of volatilities were a source of concern, a time-homogeneous model could be appropriate (Chapter 15). All these approaches are, however, not without their own drawbacks, as shown later on, and the ease of calibration of the BDT model, dealt with in Section 5 of this chapter, should not be overlooked.

11

The Hull and White approach

11.1 INTRODUCTION AND MOTIVATION

One of the most important conclusions reached in the chapter devoted to the BDT/HL models was that, within the class of the one-factor models, one of their most important shortcomings stemmed from their inability to fit, at the same time, an arbitrary term structure of volatilities *and* a pre-assigned future behaviour for the volatility of the short rate. It is true that little can be guessed, *a priori*, about the future behaviour of the volatility of the short rate, but, in general, one would like the process to display roughly stationary properties. The BDT/HL models, as it has been shown, require instead that the volatility of the short rate should decay over time, from today's time origin, for mean reversion to take place.

More precisely, it was observed in Chapter 10 that there are at least two distinct ways of imparting to the process for the short rate the mean-reverting character which is needed in order to bring about a realistic description of the dynamics of the term structure, and to reproduce the market prices for caps and swaptions (which, in turn, embody this feature): the first way is to impose a decaying behaviour to the *stochastic* component of the process (this is the approach taken by BDT and HL); the second is to assign an explicitly mean-reverting component to the *deterministic* component of the short-rate process. It is, in fact, possible to choose the parameters of the volatility-decaying process and of the deterministically mean-reverting model in such a way that, as seen from time 0, both distributions will appear indistinguishable. The same is no longer true, however, if one considers the distributions obtainable, using the same parameters, from a later time τ: if, for simplicity, one considers constant parameters for the deterministically time-reverting distribution, then a self-identical distribution will be re-obtained by restarting the drift/diffusion process from time τ. The volatility-decaying process, instead, will produce a new distribution from time τ onwards with a much lower variance per unit time than what was obtained from time 0 to time τ. If τ were very large, in order to obtain a stationary distribution, i.e. in this context, a distribution whose variance does not appreciably grow as τ goes to infinity, the forward process for the short rate would have to be virtually purely deterministic. Clearly this can have rather serious implications if one were attempting to price, for instance, long-dated American options, or options, in general, where the future distributions of rates for distant time horizons plays an important role.

Deterministically mean-reverting processes, especially if implemented with constant coefficients do, therefore, possess a valuable positive feature. Of the approaches belonging to this class, however, those which have been examined so far (i.e. the CIR/Vasicek models) had the important drawback of not being able to reproduce an arbitrary market yield curve, and, consequently, for all the qualitative illuminating insight they might provide, they have rarely, if ever, been used in actual dealing situations.

A significant breakthrough took place when Hull and White (HW) introduced a class of models which *both* incorporate deterministically mean-reverting features *and* allow perfect matching of an arbitrary yield curve. In addition, their models allow, if one so desires, an exact matching of an arbitrary term structure of volatilities, at least as seen from time 0. Since, however, this latter implementation has the undesirable effect of introducing some of the unwanted effects (i.e. potentially undesirable future behaviour of the short-rate volatility) that this class of models can successfully overcome, practitioners (and the authors themselves) have tended to favour the specification which allows perfect matching of the yield curve, and an overall satisfactory, although not perfect, match to the term structure of volatilities, without imposing any time dependence on the volatility of the short rate. Both approaches will be examined in the following.

For a particular specification of the process, Hull and White managed to obtain closed-form solutions for the prices of caps and floors, and, by applying Jamshidian's suggestion (Jamshidian (1990))[1] to the one-factor version of their model, for the prices of options on coupon-bearing bonds (i.e. swaptions). Model calibration, to which so much attention is paid in this book, could therefore, at least in principle, be carried out in a very efficient way, without having to make use of time-consuming numerical procedures. Even when computational lattices are required, the possibility of recovering, at each node, the whole future yield curve from the known values of the parameters and of the state variables constitutes a very powerful advantage.

Despite these very important positive features the Extended Vasicek (EV) model, as the normal-rates Hull and White model has often been called, is not without its shortcomings. The most obvious ones stem from the possibility for rates to attain negative values; this feature, *per se*, has probably been unduly overemphasised, and can have a rather limited impact, especially for a mean-reverting model. Potentially more serious problems can, however, arise, as will be shown in a later section, if one attempts exact calibration of a normal one-factor model to cap prices, especially for certain combinations of yield-curve shapes and market cap volatilities.

The next two sections of this chapter, as mentioned above, will first illustrate how the HW approach can produce an exact fit to a market yield curve and still allow closed-form solutions for bond options. Following sections will tackle the issue of the trinomial lattice methodology which has become intimately connected with the one-factor version of the Extended Vasicek model, and the above-mentioned problems regarding the calibration. The last sections will then explore to what extent the two-factor version of the HW approach can offer a solution to the shortcomings of the simpler one-factor model, and supply the user with a viable calibration procedure.

11.2 SPECIFICATION OF THE ONE-FACTOR VERSION OF THE MODEL

It will be recalled from Chapter 9 that the CIR and Vasicek models could be obtained starting from a common (within the exponential parameter β) specification of the process for the short rate:

$$dr = a(b - r)\, dt + \sigma r^\beta\, dz \qquad (11.1)$$

(the notation has been modified to conform with Hull and White conventions). In Equation (11.1), a, b, and σ are all positive constants, and β assumes the value of $\frac{1}{2}$ in the CIR model, and of 0 in the Vasicek approach.

Hull and White generalise this specification by allowing for a time-dependent drift $\theta(t)$, and for explicit time dependence in the reversion speed $(a \Rightarrow a(t))$ and in the volatility $(\sigma \Rightarrow \sigma(t))$:

$$dr = [\theta(t) - a(t)r]\, dt + \sigma(t)r^\beta\, dz \qquad (11.1')$$

One can notice that, by redefining $b'(t) = \theta(t)/a(t) + b$, one can rewrite Equation (11.1') as

$$dr = a(t)[b'(t) - r]\, dt + \sigma(t)r^\beta\, dz \qquad (11.2)$$

thereby showing that the specification (11.1') is equivalent to a mean-reverting model where the reversion level, $b'(t)$, is a function of time. Therefore, as anticipated in Chapter 9, both the CIR and the Vasicek models can be recovered as special cases of the HW approach, with a and b constant, and $\beta = \frac{1}{2}$ or 0, respectively. The models which correspond to these particular choices of β will be referred to in the following as the Extended CIR (EXCIR) and the Extended Vasicek (EXV) models, respectively. For clarity of exposition, the most general HW model will be written as

$$dr = [\theta(t) + a(t)[b(t) - r]]\, dt + \sigma(t)r^\beta\, dz \qquad (11.2')$$

By looking at the results of the sections devoted to the BDT model it can also be appreciated that this latter model as well can be retrieved as a special case of the HW specification (11.1), since it was there obtained that

$$d(\ln r) = \left[\theta'(t) + \frac{\partial \ln \sigma(t)}{\partial t} \ln r \right] dt + \sigma(t)\, dz \quad [\text{BDT}] \qquad (11.3)$$

which obviously corresponds to the choice of 1 for the value of β. Finally, with a β of 0 the Ho and Lee model can be retrieved, since their process can be described by an expression of the form

$$dr = \theta''(t)\, dt + \sigma(t)\, dz \quad [\text{HL}] \qquad (11.4)$$

The HW extended approach is therefore of sufficient generality to encompass as special cases most of the one-factor models analysed so far.

In order to derive the properties of the HW model both in the case of $\beta = 0$ and of $\beta = \frac{1}{2}$, one can make use of the no-arbitrage condition derived in Chapter 5, Section 1: it was there shown that, by imposing the maturity independence of the market price of risk λ, one could associate a parabolic PDE to any diffusion process for the short rate (the Feynman–Kac theorem). Slightly changing the notation there employed to conform with Hull and White's, the 'real-world' value $f(t)$ at time t of any contingent claim is given by the solution of a PDE of the type (see Equation (5.8))

$$\frac{\partial f}{\partial t} - \mu_r \frac{\partial f}{\partial r} + \frac{1}{2} \sigma_r(t)^2 \frac{\partial^2 f}{\partial r^2} = rf - \lambda(t) \frac{\partial f}{\partial r} \sigma_r(t) \qquad (11.5)$$

which gives, for the variance and drift assumed by the Extended HW models,

$$\frac{\partial f}{\partial t} [\phi(t) - a(t)r] \frac{\partial f}{\partial r} + \frac{1}{2} \sigma(t)^2 r^{2\beta} \frac{\partial^2 f}{\partial r^2} - rf = 0$$

$$\phi(t) \equiv \theta(t) + a(t)b - \lambda(t)r^\beta \sigma(t) \qquad (11.5')$$

For the special case when $\beta = 0$, i.e. for a normal short-rate model, Equation (11.5') becomes

$$\frac{\partial f}{\partial t} + [\phi(t) - a(t)r] \frac{\partial f}{\partial r} + \frac{1}{2} \sigma(t)^2 \frac{\partial^2 f}{\partial r^2} - rf = 0$$

$$\phi(t) \equiv \theta(t) + a(t)b - \lambda(t)\sigma(t) \qquad (11.5'')$$

If Equation (11.5'') is taken to refer to the value at time t of a pure discount bond of maturity T, $P(t,T)$, then the appropriate initial condition is $P(T,T) = 1$.

In this case, following Hull and White (1990a), one can conjecture a solution to (11.5'') to be of the form

$$P(t,T) = A(t,T) \exp[-B(t,T)r] \tag{11.6}$$

so long as the functions A and B are such that they satisfy the differential equations

$$\frac{\partial B}{\partial t} - a(t)B + 1 = 0 \tag{11.7}$$

$$\frac{\partial A}{\partial t} - \phi(t)AB + \frac{1}{2}\sigma(t)^2 AB^2 = 0 \tag{11.8}$$

and $A(T,T) = 1$ and $B(T,T) = 0$. One can easily verify, in fact, after taking the appropriate derivatives,

$$\frac{\partial P}{\partial r} = -A(t,T)e^{-B(t,T)r}B(t,T) = -B(t,T)P \tag{11.9}$$

$$\frac{\partial^2 P}{\partial r^2} = B(t,T)^2 P \tag{11.9'}$$

$$\frac{\partial P}{\partial t} = \frac{\partial A}{\partial t}[e^{-B(t,T)r}] - A(t,T)e^{-B(t,T)r}r\frac{\partial B}{\partial t} = P\left(\frac{1}{A}\frac{\partial A}{\partial t} - r\frac{\partial B}{\partial t}\right) \tag{11.9''}$$

that substituting Equations (11.9), (11.9') and (11.9'') into Equation (11.5'') (using Equations (11.7) and (11.8)) gives an identity. Notice that the solution has been assumed to be given by the product of a function A depending only on t and T, and a function $e^{-B(t,T)r}$, which, in turn, depends on a function of t and T only, and the short rate. It therefore belongs to the class of the affine models, discussed in Chapter 15.

Equations (11.7) and (11.8) describe two differential equations that have to be satisfied by $A(t,T)$ and $B(t,T)$ for the partial differential equation (11.6) to hold true. It will be shown later on that the information about the current term structures of rates and volatilities can determine the values of $A(0,T)$ and $B(0,T)$. In order to obtain the equation for the value of a call on a discount bond, however, an expression for the future value of the bond itself at a later time, i.e. $P(t,T)$, will be needed. By Equation (11.6) this, in turn, will require knowledge of $A(t,T)$ and $B(t,T)$. In order to be able to evaluate this quantity, let us therefore assume for the moment that $A(0,T)$ and $B(0,t)$ are known, and let us attempt to eliminate the functions $a(t)$ and $\phi(t)$ from Equations (11.7) and (11.8). To this effect, one can differentiate these two equations with respect to T, giving

$$\frac{\partial^2 A}{\partial t\, \partial T} - \phi(t)\left[\frac{\partial A}{\partial T} B + A \frac{\partial B}{\partial T}\right] + \frac{1}{2}\sigma(t)^2\left[\frac{\partial A}{\partial T} B^2 + 2AB \frac{\partial B}{\partial T}\right] = 0 \quad (11.8')$$

$$\frac{\partial^2 B}{\partial t\, \partial T} - a(t)\frac{\partial B}{\partial T} = 0 \quad\quad\quad (11.8'')$$

These two equations contain $a(t)$ and $\phi(t)$, which can therefore be eliminated from (11.7) and (11.8) at the expense of making the resulting differential equation of the second order:

$$AB \frac{\partial^2 A}{\partial t\, \partial T} - B \frac{\partial A}{\partial t}\frac{\partial A}{\partial T} - A \frac{\partial A}{\partial t}\frac{\partial B}{\partial T} + \frac{1}{2}[\sigma(t)AB]^2 \frac{\partial B}{\partial T} \quad (11.9''')$$

The boundary conditions $A(T,T) = 1$ and $B(T,T) = 0$, by construction satisfied by the chosen functions A and B, can then be invoked to obtain

$$B(t,T) = \frac{B(0,T) - B(0,t)}{\dfrac{\partial B(0,t)}{\partial t}} \quad\quad (11.10)$$

$$A'(t,T) = A'(0,t) - A'(0,t) - B(t,T)\frac{\partial A'(0,t)}{\partial t}$$

$$- \frac{1}{2}\left[B(t,T)\frac{\partial B(0,t)}{\partial t}\right]^2 \int_0^t \left[\frac{\sigma(\tau)}{\dfrac{\partial B(0,\tau)}{\partial \tau}}\right]^2 d\tau \quad (11.10')$$

where $A'(t,T)$ denotes the logarithm of $A(t,T)$. Notice that Equations (11.10) and (11.10') can both be expressed in terms of $A(0,t)$ and $B(0,t)$, which have for the moment been assumed to be known to the user ($B(t,T)$ in (11.10') can be substituted out from (11.10)).

Finally, substituting the obtained expressions for A and B in Equations (11.8') and (11.8'') one can retrieve $a(t)$ and $\phi(t)$ as

$$a(t) = \frac{\dfrac{\partial^2 B(0,t)}{\partial t^2}}{\dfrac{\partial B(0,t)}{\partial t}} \quad\quad (11.11)$$

$$\phi(t) = -a(t) \frac{\partial A'(0,t)}{\partial t} - \frac{\partial^2 A'(0,t)}{\partial t^2} + \left(\frac{\partial B(0,t)}{\partial t}\right)^2 \int_0^t \left[\frac{\sigma(\tau)}{\frac{\partial B(0,\tau)}{\partial \tau}}\right]^2 dt \quad (11.12)$$

Let us now go back for a moment to Equation (11.6), and, by using Ito's lemma, obtain the stochastic component of the discount bond price process:

$$dP(t,T) = \mu_{P(t,T)} dt + \frac{\partial P}{\partial r} \sigma dz$$

$$= \mu_{P(t,T)} dt + P(t,T)B(t,T)\sigma dz \equiv \mu_{P(t,T)} dt + v(t,T)P(t,T)\sigma dz$$

$$(11.13)$$

As Equation (11.13) shows, the process for the bond price corresponding to a normal process for the short rate is log-normal, with percentage volatility $v(t,T) = \sigma(t)B(t,T)$. But if this is the case, one can readily compute the value of a European call option C with expiry at time t on a bond maturing at time T: using as numeraire the discount bond maturing at time t, one can in fact work in the forward-neutral measure (see Chapter 5, Section 5), under which prices forwarded to time t are martingales (driftless). As shown in Chapter 5, the appropriate volatility will be the volatility of the forward bond price, $FP(t,T)$, i.e. the volatility of $P(0,T)/P(0,t)$. Since both spot discount bond prices entering the expression for the forward bond price are log-normal, the forward bond price is also log-normally distributed, with percentage volatility $v_{FP(t,T)}$ given by

$$v_{FP(t,T)} = \int_0^t v(\tau,T)^2 + v(\tau,t)^2 - 2\rho v(\tau,t)v(\tau,T) \, d\tau \quad (11.14)$$

But, since we are working in the context of a one-factor model, $\rho = 1$, and therefore

$$v_{FP(t,T)} = \int_0^t \sigma(\tau)[B(\tau,T) - B(\tau,t)]^2 \, d\tau \quad (11.14')$$

We are finally in a position to use Black's formula for the value of the call option struck at X, and to write

$$C = P(0,t)[P(t,T)N(h_1) - XN(h_2)] \quad (11.15)$$

where we have taken the liberty to denote the forward bond price by $P(t,T)$ (which strictly denotes the *future* value of the bond price), since, for this particular measure, future and forward prices coincide and, therefore, $v_{P(t,T)} = v_{FP(t,T)}$. (The same result can be arrived at using Margrabe's (1978) or

Merton's (1973) approach.) As usual

$$N(h_{1,2}) = NDTR \left[\frac{\ln \dfrac{P(t,T)}{X} \pm v(t,T)^2 t}{v(t,T)\sqrt{t}} \right] \qquad (11.16)$$

and $NDTR$ denotes the cumulative normal distribution. The quantity $v_{P(t,T)}$ can be obtained from (11.14′); the quantities $B(\tau,t)$ and $B(\tau,T)$ can be obtained from Equation (11.10); as for the bond prices $P(0,T)$ and $P(0,t)$ they are clearly available from the current yield curve, or, equivalently, within the model, from Equation (11.6). **Notice that, by the way the solution has been constructed, it automatically holds true for any arbitrary deterministic function $\theta(t)$, and, therefore, the closed form solution (11.16) holds for any arbitrary shape of the yield curve.** If the quantities $B(0,t)$ can be supplied, then the task has been accomplished of obtaining an expression as simple as Vasicek's (or, for that matter, Black's) for a model yield curve that exactly matches any given market input. The next section will therefore show how the quantities $B(0,t)$ can be obtained from the term structure of volatilities.

11.3 EXACT FITTING OF THE MODEL TO THE TERM STRUCTURE OF VOLATILITIES

Let us denote the continuously compounded yield of a T-maturity discount bond by

$$R(t,T) = -\frac{\ln P(r,t,T)}{T-t} = \frac{A'(t,T) - rB(t,T)}{T-t} \qquad (11.17)$$

where the dependence of the discount bond price on the short rate has been emphasised in the notation. Ito's lemma can therefore be applied to $R(t,T)$ seen as a function of r to obtain

$$\sigma_{R(t,T)} = \frac{\partial R(t,T)}{\partial r(t)} \, \sigma(t) = \frac{B(t,T)\sigma(t)}{T-t} \qquad (11.18)$$

whence $B(t,T)$ can be easily obtained as

$$B(t,T) = \frac{(T-t)\sigma_{R(t,T)}}{\sigma(t)} \qquad (11.18')$$

(Notice that absolute, rather than percentage, volatilities have been used in the expressions above.) At time 0 Equation (11.18') reads

$$B(0,T) = \frac{T\sigma_{R(0,T)}}{\sigma(0)} \qquad (11.18'')$$

and therefore, the **quantity $B(0,T)$, needed to evaluate, via Equation (11.10), $B(t,T)$, and, in turn, $P(t,T)$, can be expressed as a function of the current term structure of spot yield volatilities, i.e. as a function of quantities known to the user at time 0.** (Using Ito's lemma it is then just as easy, if one so desires, to translate the spot into forward rate volatilities.) The quantities $A(0,T)$, that appear in expression (11.10') and as building blocks of $P(0,T)$, can then be straightforwardly obtained from the current term structure of interest rates:

$$P(0,T) = A(0,T)\exp[-B(0,T)r] \qquad (11.19)$$

once the quantities $B(0,T)$ are known. Once the functions $B(0,T)$ and $A(0,T)$ have been obtained the user will need to interpolate between the 'observed' values in order to evaluate the derivatives appearing in Equations (11.10'), (11.11) and (11.12). As one might expect, care and some common sense must be exercised in the process if sensible results are to be obtained.

Using Equations (11.18) and (11.19) it is therefore possible to specify a normal rate model which (i) prices discount bonds exactly, (ii) displays mean reversion, (iii) allows for an arbitrary future volatility of the short rate, (iv) allows for an arbitrary term structure of volatilities and (v) gives closed-form solutions for options on discount bond options. In this formulation, the HW model can be numerically implemented using techniques closely linked to the EFD methodology and reviewed in their essence in Chapter 7 (Hull and White (1990a), (1990b)). In the form described above, however, the HW model is rarely used. The reason for this, as pointed out by HW (1995) themselves, is that the combined exact fit to the future volatility of the short rate *and* to an arbitrary term structure of volatilities has been observed, especially for markets like US$ or GP£ displaying a humped cap volatility curve, to give rise to implausible *future* term structures of volatilities (see also Chapter 15 for a discussion of this point). The preference has therefore shifted towards implementations which allow for a more direct control on the future model behaviour, as can be, for instance, enforced by imposing a constant volatility and a constant reversion speed. The price to be paid for this increase in robustness and distributional realism is that cap prices can no longer be exactly recovered. The practical effectiveness of, and the problems connected with, this procedure will be discussed in Section 11.5. Before that, the next section will present the procedure which can be employed in order to construct in a very efficient manner the tri-nomial lattice associated with the constant-volatility, constant-reversion-speed Extended Vasicek model.

11.4 CONSTRUCTING THE HW TREE FOR CONSTANT REVERSION SPEED AND VOLATILITY

The computational tri-nomial lattice used to price derivative instruments using the HW model with constant volatility and reversion speed is closely linked to the grid set up for the EFD method (see Chapter 7, Section 3). After the grid spacing has been chosen, the space/time mesh can then be subdivided into two time regions, the 'normal' region (from time 0 to time t_{sw}) and the 'switch' region (from time t_{sw} onwards); the 'switch' region, in turn, can be subdivided into upwards, normal-, and downward-switching regions. In the upward (downward) region, upward (downward) switching prevails, i.e. from node (i,j) nodes $(i+1,j)$, $(i+1,j+1)$, $(i+1,j+2)$ (nodes $(i+1,j)$, $(i+1,j-1)$, $(i+1,j-2)$) are reached, respectively (where, as usual, i denotes the time, and j the space coordinate); in the normal region branching occurs from (i,j) to $(i+1,j)$, $(i+1,j+1)$ and $(i+1,j-1)$. See Figure 11.1.

For all these different possible branching modes, p_u, p_m and p_d will always denote the probabilities of moving to the uppermost, middle or bottom node. The fitting to a set of market discount bonds is achieved by determining these probabilities.

From the previous discussion (see Equations (11.1) and (11.2)) it is clear that the burden of pricing exactly the market discount bonds is carried by the function $\theta(t)$. Hull and White therefore decouple the contribution to the drift of the short rate coming from the market-fitting function $\theta(t)$ from the contribution arising from the mean reversion $(-ar\, dt)$. Assuming, to start with, that the function θ is identically zero, the HW model becomes

$$dr = a(0 - r)\, dt + \sigma\, dz = -ar\, dt + \sigma\, dz \qquad (11.20)$$

where the first expression clearly shows that the short rate reverts to 0 with a reversion speed a $(a>0)$. The short rate is also assumed, in the first part of the construction, to start from 0. As usual, one can then proceed to determine the probabilities, say p_u and p_d, by imposing that the first two moments should be exactly recovered. More precisely, the expectation of the short rate at time $t+1$, contingent upon the short rate having value $r_0 + j\,\Delta r$ at time t, is given by

$$E[r(t+1)\,|\,r(t) = r_0 + j\,\Delta r] = r(t,j) + \mu\,\Delta t$$
$$= r_0 + j\,\Delta r - a(r_0 + j\,\Delta r)\Delta t = j\,\Delta r - aj\,\Delta t \qquad (11.21)$$

since $r_0 = 0$ in the first phase of the construction. But the expectation (normal branching) is also given by

$$E[r(t+1)\,|\,r(t) = r_0 + j\,\Delta r]$$
$$= p_u(r_0 + (j+1)\Delta r) + p_m(r_0 + j\,\Delta r) + p_d(r_0 + (j-1)\Delta r)$$
$$= [p_u + p_m + p_d]r_0 + [p_u + p_m + p_d]j\,\Delta r$$
$$+ [p_u - p_d]\,\Delta r = j\,\Delta r + [p_u - p_d]\,\Delta r \qquad (11.22)$$

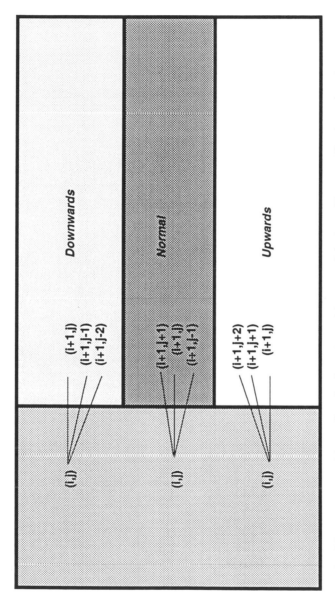

Figure 11.1 The different regions of the Hull and White tri-nomial tree, and the branching prevailing in each region

where use has been made of $[p(\text{up}) + p(\text{m}) + p(\text{down})] \equiv 1$. Equating the two expressions for the expectation, and cancelling the common $j\,\Delta r$ term, gives

$$(p_u - p_d)\,\Delta r = -aj\,\Delta r\,\Delta t \tag{11.23}$$

A similar calculation for the variance gives

$$(p_u + p_d)\,\Delta r^2 = \sigma^2\,\Delta t + a^2 j^2\,\Delta r^2\,\Delta t^2 \tag{11.23'}$$

A variety of choices can *a priori* be made for the ratio $\Delta r/\sqrt{\Delta t}$. Considerations of numerical efficiency suggest a value in the region of $\sigma\sqrt{3}$ (Hull and White (1994a)). With this value for the ratio substituted in Equations (11.23) and (11.23'), and remembering that $p_m = 1 - p_u - p_d$, one obtains, for normal branching

$$p_u = \tfrac{1}{6} + \tfrac{1}{2}aj\,\Delta t(aj\,\Delta t - 1) \tag{11.24}$$

$$p_m = \tfrac{2}{3} - (aj\,\Delta t)^2 \tag{11.24'}$$

$$p_d = \tfrac{1}{6} + \tfrac{1}{2}aj\,\Delta t(aj\,\Delta t + 1) \tag{11.24''}$$

The probabilities will all be positive as long as

$$j > -\frac{1}{\Delta ta\,\sqrt{3}} \tag{11.25}$$

$$j < \frac{1}{\Delta ta\,\sqrt{3}} \tag{11.25'}$$

Identical reasoning gives for the upward branching

$$p_u = \tfrac{1}{6} + \tfrac{1}{2}aj\,\Delta t(aj\,\Delta t + 1) \tag{11.26}$$

$$p_d = \tfrac{7}{6} + \tfrac{1}{2}aj\,\Delta t(3 + aj\,\Delta t) \tag{11.26'}$$

$$p_m = -\tfrac{1}{3} - aj\,\Delta t(aj\,\Delta t + 1) \tag{11.26''}$$

with positivity conditions

$$j > -\frac{1.816}{\Delta ta} \tag{11.27}$$

$$j < -\frac{0.184}{\Delta ta} \tag{11.27'}$$

and, for downward branching,

$$p_u = \tfrac{1}{6} + \tfrac{1}{2}aj\,\Delta t(aj\,\Delta t - 1) \tag{11.28}$$

$$p_d = \tfrac{7}{6} + \tfrac{1}{2}aj\,\Delta t(-3 + aj\,\Delta t) \tag{11.28'}$$

$$p_m = \tfrac{1}{3} - aj\,\Delta t(aj\,\Delta t - 2) \tag{11.28''}$$

with positivity conditions

$$j < \frac{1.816}{\Delta ta} \tag{11.29}$$

$$j > \frac{0.184}{\Delta ta} \tag{11.29'}$$

The probabilities for the different types of branching are shown in Figure 11.2, for a reversion speed of 0.1 and an absolute volatility σ of 0.01. Notice that these probabilities are state-dependent, not time-independent. Therefore, once evaluated, they can be stored in memory for easy access during the course of the calculation.

From Figure 11.2 it is clear that there is a variety of j coordinates that give a positive value to all three probabilities. One of the most interesting features of this approach, however, is that, by 'folding in' the rate distribution (i.e. by downward branching in the upper region, and by upward branching in the lower region) the user avoids a wasteful sampling of low-probability regions of rate space (compare, for instance, with the BDT procedure). Therefore it is advantageous to switch from regular to 'special' branching as early as possible in the region

$$0.184 < ja \, \Delta t < 0.577 \tag{11.30}$$

The first part of the procedure allows the user to determine probabilities which reflect the mean-reverting characteristics of the model. In other terms, the probabilities determined as shown above only depend on the chosen absolute volatility and reversion speed. No information from the current yield curve has been used. As discussed in Chapter 7, Section 1, the shape of the yield curve in turn depends on future expectations of rates *and* on future volatility. The process so far described therefore accounts for the volatility component to the curvature of the yield curve. This contribution is determined *a priori* from the choice of reversion speed and absolute volatility. The second (i.e. the rate expectation) component will be obtained from the current yield curve. The similarity with the BDT procedure (see Chapter 10 and Section 2 in particular) should be apparent. The construction just described usefully splits the two contributions in conceptually and transparently distinct computational phases. To ensure the correct pricing of the market discount bond, i.e. to impute the deterministic expectation of the future rates implied by the market yield curve in conjunction with the assumption made about a and σ, the Green's function formalism can be easily implemented. In addition, given the analytic features of the HW model, these Green's functions can be determined analytically, rather than having to be determined numerically as, for instance, in the BDT case. Using the concepts and the terminology employed in

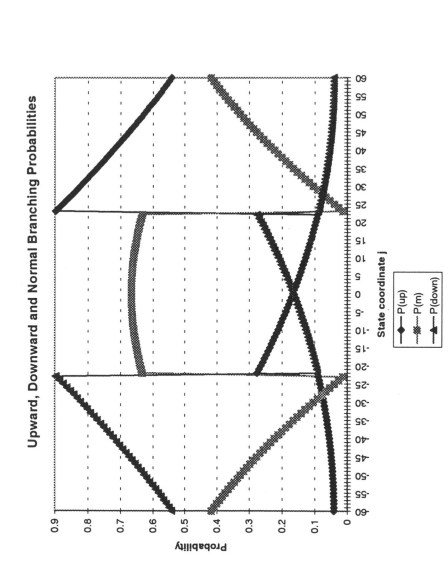

Figure 11.2 The probabilities for upward, downward and normal branching as a function of the state (rate) coordinate j for a 5-year monthly tree built with $\sigma = 0.01$ and $a = 0.1$.

Chapter 6, one can denote the value today of a certain £1 paid in state j at time i by

$$Q(i,j) \equiv G(0,0,i,j) \tag{11.31}$$

If one remembers that $G(0,0,0,0) = Q(0,0) = 1$, and one denotes the short rate today by

$$r(0,0) \equiv \alpha(0) \tag{11.32}$$

the price of a discount bond maturing at time $1\,\Delta t$ is given by

$$P(1) = Q(0,0)\exp[-\alpha(0)\,\Delta t] \tag{11.33}$$

The Green's functions $Q(1,j)$ ($j = -1,0,1$) are then given by (see Section 3 of Chapter 6)

$$Q(1,1) = Q(0,0)p_{\mathrm{u}}\exp[-\alpha(0)\,\Delta t] \tag{11.34}$$

$$Q(1,0) = Q(0,0)p_{\mathrm{m}}\exp[-\alpha(0)\,\Delta t] \tag{11.34'}$$

$$Q(1,-1) = Q(0,0)p_{\mathrm{d}}\exp[-\alpha(0)\,\Delta t] \tag{11.34''}$$

The price of a discount bond maturing at time $2\,\Delta t$, known from the market, is then given by

$$\begin{aligned} P(2\,\Delta t) = \ & Q(1,1)\exp[-r(1,1)\,\Delta t] \\ & + Q(1,0)\exp[-r(1,0)\,\Delta t] + Q(1,-1)\exp[-r(1,-1)\,\Delta t] \end{aligned} \tag{11.35}$$

The rates $r(1,j)$ ($j = 1,0,-1$) can then be expressed as a function of a (yet unspecified) 'middle' rate at time 1 as $r(1,j) = \alpha(1) + j\,\Delta r$, $j = 1,-1$ (the similarity with the BDT construction should, once again, be apparent). Therefore Equation (11.35) becomes

$$\begin{aligned} P(2\,\Delta t) = \ & Q(1,1)\exp[-(\alpha(1)+\Delta r)\,\Delta t] \\ & + Q(1,0)\exp[-\alpha(1)\,\Delta t] + Q(1,-1)\exp[-(\alpha(1)-\Delta r)\,\Delta t] \end{aligned}$$
$$\tag{11.35'}$$

From Equation (11.35') one can easily solve for the one unknown $\alpha(1)$:

$$\alpha(1) = \frac{\ln\left(Q(1,1)\exp[-\Delta r\,\Delta t] + Q(1,0) + Q(1,-1)\exp[\Delta r\,\Delta t]\right) - \ln P(2\,\Delta t)}{\Delta t}$$
$$\tag{11.36}$$

From the knowledge of $\alpha(1)$ one can then proceed to the construction of the Green's functions $Q(2,j)$ ($j = -2,-2,0,1,2$), and from the market price of $P(3\,\Delta t)$, of $\alpha(2)$. The procedure can be repeated until the whole tree has been built by forward induction. **As long as one is prepared to discount using continuous compounding** (which is computationally slightly more 'expensive' than simple compounding) **a closed-form solution can be found for the tree mid-points as a function of market quantities and of already determined variables.** There is therefore no need for the numerical search that must be employed with models like BDT. Applying the reasoning that led to Equation (11.36) recursively gives (11.35)

$$P((i+1)\,\Delta t) = \sum_{j=-n(i),n(i)} Q(i,j)\exp[-(\alpha(i)+j\,\Delta r)\,\Delta t] \qquad (11.37)$$

$$\alpha(i) = \frac{\ln\left[\displaystyle\sum_{j=-n(i),n(i)} Q(i,j)\exp(-j\,\Delta r\,\Delta t)\right] - \ln P(i+1)}{\Delta t} \qquad (11.38)$$

$$Q(i,j) = \sum_{k^*} Q(i-1,k)p(k,j)\exp[-(\alpha(i-1)+k\Delta r)\Delta t] \qquad (11.39)$$

with $\alpha(0) = r(0)$ (i.e. the initial value of the short rate as determined by $P(1\,\Delta t)$), $Q(0,0) = 0$, $p(k,j)$ is the probability of moving from node k to node j (notice that this probability is independent of time), and the summation is taken over all the probability values k^* for which $p(k,j)$ is non-zero. (It might be useful to revisit Section 3 of Chapter 6 at this point.)

The procedure just described therefore gives a forward-induction prescription for the HW Extended Vasicek model which enjoys two important advantages: it explicitly splits the contributions to the yield-curve shape coming from the volatility contribution and from the expectation of rates; and it allows the user to evaluate the Green's functions in analytic form. The former feature allows to single out in an explicit way the two variables (a and σ) which affect the cap volatilities. The latter property makes the building of the tree particularly fast, and is therefore very important in the calibration of the model. The interplay of theses two characteristics is examined in detail in the next section.

11.5 BEST-FIT CALIBRATION OF THE ONE-DIMENSIONAL HW MODEL TO MARKET DATA

The most 'natural' and intuitive procedure to fit the HW Extended Vasicek model to cap prices is to choose the couple of values for the reversion speed a and the absolute volatility σ that 'best fit' a desired series of caps. The cap fitting procedure is, however, not quite as straightforward as one might surmise, both from the technical and from the conceptual point of view. Cap prices and (percentage!) volatilities, in fact, are quoted in the market on the basis of the Black model, which assumes log-normal rates. Since the normal distribution of rates implied by the HW/Vasicek model is fitted to the first two moments of the log-normal distribution, very little price difference is to be found for at-the-money strikes. Moving away from at-the-money strikes, however, the normal assumption begins to play a more important role. For a non-flat term structure of rates and a given strike, however, not all the caplets can be at-the-money. **In matching prices of caps of different maturities it is therefore essential to disentangle the price effects arising from the mean-reverting character of the short rate process** (approximately translated, in a Black framework, by assigning percentage volatilities declining with increasing maturities), **and from the different distributional assumptions.** Large errors in the estimate of the reversion speed can otherwise be made.

More seriously, a declining *percentage* volatility does not automatically imply a declining *absolute* volatility, as displayed by any sharply upward sloping curve. If one takes as a proxy for the absolute volatility the product of the relevant forward rate and its percentage volatility, it is easy to see that commonly observed market yield curves, such as the US$ and GB£ curves in 1994 (see, e.g., Figure 9.3) coupled even with sharply declining *percentage* forward rate volatilities, fail to produce, over a very extensive range of maturities, a declining *absolute* volatility, and therefore do not give rise to a positive (absolute) reversion speed for the normal HW model. Conversely, for declining yield curves fitting to cap prices which imply a declining percentage volatility will tend to obtain a very strong normal reversion speed. Humped yield curves pose serious problems.

This feature, *per se*, simply indicates that some caution is needed when one is comparing the implications for mean reversion of log-normal and normal models. In the long run, all yield curves should become reasonably flat, and, therefore, a positive mean reversion must prevail in order to price very long caps. If one is interested in intermediate maturities, however, which can still be as long as eight or ten years for recent US$ market yield curves, any positive reversion speed could seriously fail to account for their prices.

The situation is clearly illustrated by Figures 11.3 to 11.6. For a textbook case of a flat term structure of interest rates (10%), the HW approach obtains with excellent accuracy the Black cap prices obtained not only with a flat term structure of volatilities (20%, Figure 11.3), but also with a declining volatility (Figure 11.4). Notice that in the first case the optimal reversion speed and absolute volatility turn out to be almost exactly 0 and 0.02 (= 20% × 10%). (This need not *a priori* have been the case, given the different distributional assumptions.) For the second case of a declining percentage volatility, the reversion speed that gives best overall fit is positive (0.0991) and the absolute volatility similar, although not identical, to the product of the Black volatility $\sigma(0)$ (20%) and *the* one rate (10%). It is interesting to note that, in both cases, for at-the-money options the distributional differences play a very minor role.

For a decaying term structure of interest rates the fit to the cap prices obtained using the *same* declining percentage volatility is still acceptable

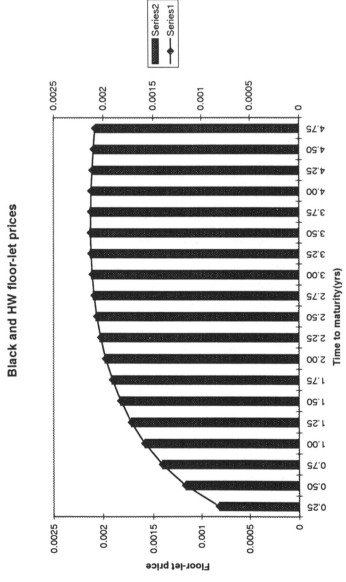

Figure 11.3 Fitting the HW parameters σ and α to log-normal floor prices for at-the-money strikes with flat term structures of interest rates (10%) and of volatilities (20%) for a variety of times to expiry (x-axis in years). The bars indicate the Black floor prices, and the continuous line the HW prices. Optimised reversion speed a = 0, σ = 0.02.

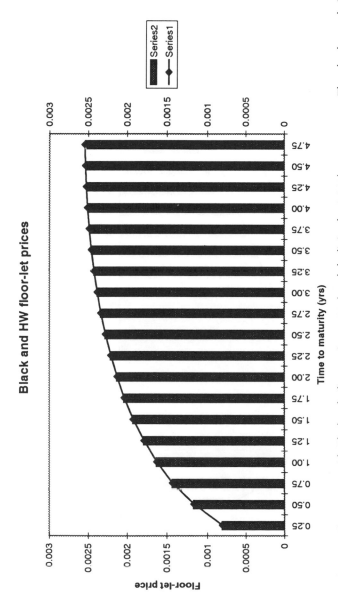

Figure 11.4 Same as Figure 11.3 with Black volatility starting at 20% and declining by 0.20% every quarter. The absolute volatility and the reversion speed were χ^2 optimised to minimise the sum of the squares of the differences between 'market' (Black) and model option prices. Optimised reversion speed $a = 0.0991$, $\sigma = 0.02072$.

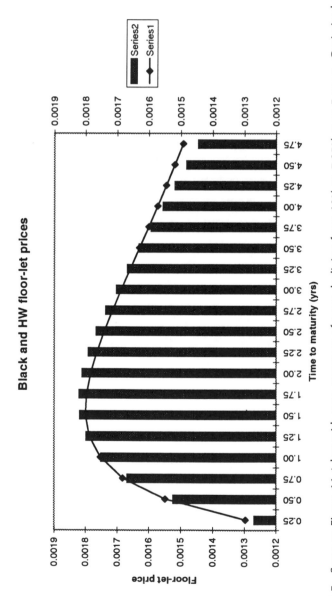

Figure 11.5 Same as Figure 11.4 but with term structure of rates declining from 10% to 7.25% over 5 years. Optimised reversion speed $a = 0.548$, $\sigma = 0.0231$.

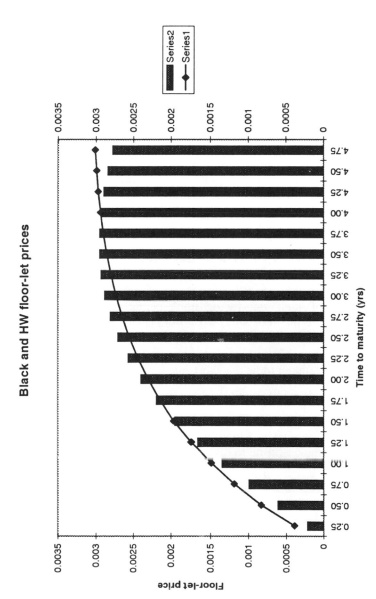

Figure 11.6 Same as Figure 11.4 but with term structure of rates rising from 10% to 16% over 5 years. Optimised reversion speed $a = -0.1275$, $\sigma = 0.0197$.

(Figure 11.5), but now the estimated reversion speed is more than five times as large (0.548). Finally, Figure 11.6 shows that for a rising term structure of rates and the same declining term structure of volatilities not only is the fit rather poor, but the estimated 'best' reversion speed turns out to be *negative* ($\sigma = 0.0197$, $a = -\mathbf{0.128}$). (Needless to say, this feature would imply an exploding (mean-fleeing), rather than mean-reverting, short-rate process.)

If one were only interested in these short-to-intermediate maturities, and therefore ready to accept the resulting model inconsistencies with very long maturity instruments, a normal negative reversion speed could be acceptable. From the implementation point of view, however, a negative mean reversion does create additional problems: the trinomial branching switching from 'normal' to 'upwards' or 'downwards', described in the previous section, totally fails to occur for negative reversion speeds; unfortunately, as discussed above, it is indeed the switching that affords a potentially attractive construction in order to avoid the wasteful sampling of rate space effected by traditional lattice constructions.

11.6 THE TWO-DIMENSIONAL FORMULATION OF THE HW MODEL

In order to overcome the intrinsic limitations of one-factor models and the specific problems of their one-factor implementation, HW have recently proposed (Hull and White (1994b)) a two-dimensional formulation of their Extended Vasicek model. The first variable could, in principle, be any (deterministic) function of the short rate, but, in order to obtain closed-form solutions, it is usually taken to be the short rate itself:

$$dr = [\theta(t) + u(t) - ar(t)] \, dt + \sigma_1 \, dz_1 \qquad (11.40)$$

the form is clearly similar to their one-dimensional model, but in the drift of r there now appears a stochastic function $u(t)$ (in addition to the deterministic $\theta(t)$ which ensures market fitting to discount bond prices), of assumed process

$$du = -bu \, dt + \sigma_2 \, dz_2 \qquad (11.41)$$

with $E[dz_1, dz_2] = \rho \, dt$ and $u(0) = 0$. In order to enhance the intuition for the model, Equations (11.40) and (11.41) can be rewritten as

$$dr = [\theta(t) + a(u'(t) - r(t))] \, dt + \sigma_1 \, dz_1 \qquad (11.40')$$

$$du'(t) = b(0 - u'(t)) \, dt + \sigma_2' dz_2 \qquad (11.41')$$

As they stand these two equations imply a short rate reverting to the time-varying level $u'(t)$ with constant reversion speed a. This reversion level, in turn, reverts to zero with constant reversion speed of b. The reversion level of this 'long-term rate' to zero might seem surprising; but the case of u' reverting to some (non-zero) constant level c can be easily accommodated in the same framework by noticing that, by a deterministic transformation of any normal variable u^* reverting to c from an initial value $u^*(0) = K$, it is always possible to recover an equation of the form (11.41′): whatever deterministic shift this procedure might entail, it will always be accommodated by a suitable change in $\theta(t)$ to $\theta'(t)$. Therefore, if interpreted this way, **Equations (11.40) and (11.41) describe the joint process of the short rate $r(t)$ following a drift $\theta'(t)$ and reverting with constant reversion speed a to a level $u^*(t)$, which, in turn, reverts to a level c with reversion speed b.**

It can also be illuminating to recast Equation (11.40) in a slightly different light, by writing

$$dr = [a(\theta'(t) - r(t))]\,dt + \sigma_1\,dz_1 \qquad (11.40'')$$

with $\theta'(t) = \theta(t) + u'(t)$, showing the short rate to revert with constant reversion speed to a variable reversion level, which is in turn the sum of a deterministic function of time (the median of the distribution) and a mean-reverting stochastic perturbation which starts at level zero, randomly fluctuates about this value, and also reverts to zero.

For the sake of simplicity, and in order to conform with HW's notation, Equations (11.40) and (11.41) will be used throughout, rather than (11.40′), (11.40″) or (11.41′), but the possibility to endow the parameters with a precise (albeit risk-neutral!) econometric interpretation should be regarded as a useful *a posteriori* check of the reasonableness of a given calibration procedure (see the following section).

Rather than discussing to what extent Equations (11.40) and (11.41) constitute a reasonable description of (risk-neutral) 'reality', one can take the more pragmatic view that the above formulation allows for a very simple closed-form solution for the price of a discount bond:

$$P(t,T) = A(t,T)\exp[-B(t,T)r - C(t,T)u] \qquad (11.42)$$

showing that the two-factor Extended Vasicek HW model belongs to the affine class (see Chapter 15). The derivation, although algebraically more involved, is effected along the same lines as for the one-factor case; the resulting expressions for $B(t,T)$ and $C(t,T)$ are given by

$$B(t,T) = \frac{1 - \exp[-a(T-t)]}{a} \qquad (11.43)$$

$$C(t,T) = \frac{b\exp[-a(T-t)] - a\exp[-b(T-t)] + a - b}{ab(a-b)} \qquad (11.44)$$

showing that the 'duration' $B(t,T)$ depends only on the reversion speed of the short rate, while the term $C(t,T)$ depends on both a and b. As for A, it is given by a rather lengthy expression, reported in the Appendix to this chapter.

In order to gain insight into the implications of the model for the yield-curve dynamics, one can easily compute the term structure of volatilities of yields of different maturities: from expression (11.42) one can straightforwardly obtain

$$\frac{\partial \ln P(0,T)}{\partial r} = -B(0,T) \qquad (11.45)$$

$$\frac{\partial \ln P(0,T)}{\partial u} = -C(0,T) \qquad (11.46)$$

Therefore, applying Ito's lemma to the T-maturity yield $y(T) = -\ln P(0,T)/T$, one obtains

$$dy(T) = \mu_y(T)\,dt + \frac{\sigma_r B(0,T)}{T}\,dz_1 + \frac{\sigma_u C(0,T)}{T}\,dz_2 \qquad (11.47)$$

giving a variance per unit time for $y(T)$ equal to

$$\text{Var}[y(t)] = \left(\frac{B(0,T)\sigma_r}{T}\right)^2 + \left(\frac{C(0,T)\sigma_u}{T}\right)^2 + \frac{2\sigma_r\sigma_u\rho B(0,T)C(0,T)}{T^2} \qquad (11.48)$$

Remembering that the forward rate from time T_1 to time T_2 seen from the yield curve at time t, $f(t,T_1,T_2)$ is given by

$$f(t,T_1,T_2) = \frac{\ln P(t_1,T_1) - \ln P(t,T_2)}{T_2 - T_1} \qquad (11.49)$$

and using Ito's lemma again one can easily obtain

$$df(t,T_1,T_2) = \mu_f\,dt + \frac{B(t,T_2) - B(t,T_1)}{T_2 - T_1}\,\sigma_r\,dz_r + \frac{C(t,T_2) - C(t,T_1)}{T_2 - T_1}\,\sigma_u\,dz_u$$

$$(11.50)$$

In the limit as T_2 approaches T_1, the forward rate (11.49) becomes the instantaneous forward rate and the terms $[B(t,T_2) - B(t,T_1)]/(T_2 - T_1)$ and $[C(t,T_2) - C(t,T_1)]/(T_2 - T_1)$ tend to the derivatives $\partial B(t,T)/\partial T$ and $\partial C(t,T)/\partial T$, respectively, allowing one to write

$$df(t,T) = \mu_f\,dt + \frac{\partial B(t,T)}{\partial T}\,\sigma_r\,dz_r + \frac{\partial C(t,T)}{\partial T}\,\sigma_u\,dz_u \qquad (11.51)$$

This gives for the variance of the forward rate $f(0,T)$

$$\text{Var}[f(0,T)] = \left(\frac{\partial B(0,T)}{\partial T}\sigma_r\right)^2 + \left(\frac{\partial C(0,T)}{\partial T}\sigma_u\right)^2 + 2\sigma_r\sigma_u\rho\,\frac{\partial B(0,T)}{\partial T}\,\frac{\partial C(0,T)}{\partial T}$$

(11.52)

Figure 11.7 shows that the functional form (11.52) can allow in a simple way for very complex shapes for the terms structure of forward rate volatilities, thus potentially allowing close fit to market data.

By evaluating $E[dy(T_1),\,dy(T_2)]$ and $E[df(0,T_1),\,dy(f,T_2)]$ and dividing by the appropriate variances one can easily obtain the covariances between different yields and forward rates, respectively, implied by the model:

$$\text{Covar}[y(T_1),y(T_2)] = \frac{B(0,T_1)B(0,T_2)\sigma_r^2}{T_1T_2} + \frac{C(0,T_1)C(0,T_2)\sigma_u^2}{T_1T_2}$$

$$+ \sigma_r\sigma_u\rho\left[\frac{B(0,T_1)C(0,T_2) + B(0,T_2)C(0,T_1)}{T_1T_2}\right]$$

(11.53)

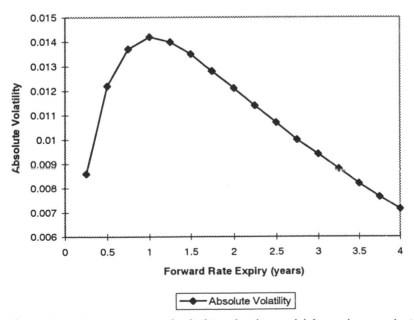

Term Structure of Forward Rate Volatilities (US$ 13 Apr 95)

Figure 11.7 Term structure of volatilities for the model forward rates, obtained after calibrating the model to the yield curve and cap data for the US$ market on 13 April 1995 (see Section 11.7 for calibration details).

$\text{Covar}[f(0,T_1)f(0,T_2)]$

$$= \frac{\partial B(0,T_1)}{\partial T} \frac{\partial B(0,T_2)}{\partial T} \sigma_r^2 + \frac{\partial C(0,T_1)}{\partial T} \frac{\partial C(0,T_2)}{\partial T} \sigma_u^2$$

$$+ \sigma_r \sigma_u \rho \left[\frac{\partial B(0,T_1)}{\partial T} \frac{\partial C(0,T_2)}{\partial T} + \frac{\partial B(0,T_2)}{\partial T} \frac{\partial C(0,T_1)}{\partial T} \right] \quad (11.54)$$

where, for instance, $\partial B(0,T_1)/\partial T$ indicates the derivative of $B(0,T)$ evaluated for $T = T_1$. It was shown in Chapter 2 that low-dimensionality models using as driving factors linear combination of rates are constrained to yield correlation functions among forward rates of roughly sigmoid shape. Section 2.2 discussed the implications for swaption pricing. This qualitative feature is again encountered for the two-factor HW model, which should come as no surprise, since the formulation of their model can be recast in terms of a linear combination of rates; however (see Figure 11.8), the region of negative convexity in the correlation function can be of rather limited extent for reasonable choices of the model parameters, thereby indicating that **a good fit to swaption data could be achieved,** *with constant model parameters,* **over a large range of swaption maturities and expiries.** This important observation

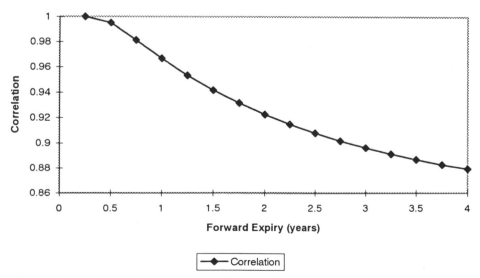

Figure 11.8 The correlation among the first forward rate and forward rates of increasing expiry for model parameters giving a good (although not the best) fit to market cap prices for 13 April 1995 (see Section 11.7 for calibration details).

will be further explored in the following section, which is devoted to the issue of calibration to market data.

Since it is possible to express the time-t price of a T-maturity discount bond as a function of the model parameters it is an easy, if algebraically tedious, matter to apply Ito's lemma in order to obtain the instantaneous variance of the discount bond price itself. Integrating this instantaneous variance from time 0 to time t one can obtain the total variance of the process of the discount bond from time 0 to time t, given by an expression of the type

$$\text{Var}[P(t,T)] = \int_0^t \sigma_r^2 [B(s,T) - B(s,t)]^2 + \sigma_u^2 [C(s,T) - C(s,t)]^2$$
$$+ 2\rho\sigma_u\sigma_r [B(s,T) - B(s,t)][C(s,T) - C(s,t)] \, ds \quad (11.55)$$

Since $B(t,T)$ and $C(t,T)$ have simple functional forms, the integration can be carried out analytically, and the lengthy but simple results can be found in Hull and White (1994b). The (square root of the) variance thus calculated, and denoted by $\sigma_{p(t,T)}$, is therefore what enters the expression for the time-0 value of a call struck at X and expiring at time t on a discount bond maturing at time T, i.e. the analytic expression for a floorlet price (the caplet expression is easily obtained from call/put parity):

$$\text{Call}(0,t,T) = P(0,T)N(h_1) - XP(0,t)N(h_2)$$

$$h_{1,2} = \frac{\ln \dfrac{P(0,T)}{P(0,t)} \pm \dfrac{1}{2}\sigma_p^2}{\sigma_p} \quad (11.56)$$

with the sign $+(-)$ referring to $h_1 (_2)$. A very simple Black-like expression is therefore available also for the two-factor HW model for pricing calls (and puts) on discount bonds. **Since a call (put) on a forward bond is equivalent (see Chapter 1) to a put (call) on the underlying rate, caps and floors can be priced analytically using the two-factor HW model.** The implications of this very important result for model calibration are explored in the next section.

11.7 CALIBRATING A TWO-FACTOR HW MODEL

It is one of the strengths of the model that in the calibration procedure the five model parameters (a, b, σ_r, σ_u and ρ) have a clearly understandable impact on cap prices (and, to some extent, on swaption prices); σ_r **and** σ_u **determine the overall volatility level, and therefore both positively contribute to the caps, floors and swaption prices.** On the other hand, the larger the reversion speeds a and b, the stronger the mean-reversion effect, and, consequently, the more 'confined' the asymptotic unconditional distribution of rates will be. The effect will become more and more pronounced for longer maturities. **Therefore, *a* and *b* will depress the value of long-dated caps and swaptions relative to short dated ones.** Finally, decreasing **the correlation** ρ will decrease the correlation among forward rates, and **will therefore have a relatively larger effect on swaption prices than on cap prices**.

In order to ascertain how this functional flexibility can be translated in actual market fitting, two relatively 'complex' market volatility curves have been chosen (the US$ and the DEM cap curves for the 13 April 1995, shown in Figure 11.9).

Using Equations (11.55) and (11.56), cap prices were then evaluated for a variety of maturities spanning 3 months to 5 years using an initial guess for the five model parameters; these latter quantities were then varied using a very fast search procedure until the χ^2 discrepancies between model and market prices were minimised. Unlike the one-factor case, very good fit could in general be found even for these complex cap curve shapes, as shown in Figure 11.10 for the US$ market (similar results were found for the DEM cap prices).

Notice that, despite the sharply upward sloping shape of the yield curve, both reversion speeds turned out to be positive, unlike what was found, for

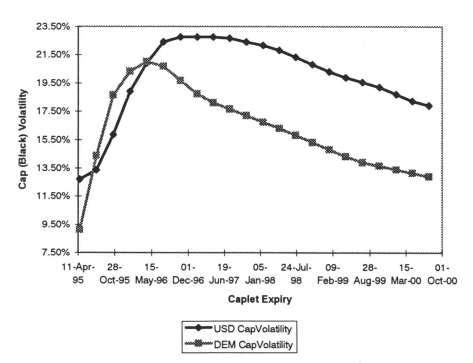

Cap Volatility Curves (DEM and USD 13 Apr 95)

Figure 11.9 The cap volatility curves for US$ and DEM on 13 April 1995.

Market (Black) and Model Caplet Prices (US$ 13 Apr 95)

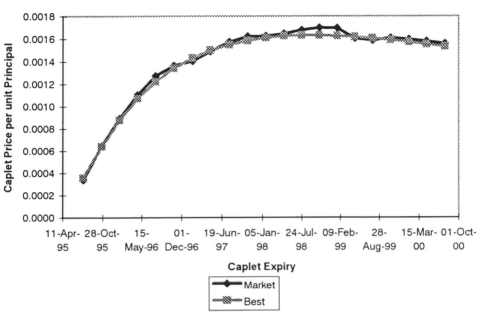

Figure 11.10 The match of model (HW2dim) and market (Black) at-the-money cap prices observed for the US$ market on 13 April 1995. 'Best' parameter set: $a = 0.46411, b = 0.96504, \sigma_r = 0.0016, \sigma_u = 0.0342, \rho = 0.65$.

similar yield-curve shapes, for the one-dimensional case (see discussion in Section 11.5). Despite this very important qualitative feature, the particular optimised set found for the US$ market displayed a probably implausibly small volatility for the short-rate. Since a zero volatility would effectively imply a one-factor model, it is not surprising that the correlation among forward rates implied by this choice of model parameters turned out to be very high, with the already discussed consequences of swaption overpricing. It is, however, very reassuring to find that a variety of solutions of very similar numerical quality (i.e. of similar good match to market prices) can be found using different combinations of the model parameters. Figure 11.11 shows the market prices, the 'best' solution, and a 'plausible' solution, which has a higher χ^2, but which is obtained from econometrically more convincing volatilities and reversion speeds. As is normally the case, an enlightened combination of fitting and foreknowledge of the expected qualitative value range for the parameters is to be preferred to blind χ^2 minimisation. **For this particular model, the procedure, besides being sensible, also produces results of very high numerical quality.** The straightforward econometric interpretation of the

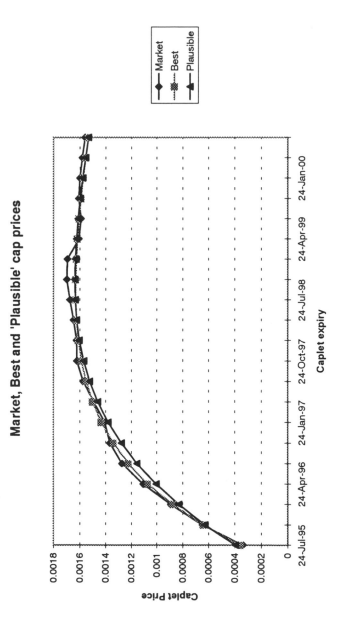

Figure 11.11 The best-fit (Best) and the 'plausible' (Plausible) match of model and market (Market) at-the-money cap prices observed for the DEM market on 13 April 1995. 'Best' parameter set: $a = 0.277$, $b = 2.188$, $\sigma_r = 0.00006$, $\sigma_u = 0.00006$, $\rho = 0.98$; 'Plausible' set: $a = 0.47$, $b = 0.38$, $\sigma_r = 0.0085$ $\sigma_u = 0.0099$ $\rho = 0.67$; the latter set was determined with just a few trial-and-error attempts, following the qualitative guidelines highlighted at the beginning of the section. Notice that the 'best' solution effectively gives rise to a one-factor model ($\sigma u/\sigma r \approx 650, \rho \approx 1$), while the 'plausible' solution truly retains the two-factor nature of the model.

model parameters outlined at the beginning of this section greatly facilitates the 'plausible' search procedure.

In order to complete the calibration, model and market European swaptions also have to compared. Unfortunately, given the two-factor nature of the model, Jamshidian's closed-form solution for an option on a coupon-bearing bond cannot be applied. One therefore has to resort to the construction of two-dimensional computational trees (which are, anyway, always needed for the pricing of the more exotic options which constitute the ultimate rationale for this type of model). Two-dimensional lattices are very often far from trivial to construct, if one wants to retain node recombination, when one state variable appears in the process for the other (as is the case for the two-factor HW model). Also in this respect, however, the HW model specification allows for important computational savings, illustrated in the following section.

11.8 NUMERICAL IMPLEMENTATION

The joint dynamics of the variables r and u are of the form:

$$dr = [\theta(t) + u(t) - ar(t)] \, dt + \sigma_1 \, dz_1 \tag{11.57}$$

$$du = -bu \, dt + \sigma_2 \, dz_2 \tag{11.58}$$

In order to map these stochastic differential equations onto a discrete two-dimensional lattice, one could naively proceed as follows. From the initial values of the state variables, $r(0,0)$ and $u(0,0)$, a two-dimensional lattice can be constructed by locating the nodes at time n as follows

$$r(n,k) = r(n,0) + k \, \Delta_r \tag{11.59}$$

$$u(n,k) = u(n,0) + k \, \Delta_u \tag{11.59'}$$

where the first index of the variables r and u indicates the time, the second the state of the world for the relevant variable,

$$-n \leqslant k \leqslant n \tag{11.60}$$

and the quantities Δ_r and Δ_u are chosen at the outset. See Figure 11.12.

Then, given that the state variables have *a priori* specified values as prescribed by (11.59) and (11.59'), the task is to determine transition probabilities from node $[r(k,n),u(j,n)]$ to the four reachable nodes

$$[r(k+1,n+1),u(j+1,n+1)] \tag{11.61}$$

$$[r(k-1,n+1),u(j+1,n+1)] \tag{11.61'}$$

$$[r(k+1,n+1),u(j-1,n+1)] \tag{11.61''}$$

$$[r(k-1,n+1),u(j-1,n+1)] \tag{11.61'''}$$

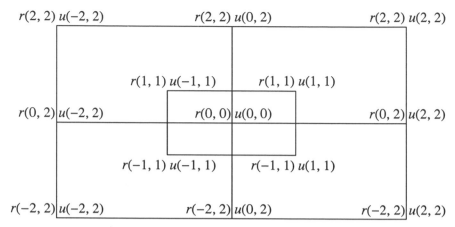

Figure 11.12 The geometry of the two-dimensional lattice. The first index denotes the state, and the second the time slice.

denoted by p_1, p_2, p_3 and p_4, respectively, such that (i) the variances of the short rate and of u, (ii) the correlation between u and r and (iii) the drift of the state variables are all correctly recovered. (If the branching were tri- rather than binomial, as HW suggest, the geometry would be slightly more complex, but all the same qualitative features would apply.) The problem with these simple constructions is that the drift for r depends on the value of the state variable u; therefore it is easy to see that, in general, there are not enough degrees of freedom to match the required moments *and* retain recombination of the lattice. However, if, following Hull and White (1994b), a new variable y is introduced

$$y = x + \frac{u}{b-a} \tag{11.62}$$

simple algebraic manipulation shows that the new stochastic differential equations become

$$dy = [\theta(t) - ay(t)]\, dt + \sigma_y\, dz_y \tag{11.63}$$

$$du = -bu\, dt + \sigma_u\, dz_u \tag{11.64}$$

with σ_y^2 given by

$$\sigma_y^2 = \sigma_r^2 + \left(\frac{\sigma_u}{b-a}\right)^2 + \frac{2\rho\sigma_u\sigma_r}{b-a} \tag{11.65}$$

and with the correlation between u and y given by

$$\rho_{y,u} = \frac{\rho\sigma_r + \dfrac{\sigma_u}{b-a}}{\sigma_y} \tag{11.66}$$

It is clear that, given the fact that the drift and the volatilities of the each new state variable does not contain the other, a trinomial (or even a skilfully implemented binomial) lattice can match the required moments, and ensure recombination. The precise details of the construction (in a trinomial framework) can be found in HW (1994b), but a variety of schemes can at this point be implemented (or slightly modified): see, e.g., Boyle (1988), Rubinstein (1994). The transformation (11.62) therefore affords the efficient computational link between the analytic specification of the model and its numerical implementation. Since, in general, European swaption prices depend to first order on the volatility level, and only as a second-order effect on the de-correlation among forward rates, virtually any sensible two-factor model which reproduces good cap prices should bring about an improvement in European swaption prices. The numerical search which requires the lattice construction can therefore be carried out in a relatively cursory way. Furthermore, the ability to evaluate the Green's functions and the swap rates at each node analytically greatly reduces the computational time. Finally, the qualitative shape of the correlation function (see Figure 11.5) indicates that the two-factor HW model has the potential to account for swaption prices more convincingly than most two-factor models, especially if the underlying variables are some simple linear combination of rates.

The two-factor HW model described above can therefore provide a useful pricing option. Its main drawback is the fact, discussed in the conclusions, that its distributional assumptions are at odds with the market tends to assume for the plain-vanilla option instruments. To what extent this should be a worry depends as much on pricing 'philosophy' as on distributional 'correctness'.

11.9 CONCLUSIONS

In view of the discussion above, it is clear that, at the present state of development, the HW approach enjoys some very important positive features, but, at the same time, requires rather careful handling. The distributional assumptions *per se* might very well be of rather limited impact, and the HW models have probably been unduly criticised and penalised for allowing negative rates: they indeed do so, but, due to the presence of mean reversion, the integrated probability of this occurrence is quite limited. (This is particularly true for the two-factor version of the model.) The distributional assumptions do play an important role, however, in the pricing of caps, since, especially in steep yield-curve environments, some of the caplets will probably be out-of-the-money. As pointed out in the previous sections, the distilled 'best' reversion speed(s) will therefore embed a very convoluted combination of actual mean reversion and distributional assumption at variance with the market log-normal model.

Probably more important is the fact that, for the favoured implementation, i.e. with constant reversion speed and absolute volatility, the one-factor model can poorly account even for the prices of at-the-money caps encountered in several yield curve/cap volatility curve environments. The implementation with time-varying reversion speed and volatility, on the other hand, has been found to imply (not unlike the BDT case, but probably more markedly so) implausible behaviour for the term structure of volatilities as seen from future points in time.

The two-factor version has been shown to be potentially free of this problem. As is always the case, however, when an unconstrained optimisation procedure is employed in order to 'best fit' model to market prices, care must be taken to ensure that the 'best' solution is indeed reasonable in view of the econometric interpretation of the model parameters. From this point of view the transparency of the model parameters, discussed in the calibration section, can be of great help.

As for the positive aspects, it is worthwhile noticing that, since discount bond prices can be obtained as a function of the model parameters and of the value of the short rate, any swap rate can be easily and analytically evaluated at any node in a tree without making use of the cumbersome and CPU-time-intensive discounting procedure required by an approach like BDT. Also, since option on discount bonds can be obtained from a given time/space node, there is no need, in order to value, say, a 2-week option on a 10-year discount bond, to construct a 10-year-and-2-week tree, since all the necessary information will be available at the different nodes at option expiry.

The fact that the shape of the correlation function displays a less markedly sigmoid shape than that found in most two-factor models has positive implications for simultaneous calibration to cap and swaption prices. There remains the problem that, since market caps and European swaptions are priced on the basis of a log-normal rate model, a good and consistent match to a set of market prices can only be achieved for at-the-money strikes. Problems therefore can arise if one wants to hedge complex instruments using a portfolio of plain-vanilla options: if one considers the 'true' value of an option the cost of its replicating portfolio, one might find disturbing that not all the hedging transactions might have to be carried out at the prices implied by the model.

If these shortcomings are recognised, the existence of analytic solutions for bond and bond option prices makes the HW models of great appeal, as long as they are judiciously and carefully implemented. It should be recalled, in fact, that the HW approach is the only one to allow closed-form solutions without having to constrain the deterministic part of the process of the factor(s): how important this apparently minor point actually is will be fully appreciated after the chapter on the Longstaff and Schwartz model.

APPENDIX

From Hull and White (1994b)

$$P(t,T) - A(t,T) \exp[-B(t,T)r \quad C(t,T)u]$$

$$\ln[A(t,T)] = \ln(P(0,T)/P(0,t)) = B(t,T)F(0,t) - \eta$$

$$\eta = \sigma_1^2(1 - \exp(-2at))B(t,T)^2/(4a) - \sigma_1\sigma_2\rho[B(0,t)C(0,t)B(t,T) + \gamma_4 - \gamma_2]$$
$$-1/2\sigma_2^2[C(0,t)^2B(t,T) + \gamma_6 - \gamma_5]$$

$$\gamma_1 = (\exp - (a+b)T[\exp((a+b)t)-1])/[(a+b)(a-b)]$$
$$- \exp(-2aT)(\exp(2at) - 1)/(2a(a-b))$$

$$\gamma_2 = [\gamma_1 + C(t,T) - C(0,T) + 1/2(B(t,T)^2 - B(0,T)^2$$
$$+ t/a - (\exp(-a(T-t)) - \exp(-aT))/(a^2)]/(ab)$$

$$\gamma_3 = (\exp(-2at) - 1)/(2a(a-b)) - (\exp(-(a+b)t - 1)/((a+b)(a-b))$$

$$\gamma_4 = [\gamma_3 - C(0,T) - 1/2B(0,T)^2 + t/a + (\exp(-at)) - 1)/(a^2)]/(ab)$$

$$\gamma_5 = [1/2(C(t,T)^2 - C(0,t)^2) + \gamma_2]/b$$

$$\gamma_6 = [\gamma_4 - 1/2C(0,t)^2]/b$$

ENDNOTES

1. Jamshidian's formula for obtaining the price of an option on a coupon-bearing bond from the price of an option on a pure discount bond is of general validity for any one-factor model, as long as the option price is a monotonic function of the state variable.

12
The Longstaff–Schwartz model

12.1 MOTIVATION

The principal component analysis presented in Chapter 2, Section 2, indicated that a large proportion of the variability across rates of different maturity could be satisfactorily explained by invoking two or three orthogonal factors. It was then argued that the first principal component could be reasonably interpreted as the average level of the yield curve, the second its slope, and the third (perhaps) its curvature. These first three factors accounted together for approximately 95–99% of the observed variability (the exact value depending on the specific market and on the period of observation), and, subject to the same qualifications, the first factor by itself explained about 85–90% of the variance.

These findings on the one hand gave justification to one-factor models, and, on the other hand, indicated that two-factor approaches should plausibly consider the slope of the yield curve as the additional factor. (Information about the curve slope can, of course, be incorporated in a variety of different ways, not necessarily by requiring the spread to be the second factor: any two rates, or linear combination thereof, can be used for the purpose.)

Dybvig (1988) challenged this view by arguing that the level and the slope might well explain 95% of the variance, if one is concerned with explaining the variability of rates or bond prices. If, however, one is interested in the pricing of contingent claims, it might very well be that an additive second factor (such as the spread) has a negligible effect on option values. If the second factor were instead taken to be the variance of the first principal component, it could have a small effect on bond prices (virtually none at short maturities, as Dybvig points out), but perhaps a significant effect on bond option pricing. (See the discussion at the beginning of Chapter 6, Section 1).

If this view were correct it would imply that a joint dynamics of the two factors of the form:

$$dr = \mu_r(r,V,t)\,dt + V(r,t)\,dZ_1 \qquad (12.1)$$

$$dV = \mu V(r,V,t)\,dt + \sigma_V\,dZ_2 \qquad (12.1')$$

could efficiently account for observed option pricing. This is the view implicitly taken by Longstaff and Schwartz (1992a) in the implementation of their two-factor model, described in this chapter. As in the case of the CIR model, they derive it by considering a (very) stylised version of the economy as a whole, in which interest rates are obtained endogenously, rather than received from empirical observation. Whatever their economic justification, however, it will be argued in this chapter that their contribution should be evaluated not on the basis of a convincing description of economic reality, but on the merits of a specification of the form (12.1), (12.1′) as a useful pricing and risk-management tool.

12.2 THE LS ECONOMY

In the model of Longstaff and Schwartz agents (investors) are faced, at each point in time, with the choice between investing or consuming *the* single good produced in the economy. There is a single stochastic constant-return-to-scale technology (i.e. a single production process: identical companies in which investors can purchase shares). If $C(t)$ represents consumption at time t, the goal of the representative investor is to maximise, subject to budget constraints, his additive preferences of the form

$$E_t\left[\int_t^\infty \exp(-\rho s)\ln(C(s))\,ds\right] \qquad (12.2)$$

Consumption at time s is 'discounted' to the present time t by a utility discounting rate ρ, which present-values the 'pleasure' of future consumption $C(s)$. $E_t[\ ]$ is the conditional expectation operator, i.e. investors maximise their expectation, subject to information available up to time t, of the discounted future consumption. In other words, by deferring consumption the investor can reinvest the single good in the economy so as to realise a greater consumption at a later time. The utility discount factor accounts for the reduction in satisfaction due to delayed consumption. Furthermore, a logarithmic utility function is assumed.

Consumption or reinvestment decisions have to be made subject to budget constraints that, given the assumptions above, have the form

$$dW = W\,\frac{dQ}{Q-C}\,dt \qquad (12.3)$$

i.e. the infinitesimal change in wealth W over time dt is due to consumption ($-C\, dt$) and returns from the production process (dQ/Q), scaled by the wealth invested in it (whence the constant-return-to-scale technology assumption).

The returns on the physical investment (the only good produced by the economy) are in turn described by a stochastic differential equation of the form

$$\frac{dQ}{Q} = (\mu X + \theta Y)\, dt + \sigma \sqrt{Y}\, dZ_1 \tag{12.4}$$

where dZ_1 is the usual increment of a Brownian motion, μ, θ and σ are constants, and X and Y are two state variables (economic factors) chosen in such a way that X is the component of the expected returns unrelated to production uncertainty (i.e. to dZ_1), and Y is the factor correlated with dQ. Both X and Y are Wiener processes described by stochastic differential equations

$$dX = (a - bX)\, dt + c\sqrt{X}\, dZ_2 \tag{12.5}$$

$$dY = (d - eY)\, dt + f\sqrt{Y}\, dZ_3 \tag{12.6}$$

Given the assumptions made, there is no correlation between the process dZ_1 and dZ_2, on the one hand, and between dZ_2 and dZ_3 on the other, i.e. $E[dZ_2\, dZ_1]$ and $E[dZ_2\, dZ_3]$ are both equal to zero. It is not easy to find an intuitive interpretation for the two factors described above; rather than economic intuition or plausibility, the main justification for the description of the economy embedded in Equations (12.1) to (12.5) is analytic tractability, as will become apparent later on.

If one accepts that the optimal consumption, given the assumption above, is ρW (see CIR (1985b) for a proof), direct substitution of Equation (12.4) and of the optimal consumption in the budget constraint Equation (12.3) gives for wealth the stochastic differential equation

$$dW = (\mu X + \theta Y - \rho)W\, dt + \sigma W \sqrt{Y}\, dZ_1 \tag{12.7}$$

12.3 THE PDE OBEYED BY CONTINGENT CLAIMS

Having obtained the Wiener process followed by the wealth of the representative investor, two results from CIR (1985b) can be drawn upon to obtain that the partial differential equation obeyed by any contingent claim H is

$$\frac{\partial^2 H}{\partial x^2}\frac{x}{2} + \frac{\partial^2 H}{\partial y^2}\frac{y}{2} + (\gamma - \delta x)\frac{\partial H}{\partial x} + (\eta - (\xi + \lambda)y)\frac{\partial H}{\partial y} - rH = \frac{\partial H}{\partial \tau} \tag{12.8}$$

where $x = X/c^2$, $y = Y/f^2$, $\gamma = a/c$, $\delta = b$, $\eta = d/f^2$, r is the instantaneous riskless rate and the market price of risk has been endogenously derived to be proportional to y, rather than exogenously assumed to have a certain functional form.

The set of equations and assumptions described above provide a general equilibrium model for the economy as a whole. Contingent claims are priced in this framework as endogenous components of the economy, and their prices are therefore *equilibrium* prices. The same cannot be said, in general, for no-arbitrage models, which dispense with any description of the economy. While this added feature of the CIR and LS models is certainly intellectually interesting, it should be kept in mind that their claim of providing a general equilibrium model is only valid within the context of the very stylised economy they assume (only one good produced, no role for money in the economy, no trade with 'foreign' economies, etc.). As it is the case with all equilibrium models, the investors' utility function, or, more specifically, the market price of risk, will appear in the PDE describing the price of any contingent claim. Since, of course, the parameters (including the market price of risk) of the model cannot in practice be determined *a priori*, the user will be faced with the need to estimate them either by a suitable best-fit procedure to some observable set of data (typically a yield curve, but the term structure of volatilities and the correlation between rates might also have to be taken into account), or by means of a mixed 'historical-implied' approach. Once again, as with many other models, the risk will be present of forcing reality into an unrealistic or oversimplified model. If that is the case, the estimated parameters will give the tell-tale indication of an ill-specified model by their 'implausible' behaviour and values. The risk is all the more present for a model that, with a few more parameters, purports to describe much more than any no-arbitrage approach. As usual, ultimately the capability to capture via hedging strategies the predicted option value will constitute the real test of the model. More about this will be said in later sections.

12.4 THE DYNAMICS OF THE TRANSFORMED VARIABLES r AND V

As it stands, the model expresses the value of any contingent claim as a function of the unobservable quantities X and Y. Fortunately a link with more directly observable financial quantities can be obtained by remembering that, given the assumed logarithmic form of the utility of wealth function, the instantaneous interest rate is simply equal to the expected return from the production process (dQ/Q) minus the variance of the production returns (notice the similarity with the drift of stock returns in a Black and Scholes world, given by the riskless rate plus a compensation proportional to the standard deviation of the stock returns). Given the definition above, the instantaneous rate is therefore equal to

$$r = \alpha x + \beta y \tag{12.9}$$

with $\alpha = \mu c^2$ and $\beta = (\theta - \sigma^2)f^2$. Since the stochastic differential equations for x and y are known, Ito's lemma can be applied to obtain the variance of r and V:

$$V = \alpha^2 x + \beta^2 y \tag{12.10}$$

Finally, the Wiener processes for r and V can also be obtained from Equations (12.9) and (12.10) by using Ito's lemma again, giving

$$dr = \left[\alpha\gamma + \beta\eta - \frac{r(\beta\delta - \alpha\xi) + V(\xi - \delta)}{\beta - \alpha} \right] dt + \sigma_{r_2}\, dz_2 + \sigma_{r_3}\, dz_3 \tag{12.11}$$

$$dV = \left[\alpha^2\gamma + \beta^2\eta - \frac{r\alpha\beta(\delta - \xi) + V(\beta\xi - \alpha\delta)}{\beta - \alpha} \right] dt + \sigma_{V_2}\, dz_2 + \sigma_{V_3}\, dz_3 \tag{12.12}$$

with

$$\sigma_{r_2} = \alpha\sqrt{\frac{\beta r - V}{\alpha(\beta - \alpha)}} \tag{12.13}$$

$$\sigma_{r_3} = \beta\sqrt{\frac{-\alpha r + V}{\beta(\beta - \alpha)}} \tag{12.13'}$$

$$\sigma_{V_2} = \alpha\sigma_{r_2} \tag{12.14}$$

$$\sigma_{V_3} = \beta\sigma_{r_3} \tag{12.14'}$$

Equations (12.9) and (12.10) imply that both r and V can only assume positive values. Notice carefully that the arguments under the square root sign in Equations (12.13) and (12.14) must be positive for these expressions to yield real values. This imposes constraints on the state variables, r and V, and on the parameters α and β, which will be discussed later on.

From the assumptions made about the factors, X and Y, affecting production, namely that there is no correlation between dZ_2 and both dZ_1 and dZ_3, it follows that there are no cross-terms (i.e. $[dZ_2\, dZ_3]$) in the products of Equations (12.11) and (12.12). This does not mean, however, that there is no correlation between r and V: this correlation can be easily computed by evaluating the variance–covariance matrix of the increments of the variables r and V. From

$$\begin{matrix} E[dr\, dr] & E[dr\, dV] \\ E[dV\, dr] & E[dV\, dV] \end{matrix} \tag{12.15}$$

and remembering that $dZ_i dZ_j = \delta_{i,j} dt$, $(i,j = 2,3)$, one can easily calculate that

$$\text{Var}[r] = \frac{\alpha^2(\beta r - V)}{\alpha(\beta - \alpha)} + \frac{\beta^2(V - \alpha r)}{\beta(\beta - \alpha)} = \alpha^2 x + \beta^2 y = V \qquad (12.16)$$

as one must expect, and that

$$\text{Var}[V] = \frac{\alpha^4(\beta r - V)}{\alpha(\beta - \alpha)} + \frac{\beta^4(V - \alpha r)}{\beta(\beta - \alpha)} \qquad (12.17)$$

(The symbol δ_{ij} (Kroeneker delta) is equal to 1 for $i = j$, and zero otherwise.) This allows one to write for ρ_{rV}

$$\rho_{r,V} = \frac{E[dr\, dV]}{\sigma_r \sigma_V} = \frac{\alpha^3 x + \beta^3 y}{\sqrt{\alpha^2 x + \beta^2 y}\,\sqrt{\alpha^4 x + \beta^4 y}} = \frac{\alpha^3 x + \beta^3 y}{\sqrt{V(\alpha^4 x + \beta^4 y)}} \qquad (12.18)$$

From this result one can verify that this correlation is always positive, or, at most, zero. The results by Chan, Karoyli, Longstaff and Sanders (1991) give empirical support to this feature of the model, i.e. to the fact that higher levels of volatility seem to be associated with higher rates. A significant advantage of a model specification in these terms is that the value of V is not uniquely determined by the level of the interest rate, as any prescription of the form $V = r^\beta \sigma$ implies. While, however, the correlation is only constrained to be between zero and one, plausible choices for the parameters tend to produce very high values of the correlation between r and V. This, *per se*, does not entail implausibly high correlations between rates of different maturities, as a later section will show, but these high values of the correlation do have important consequences for the model, which will be explored later on.

From the results obtained, it is easy to rewrite the obtained variances and expectations of r and V in terms of the parameters α, β, γ, δ, η and ξ. The (unconditional) expectation and variance of r are in fact given by

$$E[r] = \frac{\alpha\gamma}{\delta} + \frac{\beta\eta}{\xi} \qquad (12.19)$$

and

$$\text{Var}[r] = \frac{\alpha^2\gamma}{2\delta^2} + \frac{\beta^2\eta}{2\xi^2} \qquad (12.19')$$

respectively.

The mean and variance of the stationary distribution of V have the form

$$E[V] = \frac{\alpha^2\gamma}{\delta} + \frac{\beta^2\eta}{\xi} \qquad (12.19'')$$

and

$$\text{Var}[V] = \frac{\alpha^4 \gamma}{2\delta^2} + \frac{\beta^4 \eta}{2\xi^2} \qquad (12.19''')$$

respectively. The crucial importance of these relationships for model calibration will be shown in the section devoted to the 'historical' approach (Section 12.12).

From Equations (12.5)–(12.6) and (12.9)–(12.10) it can be shown that the joint distribution of the short rate and the variance is given by the product of the non-central chi-squared distribution with non-centrality parameter ω_1 for the short rate, and the identical distribution with non-centrality parameter ω_2 for the variance: this particularly simple result stems from the absence of correlation between the original variables X and Y.

If one then indicates this joint distribution as $q(r,V,t;r_0,V_0)$ it is very interesting to examine the one-dimensional distribution $Q(r,t;r_0,V_0)$ resulting from integrating $q(r,V,t;r_0,V_0)$ over all the possible values of V:

$$\int_{\alpha_r}^{\beta_r} q(r,V,T;r_0,V_0)\, \mathrm{d}V = Q(r,t;r_0,V_0) \qquad (12.20)$$

The result of this integration is shown in Figure 12.1 for several values of t, and for a 'reasonable' choice of parameters.

With t increasing from 0.3 years to 1 year and to 2 years one can readily observe a delocalisation of the initial value for the short rate of 8.00%. The spreading of the distribution, however, does not increase at the same rate over time, and, for 'realistic' values of the parameters, the rate distribution obtained for 5 years is virtually indistinguishable from the 10-year distribution. This feature should be contrasted with the type of log-normal distribution assumed, for instance, by the BDT model. In this latter type of model, the burden of avoiding rates from becoming too dispersed is taken up by imposing a time-dependent (decaying) volatility for the short rate, as discussed at length in Chapter 11. The introduction of time dependent parameters in order to prevent excessive dispersion of rates is not necessary with the LS model, which obtains more 'naturally' and consistently the same result by virtue of the mean-reverting nature of its rate distribution. The implications of these distributional features for option pricing will be examined in a later section (Section 8).

12.5 THE EQUILIBRIUM TERM STRUCTURE

As shown above, any security traded in the economy described by the LS model must satisfy the PDE (12.8). In particular, this equation will have to be

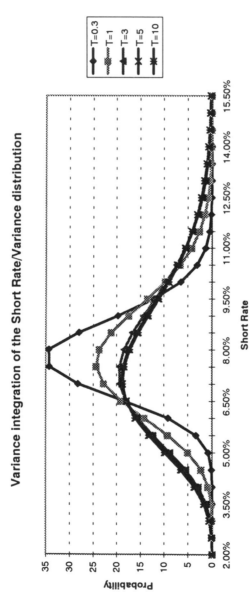

Figure 12.1 The integration of the distribution of the short rate and variance over the variance for several values of t; notice how, after an initial de-localisation, the unconditional variance of the short rate virtually stops growing.

satisfied by a zero-coupon bond, i.e. a security with terminal condition $F(r,V,0) = 1$. When this boundary condition is imposed, and a separation of variables approach is followed, the resulting expression for the value of a discount bond, F, τ years before expiry turns out to be given by (Longstaff and Schwartz (1992a))

$$F(r,V,\tau) = A^{2\gamma}(\tau)B^{2\eta}(\tau)\exp(\kappa\tau + C(\tau)r + D(\tau)V) \qquad (12.21)$$

with

$$A(\tau) = \frac{2\varphi}{(\delta + \varphi)[e^{\varphi\tau} - 1] + 2\varphi}$$

$$B(\tau) = \frac{2\psi}{(\nu + \psi)[e^{\psi\tau} - 1] + 2\psi}$$

$$C(\tau) = \frac{\alpha\varphi[e^{\psi\tau} - 1]B(\tau) - B\psi[e^{\varphi\tau} - 1]A(\tau)}{\varphi\psi(\beta - \alpha)}$$

$$D(\tau) = \frac{-\varphi[e^{\psi\tau} - 1]B(\tau) + \psi[e^{\varphi\tau} - 1]A(\tau)}{\varphi\psi(\beta - \alpha)}$$

$$\nu = \lambda + \xi$$

$$\varphi = \sqrt{2\alpha + \delta^2}$$

$$\psi = \sqrt{2\beta + \nu^2}$$

$$\kappa = \gamma(\delta + \varphi) + \eta(\nu + \varphi)$$

(To conform with LS's notation, discount bonds, elsewhere in this book denoted by $P(t,T)$, are written as $F(t,T)$.) From the above expressions one can see that the discount function depends on two state variables (r and V) and time, plus six parameters, α, β, γ, δ, η and ν. As was seen to be the case with the CIR model, the market price of risk does not appear by itself, but only in combination with the parameter ξ. It will be discussed later on in the context of the parameterisation of the LS model, that there is therefore an infinity of values λ and ξ giving rise to an identical fit to a given yield curve. Only if one supplemented information obtained from bond prices with information about the 'real' (as opposed to risk-adjusted) dynamics of the state variables, would it be possible to estimate, within the context of the model, the market price of risk.

The formal similarity of the LS and the CIR discount functions are quite apparent. The former, however, enjoys the extra flexibility of being defined in terms of more parameters, and of two, rather than one, state variables; it is therefore capable of giving rise to much more complex yield-curve shapes. Figure 12.6 in Section 10 provides a clear example.

Notice that the term structure depends on time only via the residual maturity τ: the LS model therefore belongs to the time-homogeneous class discussed in Chapter 15. This is of particular relevance for the evolution over time of the term structure of volatilities, derived in the next section. In order to do so, it is useful to derive the expression for the continuously compounded yield of a T-maturity zero-coupon bond, which can be directly obtained as the negative of $\log(F(T))/T$; a simple calculation gives

$$Y(T) = \frac{-\kappa T + 2\gamma \log A(T) + 2\eta \log B(T) + C(T)r + D(T)V}{T} \qquad (12.22)$$

The limit of this expression for T tending to 0 is obviously r, and the limit for T going to infinity is a constant (compare CIR) given by

$$Y(\infty) = \gamma(\varphi - \delta) + \eta(\psi - \nu) \qquad (12.23)$$

12.6 TERM STRUCTURE OF VOLATILITY

For practical option pricing applications, achieving a good fit to the term structure of volatility (and, to a lesser extent, to the correlation surface) can be as important as fitting the yield curve correctly. The volatility of rates of different maturities can be obtained by deriving the volatility of zero-coupon bond prices for different maturities, and then by applying Ito's lemma to convert the price volatility to a yield volatility. More precisely, remembering Equations (12.11), (12.12) and (12.21) one can write

$$dF = [\mu_F]\,dt + F_r[\sigma_{r2}\,dZ_2 + \sigma_{r3}\,dZ_3] + F_V[\sigma_{V2}\,dZ_2 + \sigma_{V3}\,dZ_3] \qquad (12.24)$$

which can be rearranged to give

$$dF = [\mu_F]\,dt + \left[\frac{\partial F}{\partial r}\sigma_{r2} + \frac{\partial F}{\partial V}\sigma_{V2}\right]dz_2 + \left[\frac{\partial F}{\partial r}\sigma_{r3} + \frac{\partial F}{\partial V}\sigma_{V3}\right]dz_3 \qquad (12.25)$$

The expectation of the square of the stochastic part of dF is then given by

$$\mathrm{Var}\,[dF] = E\left[\left\{\left[\frac{\partial F}{\partial r}\sigma_{r2} + \frac{\partial F}{\partial V}\sigma_{V2}\right]dz_2 + \left[\frac{\partial F}{\partial r}\sigma_{r3} + \frac{\partial F}{\partial V}\sigma_{V3}\right]dz_3\right\}^2\right] \qquad (12.26)$$

By direct evaluation of the derivatives, and remembering that the Brownian increments dZ_2 and dZ_3 are uncorrelated, one obtains for the instantaneous volatily of bond returns

$$
\mathrm{Var}\!\left[\frac{\mathrm{d}F(T)}{F(T)}\right] = \sigma^2_{F(T)}
$$

$$
= r\left[\frac{\alpha\beta\psi^2(\mathrm{e}^{\varphi T}-1)^2 A^2(T) - \alpha\beta\varphi^2(\mathrm{e}^{\psi T}-1)^2 B^2(T)}{\varphi^2\psi^2(\beta-\alpha)}\right]
$$

$$
+ V\left[\frac{-\alpha\psi^2(\mathrm{e}^{\varphi T}-1)^2 A^2(T) - \beta\varphi^2(\mathrm{e}^{\psi T}-1)^2 B^2(T)}{\varphi^2\psi^2(\beta-\alpha)}\right]
$$

$$
(12.27)
$$

Finally, in order to obtain yield volatilities, one has to use Ito's lemma again, this time to the function $Y(T) = -\log(F(T))/T$, giving

$$
\sigma_{Y(T)} = \frac{\partial F}{\partial Y}\,\sigma_{F(T)} = \frac{1}{TF(T)}\,\sigma_{F(T)} \qquad (12.28)
$$

Examples of the term structure of volatility thus obtained are given in Figure 12.2 for several values of β.

The crucial issue, of course, is not so much to obtain the yield-curve volatility from the model parameters, but to ascertain how the model can be calibrated using its degrees of freedom. This all-important issue is analysed in the section devoted to the parameterisation; in the meantime, however, it is interesting to notice that the term structure of volatility is not flat (it shows dependence on the yield maturity), and that, for 'reasonable' values of the parameters it displays more structure than, say, the BDT approach.

12.7 CORRELATION BETWEEN RATES

One of the most important features of a two-factor model (which will ultimately determine its ability to price swaptions correctly) is its capability to imply an imperfect degree of correlation between rates of different maturity. It is therefore very important to obtain an expression for the correlation between yields of discount bonds of different maturities. This can be accomplished by (i) considering the expression of a τ_1-maturity yield as a function of r and V, as obtained in Equation (12.22); (ii) applying the two-dimensional formulation of Ito's lemma to obtain the differential $\mathrm{d}Y_{\tau_1}$; (iii) repeating the same procedure for a yield of different maturity, τ_2; and (iv) finally evaluating the expectation $E[\mathrm{d}Y_{\tau_1}\,\mathrm{d}Y_{\tau_2}] = \rho_{\tau_1,\tau_2}\sigma_{\tau_1}\sigma_{\tau_2}\,\mathrm{d}t$.

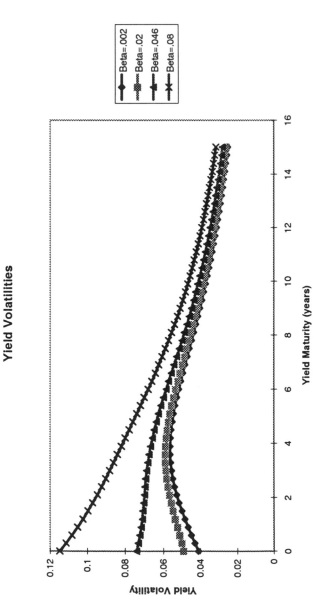

Figure 12.2 Possible shapes of the term structure of volatilities for $x = 0.208$, $y = 1.794$, $\alpha = 0.09$, $\gamma = 0.0560$, $\delta = 0.30648$, $\eta = 0.23017$, $\nu = 0.2689$ and various values of β from 0.002 to 0.08. Notice the complexity of shapes obtainable by changing just one parameter.

Looking back at Equation (12.22) that was previously obtained for the yield of a discount bond of maturity t, one can readily see that, despite the rather daunting appearance, it can be rewritten as

$$Y_t = \frac{W(t) + C(t)r + D(t)V}{t} \qquad (12.22')$$

with the term $W(t)$ collectively describing the first three terms (dependent on t, but not on r or V) in the round brackets on the left-hand side of Equation (12.22). Equation (12.22) therefore describes a linear dependence between Y_t and both r and V, and, therefore, Ito's lemma can be applied in a particularly straightforward manner. After rewriting, symbolically, Equations (12.11) and (12.12) as

$$dr = \mu_r\, dt + \sigma_{r2}\, dz_2 + \sigma_{r3}\, dz_3 \qquad (12.29)$$

$$dV = \mu_V\, dt + \sigma_{V2}\, dz_2 + \sigma_{V3}\, dz_3 \qquad (12.29')$$

one can write

$$dY(\tau) = \mu_{Y(\tau)}\, dt + \frac{\partial Y(\tau)}{\partial r}\, [\sigma_{r_2}\, dz_2 + \sigma_{r_3}\, dz_3]$$

$$+ \frac{\partial Y(\tau)}{\partial V}\, [\sigma_{V_2}\, dz_2 + \sigma_{V_3}\, dz_3]$$

$$= \mu_{Y(\tau)}\, dt + \left[\frac{\partial Y(\tau)}{\partial r}\, \sigma_{r_2} + \frac{\partial Y(\tau)}{\partial V}\, \sigma_{V_2}\right] dz_2$$

$$+ \left[\frac{\partial Y(\tau)}{\partial r}\, \sigma_{r_3} + \frac{\partial Y(\tau)}{\partial V}\, \sigma_{V_3}\right] dz_3$$

$$= \mu_{Y(\tau)}\, dt + [C(\tau)\sigma_{r_2} + D(\tau)\sigma_{V_2}]\, dz_2$$

$$+ [C(\tau)\sigma_{r_3} + D(\tau)\sigma_{V_3}]\, dz_3 \qquad (12.30)$$

Having obtained this result, one can now, easily if tediously, compute

$$E[dY_{\tau_1}\, dY_{\tau_2}] = \rho_{\tau_1,\tau_2}\sigma_{\tau_1}\sigma_{\tau_2}\, dt$$

$$= E\left[\frac{[C(\tau_1)\sigma_{r_2} + D(\tau_1)\sigma_{V_2}]\, dz_2 + [C(\tau_1)\sigma_{r_3} + D(\tau_1)\sigma_{V_3}]\, dz_3}{\tau_1}\right.$$

$$\left. \times \frac{[C(\tau_2)\sigma_{r_2} + D(\tau_2)\sigma_{V_2}]\, dz_2 + [C(\tau_2)\sigma_{r_3} + D(\tau_2)\sigma_{V_3}]\, dz_3}{\tau_2}\right]$$

$$
= \frac{[C(\tau_1)\sigma_{r_2} + D(\tau_1)\sigma_{V_2}][C(\tau_2)\sigma_{r_2} + D(\tau_2)\sigma_{V_2}]}{\tau_1\tau_2}\, dt
$$

$$
+ \frac{[C(\tau_1)\sigma_{r_3} + D(\tau_1)\sigma_{V_3}][C(\tau_2)\sigma_{r_3} + D(\tau_2)\sigma_{V_3}]}{\tau_1\tau_2}\, dt
$$

$$
+ \frac{[C(\tau_1)\sigma_{r_2} + D(\tau_1)\sigma_{V_2}][C(\tau_2)\sigma_{r_3} + D(\tau_2)\sigma_{V_3}]}{\tau_1\tau_2}\, \rho_{r,V}\, dt
$$

$$
+ \frac{[C(\tau_1)\sigma_{r_3} + D(\tau_1)\sigma_{V_3}][C(\tau_2)\sigma_{r_2} + D(\tau_2)\sigma_{V_3}]}{\tau_1\tau_2}\, \rho_{r,V}\, dt
$$

$$(12.31)$$

But, given the assumptions about the correlation among the Brownian motions, $\rho_{r,V} = 0$. Therefore

$$
\rho_{\tau_1,\tau_2} = \frac{1}{\sigma_{\tau_1}\sigma_{\tau_2}\tau_1\tau_2}
$$
$$
\times \{[C(\tau_1)\sigma_{r_2} + D(\tau_1)\sigma_{V_2}][C(\tau_2)\sigma_{r_2} + D(\tau_2)\sigma_{V_2}]
$$
$$
+ [C(\tau_1)\sigma_{r_3} + D(\tau_1)\sigma_{V_3}][C(\tau_2)\sigma_{r_3} + D(\tau_2)\sigma_{V_3}]\} \qquad (12.32)
$$

The only quantities that remain to be evaluated are σ_{τ_1} and σ_{τ_2}, i.e. the instantaneous volatility of bond returns for a discount bond of maturity 1 or 2, respectively. This, as done above, can be obtained by applying Ito's lemma to Equation (12.22), and then taking the appropriate expectations of the stochastic components.

When all of this has been carried out, correlations between rates of different maturities obtained with 'plausible' parameters are reported in Figure 12.3.

It is interesting to notice that the qualitative shape of the correlation surface **is the same as what had been observed in the case of two-factor models based on a principal component approach**. Also the choice of the variance of the short rate as the second stochastic variable therefore fails to bring about the exponentially decaying shape of the correlation function that one would like to obtain in order to price simultaneously caps and swaptions.

12.8 OPTION PRICING

One of the most appealing features of the LS model is its ability to price discount bond options in analytic form. Since, as noted in the context of the HW model, an important class of contingent claims (caps and floors) can be

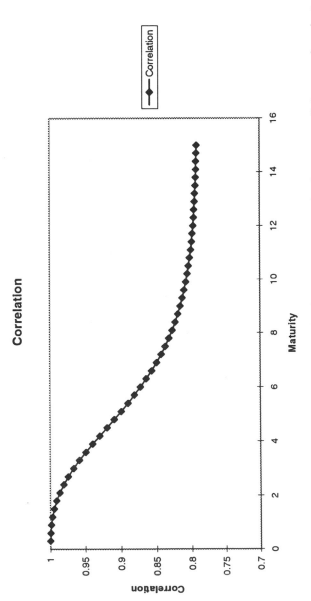

Figure 12.3 The correlation between the short rate and forwards of increasing maturity for the same coefficients used to obtain Figure 12.2. Notice the sigmoid shape of the function.

valued as put or calls on discount bonds, this feature can be of great assistance in the calibration phase, as discussed later on.

In their paper, LS give the solution to the problem of a call expiring at time t and struck at K on a discount bond with T further periods to maturity. Since the expression, of general form

$$C(r,V,t,T) = F(r,V,t+T)\Psi(\ ) - K\Psi(\ ) \qquad (12.33)$$

is rather involved, the reader is referred to LS's original paper (1992a). In the present context it will suffice to say that the function $\Psi(;p.q)$ is the bivariate non-central chi-squared distribution function (see, for instance, Johnson and Kotz (1970)).

Elegant and important as these results might be, European options on discount bounds do not exhaust the full range of options encountered in practice. To make the approach extendable to European options with generic payoffs, Longstaff and Schwartz have pointed out in a later paper (1992b) that a separation-of-variables technique is applicable to the fundamental partial differential Equation (12.8), allowing the factorisation of the solution function $H(x,y,t)$ in the product of a discount function $F(x,y,t)$ and $M(x,y,t)$, where $M(.)$ gives the forward value of the claim. (The numeraire used in this context is therefore the bond maturing at option payoff time, whence the restriction of the technique to strictly European options, where 'strictly' means that, in general, no payoff-dependent events should occur between inception of the option and its expiry). The forward value of the claim is the expectation of the payoff function $V(x,y,t)$, taken over the probability distribution of x and y. For a caplet on the short rate, for instance, the payoff function has the form

$$V(r,t) = \text{Max}[(r - X,0)] = \text{Max}[(\alpha x + \beta y) - X,0)] \qquad (12.34)$$

where X, as usual, is the strike. In order to carry out the integration, LS (1992b) point out that the distribution of x and y, contingent on an initial value x_0 and y_0, is given by

$$
\begin{aligned}
q(x,y\,|\,x_0,y_0) = \ & \frac{4}{a(\tau)c(\tau)} \left(\frac{x}{b(\tau)x_0}\right)^{\gamma-\frac{1}{2}} \left(\frac{y}{d(\tau)y_0}\right)^{\eta-\frac{1}{2}} \\
& \times \exp\left[-\frac{2}{a(\tau)}(x + b(\tau)x_0)\right] \exp\left[-\frac{2}{c(\tau)}(y + d(\tau)y_0)\right] \\
& \times I_{2\gamma-1}\left(\frac{4}{a(\tau)}\sqrt{b(\tau)xx_0}\right) \quad I_{2\eta-1}\left(\frac{4}{c(\tau)}\sqrt{d(\tau)yy_0}\right)
\end{aligned}
$$

$$(12.35)$$

where

$$a(\tau) = \frac{A(\tau)\exp(\phi\tau - 1)}{\phi}$$

$$b(\tau) = A^2(\tau)\exp(\phi\tau)$$

$$c(\tau) = \frac{B(\tau)\exp(\psi\tau - 1)}{\psi}$$

$$d(\tau) = B^2(\tau)\exp(\psi\tau)$$

and $I(\cdot)$ is the modified Bessel function of (non-integer) order p. Whilst the probability distribution is always integrable, there are combinations of values of the parameters which make the distribution diverging for x and/or y tending to 0. Specifically, if either γ or η are smaller than $\frac{1}{2}$, it is easy to see that the two terms in the first line of espression (12.35) tend to infinity. As pointed out before, the distribution remains integrable, but numerically this makes the integration procedure much more delecate. Whilst the parameter values proposed by LS in their example do give rise to a smooth and easily integrable distribution function, they give rise to a rather contrived shape for the yield curve. The coefficients obtained from the optimisations carried out using real-life discount functions (see the section) have always yielded at least one of the two parameters γ or η (and often both) smaller than $\frac{1}{2}$.

Apart from these 'technical considerations', for practical evaluation of European options more complicated than the rather contrived examples of a caplet on the short rate, the user will in general have to create the appropriate payoff functions using the necessary forward discount functions: if one wanted to value using this technique a 'real' caplet on a 6-month forward rate expiring at time t, one would have to evaluate the forward option payoff as

$$\text{Max}\left[\left(\frac{F(x, y, t)}{F(x, y, t + 6m)} - 1\right)\middle/ \tau - X, 0\right] \tag{12.36}$$

and then integrate over the appropriate probability density. In general therefore, as long as the payoff can be expressed as a combination of forward rates, which, in turn, can be written as functions of discount bonds, it is always possible to substitute for r and V the corresponding functions of x and y, and integrate over these two variables from 0 to infinity.

The present section has shown how European options can be evaluated, analytically or numerically, within the context of the LS approach. For more complex types of options the most suitable numerical procedure can be either a two-dimensional FD scheme (see Chapter 7) if the option is compound or American, or a MC approach if it is path dependent. The latter technique, in particular, can be efficiently applied because, from the values of the state variables and of the parameters, the entire yield curve can be recovered, allowing easy analytic evaluation of swap rates, discount bond values, etc. The issue still remains to be addressed, however, of how the model can be calibrated to market data. The following sections will give some insight on how this task can be accomplished, and of the possible inherent dangers.

12.9 CALIBRATING THE LS MODEL

For a model as rich as the Longstaff and Schwartz, there is a virtually endless array of tests that, at least in principle, could be devised to assess its performance and realism: the quality of the fit to market yield curves, the stability of the obtained coefficients, the capability to reproduce the observed decorrelation between rates, the predictive power for the change of the yield curve given the observed changes in r and V, to name just a few. Since the results obtainable from the model clearly depend on the acceptability of the coefficients, three different criteria can be employed: first of all, the coefficients cannot jointly assume certain values or the mathematical solution would not exist: looking at Equations (12.13) and (12.14), for instance, which describe the process for the short rate, it is clear that the argument of the square root must be greater than 0 in order to obtain a real (as opposed to a complex) solution. Therefore, for $\beta - \alpha > 0$, the short rate must be greater than β times its variance, and, in turn, the variance must be greater than α times the short rate. These conditions must at all costs be satisfied.

There are then combinations of coefficients which produce mathematically acceptable solutions, but assign to observable financial quantities unacceptable values. Little needs to be said about this case, since those users who went ahead and used the model thus parameterised would immediately find that easily observable financial quantities are seriously mispriced by the model.

There is, however, the third possibility of a set of coefficients producing a mathematically acceptable solution, assigning plausible values to all observable financial quantities, but inconsistent with the assumptions made about the economy in order to derive the general equilibrium model. In particular, for the interpretation of the six parameters to be consistent with the stylised economy described at the beginning of Section 12.2 they should all assume positive values. On the other hand, this would not be required if one were to be ready to relinquish the interesting 'story' about the equilibrium economy, and just took Equations (12.11) and (12.12) as a starting point for a plausible description of the joint dynamics of the short rate and its variance. Since not too much faith can be placed in the realism of the description of the whole economy as attempted by the very simplified assumptions made at the outset, the loss might after all be not as dire as one might initially fear. The mean-reverting features of the short rate are intrinsically interesting and plausible, and the choice of the variance as a second variable can be backed by theoretical justification (see Dybvig (1988)). Therefore, in the analysis reported in the following, solutions with negative, but otherwise acceptable, parameters, were not discarded.

12.10 FITTING THE YIELD CURVE USING THE IMPLIED APPROACH

To investigate empirically how easily the model could be calibrated and implemented using a purely implied approach (i.e. by regarding the two state variables and the six parameters as fitting quantities), the attention was focused on the UK gilt market, and on the swap markets of GBP, US$ and DEM. More precisely, for the UK gilt market, a discount function was first obtained using the available market prices and one of the methods discussed in Chapter 1 for yield-curve estimation. All the LS parameters and state variables were then fitted to the resulting discount function. For the GBP, US$ and DEM swap markets all the parameters and the two state variables were used in the fit to the discount function constructed using deposit (LIBOR) rates, futures prices and swap rates.

Starting with the analysis of the gilt data, the market discount function was obtained for the first day of each month from 1 October 1990 (when short rates in the UK were around 15%) to 1 June 1993 (the period straddles Black Wednesday of September 1992). An unconstrained optimisation was carried out by minimising the sum of the squared deviations between the model and the observed yields for maturities from 0.5 to 30 years at semi-annual intervals. In the course of this minimisation, none of the mathematically or financially unacceptable regions were ever encountered in the pre-September 1992 period, despite the fact that no explicit constraint to this effect was put in place. In this restricted sense (i.e. as long as compatibility with the equilibrium economy is not required) the coefficients were capable of 'naturally' finding acceptable regions.

As it is apparent some of the coefficients turned out to be negative. With the proviso mentioned above about the possibility of a different hidden minimum, this, of course, invalidates the stronger form of the test of the LS model as a description of the equilibrium economy, but, as pointed out before, this might be not too serious.

Overall, the variations over time of the coefficients did not seem to be as 'wild' as in the analysis of the CIR model, at least in the two subperiods before and after September 1992, as shown in Figures 12.4 and 12.5 for the case of the US$ swap market.

Any variation of these coefficients, should, from the theoretical point of view, invalidate the model altogether. The closed-form solution for the

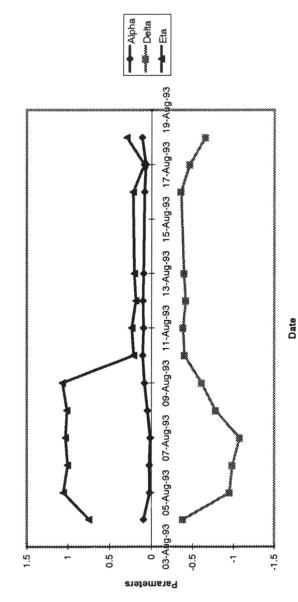

Figure 12.4 The α, β, γ, δ and η coefficients estimated using the 'implied' procedure described in the text for the US$ swap market over several consecutive dates. Notice the overall absence of very large fluctuations in the estimated values.

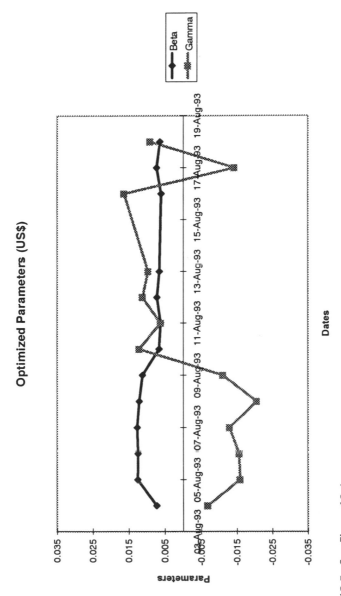

Figure 12.5   See Figure 12.4.

discount function, after all, is obtained for strictly constant coefficients. One can, however, take a more flexible, or pragmatic, standpoint and invoke some sort of 'adiabatic approximation' as long as the variation over time is slow enough.

For some realisations of the coefficients it is apparent from the figures the oscillation between two competing minima. After September 1992 (Black Wednesday) all the coefficients change radically, which is, after all, not surprising, since the yield curve changed drastically both in level and in shape. Needless to say, such a change was in no way compatible with the rate dynamics implied by the model, and should therefore be seen as a 'change of universe'.

The quality of the fit to the yield curves is in general very good to excellent, even for very complex yield-curve shapes. See, for instance, Figure 12.6.

Furthermore, since in the procedure described above the short rate was taken to be a completely free parameter in the optimisation, the fact that it turned out to assume values very close to the observed short rates is encouraging. On the

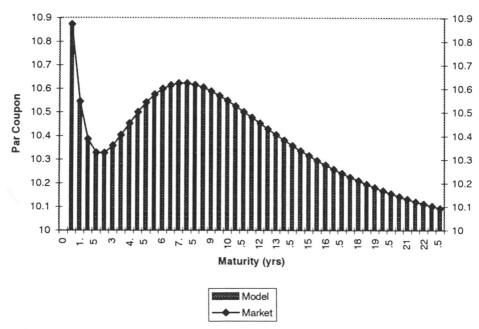

Figure 12.6 The model and market yields for a particularly complex yield-curve shape (UK gilts—July 1991).

other hand, since the coefficients were fitted to the market yield curve, and the quality of the fit was always good, the short rate is not really a 'free' parameter, since it must, for any reasonable and well-behaved model, be very similar to the shortest fitted yields. However, the model does allow for rather pathological cases of very sharp variation of the rates at short maturities (this, incidentally, is indeed the case for the choice of coefficients presented in Longstaff and Schwartz's (1992b) illustration of the method for valuing generic European options dealt with in Section 12.8), and the fact that these combination of coefficients are not borne out by the optimization procedure is encouraging.

The same considerations apply to the long yield: their closeness to observed values is, at the same time, both encouraging and, to a large extent, ensured by the optimisation procedure.

It is very interesting to calculate the degree of correlation between the two driving factors, i.e. the short rate and its variance (see Equation (12.18)): this correlation, for all the coefficients obtained, is always very high, sometimes as high as 99%. If it were exactly unity, the model would collapse to a one-factor model. Yet, these very high correlations imply the de-correlations between rates of different maturities shown, for a typical example, in Figure 12.3; as it is seen, these turn out to be much larger, and (with the usual proviso about the sigmoid shape) of very plausible magnitude. The mathematical explanation of the paradox lies in the fact that the correlation between r and V depends on the coefficients α and β only (see Equation 12.18), whilst the correlation between rates (see Equation 12.33) depends on the whole set of coefficients. The fact, however, remains that, due to this high degree of correlation between r and V, periods of high short rates are associated with periods of high rate volatility (and this, after all, is a plausible and desirable feature). What is less plausible and desirable, however, is that variance and rates should move in step with the closeness displayed by Figure 12.7. Also, the values of the 'unobservable' short-rate volatility are of the right order of magnitude if compared with some reasonable proxy, but overall no better than that.

Similar results were obtained for the US$, UK£ and DM swap/futures markets, with the interesting exception that for the DM yield curve all the coefficients naturally satisfied for the periods examined (44 observations in July and August 1993) not only the mathematical/financial constraints, but also the requirements for the theoretical treatment of the equilibrium economy to be valid (i.e. they always turned out to be positive): good or excellent fit to the yield curves was always obtained, the same pattern of overall smooth variation of these coefficients over long periods was observed, and the same features of high correlation between r and V, and larger de-correlation between rates of different maturities were observed.

Overall these first sets of empirical investigations therefore point out that,

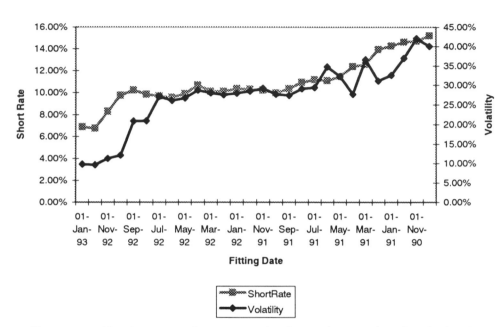

Figure 12.7   The short rate and its variance, fitted using the procedure described in the text, for the UK gilt market.

with a completely 'implied' estimation of the parameters

(i)   one can obtain a very good quality fit both to up- and downward sloping curves, and to curves with more complex shapes (UK gilt);

(ii)   the coefficients by and large assume plausible values, and change smoothly over time; however, only for the DM swap/futures market are they consistent with the description of the equilibrium economy;

(iii) short and long rates are plausible and in good agreement with empirical observation; for the volatility of the short rate the agreement is no better than at order-of-magnitude level;

(iv)   the degree of de-correlation between rates of different maturities is overall plausible, although the qualitative shape (sigmoid rather than exponentially decaying) is 'wrong'. (Notice carefully that the LS model, despite being two factor, is *not* of the type described in Chapter 2, Section 2, and therefore the sigmoid shape for the correlation function need not necessarily arise.)

However, no indication can be obtained from these tests about the more

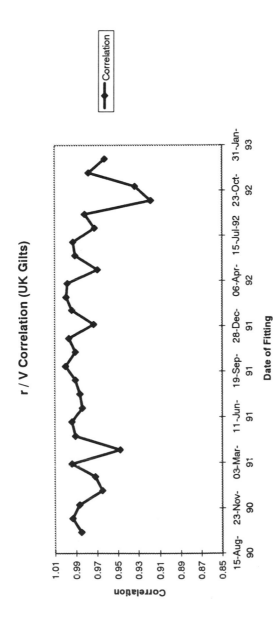

Figure 12.8 The theoretical instantaneous correlation between the short rate and its variance produced by the parameters obtained by fitting the UK gilt data using the procedure described in the text.

important issue of the correctness of the description of the yield-curve dynamics, crucial from the point of view of hedging. The following section touches upon these aspects.

12.11 TESTS OF THE JOINT DYNAMICS USING THE IMPLIED APPROACH

In order to see whether the 'implied' calibration procedure applied to the LS model produces parameters which imply the satisfactory yield-curve dynamics, a strategy similar to the one used in the analysis of the BDT model can be employed. More precisely, after obtaining as described in the previous section the optimised 'implied' parameters for a given day, the sensitivity of the yield curve to the short rate and the variance can be obtained by differentiating Equation (12.21)

$$F(r,V,\tau) = A^{2\gamma}(\tau)B^{2\eta}(\tau)\,e^{\,\kappa\tau\,+\,C(\tau)r\,+\,D(\tau)V} \tag{12.21}$$

with respect to these two variables:

$$\frac{\partial F(r,V,\tau)}{\partial r} = F(r,V,\tau)c(\tau) \tag{12.37}$$

$$\frac{\partial F(r,V,\tau)}{\partial V} = F(r,V,\tau)D(\tau) \tag{12.38}$$

Notice that unlike, for instance, the BDT case, given the closed-form solution for the discount function, these sensitivities can be obtained analytically without making use of binomial tree constructions.

The 'experienced' changes in the short rate and variance over two consecutive days can then be taken to be given by the differences of the respective optimised quantities as obtained by fitting to the market discount functions for the two days. This choice is clearly not unique, but, at least, it is the one most consistent with the chosen 'implied' analysis of the model. With this information at hand, one can then predict the change in the price of a discount bond of maturity τ, as

$$\Delta F(r,V,\tau) = F(r,V,\tau)[C(\tau)\,\Delta r + D(\tau)\,\Delta V] \tag{12.39}$$

By considering the experienced changes in the discount functions over two consecutive days the comparison can then be carried out between model predictions and 'reality'. Figures 12.9 and 12.10 show the results of two of these tests, with the model parameters obtained using the 'implied' approach described in the previous section.

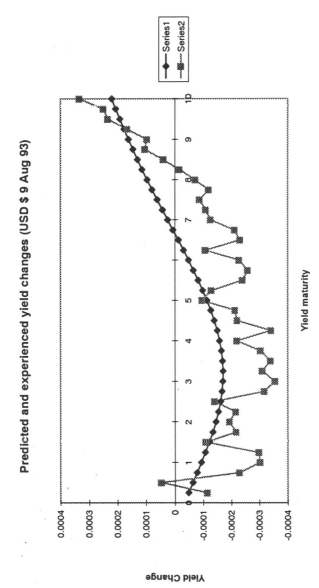

Figure 12.9 An example of a very good prediction (black dots) for a very complex pattern of yield changes (US$ curve, 9 Aug 1993), maturities out to 10 years on the x-axis. No one-factor model could reproduce such a complex pattern.

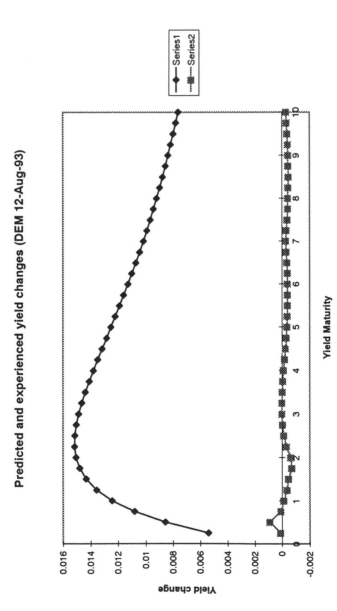

Figure 12.10 An example of a very poor prediction (black dots) for a relatively simple pattern of yield changes (DEM curve, 12 Aug 1993), same maturities as above. No reasonable one-factor model could produce such poor predictions for the market yield changes.

Despite some fortuitously suggestive results (see Figure 12.9), the correlation between experienced and predicted changes in rates is in general very low. The performance is actually often much poorer than for the simpler BDT model. The reason for this can be traced to the sensitivity of a discount bond price to the variance of the short rate, and to the very high correlation between the short rate and its variance implied by the model. This sensitivity is in fact large (of the same order of magnitude as the sensitivity to the short rate), but the daily changes in short rate volatility (forced by the very high correlation to move virtually in step with the change in the short rate itself) bear little resemblance with the 'real' changes in rate volatility. This can give rise to particularly implausible changes in correspondence with very large movements (upwards or downwards) in the short rate, thereby creating the pathological 'predictions' such as the ones shown in Figure 12.10. If one considers only changes in bond prices predicted by the 'observed' changes in short rate, the results are better behaved. However, in so doing one is giving up the very advantage that constitutes the main motivation for moving to a two-factor model.

Summarising the results, the predictions produced by carrying out a similar analysis for the BDT model (see Section 10.3) failed to have great explanatory power because rates of long maturities were forced by the model to move too much in step with the short rate. The LS model allows this decoupling, but the second factor, at least as distilled by the parameterisation procedure described above, fails consistently to account for the residual variation, and actually often produces totally unacceptable results.

The hedging implications of these findings are of course very important: in practical situations, if in-model hedging is desired, one will try to match the sensitivity to the underlying factors of a given instrument with the corresponding sensitivities of two other instruments, judiciously chosen. If the sensitivity to one of the factors is a number of dubious reliability, the reasonableness and effectiveness of the whole procedure becomes very questionable.

Of course, with a model of the complexity and richness of the LS, is it very difficult to say that 'the model' falls short of fulfilling its promise. More correctly, one can only speak about a particular implementation and parameterisation procedure. Perhaps if the coefficients were obtained from a mixed historical/fitting procedure more reasonable results could be obtained. The problem would, however, remain that the volatility of the short rate is strictly speaking not an observable quantity. In order to circumvent this problem, the cap volatility curve could be fitted by means of the following procedure: given a set of parameters (α, β, γ, δ, η, ξ and ν), however determined, one could construct a finite-difference grid with the terminal payoff of the cap, and evolve it backwards in time along the three-dimensional (two 'space' (r and V) and one time coordinate) lattice until time zero is reached; at this time, a two-dimensional array of today's cap values is obtained; for a given value of $r(0)$ this will collapse to a single vector of cap prices. One can then pick, or interpolate, the volatility V value that gives the correct cap market value. As described, the procedure is suggestively similar to obtaining an 'implied volatility' in the Black and Scholes approach.

The problem, however, is that the discount function which describes the model yield curve to be fitted to the market values is a function of the six parameters and of the two state variables. The two 'implied' procedures described above to fit the yield curve and the cap volatility curve cannot, therefore, be applied independently. The model parameters will specify a yield curve for a given choice of r and V.

The problem is, of course, theoretically not insoluble: the degrees of freedom to fit zero-coupon bond prices *and* cap volatilities *and* a lot more are all there; what is lacking is a simple procedure to fit both functions in a relatively straightforward way. Whether fitting all the available market data is desirable is, of course, a different question, whose answer ultimately depends on the confidence the user is prepared to put in a particular model, and on the judgement of the extent to which specific markets (e.g. swaptions) are sufficiently 'perfect' (e.g. liquid and/or devoid of institutional frictions) to justify the enforcement of the assumptions that generate the no-arbitrage conditions. The judgement and intuition of the user must therefore play an important part in the decision of which types of market values to use in the parameterisation, and, within a given class, which prices can actually be considered 'trustworthy'.

This issue is actually deeper than what is implied by these remarks, and leads directly to the all-important question: for what purpose is a model used? One way to trade complex options is by means of a loosely defined 'arbitrage' strategy, i.e. by attempting, as much as possible, not to take directional positions, but to construct a (dynamically rebalanced) replicating portfolio made up of plain-vanilla options and cash instruments that behaves as much as possible as the exotic instrument. Within the framework of this approach the trader would attempt to make his profit by selling (buying) at a slightly higher (lower) price than fair value, and by attempting to retain this value by a dynamic hedging strategy. To the extent that the chosen model is 'correct', i.e., in this context, capable of providing the necessary hedging parameters, the user would then be insulated from outright directional moves in the state variables of the model. If this approach is taken, the trader cannot question the 'correctness' of the prices of the underlying plain-vanilla options or of the cash instruments (bonds and swaps); rather, he must consider them as exogenous components of the price of the exotic options. Exact recovery of the market prices of the underlying instruments is therefore indispensable.

If, on the other hand, the trader uses exotic options to express complex market views, then a model indicating where, given certain assumptions about the economy, prices 'should' be is certainly more suitable than a purely no-arbitrage model. A lot of judgement will, of course, be required to establish to what extent the very stylised description of the economy that can be provided by any realistically implementable model can provide useful guidance in pointing out market mispricings. With this caveat in mind, however, the inability of a model to price exactly and simultaneously discount bonds, caps and swaptions could be viewed as a potentially desirable feature rather than an outright shortcoming. Clearly, the user will have to be particularly careful not to interpret as 'trading indications' those discrepancies between model and market prices which arise from the *intrinsic* inability of a model to account for certain real-life features (e.g. de-correlation between rates).

If exact recovery of the prices of discount bonds and caps were not considered strictly necessary, then the 'historical' procedure could produce a parameterisation procedure which would not only overcome most of the shortcomings outlined in the last two sections, but would also be more robust and conceptually more self-consistent. The next section is therefore devoted to this topic.

12.12 CALIBRATION TO THE YIELD CURVE USING THE HISTORICAL APPROACH

In order to examine a possible route towards the historical estimation of the LS model parameters, it is useful to recall that the fundamental PDE

$$\frac{\partial^2 H}{\partial x^2} \frac{x}{2} \frac{\partial^2 H}{\partial y^2} \frac{y}{2} + (\gamma - \delta x)\frac{\partial H}{\partial x} + (\eta - (\xi + \lambda)y)\frac{\partial H}{\partial y} - rH = \frac{\partial H}{\partial \tau} \quad (12.40)$$

which allows the pricing of any contingent claim in the LS model and contains (i) two state variables (x and y, or the transformed r and V), and (ii) four parameters: γ, δ, η, $(\xi + v)$ (notice that $(\xi + v)$ has been written, for reasons that will become apparent in the following, as a single parameter).

In addition two more parameters, α and β, specify the transformation from the state variables x and y to the state variables r and V:

$$r = \alpha x + \beta y \quad (12.41)$$

$$V = \alpha^2 x + \beta^2 y \quad (12.42)$$

Of these overall parameters, therefore, six (α, β, γ, δ, η, ξ) describe the 'real' (as opposed to risk-adjusted) dynamics of the two state variables, but a further parameter, v, linked to the investors' utility function, enters the PDE. As usual, without independent access to the latter it is therefore impossible to price contingent claims even if all the distributional assumptions concerning the variables r and V were perfectly correct, and the most thorough statistical analysis of real data were carried out.

In order to circumvent the problem, Longstaff and Schwartz (1993) has proposed the following two similar procedures:

PROCEDURES 1 AND 2

(i)   carry out a statistical analysis of the time series of the short rate and of the variance of the short rate;
(ii) from the constraint that x and y should be greater than zero, obtain the condition that

$$\begin{array}{c} \alpha < V \\ \hline r < \beta \end{array} \qquad\qquad (12.43)$$

and therefore choose

$$\alpha = \text{Min} \; \frac{V}{r} \qquad\qquad (12.44)$$

$$\beta = \text{Max} \; \frac{V}{r} \qquad\qquad (12.45)$$

where the minimum and maximum are taken over the observed time series;
(iii) from the relationships previously obtained:

$$E[r] = \frac{\alpha\gamma}{\delta} + \frac{\beta\eta}{\xi} \qquad\qquad (12.46)$$

$$\text{Var}[r] = \frac{\alpha^2\gamma}{2\delta^2} + \frac{\beta^2\eta}{2\xi^2} \qquad\qquad (12.47)$$

$$E[V] = \frac{\alpha^2\gamma}{\delta} + \frac{\beta^2\eta}{\xi} \qquad\qquad (12.48)$$

$$\text{Var}[V] = \frac{\alpha^4\gamma}{2\delta^2} + \frac{\beta^4\eta}{2\xi^2} \qquad\qquad (12.49)$$

determine the remaining four parameters, by solving a simple system of non-linear equations.

Up to this point the two procedures are identical. As for the evaluation of the further parameter ν related to the market price of risk two strategies are then suggested:

PROCEDURE 1

(iv) (a) solve analytically with these six parameters and a guess value for v the PDE (Equation (12.40)) with the boundary conditions appropriate to zero discount bonds, then compare the model values thus obtained with a market-obtained discount function, and vary the value of v until the one is found which affords the smallest sum of squared deviations; or

PROCEDURE 2

(iv) (b) take the first maturity of interest, t_1, solve the PDE above with the boundary condition pertaining to a zero discount bond maturing at time t_1 with a trial value for v (t_1), thereby obtaining a model price for the discount bond, $Z_{mod}(v(t_1))$; vary this trial value $v(t_1)$ until an exact match is obtained between the model and the market value; move on to the next maturity, and use the obtained value $v(t_1)$ for the numerical integration from time 0 to time t_1, and a trial value $v(t_2)$ for the period between t_1 and t_2. Vary $v(t_2)$ until a match is obtained between observed and model prices.

It is important to notice that the first strategy is much simpler, since the model discount function can be obtained analytically, as long as v is constant; however, if this approach is employed one cannot in general recover the observed discount function exactly. On the other hand, the second approach recovers the prices of zero-coupon bonds by construction, but is rather laborious due to the need to integrate the PDE (12.40) numerically, and the approach no longer enjoys the theoretical advantage of being an equilibrium model (with approaches as stylised as the CIR or LS, whether this should be regarded as a serious drawback is, of course, very debatable).

The parameterisation procedure described in this section could be used within the framework of 'positional trading' described at the end of the previous section, as long as the trader had sufficient confidence in the reliability of the model. The statistical difficulties of stage (i) of both procedures should, however, not be underestimated (see, e.g., Clewlow and Strickland (1994) and the reply by Longstaff and Schwartz (1994)).

12.13 CONCLUSIONS

The attempt has been made in this chapter to present the most salient positive and negative features of the LS model. Among the first one can certainly number an undeniable intellectual elegance and the fact that (with Fong's (1992) approach) it is one of the very few interest-rate-option models to provide closed-form solutions for the case of stochastic volatility. Once the model has been calibrated, the fact that it belongs to the affine class (see

Chapter 15) allows the user to obtain very easily a wealth of results (such as correlation among rates, yield volatilities, etc.) that can shed a lot of light on its characteristics. The time stationarity of the model further ensures that whatever features are ascribed to the yield-curve dynamics at time t, such as, for instance, the term structure of volatilities, will be found again at later times. The same cannot be said, for instance, for the BDT model, and for time-inhomogeneous models in general. The importance of this feature is also discussed in Chapter 15. Furthermore, unlike 'early' equilibrium models such as the CIR or Vasicek, even very complex yield-curve shapes can be reproduced with relative ease.

Moving to less positive aspects, the calibration procedure has been shown to be fraught with difficulties: a purely 'implied' approach cannot be guaranteed to yield a reasonable implied dynamics. The very flexibility of the functional form of the model, allowing the 'twisting' of the yield curve around virtually any market term structure is probably more of a bane than a blessing, at least in so far as a purely implied approach is adopted. As it is in general the case, what really matters in judging the quality of a fit to a given yield curve is whether the deterministic dynamics of a given model is actually capable of producing a complex yield-curve shape. This is particularly true at the short end of the maturity spectrum, where expectations of future rates play a much more important role than expectations about future volatilities in determining the shape of the term structure (see Section 9.1).

A 'historical' (as opposed to implied) approach parameter estimation procedure would be free of these dangers, but leaves the user with the usual problem of potentially mispriced 'underlying' assets. A mixed parameterisation strategy is certainly interesting, but it is not clear how to obtain a *simultaneous* fitting to nothing more 'exotic' than discount bond and cap prices. While these shortcomings are common to several models (see the discussion at the beginning of Section 9.6), the LS approach presents the added undesirable feature of forcing a very high correlation between the short rate and its own volatility, at least for a wide variety of plausible parameter choices (see Clewlow and Strickland (1994)). The consequences of these features have been discussed in the preceding sections.

Balancing these positive and negative features is not easy. It is probably fair to say that its elegance and conceptual scope make the LS model a very interesting and potentially profitable tool in order to investigate at a qualitative level general features of the yield-curve dynamics. On the other hand, to the best knowledge of the writer, exceedingly few financial institutions employ the LS model as an actual real-time trading tool, and, unfortunately, this is likely to remain the case until and unless a robust and reasonably simple parameterisation method capable of accurate pricing of the underlying instruments is found.

13

The Brennan and Schwartz model

13.1 INTRODUCTION

Of the two-factor models presented in Part Four, the Brennan and Schwartz (BS) (1982, 1983) is, with the exception of the 'historical' implementation of the Heath Jarrow and Morton methodology, probably the one that most directly embraces the principal component framework outlined in Chapter 2. As will be shown in the following, in fact, BS begin their treatment by positing that the yield-curve behaviour can be described in terms of the dynamics of two possibly unobservable and *a priori* unknown state variables, u_1 and u_2. Given this assumption, any yield or rate must be expressible as a function of these two variables. In particular, if the short and the long (consol) rates can be expressed, by inverting their implicit dependence on u_1 and u_2, as twice differentiable functions of the state variables, then they can be taken as their observable proxies. In short, no explicit claim is made about the yield curve being 'in reality' driven by these two rates, but, if the invertibility conditions are fulfilled, the analysis can proceed as if the short rate r and the long yield (L) were indeed the driving factors. Therefore the model can be interpreted as being driven by 'level' (long yield) and 'slope' (short rate–long yield) of the yield curve.

Notice that this approach does not directly imply anything about the efficiency of this particular choice in terms of explanatory power of the yield-curve variability: the only requirement for the choice to be acceptable is that the two chosen rates should not display perfect co-linearity. However, since the sum of the short and the long rate can be considered a good proxy for the average level of the yield curve, and their difference for the slope, the independent results of a principal component analysis, frequently referred to in previous sections, confer to the approach the added appeal of a statistically well-justifiable procedure.

The original choice of BS, however, was probably not motivated by statistical considerations. Their framework, originally devised as a bond model capable of testing market efficiency, is in fact of equilibrium nature: the drift and volatilities of the proxy variables, r and L, are taken to refer to the real world, and the resulting parabolic partial differential equations for the prices of traded assets therefore contain two market prices of risk. The expected return from a given security will, in general, be given by the sum of the riskless rate plus the extra return investors demand in order to bear the risks connected with the variability in both the short and the long rate. As we saw in connection with models such as the CIR, independent estimation of *one* market price of risk is arduous enough, and has rarely, if ever, yielded convincing results. Also the joint estimation of some function of a single market price of risk and the parameters describing the real-world dynamics of the state variables (capable, almost by construction, of giving more 'appealing' results) have been shown to require extreme care (see Chapters 9 and 12) if a meaningful calibration is to be obtained. The existence of two market prices of risk in the BS model would therefore seem to indicate an approach fraught with virtually insurmountable estimation problems. The greatest insight of BS, however, has been that one of these market prices of risk can be made to disappear, as long as the second variable is chosen to be the 'long' (consol) yield (more precisely defined in the following). When this is accomplished, the BS approach therefore can offer the rich dynamical behaviour of a two-factor model with the estimation complexity of a one-factor model. As a consequence, if carefully implemented and parameterised, it can offer a valid alternative for the pricing of complex interest-rate options.

An important distinction will be made in this chapter between this very useful and general result, and the specific model put forth by BS. It will be argued in the concluding section that the specific implementation recommended by BS is neither theoretically acceptable, nor practically very useful. Nonetheless the avenue opened by the general framework has wider validity and appeal, and can be very profitably explored.

13.2 THE CONDITION OF NO-ARBITRAGE AND THE MARKET PRICE OF LONG YIELD RISK

As stated in the introduction, BS assume that it is indeed possible to effect a translation from the unobservable 'true' state variables to two particular observable rates. These rates are chosen to be the short rate, r, and the yield, L, on the irredeemable bond (the consol). The latter is defined as a security paying £Δt every time interval Δt. (The irredeemable Gilts 'war loans' are, for instance, a good approximation to a consol.) Notice that if, on any given day, the yield curve tends asymptotically to a constant level (possibly different day after day), the equilibrium swap rate will tend to the yield of the consol as its maturity approaches infinity. Notice also that, from elementary bond mathematics, the price, $P(t,\infty;c) \equiv C(t;c)$, of a consol paying a coupon c is simply given by c times the reciprocal of the long yield itself:

$$C(t) = \frac{c}{L} \qquad (13.1)$$

In complete generality, the stochastic differential equations for r and L can be written as (BS's notation has been changed in order to conform with the symbols used elsewhere in the book; as for their choice of lower-case 'l' for the long yield, it was deemed to be nothing short of typographically diabolical, especially given that factors of 1 (one) also appear in the equations):

$$dr = \mu_r(r,L,t)\, dt + \sigma_r(r,L,t)\, dz_r \qquad (13.2)$$

$$dL = \mu_L(r,L,t)\, dt + \sigma_L(r,L,t)\, dz_L \qquad (13.2')$$

The notation, lightened in the following, makes clear the possibility of an explicit dependence of both drifts and volatilities on the two state variables and on calendar time. As usual

$$E[dz_r\, dz_L] = \rho\, dt \qquad (13.3)$$

From the two absolutely general Equations (13.2) and (13.2′) one can derive using Ito's lemma the return on any asset, V (possibly paying a continuous dividend c):

$$\frac{dV}{V} = \mu_V\, dt + \frac{\partial V}{\partial r}\, \sigma_r\, dz_r + \frac{\partial V}{\partial L}\, \sigma_L\, dz_L \qquad (13.4)$$

with

$$\mu_V = \left[c + \mu_r \frac{\partial V}{\partial r} + \mu_L \frac{\partial V}{\partial L} + \frac{1}{2}\left(\frac{\partial^2 V}{\partial r^2}\, \sigma_r^2 + \frac{\partial^2 V}{\partial L^2}\, \sigma_L^2 + 2\frac{\partial^2 V}{\partial r\partial L}\, \sigma_r \sigma_L \rho \right) \right] \Big/ V$$

$$(13.4')$$

(Notice that, for a security paying a continuous dividend with an annual coupon rate c, $\partial V/\partial t = c$.)

The no-arbitrage condition derived in Chapter 5, Section 1, showed that, if the price V of a security is affected by n variables $\{x\}$, then (i) its expected return can be written as:

$$\mu_V = r + \sum_i \left(\frac{\partial V}{\partial x_i} \right) \sigma_i \lambda_i \qquad (13.5)$$

with λ_i indicating the market price of risk associated with the ith variable, and (ii) that these market prices of risk can in general be a function of all the state variables and of calendar time, but of no specific characteristic of asset V:

$$\lambda_i = \lambda_i(x_1, x_2, \ldots, x_n, t) \tag{13.6}$$

If this asset, in particular, is a bond, the various market prices of risk cannot depend on the bond maturity. Notice the presence in Equation (13.5) of the 'elasticity' term $\partial V/\partial x_i$, showing how different securities can be affected to different extents by the variability in the variables x_i. In particular, should one of these elasticities, say the jth, be exactly zero, then the market price of risk associated with the jth variable would not affect the price of the security.

For the particular case of the BS model, Equation (13.5) becomes

$$\mu_r = r + \frac{\partial V}{\partial r} \sigma_r \lambda_r + \frac{\partial V}{\partial L} \sigma_L \lambda_L \tag{13.5'}$$

This equation must hold true for any security. In particular it must hold true for a consol bond paying a unit coupon. But this security, whose price is simply given (see Equation (13.1) by $1/L$, shows no dependence on the variable r. Therefore its expected return will not depend on the market price of short-rate risk. More precisely, equating expressions (13.4) and (13.5$'$) for the case of $V = C(t;1) = 1/L$, and remembering that

$$\frac{\partial C}{\partial t} = 1$$

$$\frac{\partial C}{\partial r} = \frac{\partial^2 C}{\partial r^2} = \frac{\partial^2 C}{\partial r \partial L} = 0$$

$$\frac{\partial C}{\partial L} = \frac{2}{L^2}$$

$$\frac{\partial^2 C}{\partial L^2} = \frac{2}{L^3} \tag{13.7}$$

one easily obtains

$$\lambda_L = \frac{rL - L^2 + \mu_L}{\sigma_L} - \frac{\sigma_L}{L} \tag{13.8}$$

Since a market price of risk cannot depend on any specific feature of the particular security used to obtain it, it must hold true in general for any security. Therefore Equation (13.8) can be inserted in the last term on the RHS of Equation (13.5$'$). Since this whole RHS must in turn equal the percentage drift on any asset V, it can be equated to the RHS of Equation (13.4); when the algebra is carried out one obtains the parabolic PDE

$$\frac{\partial V}{\partial t} + c + \frac{\partial V}{\partial r}(\mu_r - \lambda_r \sigma_r) + \frac{\partial V}{\partial L}\left(L^2 - rL + \frac{\sigma_L^2}{L}\right)$$

$$+ \frac{1}{2}\left[\frac{\partial^2 V}{\partial r^2}\sigma_r^2 + \frac{\partial^2 V}{\partial L^2}\sigma_L^2 + 2\frac{\partial^2 V}{\partial r \partial L}\rho\sigma_r\sigma_L\right] = rV \qquad (13.9)$$

Notice that not only is the market price of long yield risk absent from the PDE, but so is the drift of the long yield itself. (Compare this with the disappearance of the 'real-world' drift from the Black and Scholes equation.) Notice also that Equation (13.9) applies to the real world. Therefore the short-rate drift that it contains does not refer to any risk-adjusted universe, and could, in principle, be estimated by econometric (statistical) methods. The user will therefore still be left with the task of estimating the market price of short-rate risk. This, in turn, can only be arrived at by using the traded prices of securities which price this risk. This is exactly the route followed by BS: as shown in the following section, they first posited particular functional forms for the drifts and volatilities of r and L, and proceeded to estimate the free parameters of these functional specifications via statistical analysis of real data. After taking these functional forms and these parameters as 'true', they further assumed that λ_r should be an intertemporal constant, and estimated its value from the market prices of US Treasuries. Whatever the merit of this specific procedure, the results (13.8) and (13.9) are of general validity, and their usefulness should not be affected by whatever criticism one might level at the particular model specification and parameterisation that BS carried out.

13.3 THE SPECIFIC MODEL

In order to carry out a quantitative estimation, BS posited that the actual dynamics of the short and consol rates should have the form:

$$dr = (a_1 + b_1(L - r))\,dt + r\sigma_1\,dz_1 \qquad (13.10)$$

$$dL = L(a_2 + b_2 r + c_2 L)\,dt + L\sigma_2\,dz_2 \qquad (13.10')$$

The chosen functional forms assign locally log-normal behaviour to both the short and the long rate. In addition, the deterministic component of the real-world dynamics of the short rate is assumed to be of mean-reverting form, with the short rate reverting to the long yield with reversion speed b_1. As BS point out (Brennan and Schwartz (1982)), this assumption is consistent with theories of the term structure based on expectations, i.e.

theories which assume long rates to be based upon expectation of future short-rates.

In addition to this term, the presence of a constant term a_1 in the drift of r gives a contribution more difficult to justify. In particular, if a_1 is negative and sufficiently large, it will cause the short rate to become negative after a finite amount of time, even despite the locally log-normal stochastic component. This feature of the model will be revisited when discussing the parameterisation of the model, and its stability.

It is also interesting to notice that, despite the fact that the market price of long-rate risk and the drift of the consol yield do not enter the PDE satisfied by a security's price, the 'real-world' drift of L will still influence the 'real-world' drift of r via the coupled joint deterministic dynamics: L enters the drift of r, and r enters the drift of L. The specific functional form chosen for the deterministic component of the consol yield stems from BS's assumption that the market price of long yield risk should be bi-linear in r and L:

$$\lambda_L = k_0 + k_1 r + k_2 L \tag{13.11}$$

as can be verified by substituting Equation (13.11) in Equation (13.8) of the previous section. If one then solves this equation for μ_L, after inserting $\sigma_2 L$ for σ_L, one obtains

$$a_2 = k_0 + \sigma_2^2 \tag{13.12}$$

$$b_2 = \sigma_2 k_1 - 1 \tag{13.12'}$$

$$c_2 = \sigma_2 k_2 + 1 \tag{13.12''}$$

Notice that, since in all the coefficients there enter a term appearing in the unknown market price of long yield risk, one is none the wiser as to possible cross-relationships among the 'real-world' drift parameters of L and its volatility.

BS went on to estimate the parameters a_1, b_1, σ_1, a_2, b_2, c_2, σ_2 and ρ using US rates data spanning the period 1958–1979. Their statistical methodology is described in detail in BS (1982). Taking these estimates of the real-world parameters as 'true', the market price of short rate risk, λ_r, was then estimated from bond prices.

More precisely, market values of Treasury bonds were compared with the model bond prices created by multiplying each cash flow (coupon and principal) by the discount factor, in turn obtained by solving the PDE (13.9) subject to the initial condition $P(T,T) = 1$. Notice that, since no analytic solutions are known for PDE (13.9) with the coefficients of the form given by Equations (13.10), (13.10'), a rather time-consuming two-dimensional finite-differences methodology of the type described in the last section of Chapter 7 had to be employed.

The results of their analysis are reported in the Table 13.1 (taken from BS (1983)). Notice that only a_1, b_1, σ_1 and ρ enter *directly* the PDE that governs the price of discount bonds, and one might be tempted to conclude that the estimation of the other parameters should have no influence on bond pricing. As mentioned above, this would, however, be incorrect, given the joint nature of the dynamics for the state variables: a given choice of, say, b_2 will affect the evolution of L, which in turn multiplies b_1 in the drift of r.

Probably the most disturbing feature of this parameter estimation is the large and negative value of a_1, imparting a strong negative drift to the short rate. One should be very careful drawing conclusions 'by inspection' as to the joint dynamics of the two variables, since the mean-reverting term creates a dynamical system coupled in a rather complex way. An example of the paths for the short-rate and the consol yield is shown in Figure 13.1 (to obtain a reasonable behaviour the term $a1$ was reduced by one order of magnitude).

Even this couple of relatively well-behaved (if not intuitively very 'plausible') paths display a worrying proneness to instability. This behaviour is shown more clearly in Figures 13.2, 13.3 and 13.4, where the 'exploding' behaviour of the long rate becomes apparent. Notice that the negative values attained by the long yield are an artifact of the simulation, and produced by the extremely high values of the long yield coupled with the discretised equations for the reversion term.

Unfortunately, even by changing the parameters over a reasonable but wide range, the unstable behaviour of the coupled dynamics for the two variables cannot be eliminated. The tendency for the long yield to assume extremely large values, in particular, cannot be eradicated and gives rise to the resulting distribution of the consol yield displaying an upper tail (high values of L) that fails to abate at a reasonable rate. Therefore there is a finite and no negligible probability for exceedingly high values of the long yield after finite times. This 'empirical' finding is *not* an artifact of the finite-time MC simulation, since it

Table 13.1 The Coefficients Estimated by BS (1983) and Their Reported Standard Errors

Parameter	Estimate	Error
a_1	−0.0887	±0.0526
b_1	0.1102	±0.0301
σ_1	0.1133	
a_2	0.0089	±0.0069
b_2	0.00358	±0.0017
c_2	−0.0037	±0.0020
σ_2	0.0298	
ρ	0.2063	
λ_r	0.45	

Sample Paths of the Short and Consol Yields

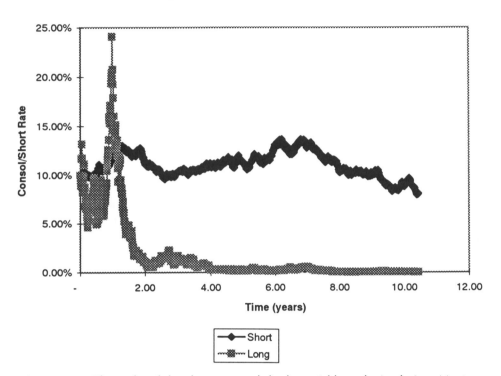

Figure 13.1 The paths of the short rate and the long yield as obtained via a Monte Carlo simulation which employed the parameters estimated by BS, but with the coefficients a1 reduced by one order of magnitude.

has been explained by Hogan (1993) in a very interesting (albeit rather technical) paper, where it is shown that the joint dynamics of the two variables is such that the long yield will explode with positive probability in finite time. This feature, Hogan points out, is not linked to the particular BS model specification. It is in fact possible to prove (Hogan (1993)) that, if the drift of the short rate is of the form

$$\mu_r = a + b(1 - r) \tag{13.13}$$

or

$$\mu_r = a + br(L - r), \quad (b < 1) \tag{13.13'}$$

or

$$\mu_r = a + br \ln \frac{L}{r} \tag{13.13'}$$

Sample paths of the Short and Consol Yields

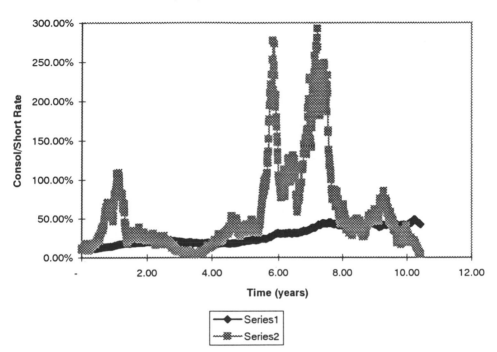

Figure 13.2 Paths of the short rate and the long yield as obtained via Monte Carlo simulations which employed the parameters estimated by BS, but with the coefficient a1 reduced by one order of magnitude. Notice the exploding behaviour of the long yield, and the extent to which the short rate can be 'dragged' by the long yield into very high regions.

then the model explodes, which is a rather dramatic way to express the fact that either r or L will reach infinity in a finite amount of time with positive probability. Notice that this problem is much more serious than, for instance, the possible existence of arbitrage for some 'naive' changes of process drifts (Cheng (1991)), which create non-equivalent measures (i.e. measures which are not equivalent to the real-world measure). Probably, these 'technical' imperfections (see Cheng (1991) for specific examples) should have little impact, from a practitioner's point of view, on option pricing. The problems outlined by Hogan, on the other hand, would be immediately encountered if one carried out, for instance, a Monte Carlo simulation of the process paths, as shown above.

The 'Hogan instability' is linked to the specific parameterisation and functional form chosen for the BS model. Further, and possibly more fundamental, problems with BS's approach stem from the following considerations: the price

Sample Paths of the Short and Consol Yields

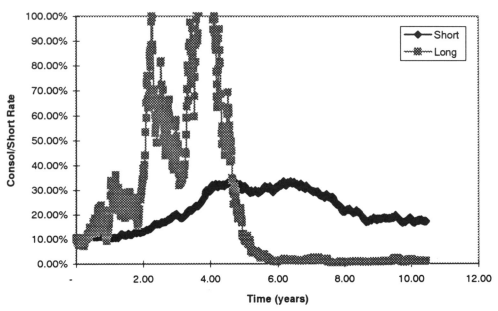

Figure 13.3   See Figure 13.2.

of any asset in a risk-neutral world is given by the expectation of the payoffs discounted along the short-rate paths:

$$V(0) = E\left[\exp\left[-\int_0^t r(s)\,\mathrm{d}s\right]V(t)\,|\,\mathfrak{F}_0\right] \qquad (13.14)$$

In particular for the case of the price of a consol bond paying £dt every time interval dt, Equation (13.14) becomes

$$C(0) = E\left[\int_0^\infty \exp\left[-\int_0^t r(s)\,\mathrm{d}s\right]\mathrm{d}t\,|\,\mathfrak{F}_0\right] \qquad (13.14')$$

The payoff $V(t)$ at each point in time is £dt, and the discounted values of all these infinitesimal payoffs are summed over (integrated) by the integral from today to infinity. Equation (13.14') clearly shows that the consol price (or rate) is determined by the process for the short rate itself, and that their dynamics are therefore more intimately linked than a superficial analysis might indicate. At an intuitive level, the origin of this link can be readily appreciated if one pictures the two variables r and L on a two-dimensional lattice (such as the one depicted in Section 11.7), and considers their respective values in, say, the

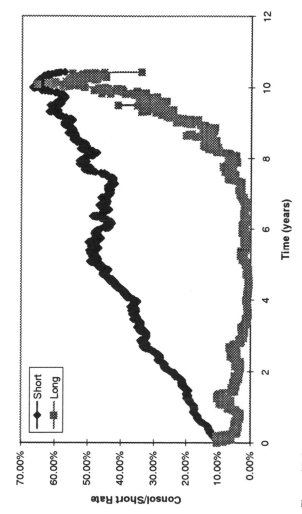

Figure 13.4 See Figure 13.2.

up/up state, as evolved from today's $r(0)$ and $C(0)$. The C(up) value thus reached could, however, also be obtained by discounting using future values of the short-rate, the known future payments from the consol occurring all the way out to the boundary of the lattice (in practice, since the series does converge, a larger and larger, but still finite, lattice would produce an answer that could be made arbitrarily close to the true one). The 'two' values of C in this state, i.e. C(up) and the sum of the discounted payoffs, must be the same for the model to be internally consistent, but there is no guarantee that this should be the case for arbitrary model parameters. Notice also that, since the (risk-adjusted) drift of C is completely determined by no-arbitrage conditions, the most likely candidate in order to ensure the compatibility of the process is the volatility of the consol itself.

Duffie, Ma and Yong (1994) made these intuitive considerations more precise by showing that, if the SDEs for the short rate and the consol price are of the general type

$$dr = \mu_r(r,C)\,dt + \sigma_r(r,C)\,dz \qquad (13.15)$$

$$dC = (r,C - 1)\,dt + A(r,C)\,dz \qquad (13.15')$$

then the volatility of the consol price A must have a specific form for the consol to be indeed linked to the short-rate process by Equation (13.14'). (Notice that the drift on C simply stems from the no-arbitrage condition derived above in discrete time.) More precisely, under technical conditions, they prove that the equations above certainly have solutions if the consol price is a function f of the short-rate itself, $C(t) = f(r(t))$. If this is the case therefore (via Ito's lemma), $A(r,C)$ must be of the form

$$A(r,C) = f'(r)\sigma_r(r,C) \qquad (13.16)$$

They also prove that the function $f(r)$ that maps the short rate into the consol must be a solution to an *ordinary* differential equation

$$f'(r)\mu_r(r,f(r)) - rf(r) + \tfrac{1}{2}f''(r)\sigma_r^2 + 1 = 0 \qquad (13.17)$$

These results have profound implications for the model: since $L = 1/C$, and $C = f(r)$, BS's apparently two-factor approach actually collapses, at least under the conditions required for the proof, to a degenerate model describable in terms of a single state variable. Notice carefully, however, that the results reported above only prove that a function A as above provides a consistent solution, not that it provides the *only* consistent solution. In other terms, for any choice of the drift and variance of the short rate there is always a function A such that the SDEs above are internally consistent; it is still possible, however, that there might exist another function A', not determined by Equations (13.16) and (13.17), such that inconsistencies between the processes do not arise. Furthermore, some of the technical conditions required to produce the results above might be, after all, not so innocuous; in particular Duffie et al require that the short rate r should stay in some interval $[r_{min} r_{max}]$, with $0 < r_{min} < r_{max}$.

13.4 CONCLUSIONS

In the light of the findings outlined in the previous section one might be tempted to conclude that the BS approach is theoretically flawed, and of little practical use. Such a conclusion would be far too harsh, and would fail to distinguish between the no-arbitrage condition pointed out by BS (Equation 13.8), and the specific model parameterisation they employ; while the latter can be (and has been) criticised on several grounds, the former offers a powerful tool in reducing the complexity of the problem of modelling the yield-curve dynamics. There are several alternative choices for the evolution of r and L which are free of the criticisms pointed out by Hogan (1993), and which give rise to very plausible descriptions of the movements of the term structure. In addition to these caveats, Duffie, Ma and Yong (1994) point out the requirements of internal consistency which stem from BS's very choice of state variables (in turn needed to eliminate one market price of risk). They show that compatibility between the consol price and short-rate processes is achieved by a particular choice for the volatility of the consol price itself; they do not prove, however, the uniqueness of this type of solution.

In view of the above, it therefore seems fair to say that, if suitably extended and carefully handled, the line of approach proposed by BS can be fruitful. On the other hand, naive implementations are likely either to produce unstable results, or to give rise to degenerate one-variable models.

BS's original intention was to create an *equilibrium* model, and they have therefore carried out their analysis in the 'real-world' measure. If the problems outlined by Hogan (1993) and Duffie, Ma and Yong (1994) are addressed, the equivalent of the no-arbitrage condition (13.8) can, however, be obtained in the risk-neutral measure. This, in turn, can lead to a no-arbitrage lattice methodology whose computational complexity can be made to be not substantially greater than, say, what is required for the BDT model. This can be important since the 'mainstream' two-factor approach, i.e. the HJM framework reviewed in the following chapter, suffers from the drawback of giving rise, in nontrivial cases, to non-recombining trees, which necessitate Monte Carlo technologies for option valuation. While this should constitute a well-suited framework for path-dependent options, the issue of the evaluation of American options using Monte Carlo (see Section 8.4) is, at the moment, probably *the* single most arduous computational challenge, and all results which have appeared in this area have been as enticing as incomplete.

One should, on the other hand, remember that lattice- or finite-differences-based methodologies can but awkwardly deal with path-dependent options in more than one dimension. The two methodologies, if carefully implemented, can therefore both be valuable and, to some extent, complement each other. For consistency of pricing and for risk-management purposes the issue clearly remains of the compatibility of Markovian models (such as BS's) and non-Markovian approaches. These issues will be explored in the last section of Chapter 16.

14

The Heath Jarrow and Morton approach

14.1 INTRODUCTION

As mentioned in the Introduction, an increasing number of exotic interest-rate instruments have appeared in the market in the last few years, whose value depends in a crucial way on the imperfect correlation among rates. Needless to say, correlation-dependent instruments have been around since European swaptions have been traded alongside caps and floors. But, in this simple case, all the complexity of the yield-curve dynamics is subsumed into a single number, i.e. the volatility of the swap rate (see Chapter 1); looking for instance at Equation (1.31), one can see that the Black 'implied volatility' for a swaption gives, at least for the most liquid markets, a direct indication of the implied covariance matrix among all the forward rates of interest. In Chapter 1, Section 4, it was also shown how, at least in principle, one could 'strip' the correlation structure for the whole yield curve from a suitable series of caps and swaptions, and in Chapter 3 it was argued that a simple analytic expression (the Black formula) could provide a theoretically sound and easy-to-implement answer to the problem of pricing European swaptions. The new generation correlation-dependent instruments, on the other hand, have added a new dimension of complexity, which will be briefly explored in this section as a motivation for the sometimes formidable computational complexity of multi-factor models in general, and of the Heath Jarrow and Morton (HJM) approach in particular.

The interest-rate market in its entirety can be regarded as a collection of instruments which price different sources of market uncertainty: swaps and FRAs price the level of (different portions of) the yield curve; caps and floors price the volatility of (i.e. the diagonal elements of the covariance matrix among) the different forward rates; swaptions assign a price both to the diagonal and to the off-diagonal elements of the same covariance matrix (i.e.

loosely speaking, price, in addition to the volatility of the correlation among the forward rates).

When a new class of products appears on the market, no 'benchmark' prices exist. The first task of the trader is therefore to understand, at first at a qualitative level, which features of the yield-curve dynamics will be of secondary relevance, which important and which absolutely essential in determining the price of the new security. To give a concrete example, in 1992/ 1993 accrual notes (which accrue a LIBOR interest for each day a reference rate sets within a pre-specified band) proved very popular among investors looking for yield 'enhancement'. Since the bands within which the note would accrue interest were fixed throughout the life of the instrument, it is clear that, to first order, the value of these first-generation accrual notes depended on the *level* of the yield curve. A one-factor model calibrated in a sensible way to cap volatilities would therefore seem to give a viable first-order approximation towards the pricing of this instrument. Following the tightening in US$ rates which took place at the beginning of February 1994, and the consequent change in level and/or slope of most yield curves, existing investors in accrual notes often found themselves holding notes with accrual bands hopelessly distant from the current levels of interest rates. Aware of these dangers, new investors therefore demanded a different type of accrual instrument, namely *chooser* accrual notes, where the band is reset, at a level chosen by the investor, at the beginning of each accrual period. This 'minor' twist completely changed the nature of the instrument: the *absolute level* of the yield curve now becomes virtually an irrelevance, since the investor always has the right to position the bands wherever he pleases in each period; on the other hand, the slope of the yield curve and its volatility become the first-order contributors to the value of the new instrument. A change in slope of the yield curve, in turn, is driven by imperfect correlation among rates (if all forward rates had the same volatility, perfect correlation can only give rise to an almost rigid shift of the yield curve; for a reasonable structure of cap volatilities, it is almost impossible to obtain a yield-curve inversion using a one-factor model).

Traders who had to make a market in, or to risk manage, chooser accrual notes therefore saw themselves forced to examine closely the correlation structure implied by swaption prices. At the same time, they had to look for models which could translate this additional information into a coherent pricing framework. Since the case of index accrual notes is by no means exceptional, but rather constitutes the norm in product development away from a pure yield-curve-level play towards slope and correlation products, at-least-two-factor models have obviously become extremely topical. Among the latter, the implementations stemming from the Heath Jarrow and Morton (HJM) approach (described in this chapter) have encountered the greatest degree of popularity. Why so much more effort has been put into implementing the HJM approach than, say, in working out suitable modifications of the

Brennan and Schwartz approach can be rationalised *a posteriori* only to some extent. Part of the reason is that the HJM approach can be extended, at least conceptually, to as many factors as required, while there is no obvious way to add a factor in, say, the Brenann and Schwartz model without introducing another market price of risk, and all the accompanying estimation problems. Furthermore, while for lattice- or finite-differences-based approaches the computational cost generally grows with the power of the number of factors, with the HJM approach, which, for non-trivial specifications, has to be implemented using the Monte Carlo technique, one is paying an approximately linear cost in the number of factors.

Given the effect of low model dimensionality on the covariance matrix which can be obtained from the model itself (as discussed in the last section of Chapter 2), one might argue that the choice of the HJM approach might have been prompted by the knowledge that, even if today two-factor models are at the very boundaries of feasibility, tomorrow more powerful computer technology might repay the conceptual investment into a pricing methodology which can 'naturally' grow to three or several factors. While there is certainly some ring of truth to this explanation, it is also undeniable that the formal elegance and generality of the HJM approach have played an non-indifferent role in tilting the balance of choices in its favour.

Whatever the reason for the popularity of the HJM approach, research into the Monte Carlo technique has received a most powerful boost by this state of affairs: as shown in the following (see also Chapter 16), the 'general' HJM process is intrinsically non-Markovian (i.e. path dependent: an 'up' move for the yield curve followed by a 'down' move does not lead to the same result as a 'down' move followed by an 'up' move); from the implementation point of view this in turn means that a non-trivial HJM process cannot be mapped onto a recombining tree; therefore bushy trees, or Monte Carlo paths, are *the* tools available to the practitioner for pricing and hedging options. Path-dependent options, awkwardly dealt with using one-dimensional trees, and almost impossibly clumsy in higher dimensions, are tackled very easily using the MC methodology. Compound, or American, options, on the other hand, efficiently and easily dealt with by backwards induction using finite-differences grids or recombining lattices, become very arduous to evaluate using Monte Carlo techniques. Some encouraging work, as of yet mostly unpublished, is beginning to appear in the United States on the topic of the evaluation of American options using the Monte Carlo methodology. (A brief discussion of the problems which arise in the evaluation of American options in a Monte Carlo framework appears in the last section of Chapter 8.) It is probably at the success or failure of these attempts that one should carefully look in order to establish whether the HJM approach will indeed become *the* general pricing and hedging tool of the future, or whether some other lattice-based methodology will ultimately win the day. The following sections will attempt to illustrate in detail the conceptual implications of the approach, and its concrete implementation.

14.2 THE HJM APPROACH

Section 5.4 showed that, if the chosen numeraire is the money market account, all assets grow at the riskless rate (Equation 5.32″), and forward rates are not martingales but display a non-zero drift term, which can be generally derived within the framework of the Heath, Jarrow and Morton (1989) approach. Two formulations are common for the latter, i.e. the price based, which takes the dynamics of discount bonds as the fundamental building block, and the forward based, which obtains the no-arbitrage stochastic differential equations obeyed by forward rates. The two approaches will be shown in the following to be equivalent (see also Carverhill (1993) for a clear, although not completely general, discussion). We shall start from the no-arbitrage condition shown in Chapter 5 to hold for the dynamics of *any* asset in order to arrive, in a non-technical fashion, at the HJM approach, and then obtain the equivalence of this formulation to the forward-rate-based one. This approach is probably more intuitively clear. It should be remembered, however, that, historically, the HJM results were first obtained in the forward-rates context.

The starting point of any implementation of the HJM approach is the observed yield curve, as described either by the collection of discount bonds given at time 0, $P(0,T)$, or by the instantaneous forward rates, $f(0,T)$), linked by

$$P(0,T) = \exp\left[-\int_0^T f(0,s)\,\mathrm{d}s\right] \tag{14.1}$$

$$f(0,T) = -\frac{\partial \ln P(0,T)}{\partial T} \tag{14.1'}$$

Either the discount bonds or the forward rates can therefore be taken as equivalent building blocks; in either case the approach therefore recovers by construction any given market yield curve. If one uses as numeraire the rolled-up money market account, all assets instantaneously grow at the riskless (short) rate. This must be true, in particular, for discount bonds, $P(t,T)$, for which one can therefore write:

$$\mathrm{d}P(t,T) = r(t)P(t,T)\,\mathrm{d}t + v(t,T,P(t,T))\,\mathrm{d}z \tag{14.2}$$

where, as usual, $v(t,T)$ is the time-t volatility of a bond of maturity T, $P(t,T)$ its price at time t, and $r(t)$ the short rate prevailing at time t. (For the sake of notational simplicity we shall deal with the case of a single driving factor; the extension to several factors is conceptually completely straightforward.) In Equation (14.2) the drift component is totally specified by the above-mentioned no-arbitrage condition, but the maximum generality has been allowed for the price volatility of the discount bond, which can depend on calendar time, on maturity time, and on the (stochastic) discount bond price at time t. Notice carefully that equations similar to (14.2) are commonly found in the literature: Hull (1993), for instance, starts his treatment of the HJM approach by positing

$$dP(t,T) = r(t)P(t,T)\,dt + v(t,T)P(t,T)\,dz \qquad (14.2')$$

i.e. by arbitrarily imposing a log-normal process for the stochastic component of the discount bond price. This assumption is less innocuous than might be surmised, since it leads directly to *normal* rates, and, as we shall see, to a totally non-stochastic volatility structure. Also Carverhill's (1993) starting point, i.e.:

$$dP(t,T) = r(t)P(t,T)\,dt + v(t,T)\,dz \qquad (14.2'')$$

is less general than one might imagine, since it precludes an explicit dependence on the (stochastic) discount bond price itself. Since the pinning of the HJM approach to a specific model is completely tantamount to the specification of the functional form for the volatility function, it is important to understand what is implied by the HJM approach in general, and what is a consequence of a particular implementation. Our Equation (14.2) is therefore taken as the most general starting point.

Let us now consider the variable $y(t,T) = \ln(P(t,T))$; straightforward application of Ito's lemma gives

$$dy(t,T) = d(\ln P(t,T)) = \left[r(t) - \frac{v(t,T,P)^2}{P(t,T)^2}\right]dt + \frac{v(t,T)}{P(t,T)}\,dz \qquad (14.3)$$

Therefore

$$
\begin{aligned}
d[\ln P(t,T_2) - \ln P(t,T_1)] &= \frac{1}{2}\left[\frac{v(t,T_1,P)^2}{P(t,T_1)^2} - \frac{v(t,T_2,P)^2}{P(t,T_2)^2}\right]dt \\
&\quad + \left[\frac{v(t,T_2,P)}{P(t,T_2)} - \frac{v(t,T_1,P)}{P(t,T_1)}\right]dz \qquad (14.4)
\end{aligned}
$$

As shown before, the continuously compounded time-t forward rate spanning the discrete period $[T_1\,T_2]$, $f(t,T_1,T_2)$, is given by:

$$f(t,T_1,T_2) = -\frac{\ln P(t,T_2) - \ln P(t,T_1)}{T_2 - T_1} \qquad (14.5)$$

Coupling this equation with Equation (14.4) therefore gives

$$
d[f(t,T_1,T_2)] = \frac{1}{2}\left[\frac{\dfrac{v(t,T_2,P)^2}{P(t,T_2)^2} - \dfrac{v(t,T_1,P)^2}{P(t,T_1)^2}}{T_2 - T_1}\right] dt + \left[\frac{\dfrac{v(t,T_1,P)}{P(t,T_1)} - \dfrac{v(t,T_2,P)}{P(t,T_2)}}{T_2 - T_1}\right] dz
$$

(14.6)

Defining $\xi(t,T,P) \equiv v(t,T,P)/P(t,T)$, and changing dz into $-dz$, one can therefore write

$$
d[f(t,T_1,T_2)] = \left[\frac{\xi(t,T_2,P(t,T_2))^2 - \xi(t,T_1,P(t,T_1))^2}{2(T_2 - T_1)}\right] dt
$$
$$
+ \left[\frac{\xi(t,T_1,P(t,T_1)) - \xi(t,T_2,P(t,T_2))}{T_2 - T_1}\right] dt
$$

(14.7)

Moving to the limit as T_2 approaches T_1 the discrete forward rate tends to the instantaneous forward rate $f(t,T)$:

$$
f(t,T) = -\frac{\partial \ln P(t,T)}{\partial T}
$$

(14.8)

and remembering that $\partial(f(x)^2)/\partial x = 2f(x)\,\partial f(x)/\partial x$, one finally obtains

$$
df(t,T) = \xi\left[\left(\frac{\partial \xi}{\partial T}\right)_P + \left(\frac{\partial \xi}{\partial P}\right)_T \frac{\partial P}{\partial T}\right] dt + \left[\left(\frac{\partial \xi}{\partial T}\right)_P + \left(\frac{\partial \xi}{\partial P}\right)_T \frac{\partial P}{\partial T}\right] dz \quad (14.9)
$$

where $(\partial f(x,y)/\partial x)_y$ indicates the partial derivative of the function f with respect to x, *when y remains constant*. In particular, $(\partial \xi/\partial P)_T$ indicates the derivative of ξ with respect to its explicit P dependence, but neglects the change in ξ due to the fact that P changes as T changes. Equation (14.9) therefore

(i) **shows that using the money market account as numeraire forward rates are not martingales, and**

(ii) **establishes the link that must exist in a risk-neutral world (if no-arbitrage is to be allowed) between the volatility of discount bonds and the drifts of forward rates.**

It is clear from the expression above that, since Equation (14.9) simply imposes a relationship between the drifts and volatilities of forward rates on the one hand, and the price volatility functions of discount bond prices on the other, there is no such thing as *the* HJM model; rather there exists a whole class of models, each characterised by a specific functional form for the volatility functions.

Notice that, for $v(t,T,P) = v'(t,T)P$ (i.e. for the Hull specification), Equation (14.9) simply becomes

$$df(t,T) = v'\frac{\partial v'}{\partial T}\,dt + \frac{\partial v'}{\partial T}\,dz \tag{14.9'}$$

i.e. for a bond price model log-normal in the volatility component, one can specify the dynamics of the forward rates as a function of the (deterministic!) percentage volatilities of discount bond prices only. In this case (and only in this case) is the volatility fully deterministic (Carverhill (1994) uses the term 'non-random'), in the sense that no yield-curve dependent (and hence stochastic) term appears in the volatility function. For a general process, however, this is not true: at the very least the stochastic part of the equation for a forward rate will also be a function of the bond price dependence on its residual maturity (i.e. on its 'duration').

Notice also that Equation (14.2) and following could have been obtained for *any* drift of $P(t,T)$ (not necessarily for $r(t)$), as long as $\mu_{p(t,T)}$ were simply a function of t and not of T.

Finally, making use of (14.6), Equation (14.9) can be re-written as

$$
\begin{aligned}
df(t,T) = \frac{v}{P}\Bigg[& \left[\frac{\left(\partial\left(\frac{v}{P}\right)\right)}{\partial T}\right]_P - \left[\left(\frac{\partial v}{\partial P}\right)_T - \frac{v}{P}\right]f(t,T)\Bigg]\,dt \\
& + \left[\left(\frac{\partial v}{\partial T}\right)_P\frac{1}{P} + \left[\frac{v}{P} - \left(\frac{\partial v}{\partial P}\right)_T\right]f(t,T)\right]\,dz
\end{aligned}
\tag{14.10}
$$

where use has been made of the fact that

$$\frac{1}{P}\frac{\partial P}{\partial T} = \frac{\partial \ln P(t,T)}{\partial T} = -f(t,T) \tag{14.11}$$

The relationships obtained so far are completely general, and embody nothing more than the conditions of no-arbitrage. The next sections will explore the implications of specific choices for the volatility functions (i.e. of different distributional assumptions).

14.3 SPECIFICATIONS OF THE HJM MODEL CONSISTENT WITH LOG-NORMAL BOND PRICES OR FORWARD RATES

If the log-normal assumption is made for discount bond prices, $v(t,T,P(t,T)) = v'P$, and, furthermore, if the percentage price volatility is assumed to be proportional to the bond maturity $v' = \sigma T$, then $v = \sigma PT$, and

$$\mathrm{d}f(t,T) = \sigma^2 T \, \mathrm{d}t + \sigma \, \mathrm{d}z \tag{14.12}$$

For this particularly simple specification, all forward rates are normal and display exactly the same volatility: the yield curve is therefore constrained to move exactly in parallel, and, therefore, the continuous-time equivalent of the Ho and Lee model has been recovered.

As mentioned above, these results are well known (so well known, in fact, that they are sometimes mistaken to apply to the HJM approach in general). For practical implementations, however, it can be desirable to parameterise a version of the HJM approach which displays *log-normal* volatility for all the forward rates. This would be very useful if one wanted to calibrate a specific HJM model to observed market prices of caps and European swaptions. It is interesting to investigate under what conditions this is possible, and what restrictions on the functional form of the discount bond volatility function are imposed by this assumption of log-normality. Let us begin by making the 'inspired guess' (Cooper (1993), private communication) that the function $v(t,T,P(t,t))$ should have the functional form

$$v(t,T,P(t,T)) = \psi(t) \ln P(t,T)P(t,T) \tag{14.13}$$

(Notice that, in so doing, we have dramatically restricted the possible functional dependence of v on the maturity time). Then, substituting (14.13) into (14.10) of the previous section after taking the appropriate derivatives and making use of (14.11), gives

$$\mathrm{d}f(t,T) = \mu_f \, \mathrm{d}t - \psi(t)f(t,T) \, \mathrm{d}z \tag{14.14}$$

which indeed corresponds to a log-normal specification for the distribution of forward rates. One can immediately check that, for any well-behaved function $\psi(t)$, the functional form (14.13) correctly entails that, since $P(T,T) = 1$,

$$v(t,t,P(t,t)) = 0 \tag{14.15}$$

as the certain redemption value to par of any discount bond requires (see discussion below). Notice, however, that, in obtaining result (14.14), it had been assumed that $\psi(t)$ should only depend on calendar time, and not on T as well. But, in this special case, i.e. if Equation (14.14) holds true, then the percentage volatility function of the forward rates $\psi(t)$ only depends on calendar time: therefore, for this particular form of ψ, for all forward rates on a given date to be log-normally distributed, they must all share the same percentage volatility. Given the market term structure of forward rate volatilities shown, for instance, in Figure 9.3, this could create practical problems in the calibration of a HJM model to market (log-normal) cap/swaption prices. In order to allow for the specification of different percentage volatilities, one can go back to Equation (14.10), make ψ a function of time and maturity,

$$v(t,T,P(t,T)) = \psi(t,T)P(t,T)\ln P(t,T) \qquad (14.13')$$

and, after equating terms in dz, write

$$f(t,T)\psi(t,T) = \left[\left(\frac{\partial v}{\partial T}\right)_P \frac{1}{P} + \left[\frac{v}{P} - \left(\frac{\partial v}{\partial P}\right)_T\right]f(t,T)\right] = \frac{\partial\left(\dfrac{v}{P}\right)}{\partial T} \qquad (14.16)$$

As in the previous derivation, the LHS is the form that the absolute volatility of f must assume for forward rates to be log-normally distributed. Remembering Equation (14.11) one can then write the LHS of Equation (14.16) as

$$-\frac{\partial \ln P(t,T)}{\partial T}\,\psi(t,T) = \frac{\partial\left(\dfrac{v}{P}\right)}{\partial T} \qquad (14.17)$$

Notice that if ψ, as assumed before, were a function only of t the same result obtained above would apply, i.e. $v = \psi \ln PP$; however, due to the T dependence of ψ necessary, as seen above, to allow for an independent specification for the volatilities of different forwards, one can verify by direct substitution that one can only write

$$v(t,T,P) = P(t,T)\ln P(t,T)\psi(t,T) - \int_t^T \ln P(t,s)\,\frac{\partial\psi(t,s)}{\partial s}\,ds \qquad (14.18)$$

To the term originally 'guessed' in Equation (14.13) an extra contribution must be added, which vanishes only for a flat term structure of forward rates volatilities $(\partial\psi(t,s)/\partial s = 0)$.

Equation (14.18) therefore shows the functional form that bond price volatilities must possess, if one wanted to make use of the priced-based HJM formulation, in order to allow for log-normal forward rates of different volatilities. While for the case of normal forward rates, therefore, the forward-based or price-based formulations lend themselves to equally straightforward specifications of the respective volatility functions, the results of the calculation above stress that the statements found in the literature as to the conceptual equivalence of the two approaches should actually be taken with a certain amount of care in practical implementations, if distributional consistency is required. In more concrete terms, the user who thought that Equations (14.2) or (14.2') constituted *general* specifications of the HJM model, and thereby proceeded to attempt calibration of the model to (log-normal rates) market prices of caps and swaptions, would soon encounter severe problems.

14.4 GENERAL CONSTRAINTS ON THE VOLATILITIES OF DISCOUNT BOND PRICES

Since, as it has been shown, absence of arbitrage directly translates in a link between forward rate drifts and discount bond volatilities, it is worthwhile commenting further on the complexity and richness of the volatility input. For the valuation of an option depending on n discrete forward rates, $(f(0,t_i,t_i + \tau)$, $i = 1, \ldots, n)$, these will have to be evolved from time 0 to the option expiry. In order to evaluate their drifts for the first time step one requires (see Equations (14.9) and (14.10)) the values of $2n$ discount bond volatility functions $(v(0,t_i), v(0,t_i + \tau), i = 1, \ldots, n)$ at time 0. Once each forward rate has been evolved over a time step Δt, the 'front' forward rate will become a spot rate, and the $2(n-1)$ volatilities at time Δt of the remaining $2\ (n-1)$ discount bonds of maturity $t_i - \Delta t$, $t_i + \tau - \Delta t$ $(i = 1, \ldots, n-1)$ will be required to evolve the remaining forward rates one step forward. In principle, unless some strong volatility constraints are imposed, this approach would leave the user with the task of specifying the price volatilities of discount bonds of continuously changing maturities at each point in the evolution of the forward rates. For practical implementations, the need to specify a functional form for the functions $v(.,.)$ is therefore clear, and to each particular choice there will correspond *a* particular HJM model.

A first and absolutely necessary condition on the function $v(t,\tau)$, in order to prevent infinite drifts, is that $v(t,t) \equiv 0 \ \forall \ t$, simply reflecting the certainty of the redemption at par of any discount bond.

The above condition is absolutely necessary in order to obtain meaningful results. Once the chosen functional form for $v(.,.)$ ensures that this requirement is satisfied, at least two choices are then open to the user as to the possible behaviour of the bond volatility functions. The first is whether or not the process for the short rate should depend on the path followed up to a given time, i.e. in more technical terms, whether the short-rate process should be Markovian or non-Markovian (see Chapter 16). Later in this chapter it will be shown that, in general, the short-rate increment $dr(t)$ at a generic time $t > 0$ will depend not only on the time-t value of the short rate, but on the whole history of the yield curve up to that time. For this general result *not* to hold true (see again Chapter 16), HW (1993a) and Carverhill (1992) prove that the function $v(t,T)$ must be of the separable form

$$v(t,T) = x(t)[y(T) - y(t)] \qquad (14.19)$$

A second possible choice for the functional form of the volatility functions

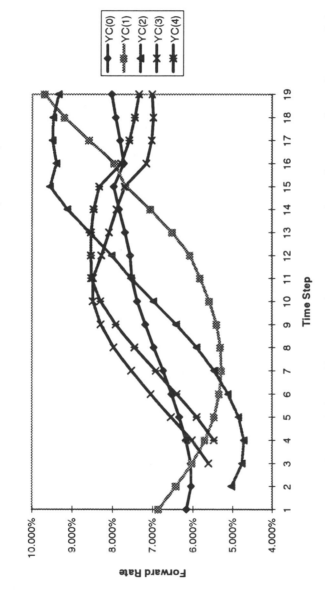

Figure 14.1 Different possible shapes of the yield curve evolving over time driven by a two-factor log-normal forwards-rates HJM model. $YC(0)$ denotes the initial yield curve and is the same for all figures. Notice how the change in shape is very complex, and the patterns are much richer than what any one-factor model could provide: in particular, Figure 14.1 shows a case of inversion of the slope, Figure 14.2 displays a pronounced steepening and Figure 14.3 highlights the degree of curvature that can be introduced in the yield curve.

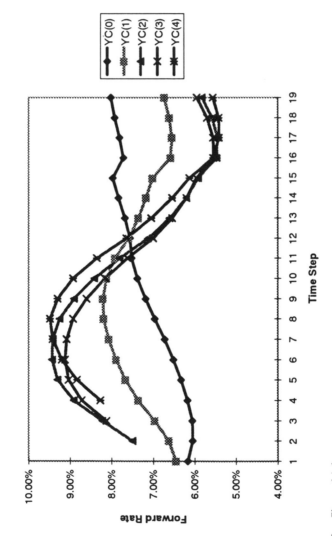

Figure 14.2 See Figure 14.1.

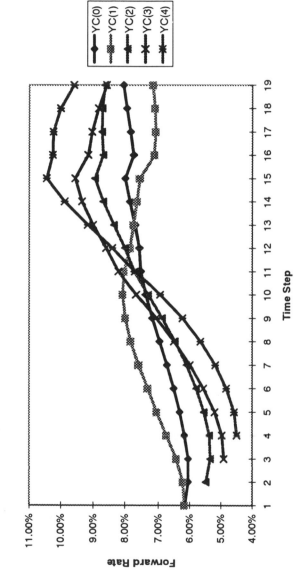

Figure 14.3 See Figure 14.1.

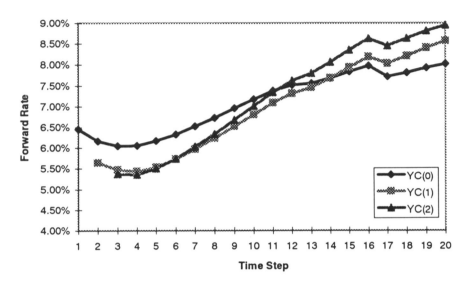

Figure 14.4 Same as for Figures 14.1 to 14.3, but with the random shocks dz_1, dz_2 from time 1 to 2 (YC(1) to YC(2)) equal in magnitude but opposite in sign to the shocks from time 0 to time 1 (YC(0) to YC(1)). Notice that, due to the non-Markovian nature of the process, there is no exact recombination of the yield curve. Notice also that the 'discrepancy' is of relatively modest magnitude.

(which, as seen, could in principle depend *both* on calendar time *and* on residual maturity) is that of time stationarity, i.e. the requirement that the volatility of the discount bond should depend only on the residual time to maturity, and not on calendar time t (see Chapter 15 for time-homogeneous models in general).

When both these two constraints (i.e. Markovian requirement for the short-rate process and time stationarity for the volatility functions) are simultaneously imposed, it is not difficult to prove (HW (1993)) that the function $v(.,.)$ must have the following functional form

$$v(t,T) = \frac{k(1 - e^{-a(T-t)})}{a} \tag{14.20}$$

whose limit as a tends to zero (i.e. in the absence of mean reversion) is simply

$$v(t,T) = k(T - t) \tag{14.20'}$$

The above equation shows that the choice for the percentage volatility function made to arrive at Equation (14.19) is actually not completely arbitrary, but is actually *the* **only allowable functional form consistent with a Markovian time-independent process**. As noticed a the beginning of this section, this latter choice for the volatility function (Equation (14.20′)) simply gives the continuous-time limit of the HL model, and the volatilities of spot rates of all maturities, $R(0,T) = -\ln[P(0,T)]/T$, are exactly the same; under this model, therefore, **the whole yield curve can only move strictly in parallel**.

It is interesting to notice that, for choice (14.20′), the condition of no-arbitrage between bonds is certainly satisfied (by the very construction of the forward rate processes); there still exists the possibility of arbitrage, however, between bonds and the money market account, since rates attain negative values with strictly positive probability in finite time under (14.20′). This no-arbitrage violation, of course, is no worse than what is found in the HL or Extended Vasicek approaches.

The requirement to make the process for the short rate Markovian (see also Chapter 15) is clearly restrictive, but has the vast computational advantage that any Markov process can always be mapped into a *recombining* lattice, whose number of nodes grows linearly with the number of time steps. Apart from the Markovian case, an 'up' move of all the forwards followed by a 'down' move will not, in general, recover the original yield curve (see Figure 14.4). In other words, the accompanying computational tree does not recombine.

This feature constitutes the most severe technical drawback connected with the general HJM approach, and it has often forced upon practitioners the use of MC techniques. Non-recombining trees have also been proposed, on the basis of the argument that it is the final number of states sampled, rather than the number of time steps, which determines the accuracy of the numerical integration. It has been argued that as few as ten or twelve time steps could give a sufficient sampling for pricing applications, but, in the absence of much published material on the matter, it is difficult to see how a five-year cap with quarterly resets (let alone an option thereon) could be priced using this technique.

Confining oneself to MC approaches, given the choice of numeraire one must be able to discount, prior to the averaging, each payoff using the value of the money market account obtained in the course of each individual realisation. To obtain this quantity one must have access to the value of the short rate at each point in time along the path. Since this is the last important ingredient missing from the explicit characterisation of the HJM approach, the task of obtaining the process for the short rate is undertaken in the next section.

14.5 THE PROCESS FOR THE SHORT RATE

The simplest way to arrive at the process for the short rate is to consider the latter as the limit of the instantaneous forward rate $f(t,s)$ as t tends to s:

$r(t) = f(t,t)$. For a given choice of discount bond volatilities $v(.,.)$, the no-arbitrage dynamics of forward rates can be symbolically written as

$$df(t,T) = \alpha(t,T)\, dt + \sigma(t,T)\, dz(t) \qquad (14.21)$$

with α and σ given, in all generality, by Equation (14.9). Expressing the SDE (14.21) in integral form

$$f(t,T) = f(0,T) + \int_0^t \alpha(s,T)\, ds + \int_0^t \sigma(s,T)\, dz(s) \qquad (14.22)$$

one can then write

$$r(t) = f(0,t) + \int_0^t \alpha(s,t)\, ds + \int_0^t \sigma(s,t)\, dz(s) \qquad (14.23)$$

Notice that, in moving from Equation (14.22) to Equation (14.23), the maturity index for the functions $\alpha(s,.)$ and $\sigma(s,.)$ under the integral sign has become the time for which the short rate is sought (i.e. the upper limit of the integral). By Equation (14.23) the future short rate at time t is expressed as the instantaneous forward rate of maturity t seen from the initial (time 0) yield curve perturbed by two distinct terms: the second is the usual sum of Brownian shocks; the first one is a deterministic function of the (possibly stochastic) variables which determine the volatilities of discount bond prices. Notice also that the dependence on t of the expression on the RHS of Equation (14.23) originates both from the upper integration limit *and* from the explicit dependence in $\alpha(s,t)$ and $\sigma(s,t)$. These double dependences will affect the differential of $r(t)$, $dr(t)$, needed to evolve the numeraire from the origin to time t. In order to obtain this differential one can make use of the ordinary calculus result (Fubini's theorem)

$$\frac{\partial}{\partial t}\left[\int_0^t f(s,t)\, ds\right] = f(t,t) + \int_0^t \frac{\partial f(s,t)}{\partial t}\, ds \qquad (14.24)$$

and of its stochastic counterpart,

$$\frac{\partial}{\partial t}\left[\int_0^t \sigma(s,t)\, dz(s)\right] = \sigma(t,t) + \int_0^t \frac{\partial \sigma(s,t)}{\partial t}\, dz(s) \qquad (14.25)$$

While this is perfectly correct, it is neither financially very illuminating nor terribly useful for practical (typically MC) discrete-time implementations. The equivalent of Equation (14.25) is therefore obtained for the case of discrete forward rates, and the result (14.25) re-obtained as the limit for the discrete short rate going to its instantaneous counterpart.

From Equation (14.23) let us generate, step by step, the process for the short rate. To this effect let us define $f(i,j)$ as the Δt-period forward rate of maturity

j, as seen from the yield curve at time i, $\alpha(i,j)$ as the drift at time i (volatility, respectively) of the j-maturity forward rate, and $\Delta z(i)$ as the Brownian increment at time i. One can then write

$$r(1) = f(0,1) + \alpha(0,1)\,\Delta t + \sigma(0,1)\,\Delta z(0) \qquad (14.26)$$

$$r(2) = f(0,2) + [\alpha(0,2) + \alpha(1,2)]\,\Delta t + \sigma(0,2)\,\Delta z(0) + \sigma(1,2)\,\Delta z(1) \quad (14.27)$$

Therefore the increment in the short rate from time 1 to time 2 is given by

$$\Delta r(1) = r(2) - r(1) = [f(0,2) - f(0,1)] + [\alpha(0,2) + \alpha(1,2) - \alpha(0,1)]\,\Delta t$$
$$+ [\sigma(0,2) - \sigma(0,1)]\,\Delta z(0) + \sigma(1,2)\,\Delta z(1) \qquad (14.28)$$

Let us pause to explore the implications of time-homogeneity on the computational burden that Equation (14.28) requires, and, to be specific, let us consider the case of log-normal bond prices, which give for the drift α expression (14.9′)

$$\alpha(t,T) = v(t,T)\,\frac{\partial v(t,T)}{\partial T} \qquad (14.29)$$

If the discount bond process is time-homogeneous, then $v(t,T) = v(T - t)$, and, therefore, $\alpha(t,T) = \alpha(T - t)$. If this is the case $\alpha(1,2) = \alpha(0,1)$ in Equation (14.28), and therefore

$$\Delta r(1) = r(2) - r(1) = [f(0,2) - f(0,1)] + [\alpha(0,2)]\,\Delta t$$
$$+ [\sigma(0,2) - \sigma(0,1)]\,\Delta z(0) + \sigma(1,2)\,\Delta z(1) \quad \textbf{(time-homogeneous)}$$
$$(14.30)$$

The drift of the short rate at time 1 can, in this case, be computed from the discount bond volatilities *at time 0*. This is, in general, not the case: in order to evolve the short rate at time $t > 0$ the evolution of quantities from time 0 to time t will be needed (the terms $\alpha(0,2)$, $\alpha(1,2)$ in Equation (14.28)).

It can also be instructive to compare the increment for the short rate at time 1 with the increment, also at time 1, of the 'next' forward rate, i.e. of the discrete forward rate spanning the period [2 3]. Since

$$\Delta f(1,2) = \alpha(1,2)\,\Delta t + \sigma(1,2)\,\Delta z(1) \qquad (14.31)$$

one can see that

$$\Delta r(1) - \Delta f(1,2) = [f(0,2) - f(0,1)] + [\alpha(0,2) - \alpha(0,1)]\,\Delta t$$
$$+ [\sigma(0,2) - \sigma(0,1)]\,\Delta z(0) \qquad (14.32)$$

Therefore, the difference in drifts at time 1 stems from (i) an obvious deterministic term linked to the shape of the yield curve at time 0: $[f(0,2) - f(0,1)]$; (ii) the difference in the drifts *at time 0* of the forward rates maturing at times 1 and 2, respectively: $[\alpha(0,2) - \alpha(0,1)]\,\Delta t$; and (iii) a term depending on past Brownian increments:

$$[\sigma(0,2) - \sigma(0,1)]\,\Delta z(0).$$

Let us now extend the analysis one step forward. Looking back at Equation (14.23) one can write

$$r(3) = f(0,3) + [\alpha(0,3) + \alpha(1,3) + \alpha(2,3)]\,\Delta t$$
$$+ \sigma(0,3)\,\Delta z(0) + \sigma(1,3)\,\Delta z(1) + \sigma(2,3)\,\Delta z(2) \qquad (14.33)$$

Subtracting Equation (14.27) from Equation (14.33) one then obtains

$$\Delta r(2) = r(3) - r(2)$$
$$= [f(0,3) - f(0,2)] + [\alpha(0,3) + \alpha(1,3) + \alpha(2,3) - \alpha(0,2) - \alpha(1,2)]\,\Delta t$$
$$+ [\sigma(0,3) - \sigma(0,2)]\,\Delta z(0) + [\sigma(1,3) - \sigma(1,2)]\,\Delta z(1) + \sigma(2,3)\,\Delta z(2)$$
$$(14.34)$$

which, after dividing and multiplying by Δt, can be rewritten as

$$\Delta r(2) = r(3) - r(2)$$
$$= \left\{ \frac{f(0,3) - f(0,2)}{\Delta t} + \frac{\alpha(0,3) - \alpha(0,2)}{\Delta t} + \frac{\alpha(1,3) - \alpha(1,2)}{\Delta t} + \alpha(2,3) \right.$$
$$\left. + \frac{\sigma(0,3) - \sigma(0,2)}{\Delta t}\,\Delta z(0) + \frac{\sigma(1,3) - \sigma(1,2)}{\Delta t}\,\Delta z(1) \right\}\Delta t$$
$$+ \sigma(2,3)\,\Delta z(2)$$
$$(14.35)$$

We are now in a position to generalise Equation (14.35) to an arbitrary time step:

$$dr(n) = r(n+1) - r(n)$$
$$= \left\{ \frac{f(0, n+1) - f(0, n)}{\Delta t} + \sum_{i=0,n-1}\left[\frac{\alpha(i, n+1) - \alpha(i, n)}{\Delta t} \right] \right.$$
$$\left. + \alpha(n, n+1) + \sum_{i=0,n-1}\left(\frac{\sigma(i, n+1) - \sigma(i, n)}{\Delta t} \right)\Delta z(i) \right\}\Delta t$$
$$+ \sigma(n, n+1)\,\Delta z(n) \qquad (14.36)$$

Notice carefully in the drift term the presence of a component (the last summation) which depends on the particular path of the Brownian motion from time 0 to time $n-1$. Expression (14.36) therefore clearly shows that **the process for the short rate is in general path dependent.**

It is now an easy matter to move to the continuous limit as Δt tends to 0 and write

$$dr(t) = \left\{ \frac{\partial f(0,t)}{\partial t} + \int_0^t \frac{\partial \alpha(s,t)}{\partial t} ds + \alpha(t,t) + \int_0^t \frac{\partial \sigma(s,t)}{\partial t} dz(s) \right\} dt$$
$$+ \sigma(t,t) dz(t) \tag{14.37}$$

Since, on the other hand, $dr(t)$ must be equal to the differential of Equation (14.23) above, *en route* to obtaining the discrete process for the short rate we have also obtained the stochastic equivalent of Fubini's theorem, mentioned in Equations (14.24) and (14.25):

$$\frac{\partial}{\partial t} \left[\int_0^t \alpha(s,t) ds \right] = \alpha(t,t) + \int_0^t \frac{\partial \alpha(s,t)}{\partial t} ds \tag{14.38}$$

and

$$\frac{\partial}{\partial t} \left[\int_0^t \sigma(s,t) dz(s) \right] dt = \sigma(t,t) dt + \left[\int_0^t \frac{\partial \sigma(s,t)}{\partial t} dz(s) \right] dt \tag{14.38'}$$

Notice that, for the case of the HJM approach, $\alpha(t,t) \equiv 0$ since $v(t,t) \equiv 0$. For the log-normal bond case explored above,

$$\alpha(t,T) = v(t,T) \frac{\partial v(t,T)}{\partial T} \tag{14.39}$$

$$\sigma(t,T) = \frac{\partial v(t,T)}{\partial T} \tag{14.40}$$

and it is therefore easy to rewrite Equation (14.37) in the form

$$dr(t) = \left\{ \frac{\partial f(0,t)}{\partial t} + \int_0^t \frac{\partial}{\partial t} \left[v(s,t) \frac{\partial v(s,t)}{\partial t} \right] ds \right.$$
$$\left. + \int_0^t \frac{\partial}{\partial t} \left[\frac{\partial v(s,t)}{\partial t} \right] ds \right\} dt + \frac{\partial v(t,t)}{\partial t} dz(t)$$
$$= \left\{ \frac{\partial f(0,t)}{\partial t} + \int_0^t \left(\frac{\partial v(s,t)}{\partial t} \right)^2 ds + \int_0^t v(s,t) \frac{\partial^2 v(s,t)}{\partial t^2} ds \right.$$
$$\left. + \int_0^t \frac{\partial^2 v(s,t)}{\partial t^2} dz(s) \right\} dt + \frac{\partial v(t,t)}{\partial t} dz(t) \tag{14.37'}$$

where $\partial v(t,t)/\partial t$ indicates the derivative of the discount bond volatility function taken at the origin. From this expression one can easily see that the process for the short rate is certainly non-Markovian if $v(\tau,t)$ depends on stochastic variables at times earlier than t (see Carverhill (1992)). Furthermore, even if $v(\tau,t)$ only depends on calendar time and time to maturity, the short-rate process will still be non-Markovian unless the integrand in the fourth term is identically equal to zero. This, however, is exactly the case which corresponds to the very special choice of the volatility functions given by $v = k(T - t)$. In this case the short-rate processes become

$$dr(t) = \left\{ \frac{\partial f(0,t)}{\partial t} + \frac{k^2(1 + \exp[-2at])}{2a} - ar + af(0,t) \right\} dt + k\, dz \qquad (14.41)$$

and

$$dr(t) = \left\{ \frac{\partial f(0,t)}{\partial t} + k^2 t \right\} dt + k\, dz \qquad (14.41')$$

in the $a \to 0$ limit. Needless to say, for these choices of the analytic form of the volatility functions, the calibration procedure will not, in general, yield an exact match to the market cap prices.

In the framework of the MC approach, once the process for the short rate obtained in this section is available, the numeraire can be accumulated along each path out to the final option expiry; as many forwards as price-sensitive resets, each in an up and a down state if one needs derivatives, plus the short rate, in the up and down state as well if sensitivity to the discounting is desired, must then be evolved along the various paths; at each reset, one forward, and its accompanying statistics, can be shed, one at a time until the last reset, at which point only the short rate has to be evolved until the option payoff time. The realisations of the forward rates along each path, evolved in parallel with the short rate using the drifts obtained in the previous sections, then provide the terminal payoff which can be discounted using the inverse of the corresponding numeraire. All the ingredients necessary in order to perform the MC evaluation of a given HJM implementation, fully characterised, as explained above, by a particular choice of the volatility function, are therefore in place.

The computational task is certainly rather daunting; it should, however, be kept in mind that an option at time t on a bond maturing at time T only requires evolution of the relevant quantities out to option expiry time; with BDT-like tree construction, instead the user must incur the computational cost associated with the building of the tree out to bond maturity for traditional lattice approaches.

14.6 CONCLUSIONS

Given the potential complexity of the calibration and option evaluation procedure, discussed in the previous sections, what is the comparative advantage, from a practical point of view, brought about by the HJM approach? The discussion can be profitably split between one- and multi-factor implementations. For one-factor models, the normal-forward-rates approach is the only one which allows mapping on a recombining tree, by virtue of its being Markovian; it is, however, virtually indistinguishable from the HW (Extended Vasicek) approach, and, therefore, the only possible advantage might stem from having a simpler procedure than the Hull and White (1993b) tree methodology to tackle path-dependent options. If a log-normal assumption is chosen for the forward rates, the underlying tree ceases to recombine. Empirically, it has, however, been observed that the pricing differences arising from the non-Markovian character of the model *vis-à-vis* a recombining log-normal approach such as BDT are very small indeed (see Chapter 16). Again, the only advantage of a HJM implementation could be the greater ease with which path-dependent options can be tackled. Other, more complex, volatility specifications are, of course, possible within the HJM framework, but the advantage that could be reaped by implementing econometrically more appealing volatility specifications is probably more than offset by the increased difficulties in pricing the plain-vanilla instruments over a large range of strikes, by and large priced in the market on the basis of Black's formula.

In view of the above, for one-factor models the arguments tilting the balance in favour of the HJM approach therefore lack great cogency. The picture changes radically in moving to multi-factor approaches. To begin with, the principal component analysis reported in Chapter 2 provides a direct indication of the factors (level and slope) that could be taken to drive the yield-curve dynamics. Furthermore, with appropriate scaling, the loadings (weights) which result from the PC analysis provide a direct route towards the historical estimation of the volatility functions of the driving factors. As shown in Figures 14.1 to 14.3, a principal component-based version of HJM can produce moves for the yield curve which are both econometrically well justifiable, and of 'convincingly' rich shape. While this approach is conceptually straightforward, and bound to make the volatility inputs not only reasonably robust, but also of direct financial appeal (e.g. volatility of the level and of the spread), it will share the shortcomings of all historical approaches, in that it will not recover exactly market option prices. The alternative, as usual, is to embrace an 'implied' procedure, perhaps after imposing functional constraints on the volatility inputs which embody the gist, if not the numerical output, of the principal component analysis. In this case, however, the calibration to market prices can become very time consuming, especially given the fact that the noise in the price estimates makes the evaluation of the derivatives with respect to the model parameters (needed for Newton–Raphson-like procedures) very arduous. The variance-reduction techniques mentioned in Chapter 8 in the context of MC procedures, and the contravariate technique in particular, can be of great help in the calibration process.

From the technical side, the computational slow-down of MC techniques with increasing number of dimensions is less than the speed reduction of finite-differences- or tree-based approaches. Furthermore, the analysis carried out in the previous sections of this chapter, which gives the drift and variance for the forward rates, can be translated almost by inspection into a multi-factor formalism (only the process for the short rate becomes somewhat involved).

Therefore, for those users who feel that the options they have to price and risk manage indeed require that the imperfect correlation among rates should be accounted for, the HJM approach has a very strong appeal. In practice, virtually all the exotic interest-rate products *do* depend in an important way on the correlation structure; while one-factor models can be 'forced', by skilful manipulation of the volatility input, to price some correlation-dependent instruments correctly (see the last section of Chapter 10), there is no guarantee that the resulting risk statistics should capture the true interest-rate exposure. An approach, such as the HJM, which can ensure the simultaneous pricing of caps and (at least of some[1]) European swaptions is therefore of great value. The price to be paid is the potential complexity of the calibration, and the difficulty to evaluate American options.

In the context of one-factor HJM models it was mentioned above that the non-Markovian character of the process has very limited pricing impact. If this result still holds true for two-factor approaches, it might be very useful to use 'in parallel' a tree-based model, possibly developed using the conceptual insight furnished by the Brennan and Schwartz approach, which displays distributional assumptions as close as possible to the chosen HJM model. This 'germane' model mapped onto a recombining tree could be of great assistance in pricing American options, and could provide an (almost) internally consistent approach to pricing and risk managing a complex option book.

It is therefore indubitable that the HJM framework has great financial and intellectual appeal, not to mention a certain undeniable elegance; it is also fair to say that, at the present stage of computer technology, its practical multi-factor implementation for actual pricing and risk management applications is one of the most challenging (and exciting) tasks with which the trading community is faced.

ENDNOTE

1. The limitations of *all* principal-component-based models in so far as the possible shape of the correlation function that they can reproduce (see Section 2.2) is concerned still hold for the HJM approach; therefore only a selection of European swaptions can be simultaneously fitted at any one time.

PART FIVE
GENERAL TOPICS

15
Affine models

15.1 DEFINITION OF AFFINE MODELS

The chapters of Part Four have dealt with a number of different models, characterised by a variety of (implicit or explicit) functional forms for the dynamics of their respective state variables. Among these models, a class stands out for the wealth of analytic results that can be derived and for the intuitional understanding that can be glimpsed into the 'workings' of the models almost by inspection. These models, referred to as 'affine' in the literature, are the topic of the present chapter.

In Chapter 5 it was shown that, for any diffusive stochastic differential equation for the short rate of the form

$$dr = \mu_r'(r,t)\, dt + \sigma_r(r,t)\, dz \tag{15.1}$$

(where μ_r' denotes the drift in the 'real world'), absence of arbitrage requires that for any asset V there should correspond a parabolic partial differential equation (PDE) (with appropriate initial and boundary conditions) of the form

$$\frac{\partial V(r,t)}{\partial t} + \frac{\partial V(r,t)}{\partial r}\,\mu_r + \frac{1}{2}\,\frac{\partial^2 V(r,t)}{\partial r^2}\,\sigma_r^2 = r(t)V(r,t) \tag{15.2}$$

with μ_r now denoting the drift in the risk-adjusted measure. Each conceivable one-factor model is characterised (within the diffusive framework) by a specific functional form for μ_r and σ_r. (The extension of the following discussion to many factors follows the same conceptual lines: see, e.g., Duffie and Kahn (1993).)

Equations (15.1) and (15.2) are completely general. If, however, one is ready to impose restrictions on μ_r and σ_r, very useful results can be obtained as to the possible functional form of discount bond prices. More precisely, if the functions μ_r and σ_r are of the affine (linear) form

$$\sigma_r^2(r) = b(t)_0 + b(t)_1 r \qquad (15.3)$$

$$\mu_r(r) = a(t)_0 + a(t)_1 r \qquad (15.3')$$

it can be shown (see, e.g., Brown and Schaefer (1993)) that solutions of the PDE for discount bonds $P(t,T)$ (i.e. with initial conditions $P(T,T) = 1$) must be of the form

$$P(r,t,T) = \exp[A(t,T) - B(t,T)r(t)] \qquad (15.4)$$

Notice that, despite the apparently very specialised functional form for the short rate and its variance, many of the models encountered in Part Four actually belong to the affine class: as for the drift component, any mean-reverting model of the form

$$dr = k(t)[x(t) - r(t)]\,dt + \sigma_r(r,t)\,dz \qquad (15.5)$$

describing a short rate reverting with reversion speed $k(t)$ to a (possibly time-dependent) reversion level $x(t)$, satisfies condition (15.3') (with $k(t)x(t) = a_0$, and $k(t)r(t) = a_1 r(t)$; and as far as the stochastic component is concerned, not only do the Vasicek/Hull and White models clearly satisfy condition (15.3) with $b_1 = 0$; but also the CIR approach, with its dependence of the volatility on $\sqrt{r}$, belongs to the affine class. Notice, however, that a relatively simple model such as BDT (or, for that matter, *any* log-normal model) does *not* belong to the affine class.

In order to explore what the implications of these conditions are, it is useful to split the discussion into the time-homogeneous and time-inhomogeneous cases.

15.2 TIME-HOMOGENEOUS AFFINE MODELS

If the further constraint is imposed on the coefficients of Equations (15.3) and (15.4) that they should not depend on calendar time, i.e.

$$\sigma_r^2(r) = b_0 + b_1 r \qquad (15.6)$$

$$\mu_r(r) = a_0 + a_1 r \qquad (15.6')$$

then is easy to show that the price of a discount bond must depend in the coefficients A and B only on the *residual* time to maturity:

$$P(r,t,T) = \exp[A(T - t) - B(T - t)r(t)] \qquad (15.7)$$

Notice that any mean-reverting model (in the short rate and/or in the variance) with constant reversion speed and reversion level can be regarded as a special case of (15.6) and (15.6'), since, to any drift of the form

$$dr = [a + k(u - r)]\, dt + \sigma_r(r,t)\, dz \qquad (15.8)$$

one can associate an equivalent process of the form

$$dr = [a + k(u - r)]\, dt + \sigma_r(r,t)\, dz = [a + ku - kr]\, dt + \sigma_r(r,t)\, dz$$
$$= [a_0 + a_1 r]\, dt + \sigma_r(r,t)\, dz \qquad (15.9)$$

with $a_0 = a + ku$ and $a_1 = -k$.

The requirements embodied by Equations (15.6) and (15.6') exclude from the time-homogeneous affine class not only the Extended Vasicek approach with time-dependent volatility; but, because of the term $\theta(t)$ which ensures exact pricing of market discount bonds, also the market-fitting, constant-volatility, one-factor Hull and White approach does not belong to the time-homogeneous affine class.

This observation is actually of general character: a simple way to turn a non-market-fitting time-homogeneous mean-reverting model like Vasicek's or CIR's into a model that fits exactly an exogenous term structure of discount bond prices is simply to insert a time-dependent level of reversion; and if, in addition, also the term structure of volatilities is to be matched, also the process variance can be allowed to display an explicit dependence on time. The chapters devoted to the Hull and White model, and to Markovian rates deal in detail with the issue of the *a priori* desirability of achieving a fit to a large number of exogenous quantities by allowing for time-dependent model parameters.

One can therefore say that, in general, time-homogeneous affine models are intrinsically incapable of fitting an arbitrary exogenous term structure of interest rates. Historically, they tend to belong to the class of equilibrium models, which attempt to explain what values rates should assume, given a model for the economy and today's known values of the state variables. (See, for instance, the first section of the chapter devoted to the Longstaff and Schwartz model.) Given these intrinsic fitting limitations, they can be of great academic interest, since they can provide a terse and parsimonious description of a 'model' equilibrium economy, but one might well wonder about their practical relevance. From the quantitative (trading) point of view, their use is indeed probably very limited. Nonetheless these affine time-homogeneous models do allow some very powerful qualitative insight about the dynamics of the yield curve, as explored in the following part of this section, that is of valuable help to enhance the understanding of more complex models.

From Equation (15.4) one can immediately derive the yield, $R(t,T)$, of any bond. From the definition

$$P(t,T) \equiv \exp[-R(t,T)(T-t)] \qquad (15.10)$$

in fact, one directly obtains

$$R(\tau) = -\frac{A(\tau)}{\tau} + \frac{B(\tau)}{\tau r(t)} \tag{15.11}$$

with $\tau \equiv (T - t)$. Ito's lemma then provides the term structure of volatilities as

$$\sigma_R = \sigma_r \frac{B(\tau)}{\tau} \tag{15.12}$$

Therefore, for affine models in general, **the 'duration' function $B(t,T)$ fully characterises the term structure of volatilities**. If, in addition, this duration function does not depend on calendar time (as is the case for time-homogeneous models), then the term structure of volatilities retains the same shape over time. The last section of Chapter 16 discusses both the desirability and the inherent shortcomings of this time invariance.

For time-homogeneous affine models $\partial/\partial T = -\partial/\partial t$; therefore, employing the by-now-familiar notation, one can write for an instantaneous forward rate

$$f(t,T) = -\frac{\partial \ln P(t,T)}{\partial T} = \frac{\partial \ln P(t,T)}{\partial t} = \frac{1}{P}\frac{\partial P}{\partial t} \tag{15.13}$$

But since, from Equation (15.7), one can write

$$\frac{\partial P}{\partial r} = -P(\tau)B(\tau) \tag{15.14}$$

$$\frac{\partial^2 P}{\partial r^2} = P(\tau)B(\tau)^2 \tag{15.15}$$

from Equation (15.2) one obtains

$$f(r,t) = r(t) + \mu_r B(\tau) - \tfrac{1}{2}\sigma_r^2 B^2(\tau) \tag{15.16}$$

Notice again that, since for time homogeneous models we require μ_r not to depend on calendar time, **the duration function $B(\tau)$ also determines, via the constant coefficients a_0 and a_1, the possible forms of the obtainable yield curves**. If the variance of the short rate is simply a constant (which is *not* required by a time-homogeneous model) then the model is, in the terminology of Chapter 16, stochastically deterministic, and **the function $B(\tau)$ completely determines the shape of the yield curve**.

Finally, from Equation (15.16) one immediately obtains a link, for this class of models, between the forward rates implied by the model and its parameters and the volatility of a given yield curve: differentiating (15.16) twice with respect to B one in fact obtains

$$\frac{\partial^2 f}{\partial B^2} = \sigma^2(t) \tag{15.17}$$

Given the remarks made above regarding the link between the functional forms (15.6) and (15.6') and mean-reverting specifications of the drift or the variance (see Equations (15.8) and (15.9)) one can, without prejudice to generality, always consider a case where the dynamics of the short rate is given by an explicitly mean-reverting equation of the form

$$dr = [k(u - r)]\, dt + \sigma_r(r,t)\, dz \tag{15.18}$$

But if this is the case, direct substitution readily gives for $B(\tau)$ the expression

$$\frac{\partial B}{\partial t} = -1 + \frac{1}{2} b_1 B^2 \tag{15.19}$$

For the special case when b_1 is equal to zero, then

$$B(\tau) = \frac{1 - \exp(-k\tau)}{k} \tag{15.20}$$

yielding an expression already encountered for the Vasicek models (and, despite their being time-inhomogeneous in the drifts, for the Hull and White and Ho and Lee ($k = 0$) models). Therefore, for the Vasicek approach one can immediately see that the obtainable shapes of the yield curve, as described by the collection of instantaneous forward rates, must be of the type:

$$f(0,T) = f(\tau) = r(0) + [u - r(0)]\left(1 - \exp(-k\tau) - \frac{1}{2}\sigma^2 \frac{1 - \exp(-k\tau)}{k^2}\right) \tag{15.21}$$

For very short maturities, i.e. for $\tau \ll 1$, Equation (15.21) becomes

$$f(\tau) = r(0) + (u - r(0))k\tau \tag{15.22}$$

Therefore, close to the origin, forward rates of increasing (but small) maturity must 'point' in the direction of the reversion level, with a slope given by the reversion speed. Just from this simple observation one can immediately see that a yield curve whose initial slope is such that a short-maturity forward rate moves 'away from' the reversion level is not recoverable by a Vasicek-type model. More in general, the admissible shapes of the yield curve are shown in Figures 15.1 and 15.2.

Qualitatively similar results hold for the CIR model, although the obtainable shapes are somewhat more complex.

Forward Rates of Increasing Expiries

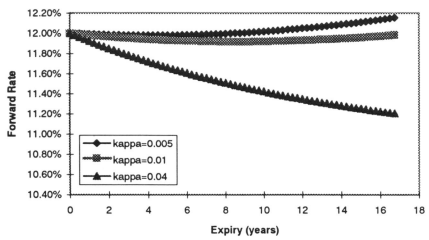

Figure 15.1 Instantaneous forward rates as a function of maturity for several values of the reversion speed κ ($r(0) = 12.00\%$, $u = 10\%$, $\sigma = 0.035$).

This discussion has provided a more quantitative grounding for the statements, often made throughout the book, about the 'volatility contribution to the shape of the yield curve'. The words of caution against blind cross-sectional fitting of model parameters to market prices should now have a more precise meaning and justification: for time-homogeneous affine models there is an inextricable link between the variance of the short rate and the shape of the yield curve (see, e.g., Equations (15.21), (15.17) and (15.15), and Figures 15.1 and 15.2). From an exogenous set of market prices for discount bonds, which might reflect a deterministic dynamics not compatible with what an affine model can allow, one can easily 'estimate' volatility parameters totally inconsistent with any plausible time-series behaviour of short rate.

While the results proven above have, strictly speaking, been shown to hold for time-homogeneous models, the general message applies to time-dependent affine models as well, as the following section will show.

15.3 TIME-INHOMOGENEOUS AFFINE MODELS

If the crucial assumption of time-homogeneity is relaxed, the all-important result that allowed to equate a derivative with respect to maturity with (the opposite of) a derivative with respect calendar time (see Equation (15.13)) no longer holds true. In order to obtain instantaneous forward rates from discount

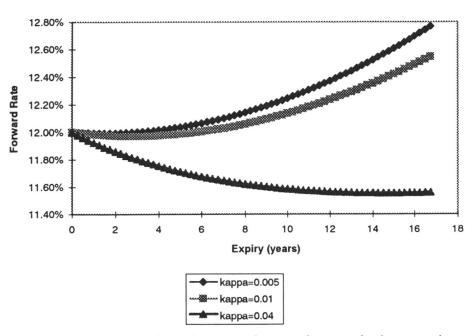

Figure 15.2 Instantaneous forward rates as a function of maturity for the same values of the reversion speed κ, and of the remaining parameters ($r(0) = 12.00\%$, $u = 10\%$, $\sigma = 0.06$). Notice how more complex shapes can be obtained by changing the volatility parameter. See the text for a discussion of the implications of this observation.

bond prices one must take the limit as T_2 goes to T_1 of

$$f(t,T_1,T_2) = -\frac{\ln P(t,T_2) - \ln P(t,T_1)}{T_2 - T_1} \tag{15.23}$$

Since for general (i.e. not necessarily time-homogeneous) affine models one can write

$$P(t,T) = \exp[-A(t,T) - B(t,T)r] \tag{15.24}$$

equation (15.23) becomes

$$f(t,T_1,T_2) = -\frac{A(t,T_2) - A(t,T_1) - [B(t,T_2) - B(t,T_1)]r(t)}{T_2 - T_1} \tag{15.25}$$

$$f(t,T) = -\frac{\partial A(t,T)}{\partial T} - \frac{\partial B(t,T)}{\partial T}r(t) \tag{15.25'}$$

The volatility of a forward rate is also immediately obtainable using Ito's lemma from the stochastic part of the process for df:

$$df = \mu_f\, dt + \frac{\partial f}{\partial r}\, \sigma_r\, dz = \mu_f\, dt - \frac{\partial B}{\partial T}\, \sigma_r\, dz \qquad (15.26)$$

where μ_f depends on the particular choice of numeraire. Notice again that the term structure of volatilities only depends on (the derivative of) B, and not on A.

In the case of a two-factor time-inhomogeneous affine model, characterised by an expression for the discount bond price of the form

$$P(t,T) = \exp[-A(t,T) - B(t,T)r - C(t,T)u] \qquad (15.27)$$

the same type of analysis gives for the instantaneous forward rate

$$f(t,T) = -\frac{\partial A(t,T)}{\partial T} - \frac{\partial B(t,T)}{\partial T}\, r(t) - \frac{\partial C(t,T)}{\partial T}\, u(t) \qquad (15.28)$$

The volatility of the forward rates can be easily obtained as

$$df = \mu_f\, dt - \frac{\partial B}{\partial T}\, \sigma_r\, dz_r - \frac{\partial C}{\partial T}\, \sigma_u\, dz_u \qquad (15.29)$$

Therefore

$$\mathrm{Var}[df] = \left(\frac{\partial B}{\partial T}\, \sigma_r\right)^2 + \left(\frac{\partial C}{\partial T}\, \sigma_u\right)^2 + 2\rho\, \frac{\partial B}{\partial T}\, \frac{\partial C}{\partial T}\, \sigma_r \sigma_u \qquad (15.30)$$

The covariance between any two forward rates is easily obtainable as

$$\mathrm{Covar}[df(t,T_1),\, df(t,T_2)] = E[df(t,T_1)\, df(t,T_2)]$$

$$= \frac{\partial B(T_1)}{\partial T_1}\, \frac{\partial B(T_2)}{\partial T_2}\, \sigma_r^2 + \frac{\partial C(T_1)}{\partial T_1}\, \frac{\partial C(T_2)}{\partial T_2}\, \sigma_u^2$$

$$+ 2\sigma_r \sigma_u \rho \left[\frac{\partial B(T_1)}{\partial T_1}\, \frac{\partial C(T_2)}{\partial T_2} + \frac{\partial B(T_2)}{\partial T_2}\, \frac{\partial C(T_1)}{\partial T_1}\right] \qquad (15.31)$$

Dividing by the square root of the product of the appropriate variances (given by expression (15.30)) one can easily compute the correlation among any two forward rates. This procedure was followed in order to obtain, for instance, the correlation structure discussed in the context of the two-factor HW model.

Apart from the intrinsic interest, these results, and those presented in the previous section, can be of great value in model calibration. The simple intuitive understanding, possible for affine models, of the qualitative behaviour of model yield curve, volatility term structure and correlation surface due to the different model parameters makes it easier to fit, for instance, cap volatility curves, European swaption prices or an observed market yield curve. The important issues of calibration to market prices are further explored in the next section.

15.4 GENERAL CONSIDERATIONS

The distinction between a time-homogeneous and a time-inhomogeneous affine model might seem a rather 'technical' one. In reality, the relevance of this feature for model calibration can be very far reaching. In order to discuss the point in greater depth, let us consider once again the statement, often made throughout this book, that the shape of a given market yield curve is influenced both by expectations of future rates and by (expectations of) future volatilities. It might be useful, at this point, to revisit the example of the two 'universes' with identical market yield curves but different volatilities, presented in Section 1 of Chapter 7. To give a concrete focus to the discussion, let us consider a market yield curve such as the one shown in Figure 15.3.

Let us analyse how different affine models might be calibrated to such a yield curve. For a one-dimensional affine model time-homogeneous both in rates and in variance, given the complexity of the yield-curve shape, the user would probably not get very far: as discussed in Sections 2 and 3, for a time-homogeneous model the forward rates of increasing but short maturity must point in the direction of the reversion level (see Equation (15.22), and the discussion thereafter). Therefore, for the case depicted in Figure 15.3, either the short end of the maturity spectrum is fitted in an acceptable way, in which case the long-maturity part of the model curve will be significantly lower than the market one, or the long yields are fitted more satisfactorily, in which case the mispricing for short maturities will be severe. In any case, whatever the specific form of the time-homogeneous model, the restricted functional form of the deterministic part of the process (of the constant-coefficients mean-reverting type in order for time-homogeneity to hold) would promptly bring about clear inadequacies in pricing the discount bonds.

If a two-dimensional time-homogeneous affine model were employed, on the other hand, the situation might be not so clear-cut. To see where problems might arise, let us try to read some financial/economic interpretation in the market yield curve of Figure 15.3. A plausible 'explanation' of the observed shape might be attempted along the following lines: the markets, at the beginning of September 1995, were discounting the possibility of a rate cut by the German authorities, but the monetary loosening was perceived to be short-lived, and substantial tightening was expected to occur after approximately six months. This 'interpretation' could account convincingly for the observed term structure, but, strictly speaking, one could not rule out the theoretical

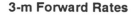

3-m Forward Rates

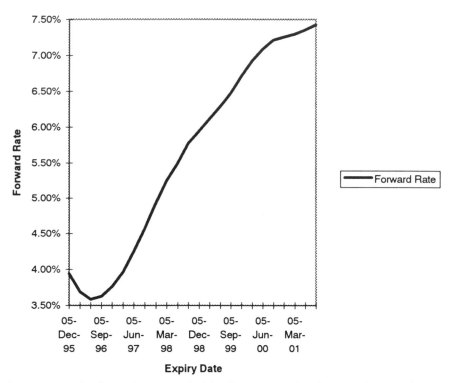

Figure 15.3 The forward rates implied by the swap market discount function for DEM (7 Sept 1995). Notice the pronounced change in slope of the curve at short maturities.

possibility that market expectations of rates might be very different from what was outlined, and that a very pronounced change in future volatilities might be discounted by the market. For this particular case, especially given the short horizon over which the change in yield-curve shape takes place, any 'interpretation' that did not take into account in a substantial way the role played by expectation of rates would probably be highly implausible. What is intuitive and plausible for a trader might, however, be beyond the reach of the optimisation procedure employed to 'best'-fit the parameter of the model (which for a two-dimensional case might be as many as a dozen). This was the danger highlighted in the 'implied' approach to the calibration of the Longstaff and Schwartz model (which indeed is of the time-homogeneous, two-dimensional type): the fitting (possibly of high numerical 'quality') of a complex yield curve might well be achieved by finding combinations of the parameters which attempt to 'conceal' the fundamental inability of the deterministic model dynamics to account for the 'expectation' of future rates. When this is the case, the ability to reproduce a virtually arbitrary yield curve can be a very undesirable feature. The alternative, i.e. to constrain the volatility inputs to yield 'reasonable' values, would enhance the 'plausibility' of the model, but, at the same time, the price would have to be paid of a possibly serious mispricing of the underlying plain-vanilla instruments.

Moving from time-homogeneous to time-inhomogeneous models, such as the one- or two-factor HW models presented in Chapter 11, the situation becomes fundamentally different: due to the presence of the 'market-fitting' function $\theta(t)$, the burden of accounting for however complicated a market yield curve can be easily accommodated by an affine model for *any a priori* choice of the volatility inputs. The other side of the coin is that the appropriateness of the input volatilities cannot be gauged from the quality of the fit to discount bond prices, which is ensured to be perfect by construction. The correctness of the volatility choice therefore requires the independent pricing of a different set of volatility-dependent instruments. (This state of affairs has already been encountered in the case of the BDT model.) In other words, time-inhomogeneous models do not 'explain', but rather *account for* the shape of the yield curve.

Exactly the same considerations can be, and have been, repeated for the fitting to cap prices: in the section devoted to the two-factor HW model it was argued that blind 'best-fitting' of the reversion speed and absolute volatility parameters can easily produce implausible curve dynamics. An enlightened combination of fitting, econometrical constraints and intuition can produce more satisfactory, and far more robust, results.

16

Markovian and non-Markovian interest-rate models

16.1 DEFINITION OF MARKOVIAN RATE PROCESSES

In Part four of this book a number of important interest-rate models have been reviewed. Several 'taxonomic' criteria could have suggested different classifications: one- versus many-factor models; analytical or numerical approaches; market-fitting versus 'market-describing' models; etc. Given that different perspectives could have given rise to equally (un)satisfactory classifications, no special effort has been devoted to the grouping of the models, apart from an understandable effort to introduce more complex models after simpler ones had already been described.

One criterion, however, *could* have provided a particularly meaningful criterion of differentiation: the Markovian or non-Markovian character of the short-rate process. The implications of this important feature of the yield-curve dynamics are explored in this chapter. (See also Carverhill (1992).)

Given a stochastic differential equation of the form

$$dx = \mu \, dt + \sigma \, dz \tag{16.1}$$

the process for dx will be said to be Markovian if the probability of dx assuming a given value $d\tilde{x}(t_n)$ at time t_n in the future, contingent on dx having assumed at past times $t_{-N}, t_{-(N-1)}, \ldots$, values $d\tilde{x}(t_{-N}), d\tilde{x}(t_{-(N-1)}), \ldots$, up to $d\tilde{x}(t_0)$ today, i.e. $p(d\tilde{x}(t_n) \,|\, dx(t_{-N}) = d\tilde{x}(t_{-N}), \; dx(t_{-(N-1)}) = d\tilde{x}(t_{-(N-1)}), \ldots, dx(t_0) = d\tilde{x}(t_0))$, is simply equal to

$$p(d\tilde{x}(t_n) \,|\, dx(t_{-N}) = d\tilde{x}(t_{-N}), \; dx(t_{-(N-1)}) = d\tilde{x}(t_{-(N-1)}), \ldots, dx(t_0) = d\tilde{x}(t_0))$$
$$= p(d\tilde{x}(t_n) \,|\, dx(t_0) = d\tilde{x}(t_0)) \tag{16.2}$$

Therefore, for the particular case of x being, for instance, the short-rate, the short-rate process is said to be Markovian if past realisations are immaterial in determining (in a stochastic sense) its future evolution. If this happens to be the case, then the short-rate process is, to use Carverhill's apt oxymoron, *randomly determined*. More precisely, this means that, given the value of the short rate at time t, the evolution of the short rate out to a later time T is completely determined by the exogenous elements of the term structure (i.e. the values of the discount bonds and by the term structure of volatilities) and by the (yet-to-occur) realisations of the Brownian motion between time t and time T. In more technical terms, the filtration $\mathfrak{F}_t$ with respect to which all expectations are calculated and which in all generality describes the process of learning *without forgetting*, in the special case of a Markovian short-rate process simply consists of the value of the short rate itself at time t.

We know from Chapter 5 that, if one chooses as numeraire the rolled-over money market account, the value at time t, $V(t)$, of any security can be evaluated by

$$V(t) = E[V(T) \exp - \int_t^T r(s)\, ds \,|\, \mathfrak{F}(t)] \tag{16.3}$$

where $V(T)$ indicates the payoff of security V at time T, $r(t)$ is the short rate, and, as usual, $\mathfrak{F}(t)$ indicates that the (risk-neutral) expectation is taken contingent upon information available at time t. Therefore, **if the short rate is Markovian, then the value at time t of any security is also completely (randomly) determined by the realisations of $r(t)$.**

Before examining in a more formal manner the conditions for the short-rate process to be Markovian, a few examples might enhance the financial intuition.

Let us consider, to begin with, any recombining tree lattice, for instance the binomial BDT procedure. By its very construction an up move from state, say, A, for the state variable followed by a down move reaches the same state of the world (i.e. the same future yield curve) as a down move followed by an up move. Let us denote this common node by D.

The prices of all future securities at D are obtained by the usual discrete averaging/discounting procedure which constitutes the finite-time counterpart of

$$V(t_D) = E\left[\exp\left(-\int_{t_D}^T r(s)\, ds\right) V(T)\right] \tag{16.4}$$

where T is the payoff time of security V, and t_D is the time corresponding to node D. Notice that there is no dependence in expression (16.4) above on whether D has been reached via the upper or the lower route. Given the deterministic drift of the (logarithm of) the short rate and its (possibly time-dependent) volatility, the state D, and the time-t_D values of all securities, simply depend on the cumulative value of the Brownian walk out to D. This is the strength and the weakness of any recombining-tree construction: on the one hand the exponential explosion of the number of nodes is avoided, but memory of where the path 'came from', needed to evaluate a path-dependent option, is lost.

As will be shown in the following, tree recombination, which, roughly speaking, ensures the Markov character of the underlying process, depends on constraints on the drifts and on the volatilities of the state variable(s) in different states of the world at different times. If, in particular, the variables used as building blocks for a model are the forward rates, as it is the case for the HJM model, we also know (see Chapter 14, Section 2) that drifts themselves are simply a function of the volatilities, either of the forward rates, or of discount bonds. Therefore, in this case, tree recombination will ultimately depend on restrictions to be imposed on the volatility functions themselves. This is indeed the case examined in the next section, for a particular (normal) choice of process for the forward rates.

16.2 CONDITIONS FOR THE RATE PROCESS TO BE MARKOVIAN

In his 1992 paper, Carverhill (1992) posits a process for discount bond prices of the form

$$\frac{\mathrm{d}P(t,T)}{P(t,T)} = r(t)\,\mathrm{d}t + v(t,T)\,\mathrm{d}z(t) \tag{16.5}$$

where all the symbols have the by-now-familiar meaning, and Carverhill's rather idiosyncratic choice of symbols (such as μ for volatilities) has been changed for consistency with this work. It will be remembered from Chapter 14 that specification (16.5) corresponds to a log-normal discount bond/normal rates assumption, and that, in this particular case, the (absolute) volatility at time t of the instantaneous forward rate maturing at time T, $\sigma(t,T)$, is linked to the volatility of the discount bond maturing at time T by

$$\sigma(t,T) = \frac{\partial v(t,T)}{\partial T} \tag{16.6}$$

Carverhill then proves that, if Equation (16.5) holds, and **if the short rate is**

indeed Markovian, then

(i)   the price volatility function must separate in a function of calendar time only and a function of maturity only:

$$\frac{\partial v(t, T)}{\partial T} = x(t)y(t) \qquad (16.6')$$

Given Equation (16.6'), Equation (16.6) can be rewritten as

$$\sigma(t, T) = x(t)y(T) \qquad (16.6'')$$

Therefore *for a log-normal bond price model*, **the admissible volatilities of forward rates must have the separable form (16.6″). In particular, no dependence on the forward rate itself is permissible.**

This shows clearly the equivalence between the Markovian property and the ability of the tree to recombine: making reference again to the diagram above, for any forward rate f_i at time t_A, the up state B will be reached by

$$f_i(B) = f_i(A) + \mu_{A,i}\, dt + \sigma_i\sqrt{\Delta t} \qquad (16.7)$$

where σ_i denotes the volatility of the forward rate of maturity T_i, f_i, and $\mu_{A,i}$ is the drift of forward rate f_i from A to B. Similarly,

$$f_i(C) = f_i(A) + \mu_{A,i}\, dt - \sigma_i\sqrt{\Delta t} \qquad (16.8)$$

For each forward rate, the down move from B to D will be given by

$$f_i(D) = f_i(B) + \mu_{B,i}\, dt - \sigma_i\sqrt{\Delta t} \qquad (16.9)$$

and, in general, for the up move from node C one can write

$$f_i(D') = f_i(C) + \mu_{C,i}\, dt + \sigma_i\sqrt{\Delta t} \qquad (16.10)$$

Notice, however, that, as long as $\mu_{C,i} = \mu_{B,i}$ the same value will be reached from B and from C *by each forward rate*, i.e. $D' = D$. This, in turn, will occur as long as the drifts $\mu_{B,i}$, $\mu_{C,i}$ only depend on time t, but not on the states B or C. If this is the case, then an up move followed by a down move will generate exactly the same yield curve. From Chapter 14, however, we know that the drifts of the forward rates are simply a function of their volatilities. Therefore conditions (16.6) and (16.6') above, and the equivalence between Markovian processes and recombining lattices, are both intimately linked and intuitively understandable.

Something farther-reaching can be shown about the implications or restrictions on the volatilities. If, in fact, in addition to the short rate being Markovian, the discount bond volatility, $v(t, T)$, is time-homogeneous (i.e. if it only depends on the residual time to maturity $(T - t)$ and not on calendar time t

by itself), then

(ii) it must have the functional form

$$v(t,T) = \rho \, \frac{1 - \exp[-a(T-t)]}{a} \tag{16.11}$$

which in the limit as a goes to 0, simply becomes

$$v(t,T) = \rho(T-t) \tag{16.11'}$$

It is easy to see that Equations (16.11) and (16.11') correspond to the Vasicek and Ho and Lee specifications, respectively.

Let us consider the implications of these results. From Equation (16.6') it follows that, under the above assumptions, the time-t price volatility of a bond of maturity T is given by

$$v(t,T) = v(t,t) + x(t) \int_t^T y(s) \, ds = x(t) \int_t^T y(s) \, ds \tag{16.12}$$

since $v(t,t) = 0 \, \forall \, t$. If one then defines as $\sigma(t) \equiv \sigma(t,t)$ the future (time-t) volatility of the short-rate, from Equation (16.6') it follows that

$$\sigma(t) = x(t)y(t) \tag{16.13}$$

Substituting for $x(t)$ in (16.12) $x(t) = \sigma(t)/y(t)$, Equation (16.12) becomes

$$v(t,T) = \frac{\sigma(t)}{y(t)} \int_t^T y(s) \, ds \tag{16.14}$$

The function $y(s)$ appearing in the integrand can be written from Equation (16.6') as

$$y(s) = \frac{\partial v(0,s)}{\partial s} \bigg/ x(0) \tag{16.15}$$

and, therefore, Equation (16.10) becomes

$$v(t,T) = \frac{\sigma(t)}{y(t)x(0)} \int_t^T \frac{\partial v(0,s)}{\partial s} ds$$

$$= \frac{\sigma(t)}{y(t)x(0)} [v(0,T) - v(0,t)] \tag{16.16}$$

But since, by Equation (16.6) again,

$$x(0)y(t) = \frac{\partial v(0,t)}{\partial t} \tag{16.17}$$

it follows that

$$v(t,T) = \frac{\sigma(t)}{\dfrac{\partial v(0,t)}{\partial t}} [v(0,T) - v(0,t)] = \frac{\sigma(t)}{\sigma(0,t)} [v(0,T) - v(0,t)] \qquad (16.18)$$

Notice that, in Equation (16.18), all the terms but the first are known as of today. In other words, under the assumptions made about the process (Equation (16.5)), i.e. for a normal forward-rates model, **the future volatilities of discount bond prices (and hence the future term structures of volatilities) are completely determined by the term structure of volatilities today and by the future volatility of the short rate**. This can therefore have an important effect on the future dynamics of the yield curve, which can be neither desirable nor easy to guess from today's specifications of the yield curve and of the volatilities curves. The issue will be looked at in greater detail in Section 16.4.

16.3 NON-MARKOVIAN MODELS ON RECOMBINING TREES

From the previous discussion it is clear that, in general, non-Markovian interest-rate models do not lend themselves to a mapping on a recombining lattice, and, more specifically, that the only class of models that completely removes the path-dependence for HJM forward rate processes is the case where the volatility structure is purely deterministic, i.e. for normal forward rates. There exists, however, as Li, Ritchken and Sankarasubramanian (1995) point out, a large and important class of models for which these general conclusions do not hold. For these models the entire term structure at future times can in fact be recovered if the values of as few as two state variables (for a one-factor model) at a future time t are known. The evolution of the term structure can therefore be made Markovian with respect to these two state variables. More precisely, if the volatility $\sigma(t,T)$ of an instantaneous forward rate $f(t,T)$ is of the functional form

$$\sigma(t,T) = \sigma(t,t)k(t,T) \qquad (16.19)$$

with

$$k(t,T) = \exp - \int_t^T \kappa(s)\, ds \qquad (16.20)$$

(with $\kappa(t)$ an arbitrary but deterministic function of time) then it can be shown (Li, Ritchen and Sankarasubramanian (1995)) that one can write the entire term structure as

$$P(t,T) = \frac{P(0,T)}{P(0,t)} \exp\left[-\beta(t,T)(r(t) - f(0,t)) - \frac{1}{2}\beta^2(t,T)\phi(t)\right] \quad (16.21)$$

with

$$\phi(t) = \int_0^t \sigma(s,t)^2 \, ds = \int_0^t \sigma(s,s)^2 k(s,t)^2 \, ds \quad (16.22)$$

$$\beta(t,T) = \int_t^T k(t,s) \, ds \quad (16.24)$$

As shown later on, the shape of the function $\kappa(t)$ can be of assistance in reproducing complex term structure of forward rate volatilities. As for the variable $\phi(t)$, which represents the accumulated variance out to time t for the instantaneous forward rate of maturity t, it uniquely determines $\beta(t,T)$, which, in turn, allows the evaluation (Equation (16.21)) of any discount bond at time t. By this expression, the future value of a discount bond is equal to its forward value today, $P(0,T)/P(0,t)$, times an adjustment factor; this, in turn, depends on the difference between the time-0 forward rate of maturity t and the realisation at time t of the short rate, on the accumulated variance out to time t for the short rate, $\sigma(s,s)^2$, and on the pre-specified (deterministic) function $k(\cdot,\cdot)$. Notice that the volatility of the short rate can depend on both the state variables, $r(t)$ and $\phi(t)$; since the latter represents the accumulated variance, and since $\sigma(t,t)$ can depend on the level of the rate itself, the time-t value of ϕ is, in general, path dependent. The path dependency, however, is of the type that can be progressively resolved using a backward-induction procedure from the knowledge of earlier and earlier values of the state variable(s) encountered in the lattice, following, for instance, the procedure suggested by Hull and White (Section 8.1). A possible functional form for the volatility of the short rate could be

$$\sigma(t,t) - \sigma_0[r(t)]^\gamma \quad (16.24)$$

With $\gamma = 0$, $1/2$, or 1 the generalised Vasicek, CIR and BDT models are recovered, respectively. A variety of shapes can be obtained for the volatility of the short rate by assigning a suitably complex shape to the function $\kappa(t)$: as Li, Ritchken and Sankarasubramanian (1995) suggest, by choosing negative values for $\kappa(t)$ for small values of t, and positive values for large t, a humped shape can be recovered for the volatility of the short rate. Notice, however, that the required functional form for the volatility of the forward rates (Equation (16.19) above) does not allow their volatility to depend on the level of the forward rates themselves, since $k(t,T)$ must be a deterministic function of time; in particular, a log-normal forward rate model does not belong to the class of models here discussed. On the other hand, experience with the BDT model shows that the discrepancy from forward rate log-normality for a log-normal short-rate model can be very modest. This procedure can therefore offer an almost-log-normal-rates model which could be mapped onto a recombining lattice of dimensionality $n + 1$ (where n is the number of driving factors). The price relevance of assigning a log-normal behaviour to the short rate rather than to the forward rates is explored at the end of the next section.

16.4 IMPLICATIONS FOR THE CHOICE OF INTEREST-RATE MODELS

The results reported in the preceding sections have important implications for approaches (such as Ho and Lee among the normal-rate models, or BDT among the log-normal ones[1]) which allow exact calibration to today's market prices of caps by imposing a particular behaviour for the future volatility of the short rate. As discussed in previous chapters, the customary way to achieve this goal is to impose a time-declining short-rate volatility, which can produce an *unconditional* distribution originating from time 0 indistinguishable from what would have been obtained using a constant-volatility mean-reverting process. While this procedure might indeed produce the desired market prices at calibration time, Equation (16.14) shows that it also implies something very strong about future volatilities of discount bonds, which are also constrained to decline over time. Clearly, this can have very profound consequences for option pricing.

This result can be contrasted with the case of a mean-reverting process with constant-volatility parameters (for instance an approach such as the two-factor HW model presented in Section 11.6). Due to the constant nature of the coefficients, one can rest assured, in this case, that the term structure of volatilities originating from a generic future time t will have the same qualitative shape as that seen from today. On the other hand, as previously discussed, models with time-independent parameters are often incapable of reproducing exactly market prices, or, if they do so, they might accomplish the task by assigning econometrically implausible values to the model coefficients. Once again, the user faces difficult choices, based at least as much on personal pricing philosophy as on hard and fast rules.

As already pointed out, the results obtained above were, strictly speaking, shown to hold true for a particular specification of bond price dynamics (Equation (16.5)). The conclusions that can be drawn from them, however, have a wider range of validity. By and large, assigning time-dependent parameters to a model indicate a (risky, albeit sometimes necessary) attempt to make the model itself give answers it is not 'willing' to yield. The simplest example is the case of the BDT declining short-rate volatility needed to price market cap prices (which in turn reflect the market's belief in mean reversion of rates).

Another example of the dangers inherent in trying to override the intrinsic limitations of a model can be found by moving to more complex two-factor models. In this case, it has been shown in previous chapters (see Section 2.2 in particular) that, as long as the driving factors are linear combinations of rates, the implied correlation structure (important, for instance, for the pricing of swaptions) is constrained to have the 'wrong' (sigmoid rather than decaying exponential) shape. However, this unwanted effect can be to some extent 'camouflaged' by assigning (strongly) time-dependent behaviour to the elements of the factors' variance–covariance matrix. Not surprisingly, this is likely to introduce the type of undesirable future behaviour highlighted by the discussion that led to Equation (16.14). In particular, if one were to force 'better' pricing of the, say, $n \times m$ swaption series (with n fixed and m ranging from $n + 1$ to $n + k$), one would probably find that the swaptions of the $r \times m$ series (for $r > n$) are actually priced much worse than if coefficients had been left undoctored. Research (Rebonato and Cooper (1995b)) carried out on a model of the Brennan and Schwartz family (modified so as to overcome the instability highlighted in Chapter 13) has shown that, by making the correlation time dependent, it is indeed possible to obtain a correlation function as seen from today of approximately exponentially decaying shape. If, however, one then examines the *future* correlation implied by the model thus calibrated, this turns out to tend to unity, thus making the model essentially one factor. The analogy with the BDT case is quite interesting: just as a time-decaying volatility turns this one-factor stochastic model into an almost deterministic (zero-forward-variance) forward description of the evolution of rates, so time-dependent correlation can turn a two-factor model into a virtually perfect-correlation (hence one-factor) description of the future yield-curve dynamics.

The 'cleanest' solution is probably to allow for more and more factors (with time-independent volatility parameters), allowing for the description of finer and finer features of the yield-curve dynamics. Such a recommendation, however correct, is not likely to win many friends among practitioners who might have tried to price and risk-manage a 10-year, quarterly reset indexed-principal swap. The only consolation is that, with the Monte Carlo approach, the computational cost grows (approximately) linearly with the number of factors. Cynics might say this can sometimes simply make an already almost unattainable task 'only' linearly more distant. Optimists will instead point to the ever-increasing power of computers as the solution to these 'transitory' problems. The user in the middle will probably hope that the 'transitory' problems will at least be resolved before his deal reaches maturity.

Another important feature to explore is what impact the Markovian or non-Markovian character of an interest-rate model *per se* can have on option prices. To investigate this feature, one can compare the results from, say, the BDT (log-normal short rate) model with a one-factor HJM log-normal forward rates implementation. After calibrating both models to the same European swaption prices, tests were conducted by evaluating American swaptions using both approaches. For all types of swaptions (in-, at- or out-of-the-money) the discrepancies were always observed to be within numerical noise (see Figure 16.1). *This points to the fact that, at least for one-factor models, as far as option pricing is concerned, the distributional features play a much more important role than the Markovian character of the process.*

These distributional features warrant a more careful analysis; it is often claimed that the BDT implies 'approximately' log-normal forward rates, thereby lending itself very readily to calibration of market caps. (See Section 10.5.) Further insight into their distributional features can be gained by repeating the argument carried out in Equations (16.7) to (16.10), and substituting the logarithm of each forward rate for the forward rate itself. As before, one can then obtain that the *percentage* drift from the B and from the C states must be identical if recombination is to be achieved. The following apparent paradox therefore seems to arise: given (i) that both the BDT and the

American Swaption Prices

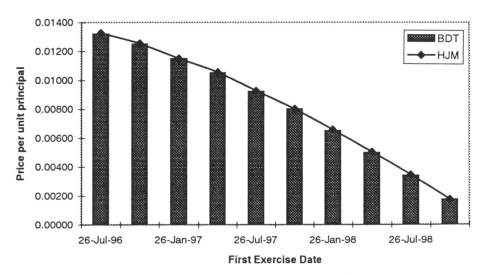

Figure 16.1 American Receivers' Swaptions for the same final swap maturity (26 Jan 1999, US$ curve of 23 Oct 1995) and different dates of the first exercise opportunity. The underlying swap frequency is quarterly, the strike was close to at-the-money (6.20%) and each exercise occurs on the relative reset date. The BDT results were obtained using a tree calibrated so as to imply approximately log-normal forward rates, and calibrated so as to obtain each individual European swaption correctly. The American swaptions were evaluated using MC simulations of a log-normal forward rate HJM model and one of the variance-reduction techniques mentioned in the last section of Chapter 8.

HJM models are arbitrage-free; (ii) that they seem to have the same (log-normal) volatilities; and (iii) that the drifts on the forward rates only depend on the volatilities themselves, **how can one model produce a recombining tree, and the other fail to do so?** The answer to this paradox can be arrived at by valuing a generic contingent claim with payoff occurring, for instance, after two time steps, using a construction consistent with the BDT distributional assumptions, but such that forward rates, rather than the short-rate, are evolved through time. To be more precise, let us assume that one wants to calculate the value at the origin (node A) of a contingent claim depending on the realisation of the short rate after two time steps. At time 0 the whole yield curve is assumed to be known, and, in particular, the value of the forward rate $f(t_A, t_D, t_D + \tau)$ is available (where τ is the tenor of the FRA, and, as usual, $f(t_A, t_D, t_D + \tau)$ is the discrete forward rate as seen from the yield curve at time t_A, spanning the period $[t_D t_D + \tau]$). If one chose as numeraire the bond expiring at time $t_D + \tau$ we know that this forward rate would be driftless. In the context of a tree methodology, however, one uses as numeraire the discrete-time counterpart of the money-market account. In other terms, one uses the one-period discount bond maturing at time t_B in order to discount payoffs occurring one time step after time t_A. The values at time t_B of the one-period bond maturing at time t_D is then used in order to discount payoffs occurring at time t_D back to time t_B. Given this choice of numeraire, for both steps drift corrections will have to be applied to the plain-vanilla forward rate resetting at time t_D. More precisely, from node A the projected values in the 'up' (B) and 'down' (C) states for the forward rate resetting at time t_D can be obtained as follows: to the value at node A of the plain-vanilla forward rate resetting at time t_D the usual 'up' and 'down' shocks by one standard deviation are first imparted (of the form $f_A \exp[\pm\sigma\sqrt{\Delta t}]$). In addition, the drift term (of the form $\exp[\mu_A \Delta t]$) has to be used in order to move the forward rate, originating from the fact that the money market account is being used as numeraire. (See Chapter 5.) Notice that, as long as the appropriate drift correction is applied, *any* forward rate can thus be evolved from time t_A to time t_B. For log-normal forward rates, whatever the precise functional form for the drift correction might be, the overall resulting forward rates at time t_B in the 'up' and 'down' states will be given by

$$f_i(B) = f_i(A) \exp[\mu_{A,i} \, dt + \sigma_i\sqrt{\Delta t}] \tag{16.25}$$

$$f_i(C) = f_i(A) \exp[\mu_{A,i} \, dt - \sigma_i\sqrt{\Delta t}] \tag{16.25'}$$

Similar drifts can then be imparted from states B and C onwards to all the forwards. In particular, for the forward rate resetting at time t_D (which would be driftless if the payoffs were discounted by the discount bond maturing at time $t_D + \tau$) the drift corrections can be obtained explicitly, since they are simply given by the terms obtained for the LIBOR-in-arrears case: the percentage drifts on the one-period forward rate in state C (B) were shown in Section 5.8 to be given by

$$\mu_{C(B)} = \frac{\tau\sigma^2 f_{C(B)}}{1 + f_{C(B)}\tau} \tag{16.26}$$

Given that the two drifts from the B and the C states are state dependent (i.e. f dependent), and therefore different, how can recombination take place, since we saw before that the necessary condition for $D = D'$ is that $\mu_C = \mu_B$? The answer is to be found in the fact that Equation (16.26) (see Section 5.8) was obtained under log-normal assumptions for the *forward rates* (as opposed to the short rate). As is well known, forward rates in the BDT framework are not exactly log-normal. What is generally not as clearly appreciated, however, is that the deviation from exact log-normality for forward rates implied by the BDT procedure by enforcing recombination is achieved by implicitly (slightly) changing the volatilities of the forward rates (i.e. by making them state dependent) in such a way that $\mu_C = \mu_B$. This must be the case (by construction), otherwise the tree would not recombine. Some algebra easily gives that the ratio K of the squares of the volatilities in states B and C is given by

$$K = \frac{1 + f_B\tau}{1 + f_C\tau} \tag{16.27}$$

Notice that, for typical applications, f is of the order of, say, 10%, and τ could be as small as $1/52$ for weekly steps. Therefore the ratio K is extremely close to 1, and, indeed, the forward rates *locally* do have an approximately log-normal distribution. The BDT tree construction therefore implicitly converts the percentage volatility σ *of the short-rate* into the volatility of the forward rates by making it state- (i.e. f-) dependent exactly to the extent required to enforce recombination. As observed above and in Chapter 10, the pricing implications of this discrepancy from exact log-normality are very small.

This final observation makes the procedure described in Section 16.3 potentially very interesting: as mentioned above, in fact, the Li, Ritchken and Sankarasubramanian procedure for mapping a non-Markovian model into a recombining tree is applicable to a log-normal short-rate process (like the BDT) but not to a log-normal forward rates model.

As usual, every simplifying feature embedded in a model tends to have some 'hidden drawbacks', which come to the surface, usually after rather careful analysis, in the form of potentially undesirable features imposed on reality stemming from apparently innocuous computational assumptions. The case just explored is one further reminder of this truth; it is reassuring, and fortunate for practical implementations, that the 'violence' made by enforcing recombination in the BDT procedure turns out to be very mild, and that, therefore, the pricing discrepancies arising from imparting a log-normal behaviour to the short-rate or to the forward rates tend to be small.

ENDNOTE

1. The results obtained in Section 16.2 pertain to the normal-rates case; similar reasoning can, however, be applied to the case of volatilities of the logarithm of the short rate. In particular, it can be shown that the condition for the recombination of a tree is that the *percentage* volatility should be independent of the state.

Bibliography

Ames W.F. (1977) *Numerical Methods for Partial Differential Equations*, New York, Academic Press

Barone E., Cuoco D., Zautzik E. (1990) 'The term structure of interest rates: a test of the Cox, Ingersoll and Ross model on Italian Treasury Bonds', unpublished working paper, Research Department, Bank of Italy, March

Barraquand J., Martineau D. (1995) 'Numerical evaluation of high-dimensional multivariate American securities', working paper, Solomon Brothers Int.

Black F., Derman E., Toy W. (1990) 'A one-factor model of interest rates and its application to Treasury bond options', *Fin. An. Jour.*, 33–339

Black F. (1976) 'The pricing of commodity contracts', *Jour. Fin. Econ.*, **3**, 167–179

Black F., Scholes M. (1973) 'The pricing of options and corporate liabilities', *Jour. Pol. Ec.*, **81**, 637–653

Boyle P.P. (1977) 'Options: a Monte Carlo approach', *Jour. Fin. Econ.*, **4**, 323–338

Boyle, P.P., Broadie, M., Glasserman, P., 'Monte Carlo Methods for security pricing' (1995) working paper, University of Waterloo, Waterloo, Ontario, Canada

Boyle, P.P., Evnine J., Gibbs S. (1994) 'Valuations of options on several underlying assets', working paper, University of Waterloo, Ontario, Canada N2L 3G1

Brennan M.J., Schwartz E.S. (1982) 'An equilibrium model of bond pricing and a test of market efficiency', *Jour. Fin. Quan. An.*, **17**, 301–329

Brennan M.J., Schwartz E.S. (1983) 'Alternative methods for valuing debt options', *Finance*, **4**, 119–138

Brown R.H., Schaefer S.M. (1991) 'The term structure of real interest rates and the Cox, Ingersoll and Ross model', unpublished working paper, London Business School, May

Brown R.H., Schaefer S.M. (1993) 'Interest rate volatility and the shape of the term structure', unpublished IFA working paper 177, London Business School, first draft July 1991, latest draft October 1993

Brown R.H., Schaefer S.M. (1994) 'Why do long term forward rates (almost always) slope downwards?', London Business School working paper, November

Brown S.J., Dybvig P.H. (1986) 'The empirical implications of the Cox, Ingersoll, Ross theory of the term structure of interest rates', *Jour. Fin.*, **41**, 617–629

Carverhill A. (1992) 'A binomial procedure for term structure options; when is the short rate Markovian?', working paper, Hong Kong University of Science and Technology, Clear Water Bay, Hong Kong, January

Carverhill A. (1993) 'A simplified exposition of the Heath Jarrow and Morton model', working paper, Department of Finance, University of Science and Technology, Hong Kong, October 4

Carverhill A. (1994) 'A note on the models of Hull and White for pricing options on the term structure', working paper, Department of Finance, University of Science and Technology, Hong Kong, July

Chatfield C., Collins A.J. (1989) *Introduction to Multivariate Analysis*, London, Chapman and Hall

Chan K.C., Karoyli G.A., Longstaff F.A., Sanders A.B. (1991) 'The volatility of short-term interest rates: an empirical comparison of alternative models of the term structure of interest rates', working paper, The Academic Faculty of Finance, Ohio State University, April

Cheng S.T. (1991) 'On the feasibility of arbitrage-based option pricing when stochastic bond price processes are involved', *Jour. Econ. Theory*, **53**, 185–198

Clewlow L., Carverhill A. (1994) 'Quicker on the curves', *Risk*, Vol. 7, No. 5

Clewlow L., Carverhill A. (1994) 'On the simulation of contingent claims', *Jour. of Der.*, Winter, 66–74

Clewlow, L. and Strickland, C. (1994) *A note on the parameter estimation in the two-factor Longstaff and Schwartz interest rate model*, Jour. Fixed Inc., March, 95–100

Cox J.C., Ingersoll J.E., Ross S.A. (1985) 'A theory of the term structure of interest rates', *Econom.*, **53**, 385

Cox J.C., Ingersoll J.E., Ross S.A. (1985) 'An intertemporal general equilibrium model of asset prices', *Econom.*, **53**, 363

Cox J.C., Ross S.A., Rubinstein M. (1979) 'Option pricing: a simplified approach', *Jour. Fin. Econ.*, **7**, 229–263

deMunnick J., Schotman, S. (1992) 'Fitting the Dutch yield curve using the Vasicek Mode' – presented at the European Finance Association Conference in Lisbon, 1992

Dothan M.U. (1990) *Process in Financial Markets*, Oxford, Oxford University Press

Doust P. (1995) 'Relative pricing techniques in the swaps and option markets', *Jour. Fin. Eng.*, March

Duffie D., Kan, R. (1992) working paper, Graduate School of Business, Stanford University

Duffie D. (1992) *Dynamic Asset Pricing Theory*, Princeton, NJ, Princeton University Press

Duffie D., Ma J., Yong J. (1994) 'Black's consol rate conjecture', working paper, Stanford University, Stanford, CA, The Graduate School of Business

Dybvig P.H. (1988) 'Bond and bond option pricing based on the current term structure', working paper, Washington University in St Louis

Elton E.J., Gruber M.J. (1991) *Modern Portfolio Theory and Investment Analysis*, 4th Edition, Chichester, John Wiley & Sons

Fisher M., Nyehka D., Zevros D. (1994) 'Fitting the term structure of interest rates with smoothing splines', US Federal Reserve Board working paper, January

Fong H.G. (1992) 'Interest rate volatility as a stochastic factor', working paper, Gifford Fong Associates

Gardiner C.W. (1990) *Handbook of Stochastic Methods*, 2nd Edition, Springer-Verlag

Geman H., El Karoui N., Rochet J.-C. (1995) 'Changes of numeraire, changes of probability measure and option pricing', forthcoming in *Jour. Appl. Prob.*

Gourlay A.R., McKee S. (1977) 'The construction of Hopscotch methods for parabolic and elliptic equations in two space dimensions with a mixed derivative', *Jour. Comp. and Appl. Math.*, **3**, 201–206

Gustavsson T. (1992) 'No-arbitrage pricing and the term structure of interest rates', working paper, Department of Economics, Uppsala University, *Economic Studies*, **2**

Harrison J.M., Kreps D. (1979) 'Martingales and arbitrage in multiperiod securities markets', *Jour. Econ. Theory*, **20**, 381–408

Harrison J.M., Pliska S. (1981) 'Martingales and stochastic integrals in the theory of continuous trading', *Stoch. Proc. and Their Appl.*, **11**, 215–260

Hatgioannides Y. (1995) 'Stochastic calculus and its applications in continuous-time arbitrage-free valuation models of financial securities: theory and estimation', lecture notes, Department of Economics, Birkbeck College, London

Heath D., Jarrow R.A., Morton A. (1987) 'Bond pricing and the term structure of interest rates: a new methodology', working paper, Cornell University, Ithaca, NY

Heath D., Jarrow R.A., Morton A. (1989) 'Bond pricing and the term structure of interest rates: a new methodology', working paper, (revised edition), Cornell University, Ithaca, NY

Ho T.S.Y., Lee S.-B. (1986) 'Term structure movements and pricing interest rate contingent claims', *Jour. Fin.*, **41**, 1011–1028

Hogan M. (1993) 'Problems in certain two-factor term structure models', *Ann. Appl. Prob.*, 3, 2, 576

Hull J. (1993) *Options, futures and other derivative securities*, 2nd Edition, Prentice Hall International Editions

Hull J., White A. (1987) 'The pricing of options on assets with stochastic volatility', *Journal of Finance*, **42**, June, 281–300

Hull J., White A. (1988) 'The use of control variate technique in option pricing', *Jour. Fin. Quan. An.*, **23**, 237–251

Hull J., White A. (1990a) 'Pricing interest-rate derivative securities', *Rev. Fin. Stud.*, **3**, 573–592

Hull J., White A. (1990b) 'Valuing derivative securities using the explicit finite differences method', *Jour. Fin. Quan. An.*, **25**, 87–100

Hull J., White A. (1993a) 'Bond option pricing based on a model for the evolution of bond prices', *Adv. in Fut. and Opt. Res.*, **6**

Hull J., White A. (1993b) 'Efficient procedures for valuing European and American path-dependent options', *Jour. of Der.*, Fall, 21–31

Hull J., White A. (1994a) 'Numerical procedures for implementing term structure models I: single factor models', *Jour. of Der.*, Fall, 7–16

Hull J., White A. (1994b) 'Numerical procedures for implementing term structure models II: two-factor models', *Jour. of Der.*, Winter, 37–49, 16

Hull J., White, A. (1995) '"A note on the models of Hull and White for pricing options on the term structure": Response', Jour. Fix. Inc., September issue, 97–102

Jamshidian F. (1990) 'Bond and option evaluation in the Gaussian interest rate model', working paper, Financial Strategies Group, Merryll Lynch Capital Markets, World Financial Center, New York, USA

Jamshidian F. (1991) 'Forward induction and construction of yield curve diffusion models', working paper, Financial Strategies Group, Merryll Lynch Capital Markets, World Financial Center, New York, USA

Johnson N.L., Kotz S. (1970) *Continuous Univariate Distributions – 1 and 2*, Boston, MA, Houghton Mifflin

Lamberton D., Lapeyre B. (1991) 'Introduction au calcul stochastique appliqué à la finance', Ecole Nationale des Ponts et Chaussées, March

Li A., Ritchken P., Sankarasubramanian L. (1995) 'Lattice models for pricing American interest rate claims', *Jour. Fin.*, **50**, 719–737

Longstaff F.A., Schwartz E.S. (1992a) 'Interest rate volatility and the term structure: a two-factor general equilibrium model', *Jour. Fin.*, **XLVII**, 1259–1282

Longstaff F.A., Schwartz E.S. (1992b) 'A two-factor interest rate model and contingent claim valuation', *Jour. Fix. Inc.*, **3**, December, 16–23

Longstaff F.A., Schwartz E.S. (1993) 'Implementation of the Longstaff–Schwartz interest rate model', *Jour. Fix. Inc.*, September, 7–14

Longstaff F.A., Schwartz E.S. (1994) 'Comments on: A note on parameter estimation in the two-factor Longstaff and Schwartz interest rate model', *Jour. Fix. Inc.*, March, 101–102

Malliaris A.G., Brock, W.A. (1982) *Stochastic Methods in Economics and Finance*, North Holland Publishing

Margrabe W. (1978) 'The value of an option to exchange one asset for another', *Journ. Fin.* **33**, 177–186

Merton R.C. (1973) 'Theory of rational option pricing', *Bell Jour. Econ. Man. Sc.*, **4**, 141–183

Miron P., Swannell P. (1991) *Pricing and Hedging Swaps*, Euromoney Publications

Morrison D.F. (1990) *Multivariate Statistical Methods*, 3rd Edition, New York, McGraw Hill

Nelson D.B., Ramaswamy K. (1990) 'Simple binomial approximations in financial models', *Rev. Fin. Stud.*, **3**, 393–430

Oksendal B. (1995) *Stochastic Differential Equations*, 5th Edition, Springer Verlag

Rebonato R. (1995) 'A two-state variable preference-free model of the evolution of interest rates', BZW working paper

Rebonato R., Cooper I.A. (1995) 'The limitations of simple two-factor interest rate models', *Jour. Fin. Eng.* (accepted for publication)

Ritchken P., Sankarasubramanian L. (1995) 'The importance of forward rate volatility structures in pricing interest rate-sensitive claims', *Jour. Der.*, **3**, Fall, 25–40

Rubinstein M. (1994) 'Implied Binomial Trees', working paper, University of California at Berkely

Schaefer S.M. (1977) 'The problem with redemption yields', *Fin. An. Jour.*, July–August, 59–67

Tilley J.A. (1993) 'Valuing American options in a path simulation model', *Trans. Soc. Act.*, **45**, 83–104

Vaillant N. (1995) 'Convexity adjustment between futures and forward rates using a martingale approach', DCM B2W, Internal Report

Vasicek O. (1977) 'An equilibrium characterization of the term structure', *Jour. Fin. Econ.*, **5**, 177–188

Willinger W., Taqqu M.S. (1991) 'Toward a convergence theory for continuous stochastic securities market model', *Math. Fin.*, **1**, 55–99

Willmott P., Dewynne J., Howison S. (1993) *Option Pricing*, Oxford, Oxford Financial Press

Wilson T. (1994) 'Debunking the myths', *Risk*, **7**, April, 67–73, and references therein

Index